SGT FROG™

KERORO GUNSO

VOL #19 BY
MINE YOSHIZAKI

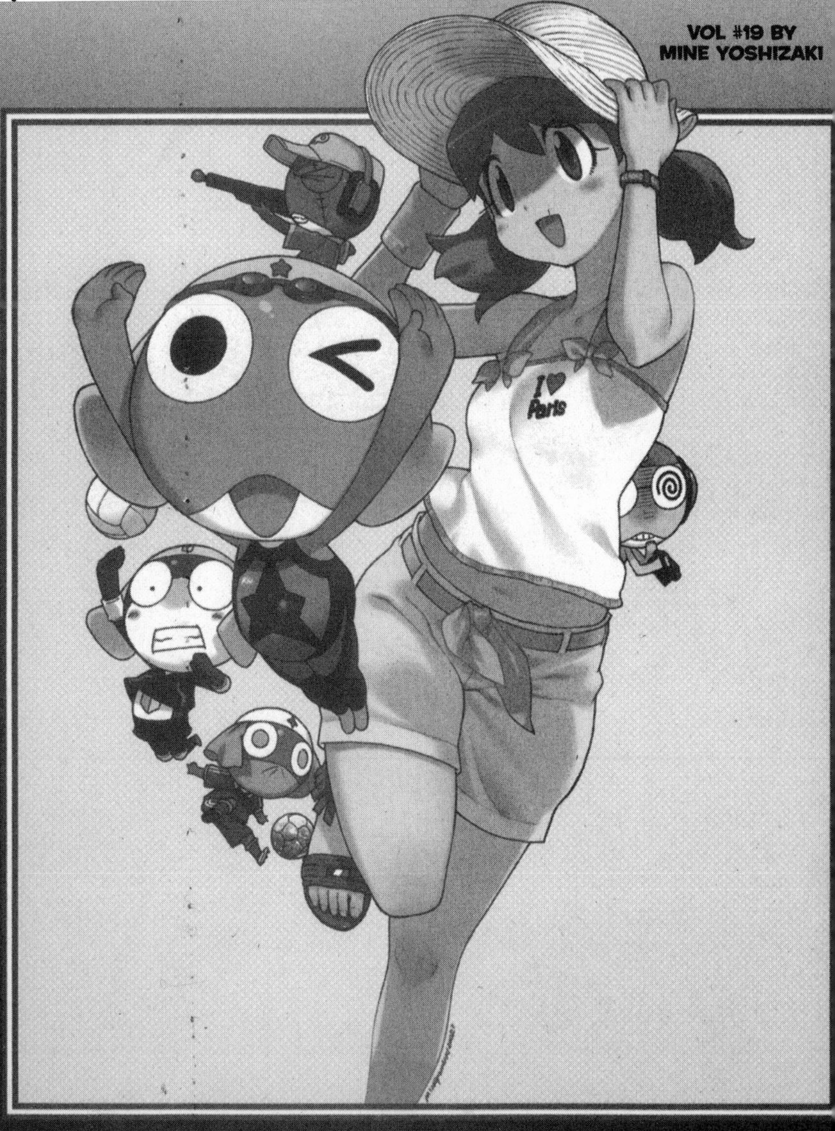
I ♥ Paris

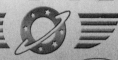

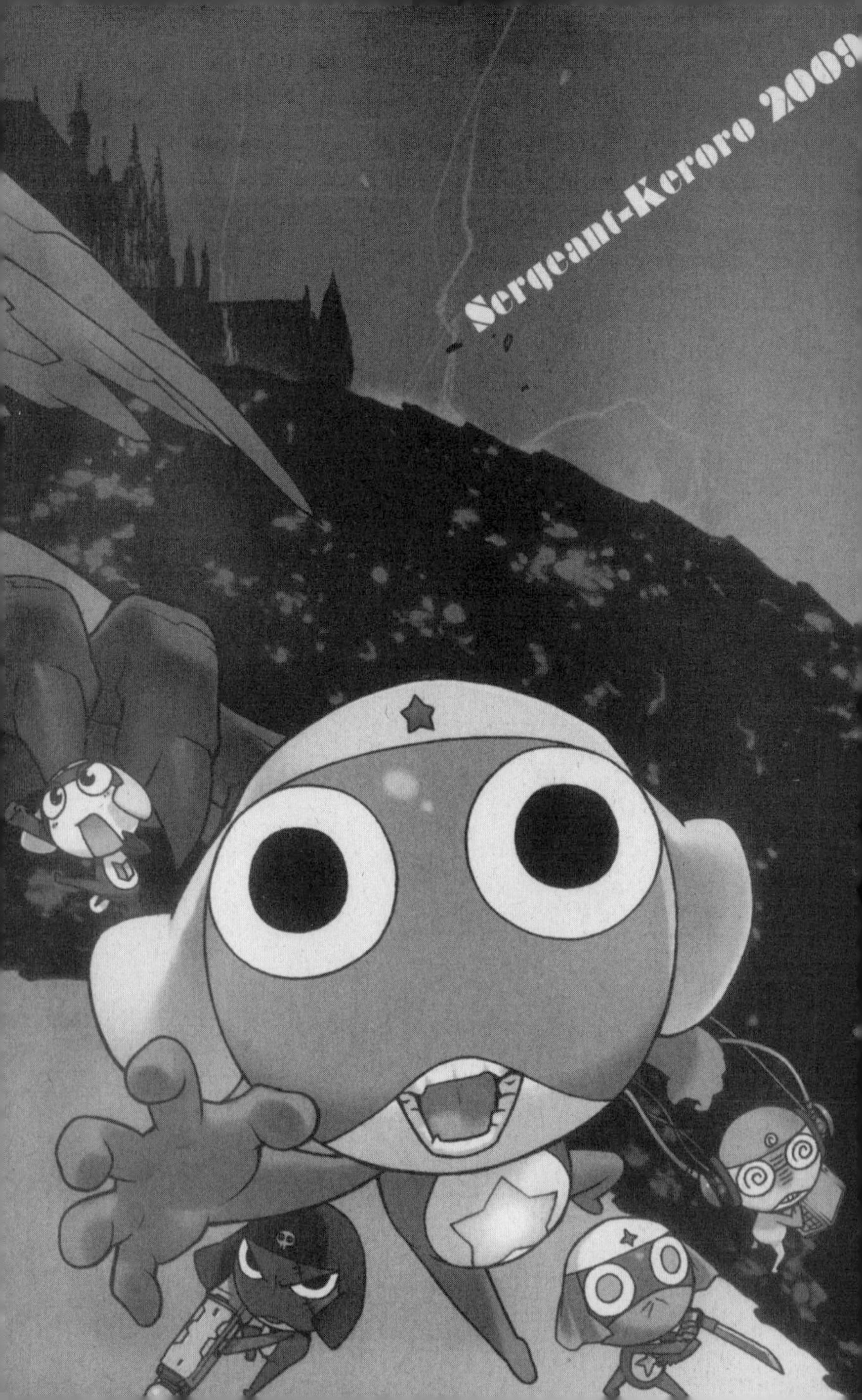
Sergeant-Keroro 2009

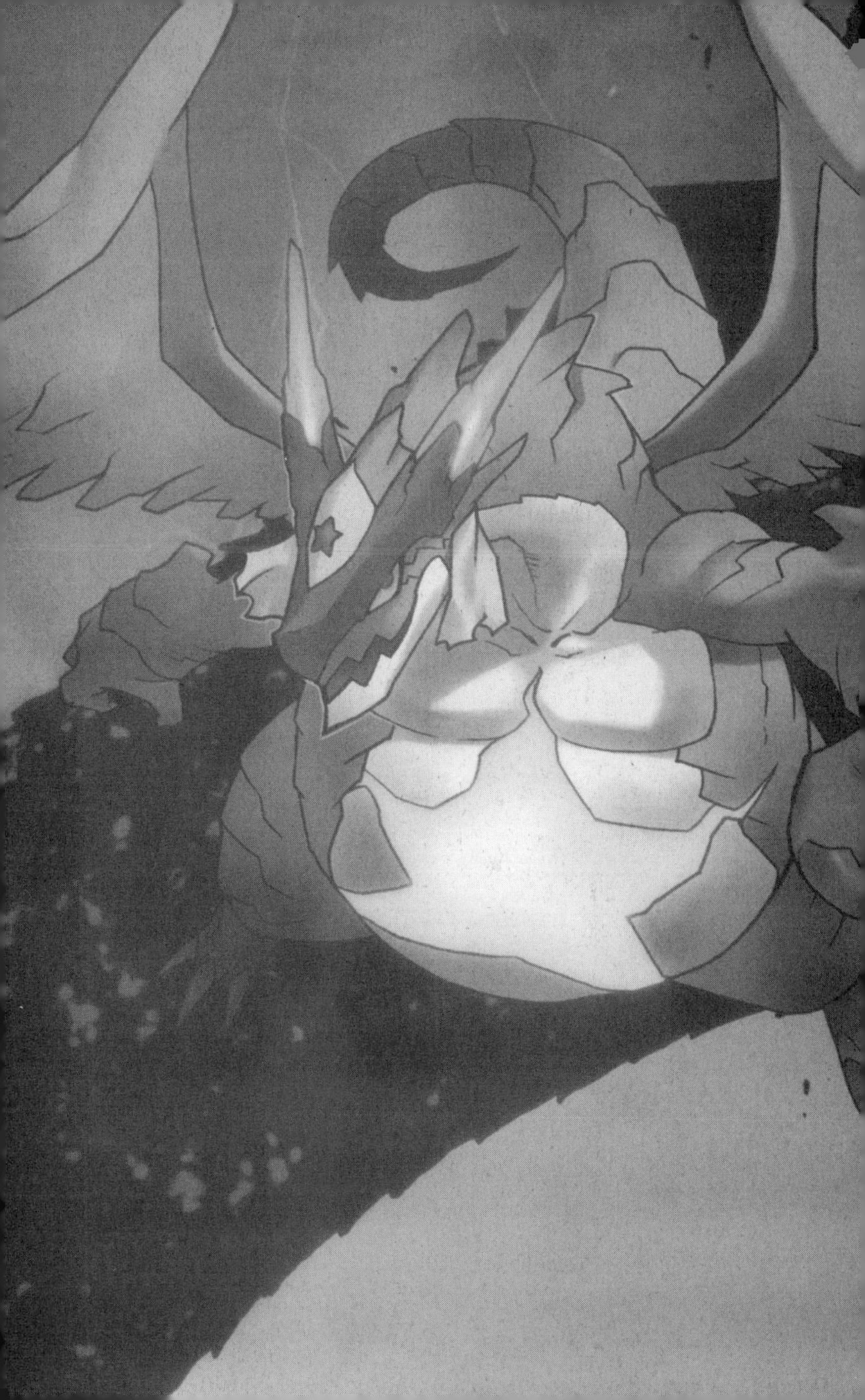

SGT. FROG 19 TABLE OF CONTENTS

SGT FROG
KERORO GUNSOU

VOLUME #19

BY
MINE YOSHIZAKI

Sgt. Frog Volume 19
Created by Mine Yoshizaki

Translation - Yuko Fukami
English Adaptation - Ysabet Reinhardt MacFarlane
Retouch and Lettering - Star Print Brokers
Copy Editor - Hope Donovan
Production Artist - Rui Kyo
Graphic Designer - Louis Csontos

Editor - Daniella Orihuela-Gruber
Print Production Manager - Lucas Rivera
Managing Editor - Vy Nguyen
Senior Designer - Louis Csontos
Art Director - Al-Insan Lashley
Director of Sales and Manufacturing - Allyson De Simone
Associate Publisher - Marco F. Pavia
President and C.O.O. - John Parker
C.E.O. and Chief Creative Officer - Stu Levy

A  Manga

TOKYOPOP Inc.
5900 Wilshire Blvd. Suite 2000
Los Angeles, CA 90036

E-mail: info@TOKYOPOP.com
Come visit us online at www.TOKYOPOP.com

KERORO GUNSO Volume 19
© Mine YOSHIZAKI 2009
First published in Japan in 2009 by KADOKAWA SHOTEN
PUBLISHING CO., LTD., Tokyo.
English translation rights arranged with KADOKAWA SHOTEN
PUBLISHING CO., LTD., Tokyo
through TUTTLE–MORI AGENCY, INC., Tokyo.
English text copyright © 2010 TOKYOPOP Inc.

ISBN: 978-1-4278-1783-9

First TOKYOPOP printing: July 2010
10 9 8 7 6 5 4 3 2 1
Printed in the USA

CHARACTER INTRODUCTIONS AND STORY SO FAR

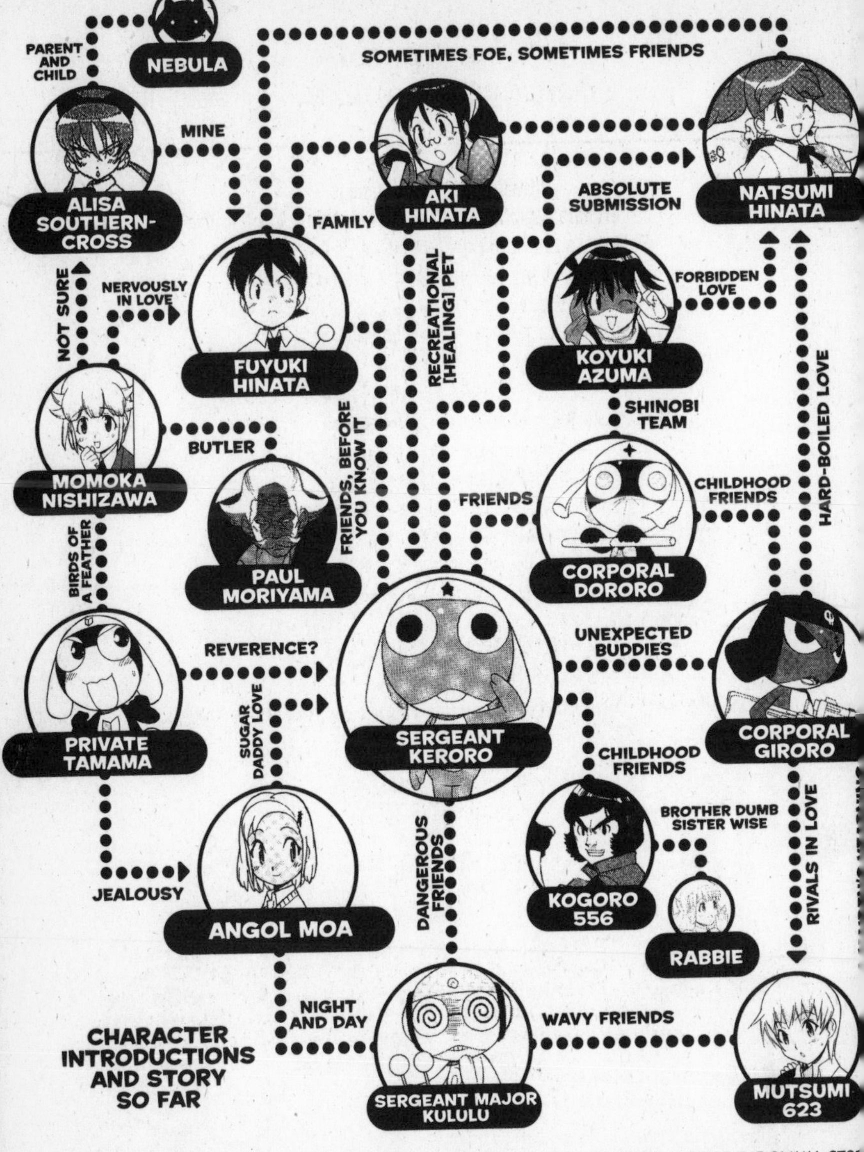
NEBULA
PARENT AND CHILD
SOMETIMES FOE, SOMETIMES FRIENDS
MINE
ALISA SOUTHERN-CROSS
AKI HINATA
FAMILY
NATSUMI HINATA
ABSOLUTE SUBMISSION
NOT SURE
NERVOUSLY IN LOVE
FUYUKI HINATA
RECREATIONAL [HEALING] PET
FORBIDDEN LOVE
KOYUKI AZUMA
HARD-BOILED LOVE
SHINOBI TEAM
BUTLER
MOMOKA NISHIZAWA
FRIENDS, BEFORE YOU KNOW IT
FRIENDS
CHILDHOOD FRIENDS
PAUL MORIYAMA
CORPORAL DORORO
BIRDS OF A FEATHER
REVERENCE?
UNEXPECTED BUDDIES
SUGAR DADDY LOVE
PRIVATE TAMAMA
SERGEANT KERORO
CORPORAL GIRORO
CHILDHOOD FRIENDS
BROTHER DUMB SISTER WISE
RIVALS IN LOVE
DANGEROUS FRIENDS
JEALOUSY
ANGOL MOA
KOGORO 556
RABBIE
NIGHT AND DAY
WAVY FRIENDS
SERGEANT MAJOR KULULU
MUTSUMI 623

AS CAPTAIN OF THE SPACE INVASION FORCE'S SPECIAL ADVANCE TEAM OF THE 58TH PLANET OF THE GAMMA STOR CLOUD SYSTEM, SGT. KERORO ENTERED THE HINATA FAMILY WHEN HIS PRE-ATTACK PREPARATION FOR THE INVASI OF EARTH RAN AFOUL VIA HIS EASY CAPTURE BY THE HINATA CHILDREN, FUYUKI AND NATSUMI. THANKS TO FUYUK KINDNESS, OR RATHER HIS CURIOSITY, SGT. KERORO SOON BECAME A WARD OF THE HINATA HOME, WITH FREE ROOM A BOARD IN EXCHANGE FOR HOUSEWORK. FROM THIS UNLIKELY BASE, HE AND HIS FOUR SUBORDINATES CONTINUE TO DEVI THEIR STRATEGY FOR THE IMPENDING INVASION OF POKOPEN...OR NOT.

KERORO'S PLATOON SEIZED THE OPPORTUNITY TO JOIN NATSUMI ON HER SCHOOL TRIP TO KYOTO, AND SUCCESSFUL RESCUED NATSUMI WHEN SHE WAS KIDNAPPED BY TAIREN, A SPLINTER NINJA GROUP. WHAT NEW CHALLENGES WILL FA KERORO AS THE FAMILY'S NORMAL LIFE RESUMES...?

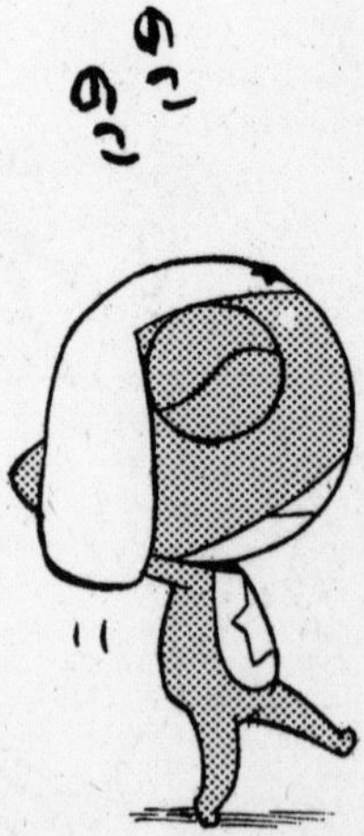
のこ のこ

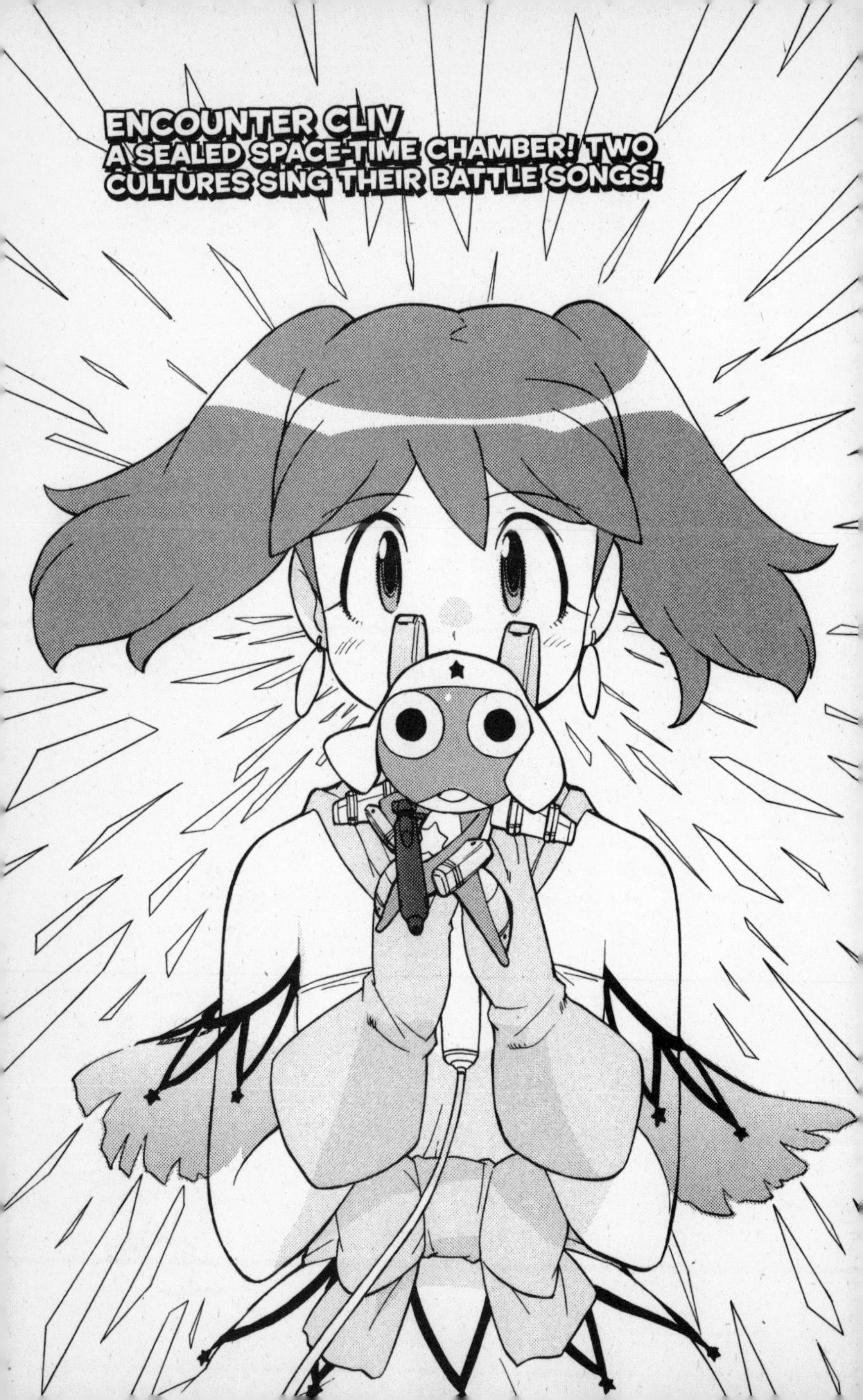
ENCOUNTER CLIV
A SEALED SPACE-TIME CHAMBER! TWO CULTURES SING THEIR BATTLE SONGS!

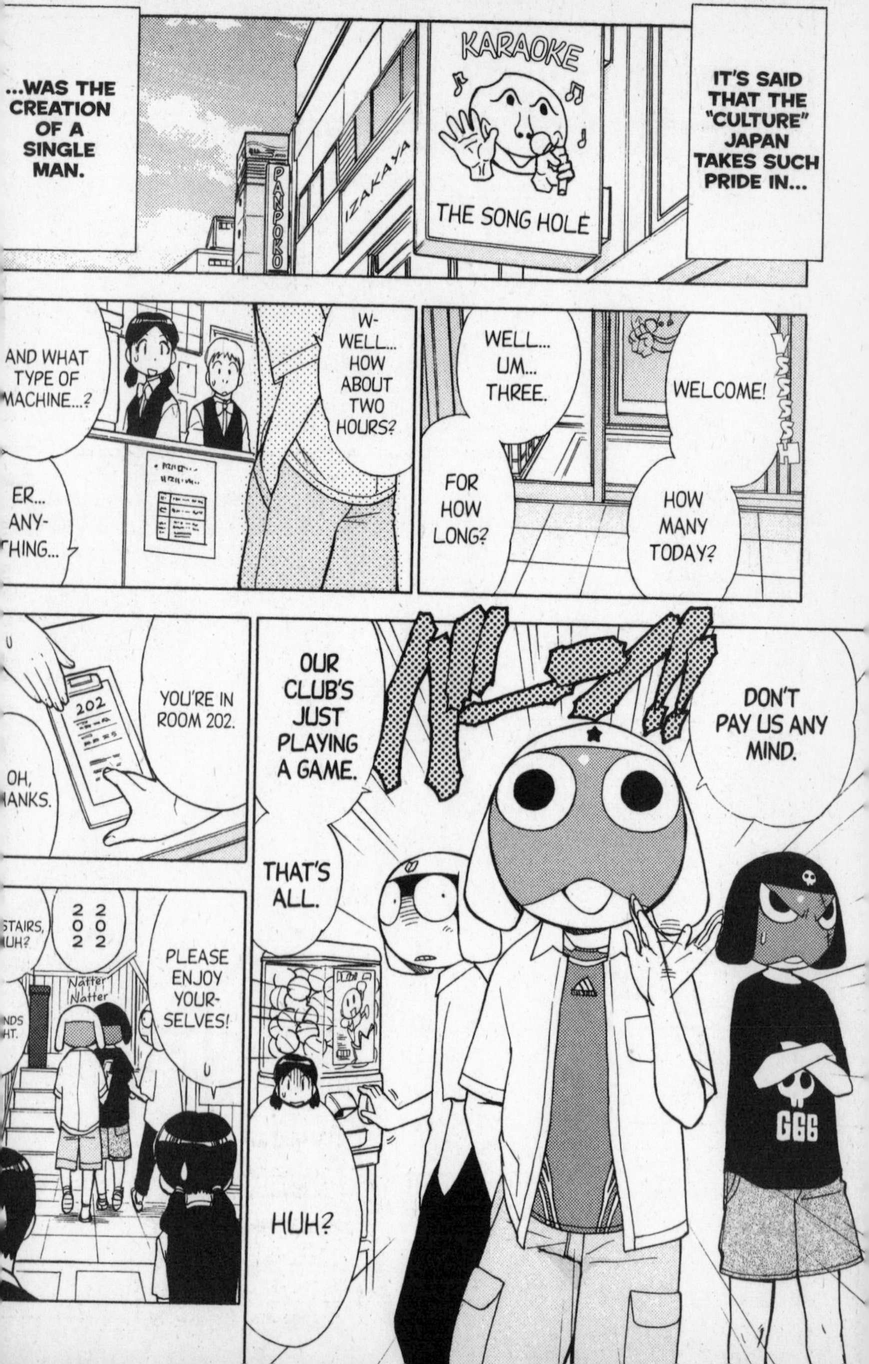
IT'S SAID THAT THE "CULTURE" JAPAN TAKES SUCH PRIDE IN...
KARAOKE
THE SONG HOLE
IZAKAYA
PANPOKO
...WAS THE CREATION OF A SINGLE MAN.
WELCOME!
HOW MANY TODAY?
WELL... UM... THREE.
FOR HOW LONG?
W-WELL... HOW ABOUT TWO HOURS?
AND WHAT TYPE OF MACHINE...?
ER... ANYTHING...
DON'T PAY US ANY MIND.
OUR CLUB'S JUST PLAYING A GAME.
THAT'S ALL.
HUH?
GGG
YOU'RE IN ROOM 202.
OH, ANKS.
202
202
PLEASE ENJOY YOURSELVES!
STAIRS, UH?
Natter Natter

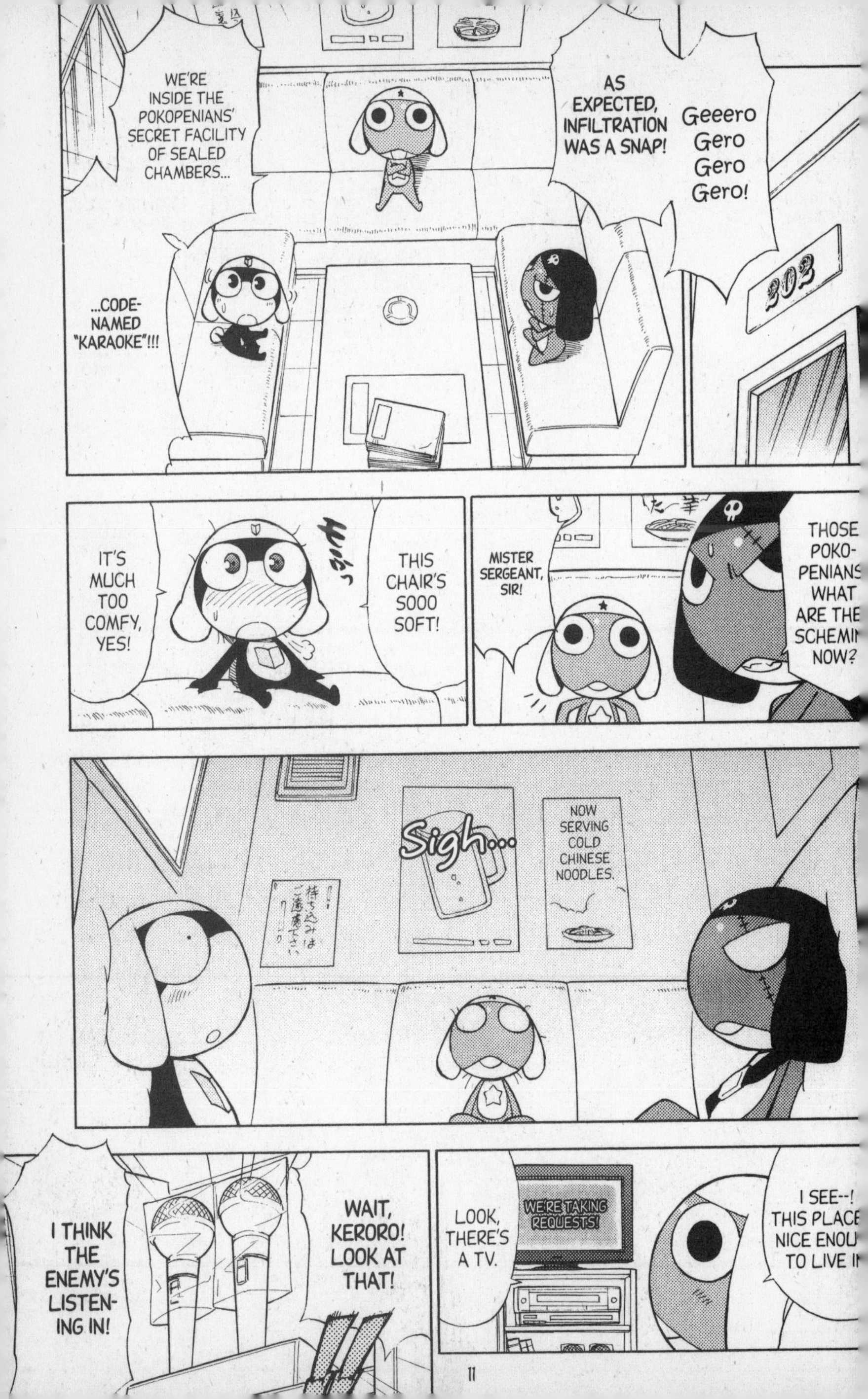
Geeero Gero Gero Gero!
AS EXPECTED, INFILTRATION WAS A SNAP!
WE'RE INSIDE THE POKOPENIANS' SECRET FACILITY OF SEALED CHAMBERS...
202
...CODE-NAMED "KARAOKE"!!!
THOSE POKO-PENIANS WHAT ARE THE SCHEMIN NOW?
MISTER SERGEANT, SIR!
THIS CHAIR'S SOOO SOFT!
IT'S MUCH TOO COMFY, YES!
NOW SERVING COLD CHINESE NOODLES.
Sigh...
I SEE--! THIS PLACE NICE ENOU TO LIVE IN
WE'RE TAKING REQUESTS!
LOOK, THERE'S A TV.
WAIT, KERORO! LOOK AT THAT!
I THINK THE ENEMY'S LISTEN-ING IN!

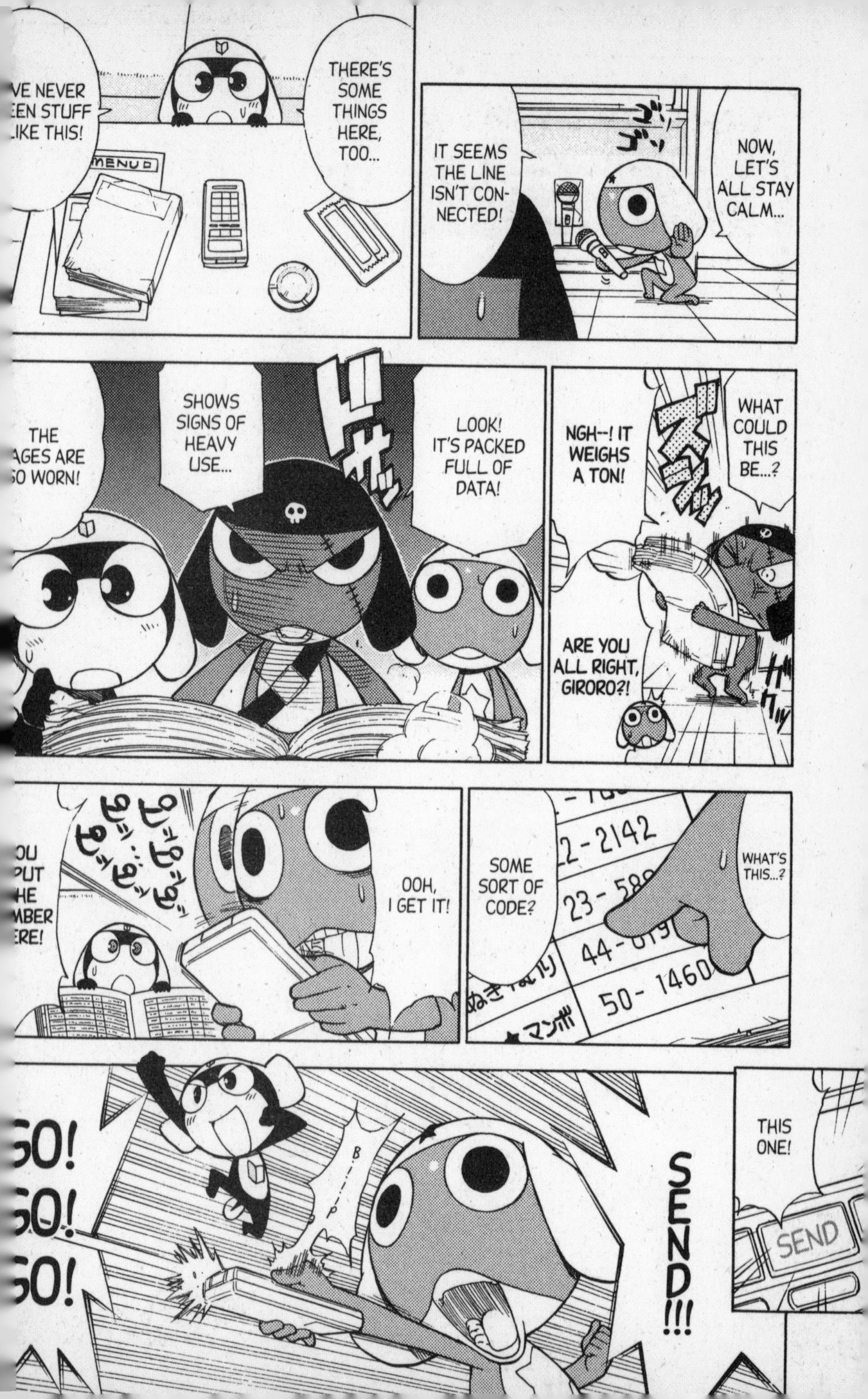
NOW, LET'S ALL STAY CALM...
IT SEEMS THE LINE ISN'T CON-NECTED!
THERE'S SOME THINGS HERE, TOO...
VE NEVER
EEN STUFF
LIKE THIS!
MENU
WHAT COULD THIS BE...?
NGH--! IT WEIGHS A TON!
ARE YOU ALL RIGHT, GIRORO?!
LOOK! IT'S PACKED FULL OF DATA!
SHOWS SIGNS OF HEAVY USE...
THE
AGES ARE
O WORN!
WHAT'S THIS...?
SOME SORT OF CODE?
2-2142
44-019
50- 1460
OOH, I GET IT!
OU
PUT
HE
MBER
ERE!
THIS ONE!
SEND
SEND!!!
GO!
GO!
GO!

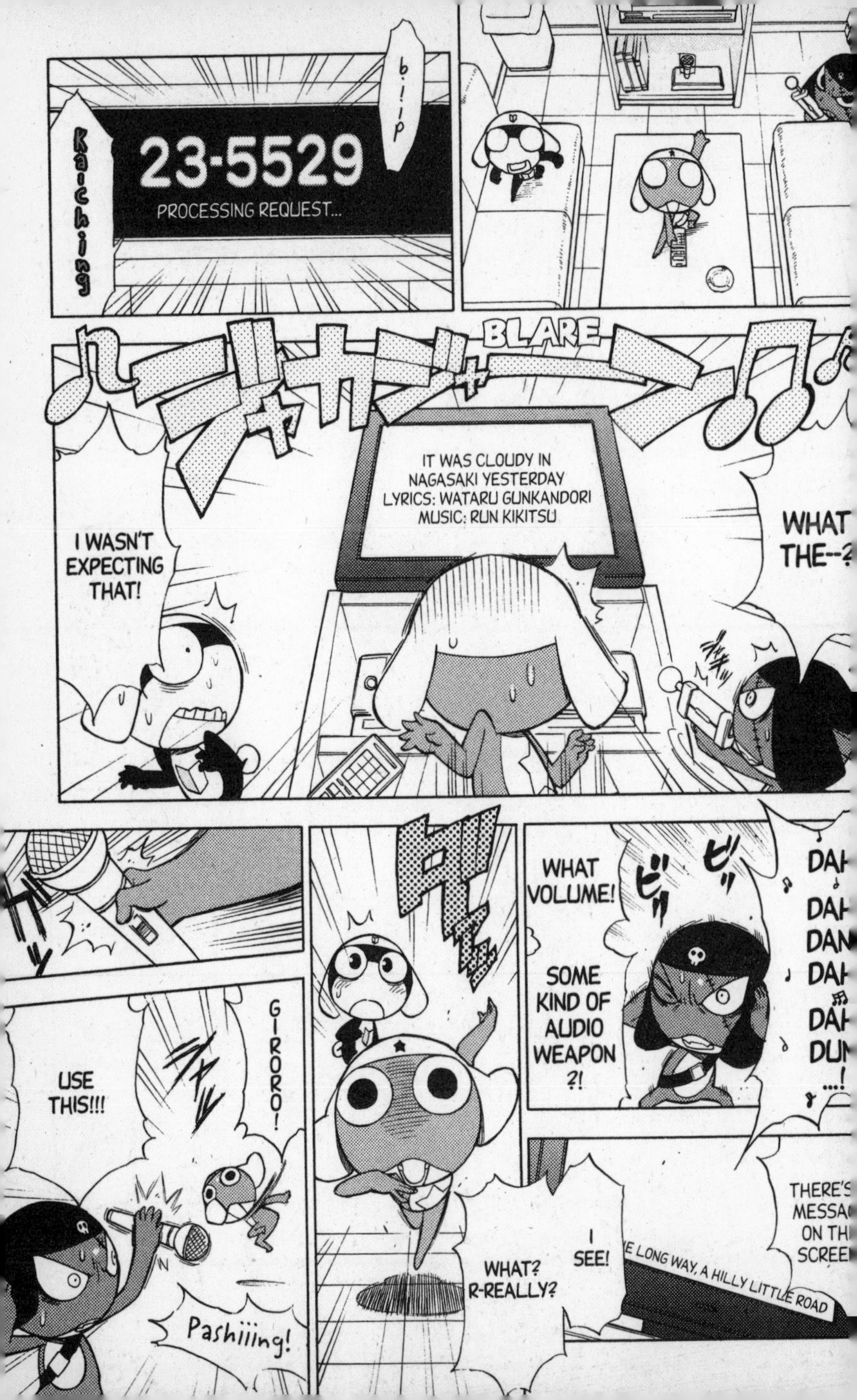
b..i..p
23-5529
PROCESSING REQUEST...
Kaiching
BLARE
IT WAS CLOUDY IN NAGASAKI YESTERDAY
LYRICS: WATARU GUNKANDORI
MUSIC: RUN KIKITSU
WHAT THE--?
I WASN'T EXPECTING THAT!
DAH DAH DAN DAH DAH DUN ....!
WHAT VOLUME!
SOME KIND OF AUDIO WEAPON ?!
THERE'S MESSAG ON TH SCREE
I SEE!
WHAT? R-REALLY?
E LONG WAY, A HILLY LITTLE ROAD
GIRORO!
USE THIS!!!
Pashiiing!

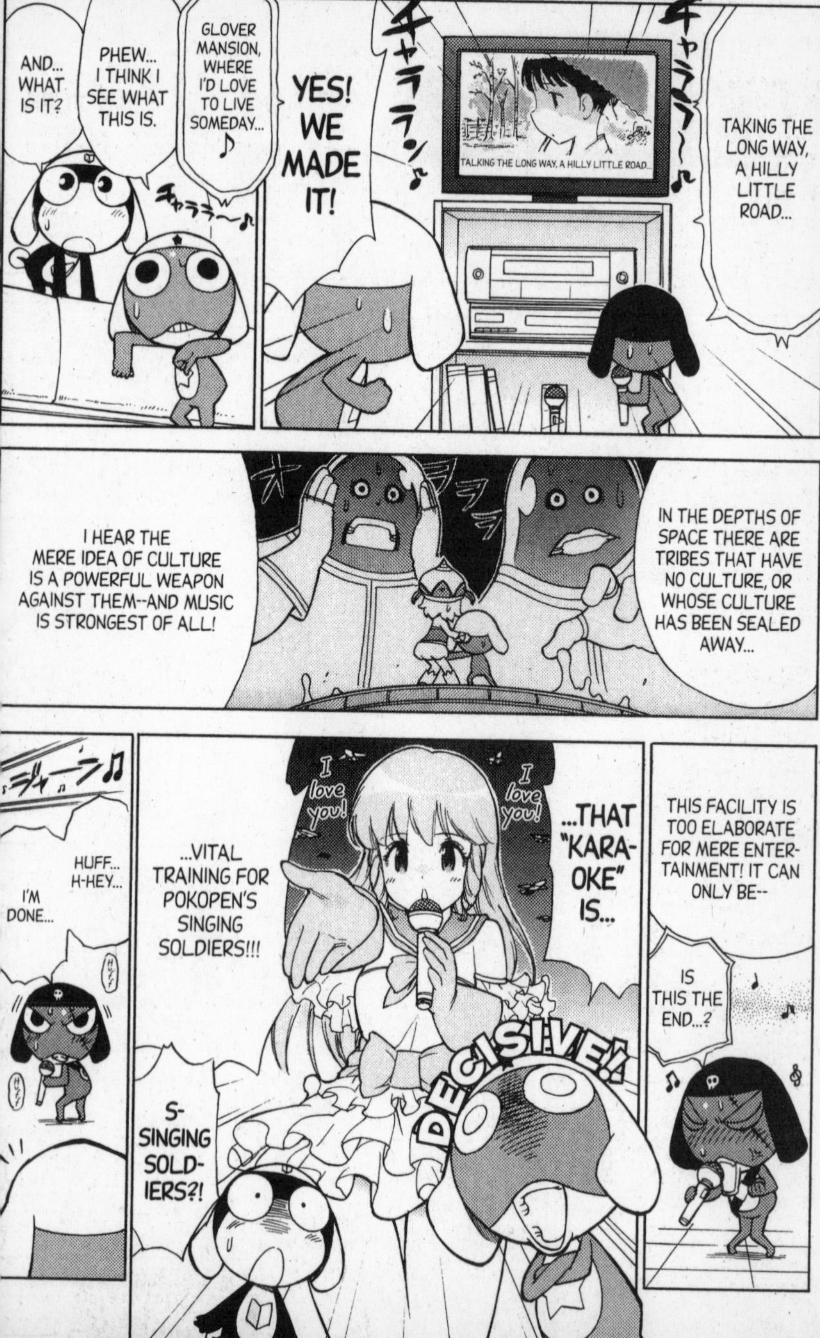
チャララ〜♪
TAKING THE LONG WAY, A HILLY LITTLE ROAD...
TALKING THE LONG WAY, A HILLY LITTLE ROAD...
チャララン♪
YES! WE MADE IT!
GLOVER MANSION, WHERE I'D LOVE TO LIVE SOMEDAY... ♪
チャララ〜♪
PHEW... I THINK I SEE WHAT THIS IS.
AND... WHAT IS IT?
IN THE DEPTHS OF SPACE THERE ARE TRIBES THAT HAVE NO CULTURE, OR WHOSE CULTURE HAS BEEN SEALED AWAY...
I HEAR THE MERE IDEA OF CULTURE IS A POWERFUL WEAPON AGAINST THEM--AND MUSIC IS STRONGEST OF ALL!
THIS FACILITY IS TOO ELABORATE FOR MERE ENTER-TAINMENT! IT CAN ONLY BE--
IS THIS THE END...?
...THAT "KARA-OKE" IS...
I love you!
I love you!
...VITAL TRAINING FOR POKOPEN'S SINGING SOLDIERS!!!
DECISIVE!!
S-SINGING SOLD-IERS?!
ジャーラ♫
HUFF... H-HEY...
I'M DONE...

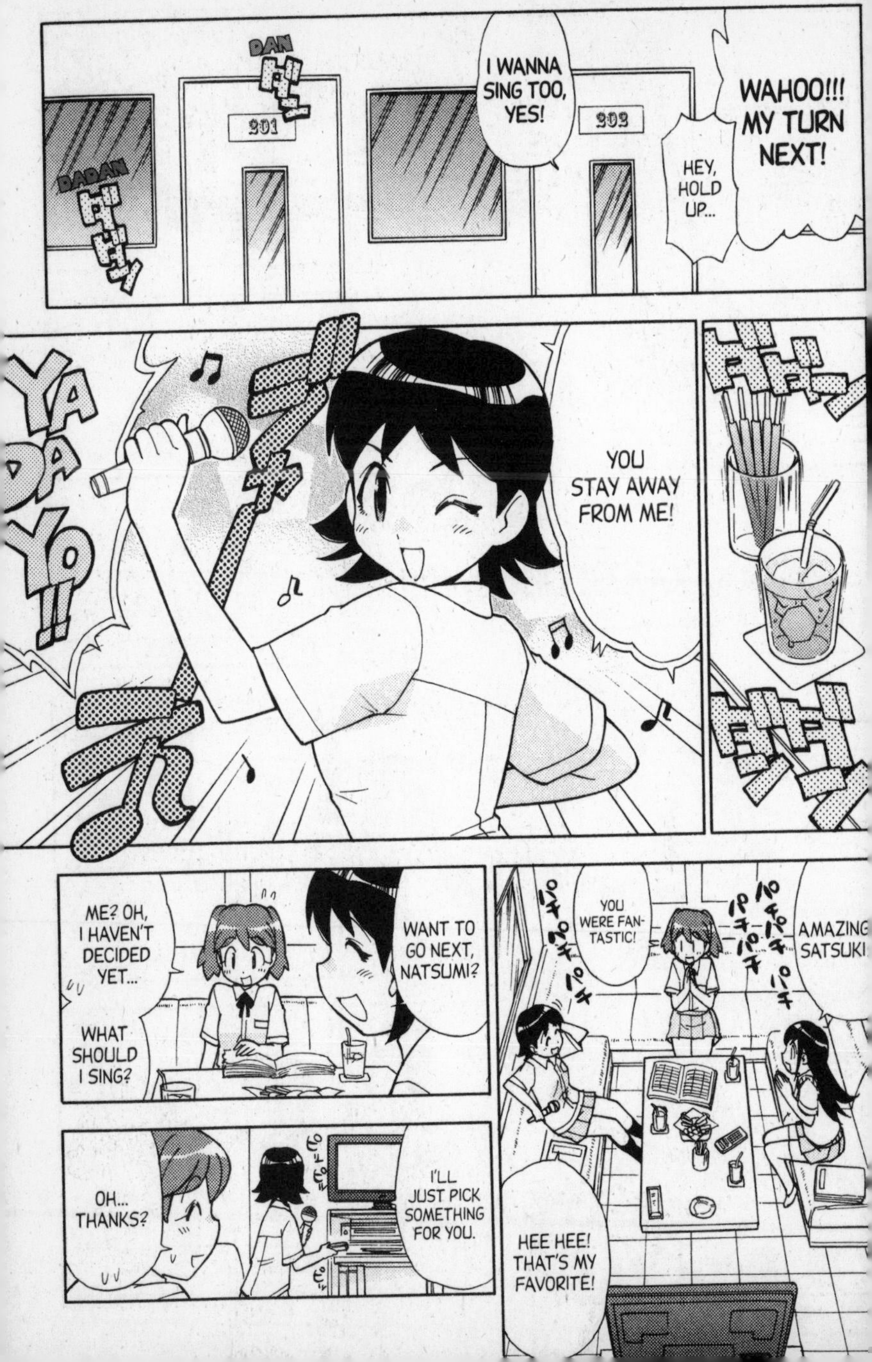
WAHOO!!! MY TURN NEXT!
HEY, HOLD UP...
I WANNA SING TOO, YES!
202
DAN
201
DADAN
YOU STAY AWAY FROM ME!
YA DA YO!!
AMAZING SATSUKI
YOU WERE FAN-TASTIC!
HEE HEE! THAT'S MY FAVORITE!
WANT TO GO NEXT, NATSUMI?
ME? OH, I HAVEN'T DECIDED YET...
WHAT SHOULD I SING?
I'LL JUST PICK SOMETHING FOR YOU.
OH... THANKS?

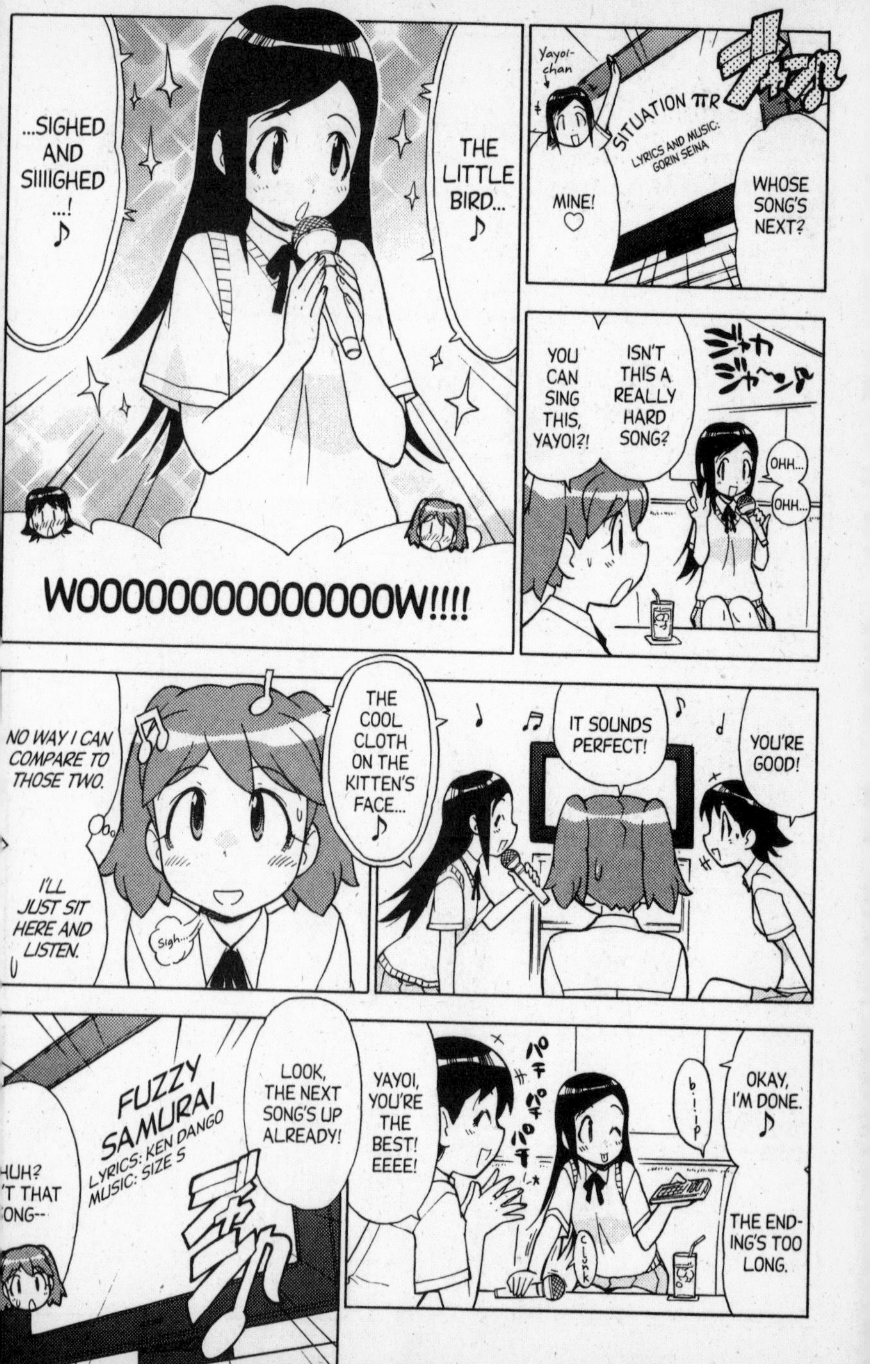
WHOSE SONG'S NEXT?
MINE! ♡
Yayoi-chan
SITUATION πR
LYRICS AND MUSIC: GORIN SEINA
ISN'T THIS A REALLY HARD SONG?
YOU CAN SING THIS, YAYOI?!
OHH...
OHH...
THE LITTLE BIRD... ♪
...SIGHED AND SIIIGHED ...! ♪
WOOOOOOOOOOOOOOOW!!!!
YOU'RE GOOD!
IT SOUNDS PERFECT!
THE COOL CLOTH ON THE KITTEN'S FACE... ♪
NO WAY I CAN COMPARE TO THOSE TWO.
I'LL JUST SIT HERE AND LISTEN.
Sigh...
OKAY, I'M DONE. ♪
THE ENDING'S TOO LONG.
b!!p
YAYOI, YOU'RE THE BEST! EEEE!
Clunk
LOOK, THE NEXT SONG'S UP ALREADY!
FUZZY SAMURAI
LYRICS: KEN DANGO
MUSIC: SIZE S
HUH?

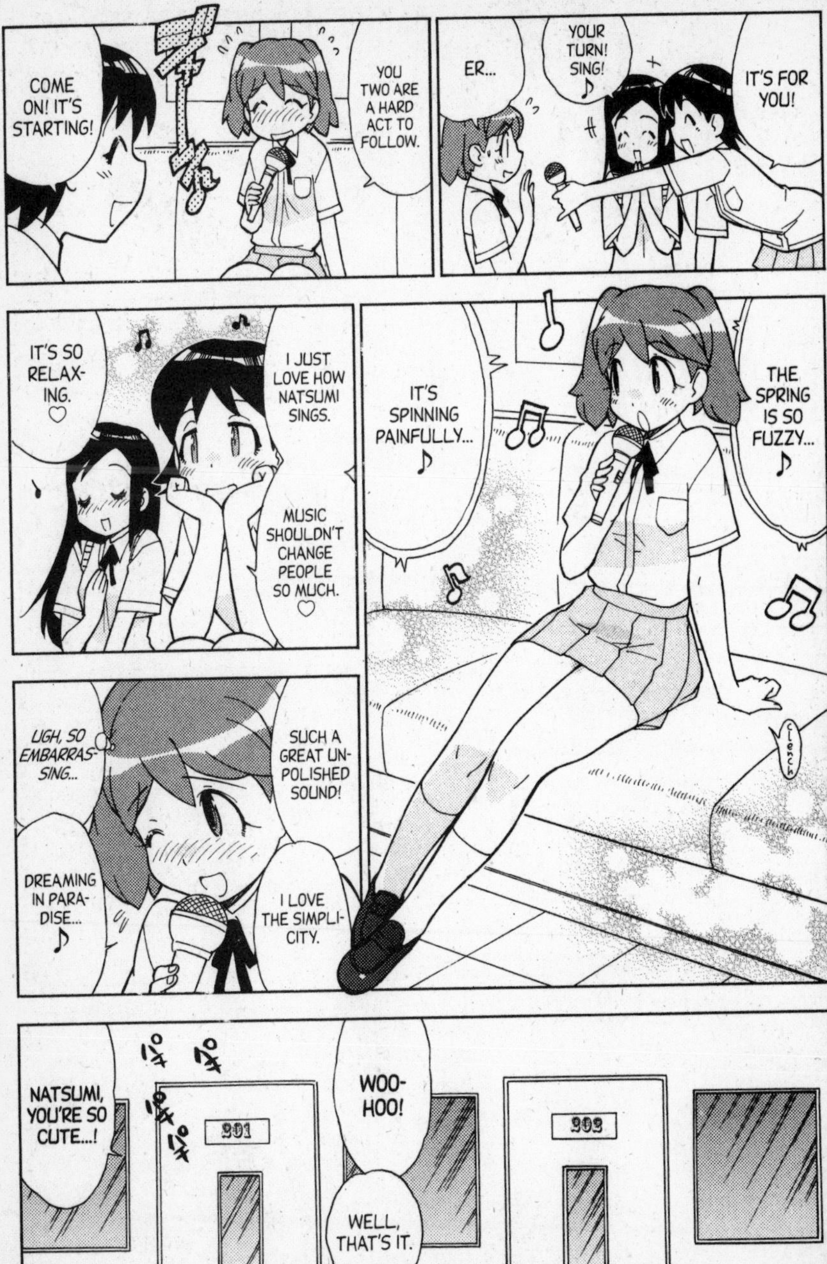
IT'S FOR YOU!
YOUR TURN! SING! ♪
ER...
YOU TWO ARE A HARD ACT TO FOLLOW.
COME ON! IT'S STARTING!
THE SPRING IS SO FUZZY... ♪
IT'S SPINNING PAINFULLY... ♪
Clench
I JUST LOVE HOW NATSUMI SINGS.
MUSIC SHOULDN'T CHANGE PEOPLE SO MUCH. ♡
IT'S SO RELAX-ING. ♡
SUCH A GREAT UN-POLISHED SOUND!
I LOVE THE SIMPLI-CITY.
UGH, SO EMBARRAS-SING...
DREAMING IN PARA-DISE... ♪
WOO-HOO!
WELL, THAT'S IT.
202
201
NATSUMI, YOU'RE SO CUTE...!

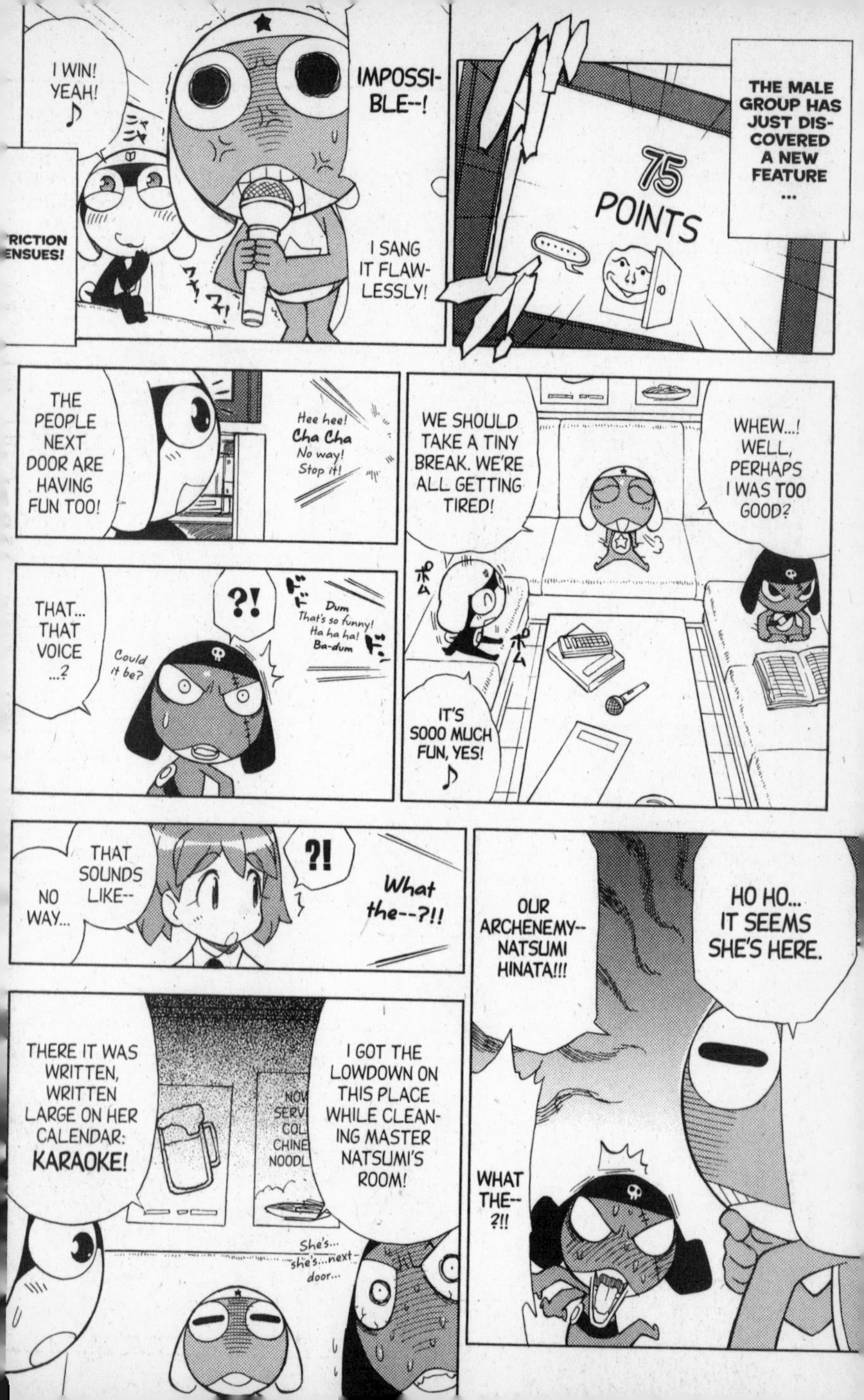
THE MALE GROUP HAS JUST DISCOVERED A NEW FEATURE ...
75 POINTS
IMPOSSIBLE--!
I SANG IT FLAWLESSLY!
I WIN! YEAH! ♪
RICTION ENSUES!
WHEW...! WELL, PERHAPS I WAS TOO GOOD?
WE SHOULD TAKE A TINY BREAK. WE'RE ALL GETTING TIRED!
IT'S SOOO MUCH FUN, YES! ♪
Hee hee! Cha Cha No way! Stop it!
THE PEOPLE NEXT DOOR ARE HAVING FUN TOO!
Dum That's so funny! Ha ha ha! Ba-dum
?!
THAT... THAT VOICE ...?
Could it be?
HO HO... IT SEEMS SHE'S HERE.
OUR ARCHENEMY-- NATSUMI HINATA!!!
WHAT THE-- ?!!
What the--?!!
?!
THAT SOUNDS LIKE--
NO WAY...
I GOT THE LOWDOWN ON THIS PLACE WHILE CLEANING MASTER NATSUMI'S ROOM!
THERE IT WAS WRITTEN, WRITTEN LARGE ON HER CALENDAR: KARAOKE!
She's... she's...next-door...

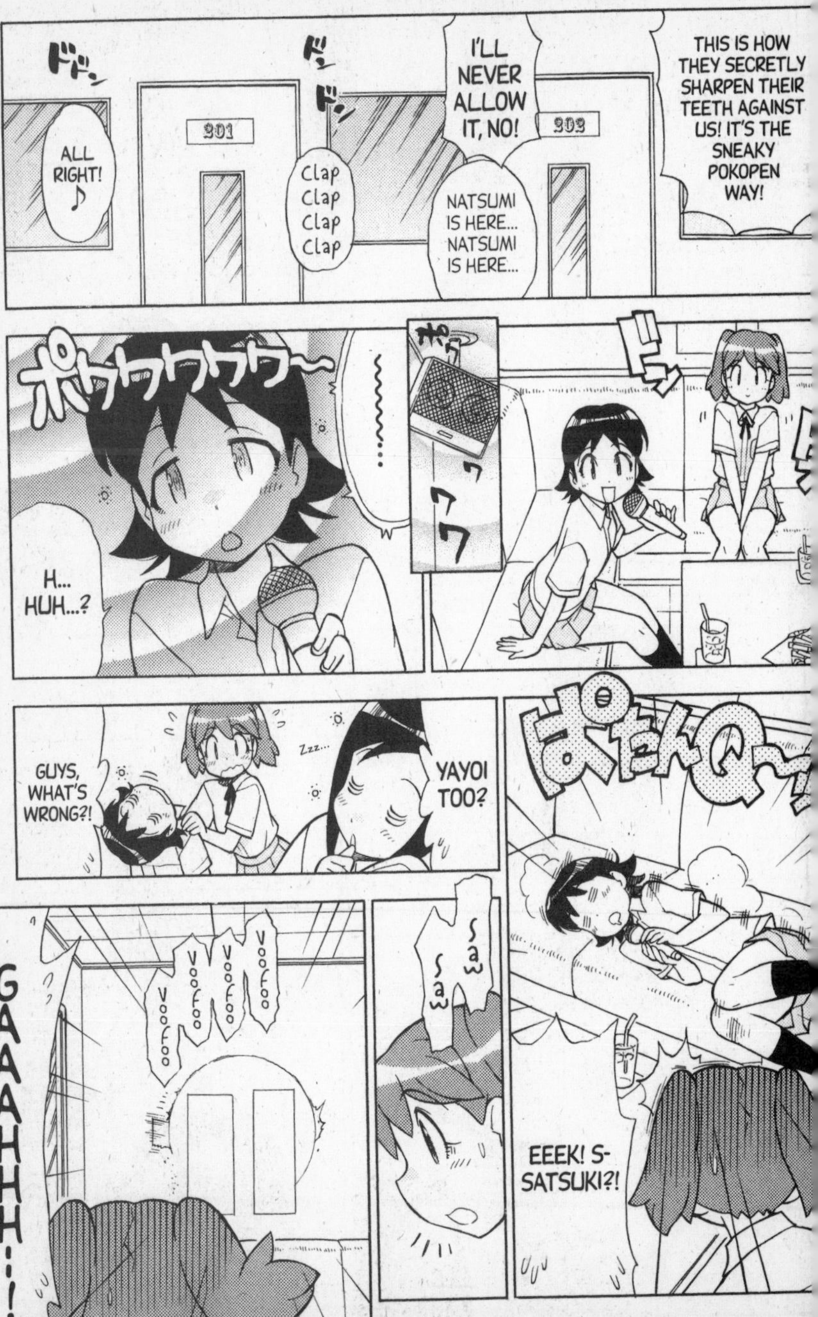
THIS IS HOW THEY SECRETLY SHARPEN THEIR TEETH AGAINST US! IT'S THE SNEAKY POKOPEN WAY!
I'LL NEVER ALLOW IT, NO!
302
NATSUMI IS HERE... NATSUMI IS HERE...
Clap Clap Clap Clap
201
ALL RIGHT! ♪
ドドン
H... HUH...?
YAYOI TOO?
Zzz...
GUYS, WHAT'S WRONG?!
EEEK! S-SATSUKI?!
saw saw
Voofoo Voofoo Voofoo
GAAAHHH..!

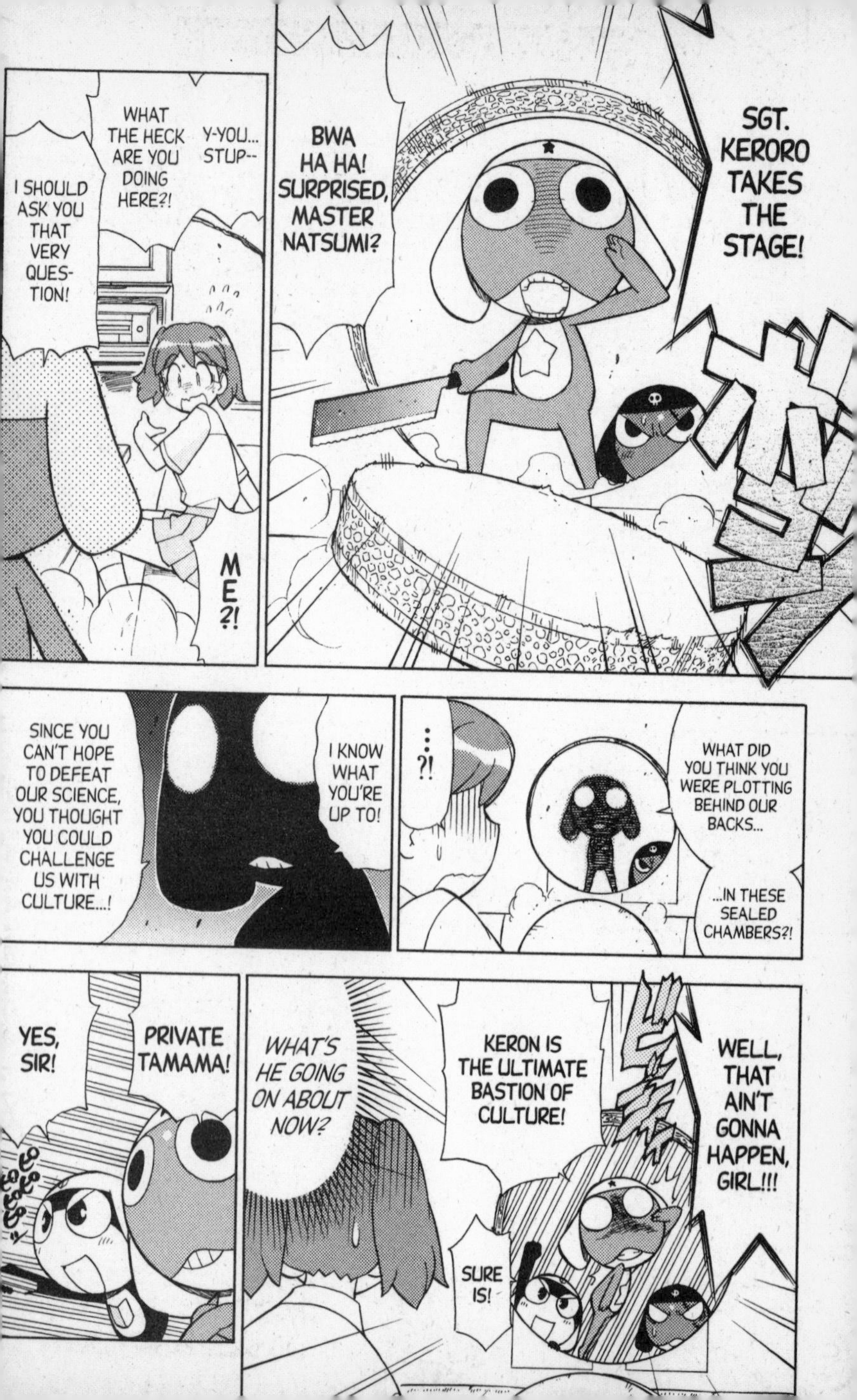

SGT. KERORO TAKES THE STAGE!
BWA HA HA! SURPRISED, MASTER NATSUMI?
Y-YOU... STUP--
WHAT THE HECK ARE YOU DOING HERE?!
I SHOULD ASK YOU THAT VERY QUES-TION!
ME?!
WHAT DID YOU THINK YOU WERE PLOTTING BEHIND OUR BACKS...
...IN THESE SEALED CHAMBERS?!
...?!
I KNOW WHAT YOU'RE UP TO!
SINCE YOU CAN'T HOPE TO DEFEAT OUR SCIENCE, YOU THOUGHT YOU COULD CHALLENGE US WITH CULTURE...!
WELL, THAT AIN'T GONNA HAPPEN, GIRL!!!
KERON IS THE ULTIMATE BASTION OF CULTURE!
WHAT'S HE GOING ON ABOUT NOW?
SURE IS!
PRIVATE TAMAMA!
YES, SIR!

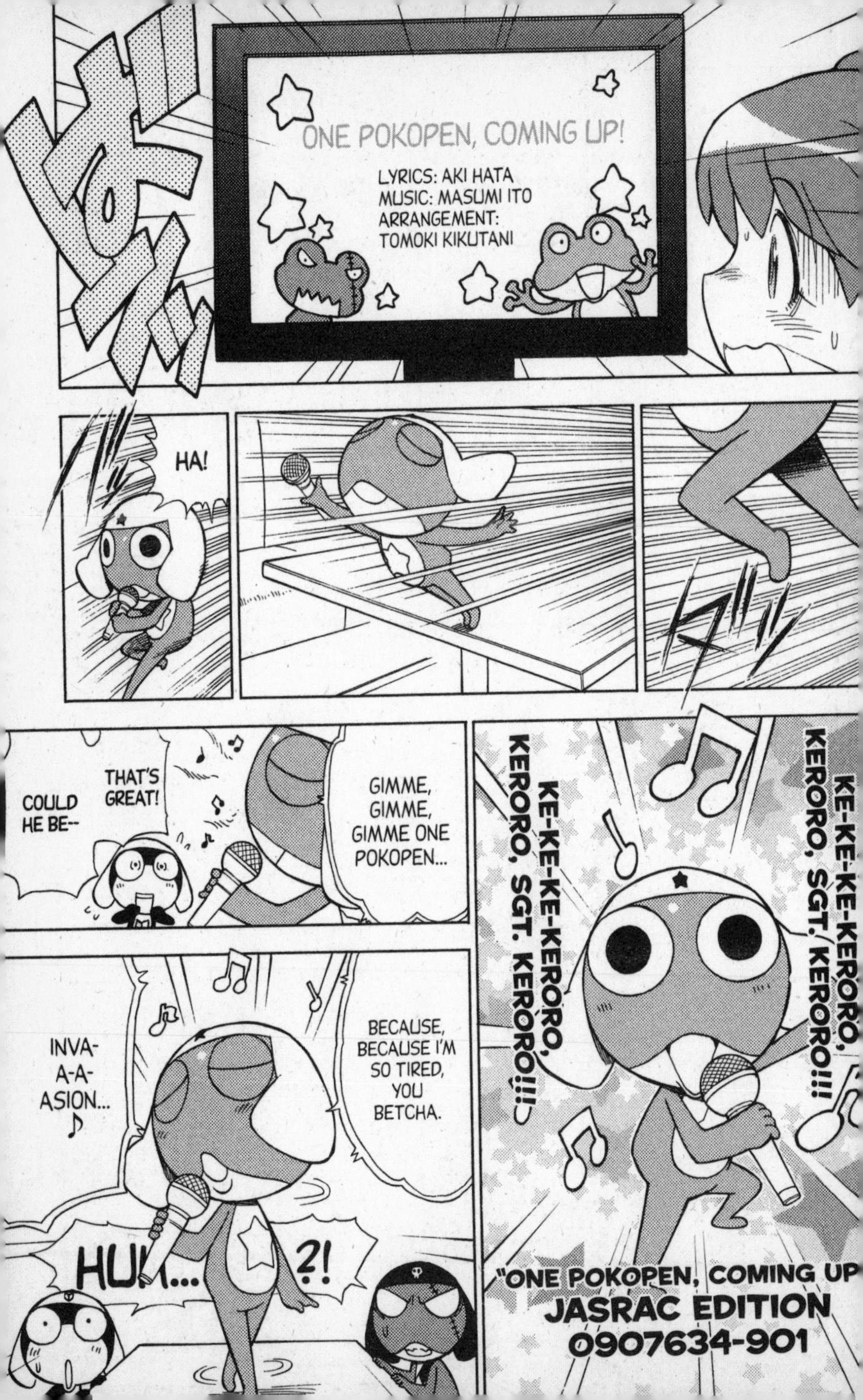
ONE POKOPEN, COMING UP!
LYRICS: AKI HATA
MUSIC: MASUMI ITO
ARRANGEMENT:
TOMOKI KIKUTANI
HA!
KE-KE-KE-KERORO, KERORO, SGT. KERORO!!!
KE-KE-KE-KERORO, KERORO, SGT. KERORO!!!
"ONE POKOPEN, COMING UP
JASRAC EDITION
0907634-901
GIMME, GIMME, GIMME ONE POKOPEN...
THAT'S GREAT!
COULD HE BE--
BECAUSE, BECAUSE I'M SO TIRED, YOU BETCHA.
INVA-A-A-ASION... ♪
?!
HUH...

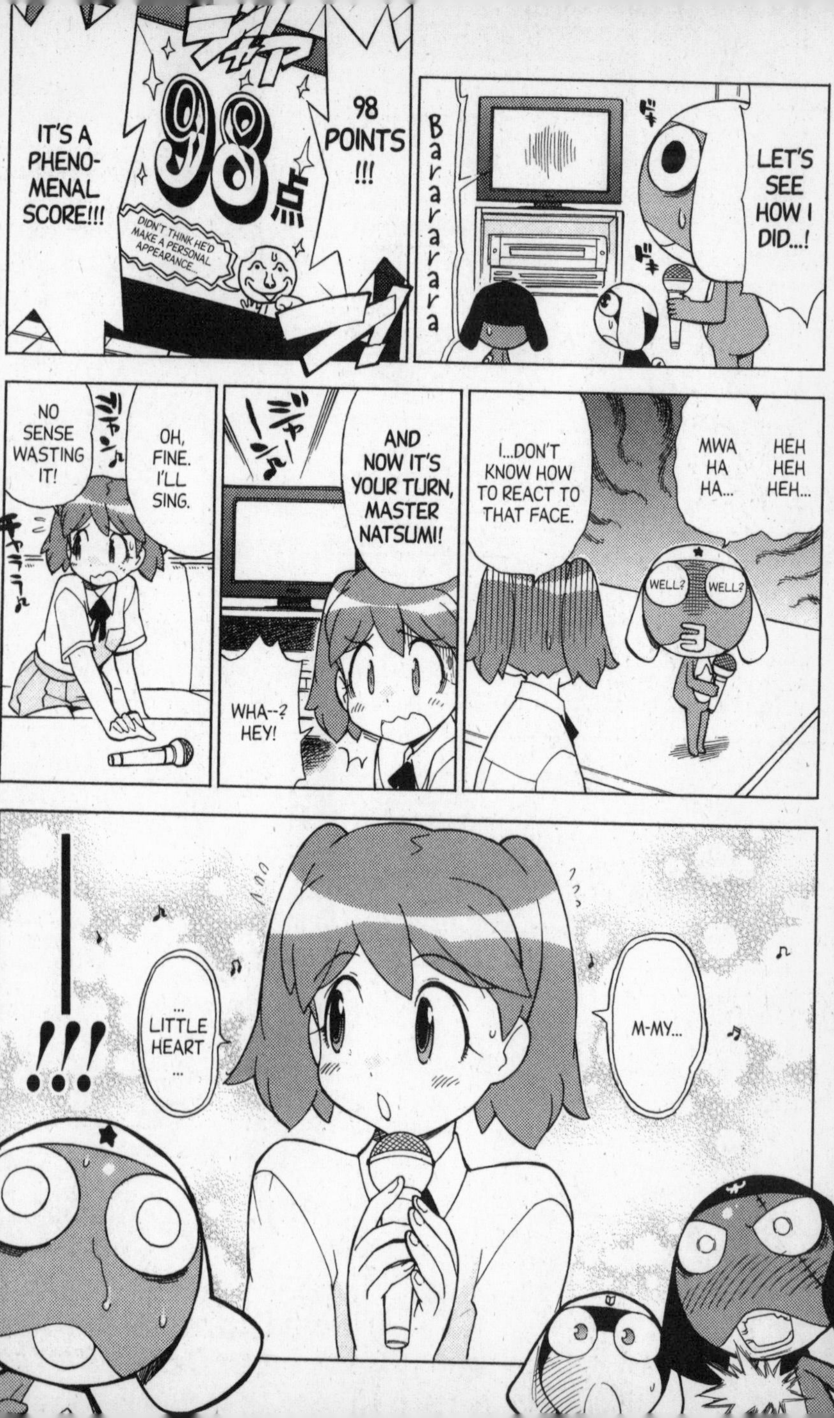
LET'S SEE HOW I DID...!
Bararararara
98 POINTS!!!
98点
IT'S A PHENOMENAL SCORE!!!
DIDN'T THINK HE'D MAKE A PERSONAL APPEARANCE...
HEH HEH HEH...
MWA HA HA...
WELL?
WELL?
I...DON'T KNOW HOW TO REACT TO THAT FACE.
AND NOW IT'S YOUR TURN, MASTER NATSUMI!
WHA--? HEY!
OH, FINE. I'LL SING.
NO SENSE WASTING IT!
M-MY...
...LITTLE HEART...
!!!

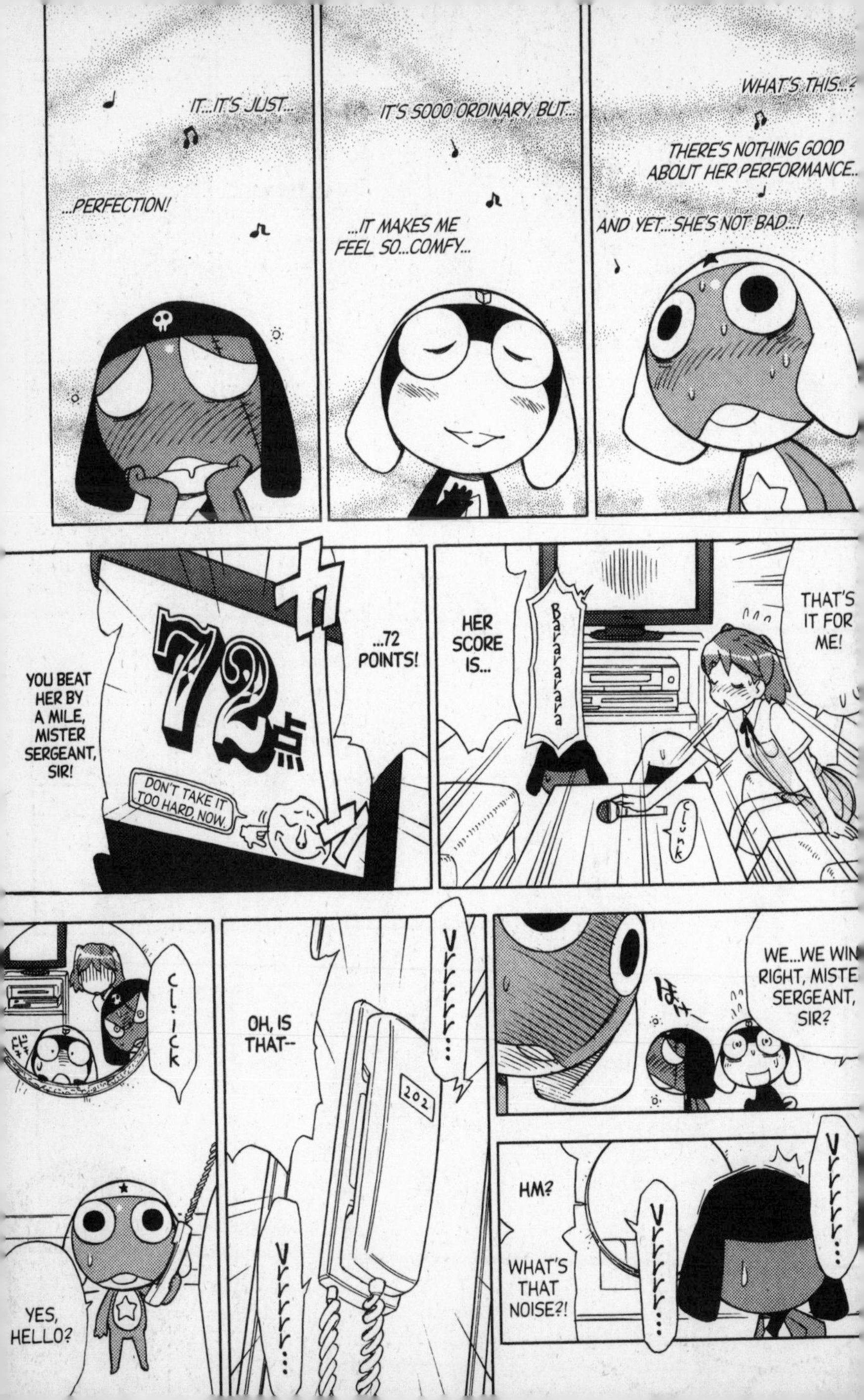
WHAT'S THIS...?
THERE'S NOTHING GOOD ABOUT HER PERFORMANCE...
AND YET...SHE'S NOT BAD...!
IT'S SOOO ORDINARY, BUT...
...IT MAKES ME FEEL SO...COMFY...
IT...IT'S JUST...
...PERFECTION!
THAT'S IT FOR ME!
Clunk
Barararara
HER SCORE IS...
...72 POINTS!
72点
DON'T TAKE IT TOO HARD, NOW.
YOU BEAT HER BY A MILE, MISTER SERGEANT, SIR!
WE...WE WIN RIGHT, MISTE SERGEANT, SIR?
Vrrrrr...
HM?
Vrrrrr...
WHAT'S THAT NOISE?!
Vrrrrr...
OH, IS THAT--
202
Vrrrrr...
Click
YES, HELLO?

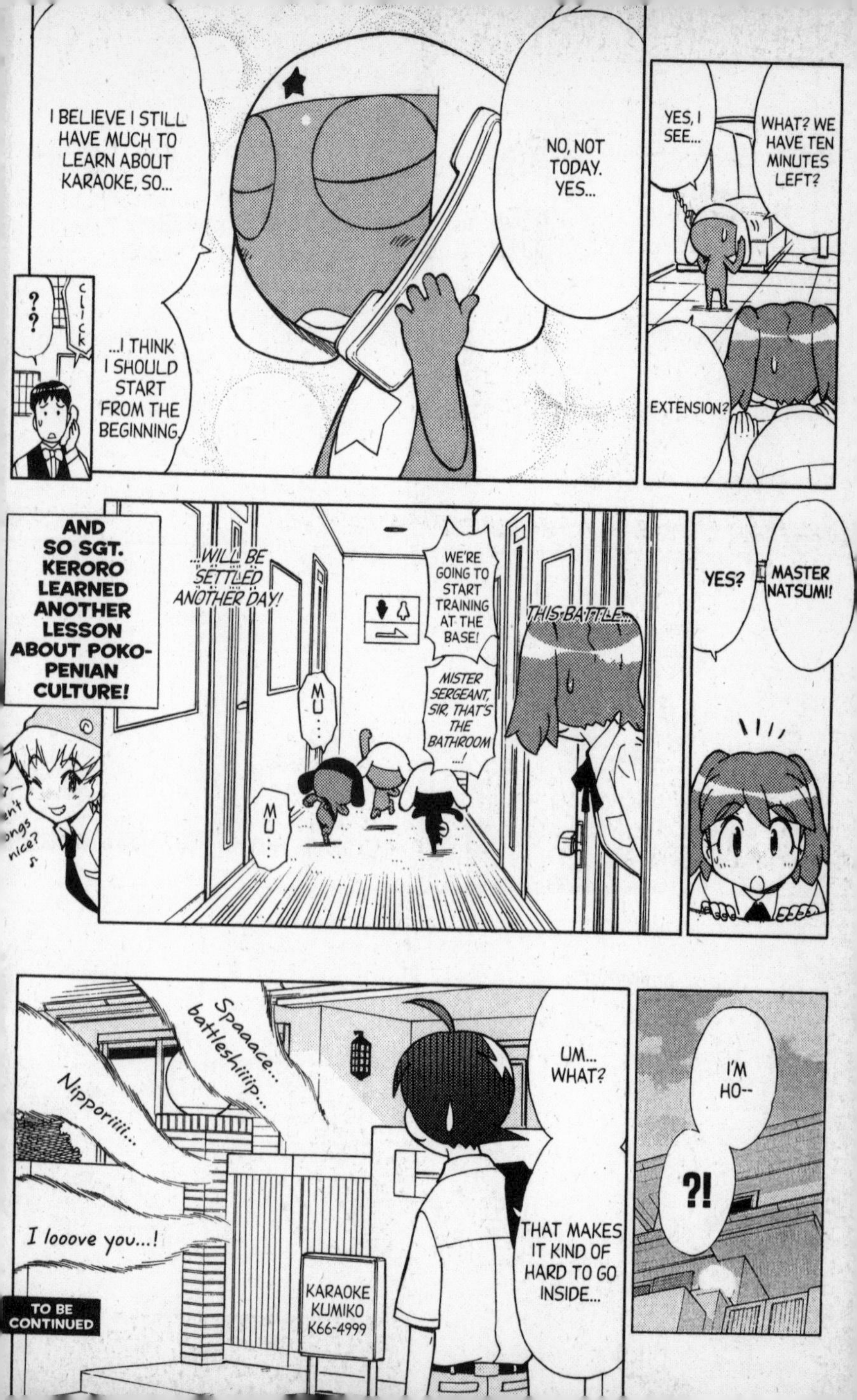
WHAT? WE HAVE TEN MINUTES LEFT?
YES, I SEE...
EXTENSION?
NO, NOT TODAY. YES...
I BELIEVE I STILL HAVE MUCH TO LEARN ABOUT KARAOKE, SO...
...I THINK I SHOULD START FROM THE BEGINNING.
CLICK
??
MASTER NATSUMI!
YES?
THIS BATTLE...
...WILL BE SETTLED ANOTHER DAY!
WE'RE GOING TO START TRAINING AT THE BASE!
MISTER SERGEANT, SIR, THAT'S THE BATHROOM...!
MU...
MU...
AND SO SGT. KERORO LEARNED ANOTHER LESSON ABOUT POKO-PENIAN CULTURE!
I'M HO--
?!
UM... WHAT?
THAT MAKES IT KIND OF HARD TO GO INSIDE...
Spaaace... battleshiiiip...
Nipporiiii...
I looove you...!
KARAOKE KUMIKO K66-4999
TO BE CONTINUED

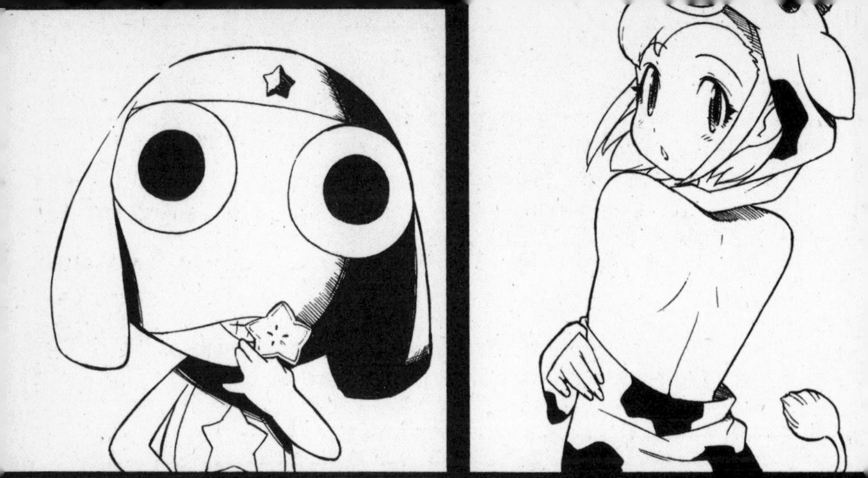

The earth was aimed at by the cruel alien. But they were HEPPOKO.

"KERORO GUNSO

ENCOUNTER CLV
A MAD COW?! OVERRUN BY A BULL-HEADED PLAN!

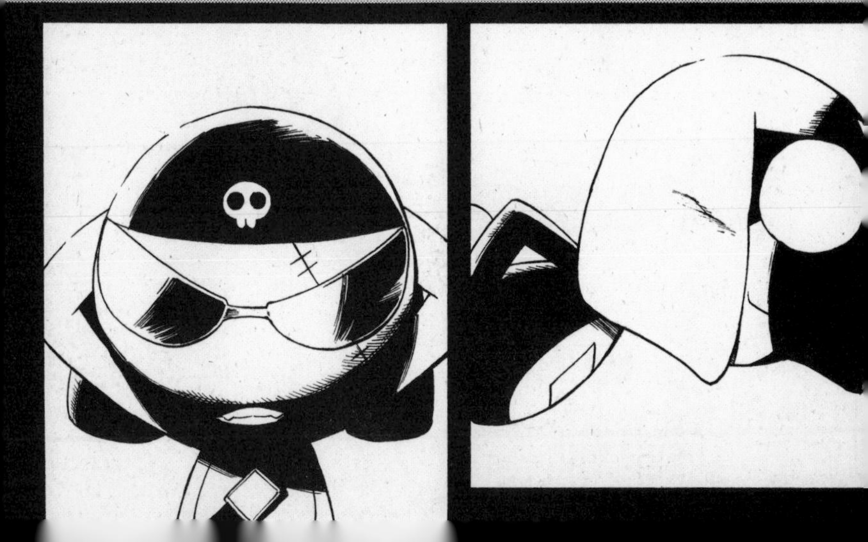

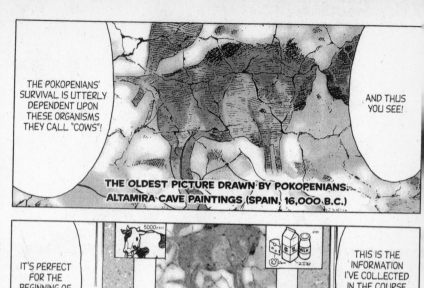

AND THUS YOU SEE!

THE POKOPENIANS' SURVIVAL IS UTTERLY DEPENDENT UPON THESE ORGANISMS THEY CALL "COWS"!

THE OLDEST PICTURE DRAWN BY POKOPENIANS: ALTAMIRA CAVE PAINTINGS (SPAIN, 16,000 B.C.)

THIS IS THE INFORMATION I'VE COLLECTED IN THE COURSE OF MY DETAILED RESEARCH!

IT'S PERFECT FOR THE BEGINNING OF THE YEAR!

Oh!

(DETAILED)

SO IF WE TAKE POSSESSION OF THEM, IT'S AN EASY VICTORY FOR US!

IT'S A WONDERFUL IDEA, YES!

WELL, NO... SEE, I THOUGHT IF WE BECAME COWS...

I KNEW IT--HE'S DRAGGING US ON ONE OF HIS TANGENTS...

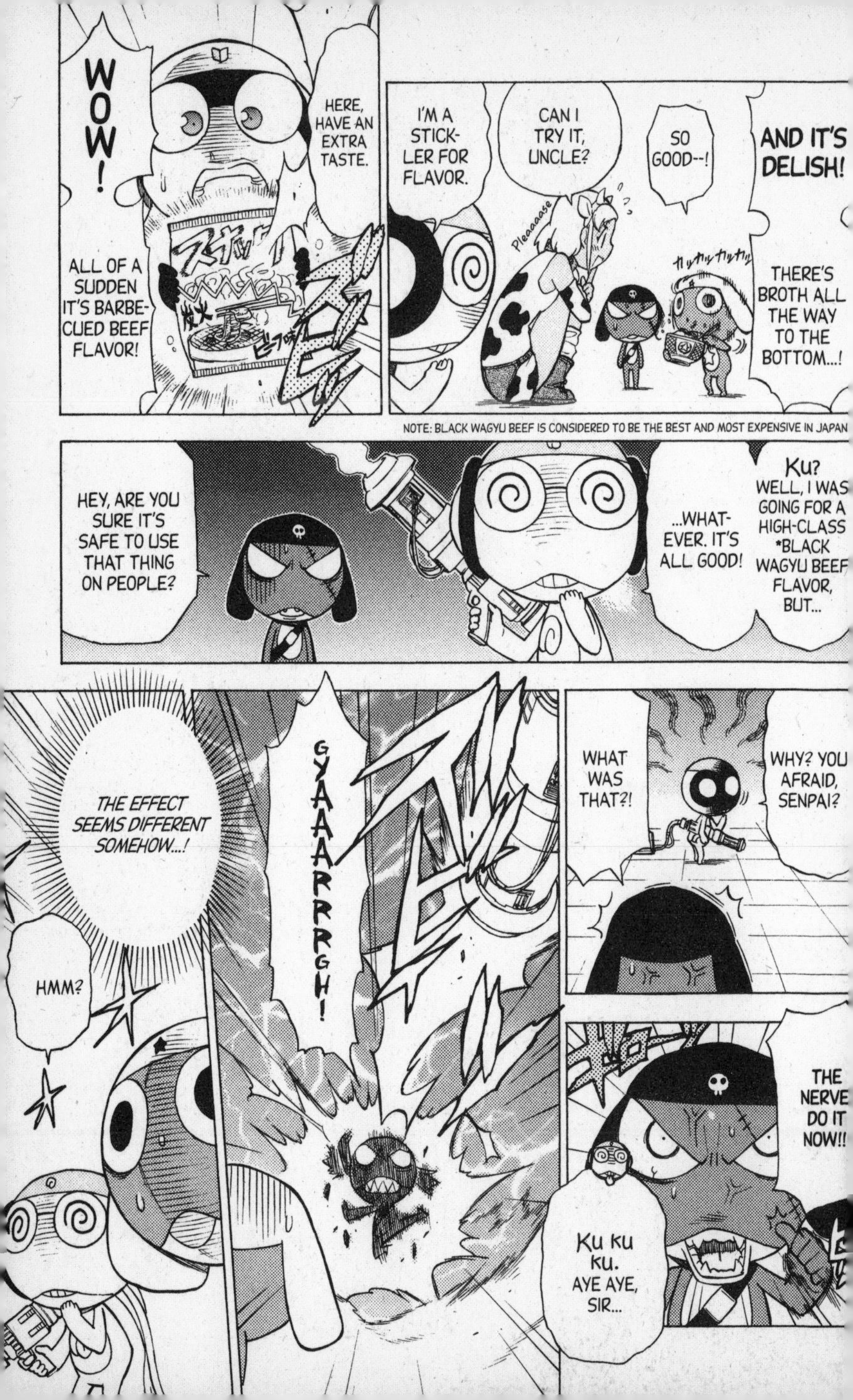
AND IT'S DELISH!
THERE'S BROTH ALL THE WAY TO THE BOTTOM...!
SO GOOD--!
CAN I TRY IT, UNCLE?
Pleaaaase
I'M A STICKLER FOR FLAVOR.
HERE, HAVE AN EXTRA TASTE.
WOW!
ALL OF A SUDDEN IT'S BARBECUED BEEF FLAVOR!
NOTE: BLACK WAGYU BEEF IS CONSIDERED TO BE THE BEST AND MOST EXPENSIVE IN JAPAN
Ku? WELL, I WAS GOING FOR A HIGH-CLASS *BLACK WAGYU BEEF FLAVOR, BUT...
...WHATEVER. IT'S ALL GOOD!
HEY, ARE YOU SURE IT'S SAFE TO USE THAT THING ON PEOPLE?
WHY? YOU AFRAID, SENPAI?
WHAT WAS THAT?!
THE NERVE DO IT NOW!!
Ku ku ku. AYE AYE, SIR...
GYAAAARRRRGH!
THE EFFECT SEEMS DIFFERENT SOMEHOW...!
HMM?

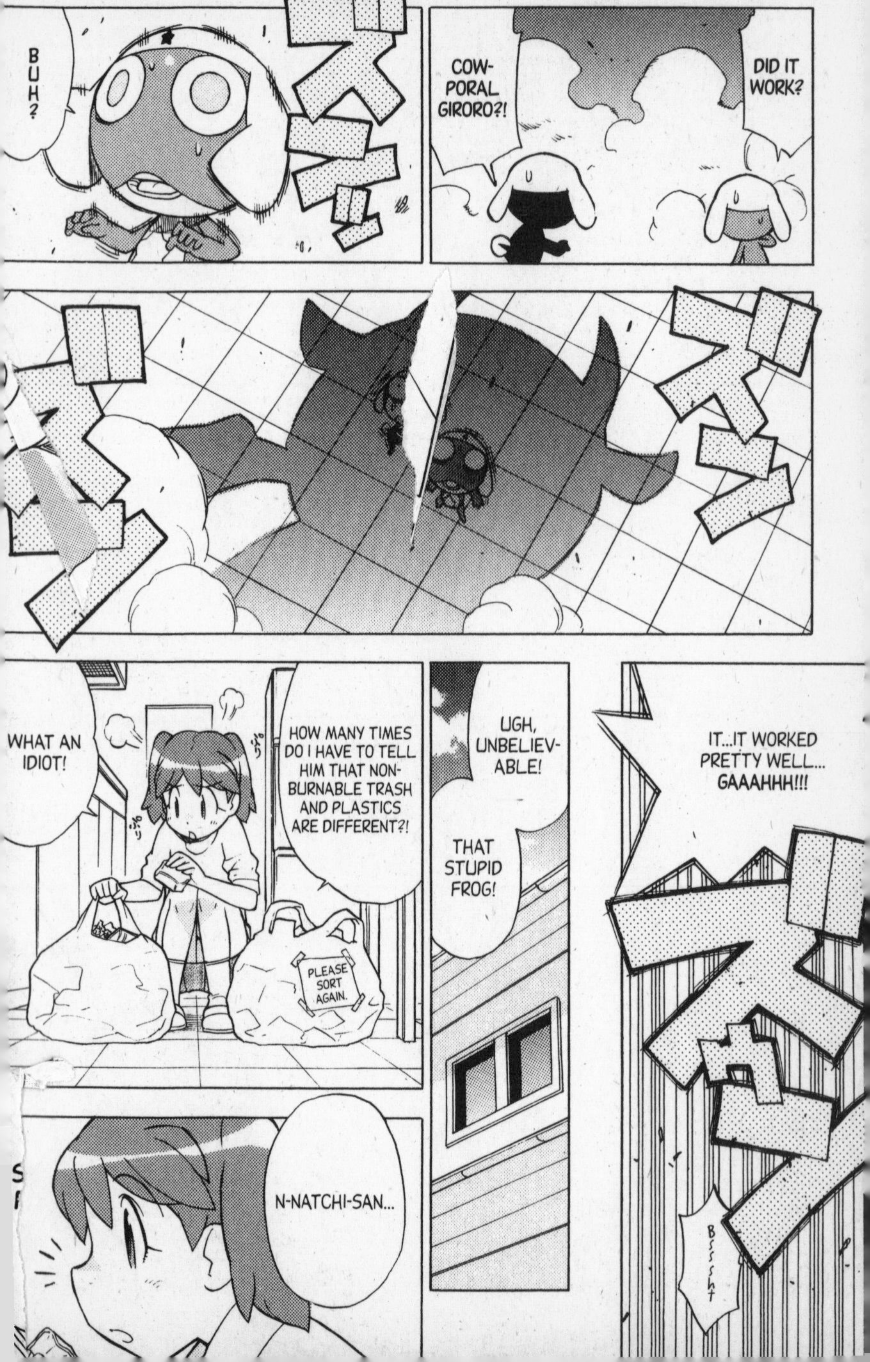
DID IT WORK?
COW-PORAL GIRORO?!
BUH?
IT...IT WORKED PRETTY WELL... GAAAHHH!!!
Bsssht
UGH, UNBELIEV-ABLE!
THAT STUPID FROG!
HOW MANY TIMES DO I HAVE TO TELL HIM THAT NON-BURNABLE TRASH AND PLASTICS ARE DIFFERENT?!
WHAT AN IDIOT!
PLEASE SORT AGAIN.
N-NATCHI-SAN...

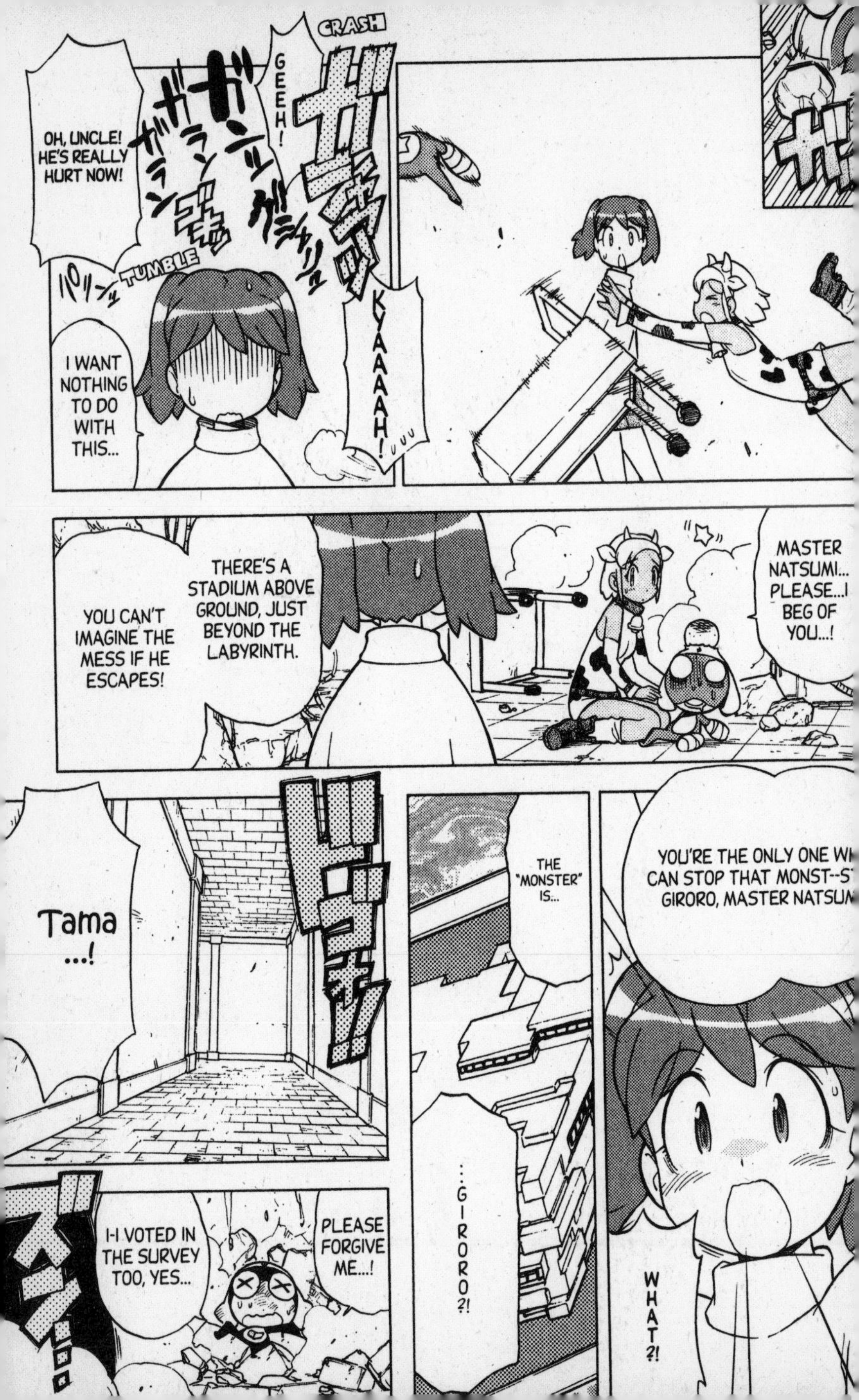

KYAAAAAH!
CRASH
GEEH!
TUMBLE
OH, UNCLE! HE'S REALLY HURT NOW!
I WANT NOTHING TO DO WITH THIS...
MASTER NATSUMI... PLEASE...I BEG OF YOU...!
THERE'S A STADIUM ABOVE GROUND, JUST BEYOND THE LABYRINTH.
YOU CAN'T IMAGINE THE MESS IF HE ESCAPES!
YOU'RE THE ONLY ONE WH
CAN STOP THAT MONST--ST
GIRORO, MASTER NATSUM
WHAT?!
THE "MONSTER" IS...
...GIRORO?!
Tama ...!
PLEASE FORGIVE ME...!
I-I VOTED IN THE SURVEY TOO, YES...

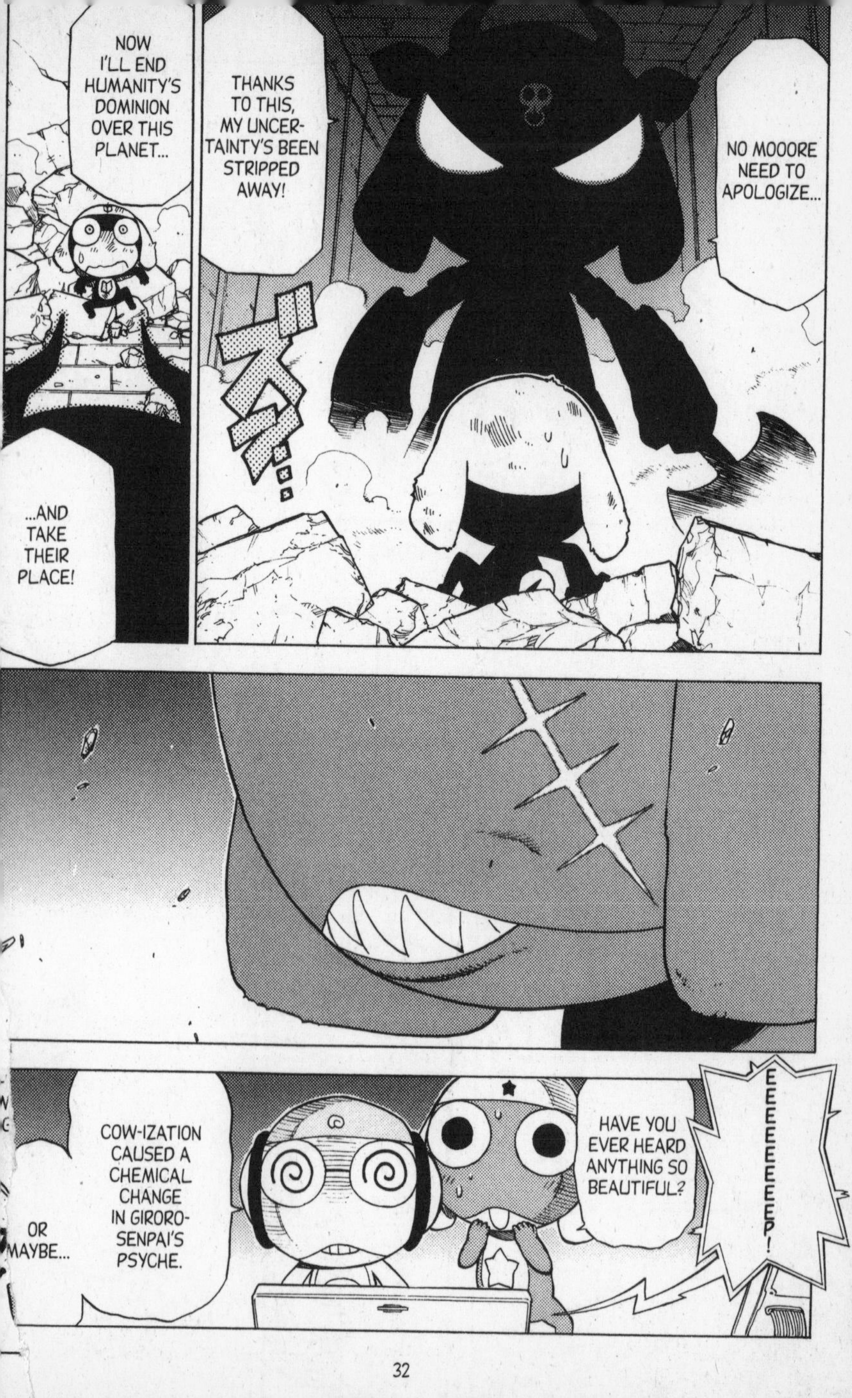
NO MOOORE NEED TO APOLOGIZE...
THANKS TO THIS, MY UNCERTAINTY'S BEEN STRIPPED AWAY!
NOW I'LL END HUMANITY'S DOMINION OVER THIS PLANET...
...AND TAKE THEIR PLACE!
EEEEEEEEP!
HAVE YOU EVER HEARD ANYTHING SO BEAUTIFUL?
COW-IZATION CAUSED A CHEMICAL CHANGE IN GIRORO-SENPAI'S PSYCHE.
OR MAYBE...

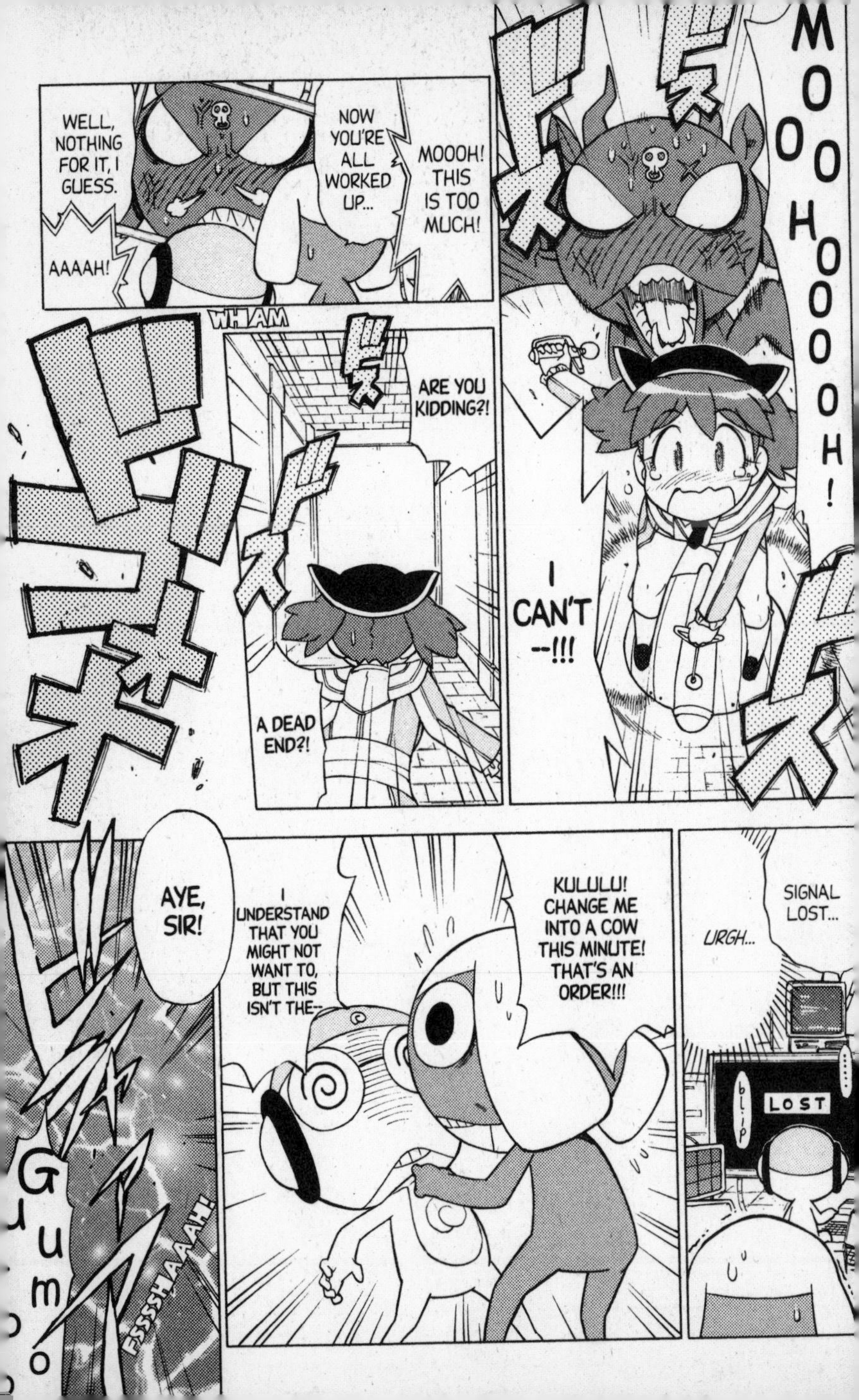
MOOOH HOOOOOOH!
I CAN'T --!!!
MOOOH! THIS IS TOO MUCH!
NOW YOU'RE ALL WORKED UP...
WELL, NOTHING FOR IT, I GUESS.
AAAAH!
WHAM
ARE YOU KIDDING?!
A DEAD END?!
SIGNAL LOST...
URGH...
blip
LOST
KULULU! CHANGE ME INTO A COW THIS MINUTE! THAT'S AN ORDER!!!
I UNDERSTAND THAT YOU MIGHT NOT WANT TO, BUT THIS ISN'T THE--
AYE, SIR!
FSSSHAAAH!
Gumoo

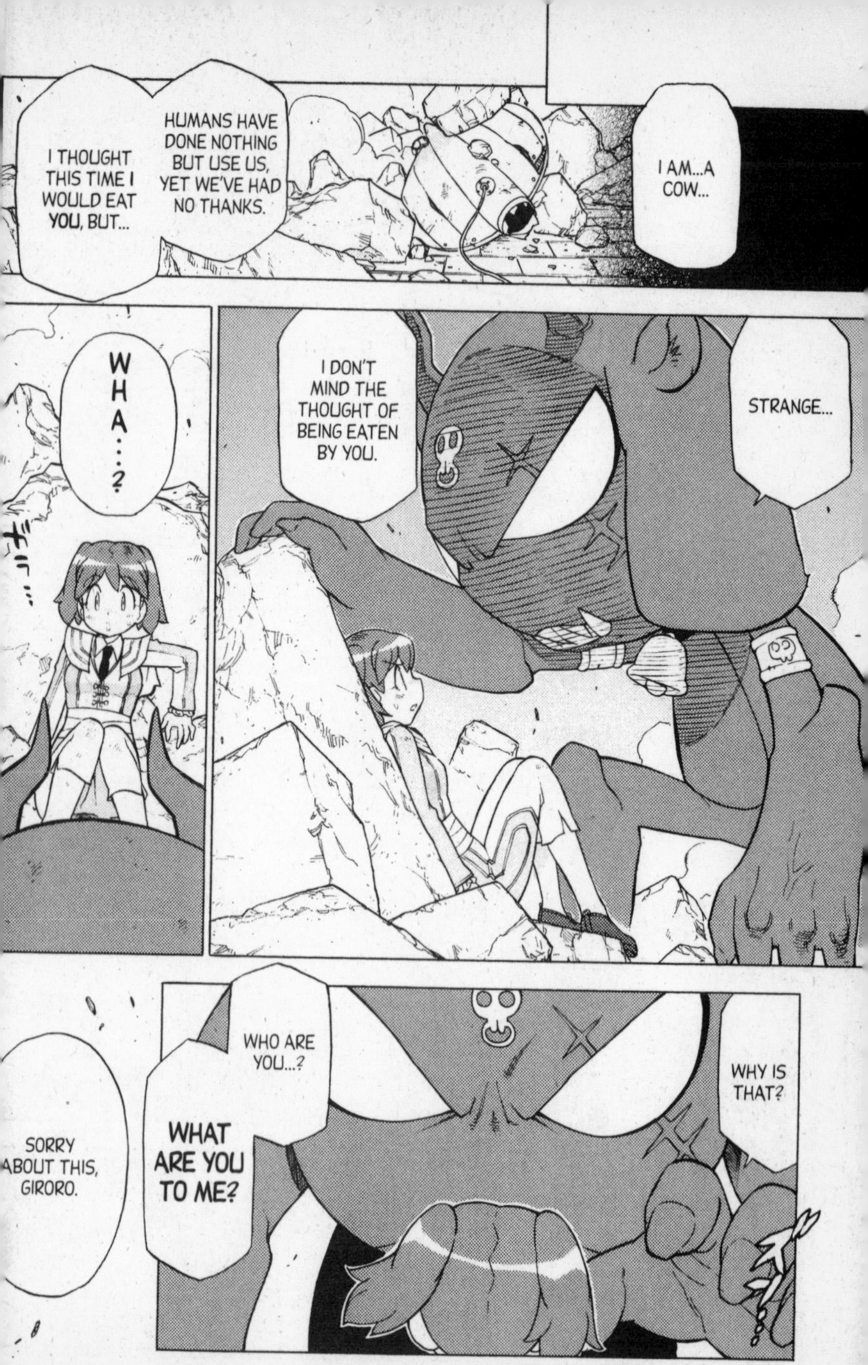
I AM...A COW...
HUMANS HAVE DONE NOTHING BUT USE US, YET WE'VE HAD NO THANKS.
I THOUGHT THIS TIME I WOULD EAT YOU, BUT...
STRANGE...
I DON'T MIND THE THOUGHT OF BEING EATEN BY YOU.
WHA...?
WHY IS THAT?
WHO ARE YOU...?
WHAT ARE YOU TO ME?
SORRY ABOUT THIS, GIRORO.

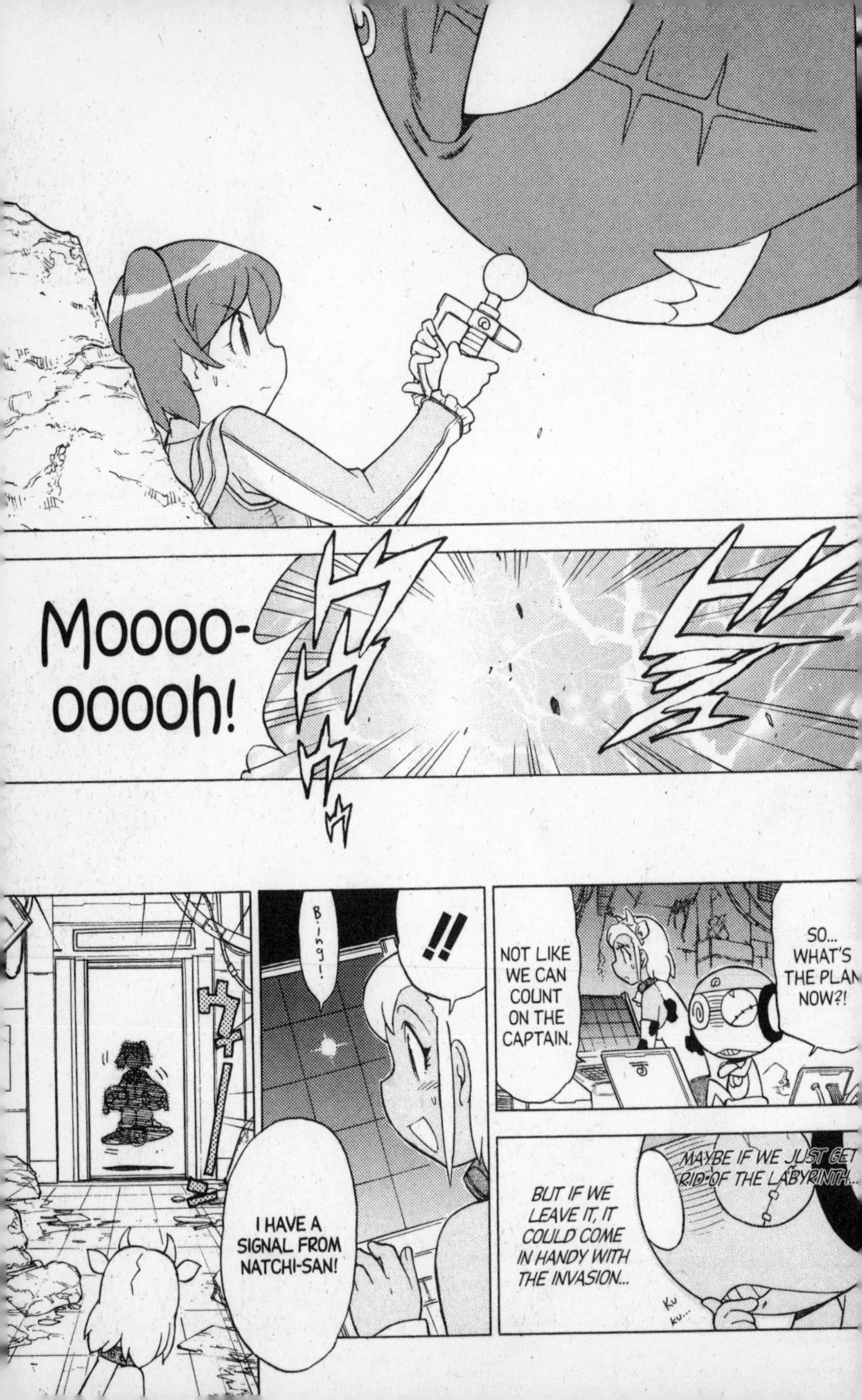
Moooo-oooooh!
SO... WHAT'S THE PLAN NOW?!
NOT LIKE WE CAN COUNT ON THE CAPTAIN.
MAYBE IF WE JUST GET RID OF THE LABYRINTH...
BUT IF WE LEAVE IT, IT COULD COME IN HANDY WITH THE INVASION...
KU KU...
Bing!
!!
I HAVE A SIGNAL FROM NATCHI-SAN!

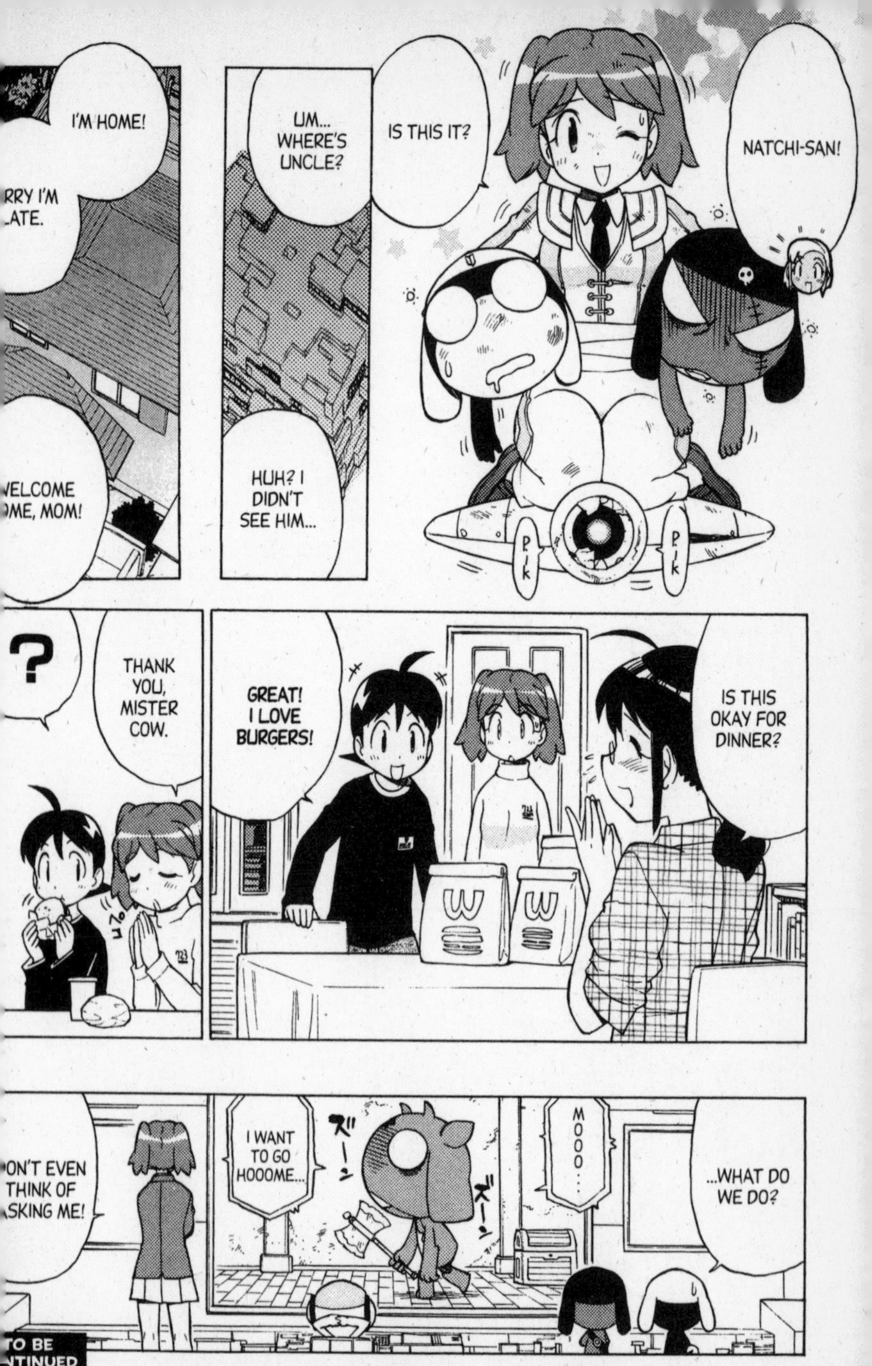
NATCHI-SAN!
IS THIS IT?
PIK
PIK
UM... WHERE'S UNCLE?
HUH? I DIDN'T SEE HIM...
I'M HOME!
RRY I'M LATE.
VELCOME
OME, MOM!
IS THIS OKAY FOR DINNER?
GREAT! I LOVE BURGERS!
THANK YOU, MISTER COW.
?
...WHAT DO WE DO?
MOOO...
I WANT TO GO HOOOME...
ON'T EVEN THINK OF
SKING ME!
TO BE
NTINUED

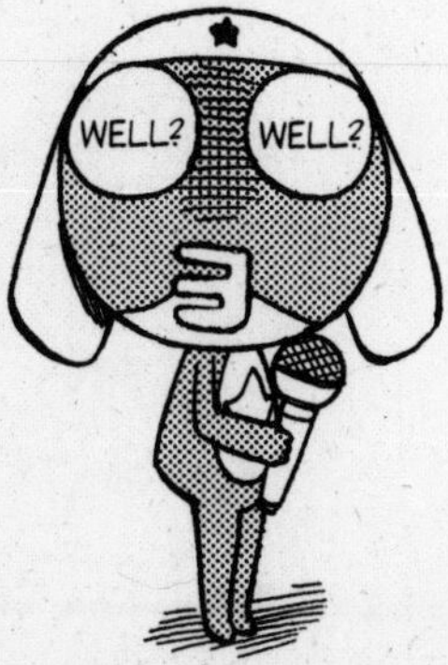
WELL? WELL?

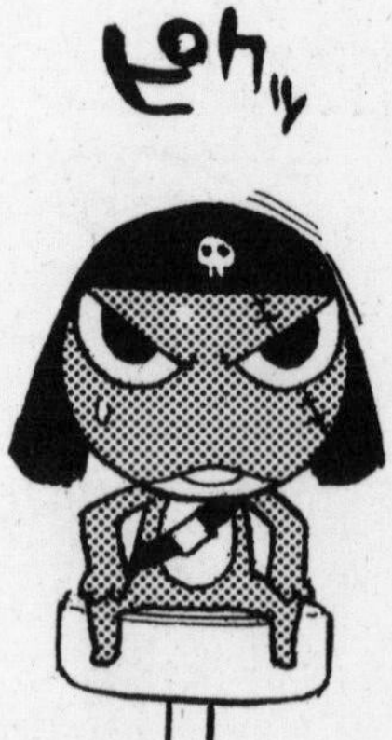
ピクッ

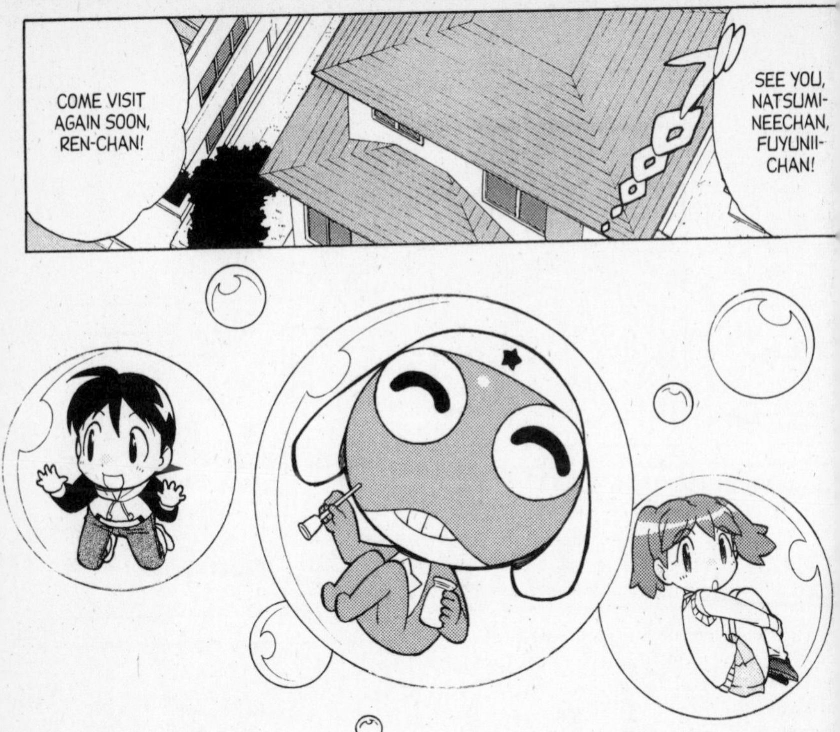
SEE YOU, NATSUMI-NEECHAN, FUYUNII-CHAN!
COME VISIT AGAIN SOON, REN-CHAN!

ENCOUNTER CLVI
KERON BUBBLES OVER

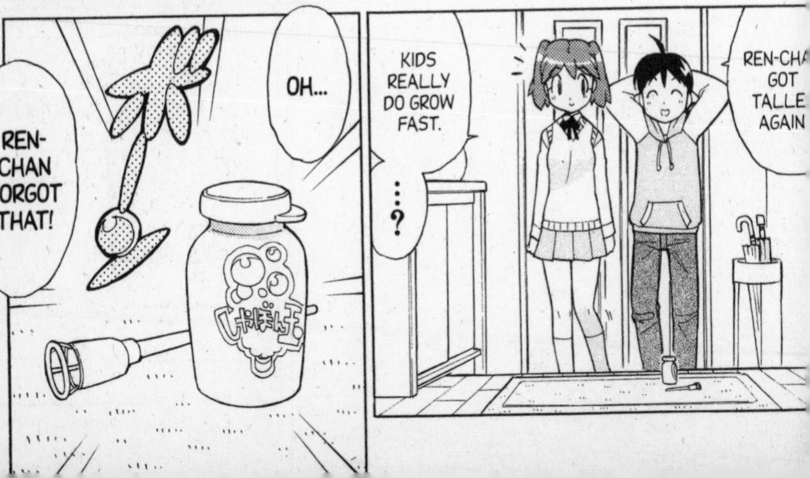
REN-CHA GOT TALLE AGAIN
KIDS REALLY DO GROW FAST.
...?
OH...
REN-CHAN FORGOT THAT!

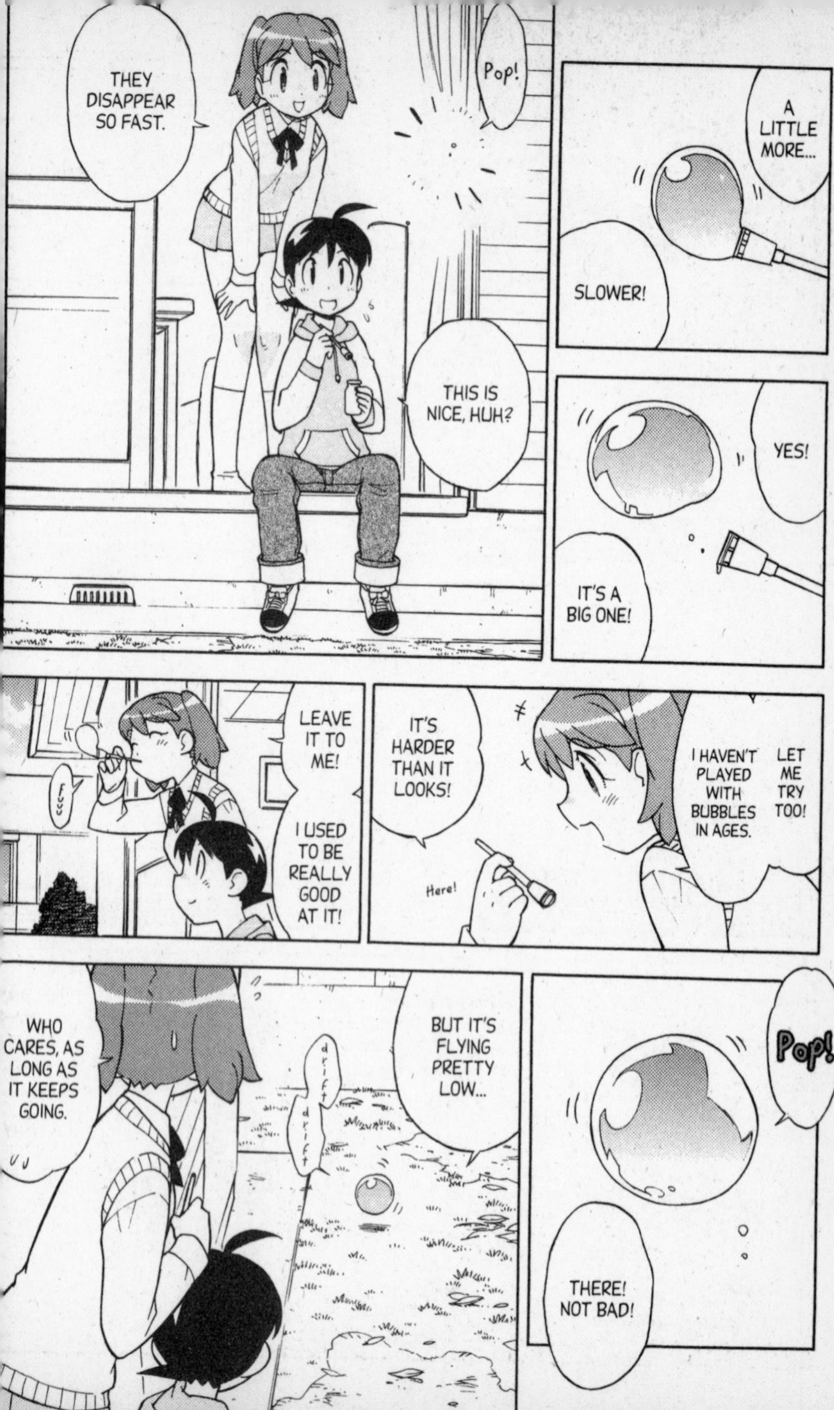
A LITTLE MORE...
SLOWER!
YES!
IT'S A BIG ONE!
Pop!
THEY DISAPPEAR SO FAST.
THIS IS NICE, HUH?
LET ME TRY TOO!
I HAVEN'T PLAYED WITH BUBBLES IN AGES.
IT'S HARDER THAN IT LOOKS!
Here!
LEAVE IT TO ME!
I USED TO BE REALLY GOOD AT IT!
Pop!
THERE! NOT BAD!
BUT IT'S FLYING PRETTY LOW...
drift drift
WHO CARES, AS LONG AS IT KEEPS GOING.

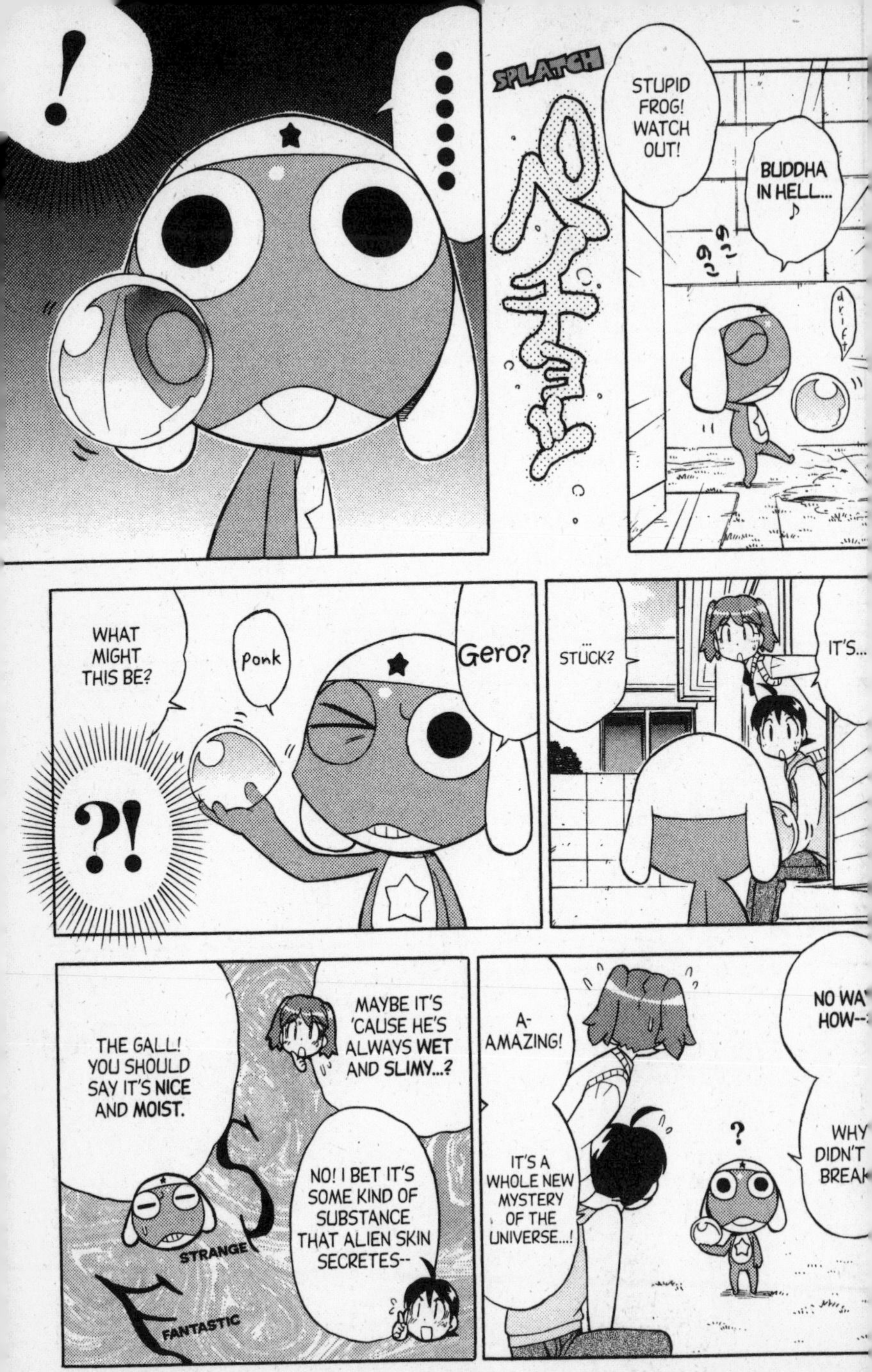
BUDDHA IN HELL... ♪
drift
STUPID FROG! WATCH OUT!
SPLATCH
!
......
IT'S...
... STUCK?
Gero?
ponk
WHAT MIGHT THIS BE?
?!
NO WA
HOW--
WHY DIDN'T BREA
A-AMAZING!
IT'S A WHOLE NEW MYSTERY OF THE UNIVERSE...!
?
MAYBE IT'S 'CAUSE HE'S ALWAYS **WET** AND **SLIMY**...?
NO! I BET IT'S SOME KIND OF SUBSTANCE THAT ALIEN SKIN SECRETES--
THE GALL! YOU SHOULD SAY IT'S **NICE** AND **MOIST**.
STRANGE
FANTASTIC

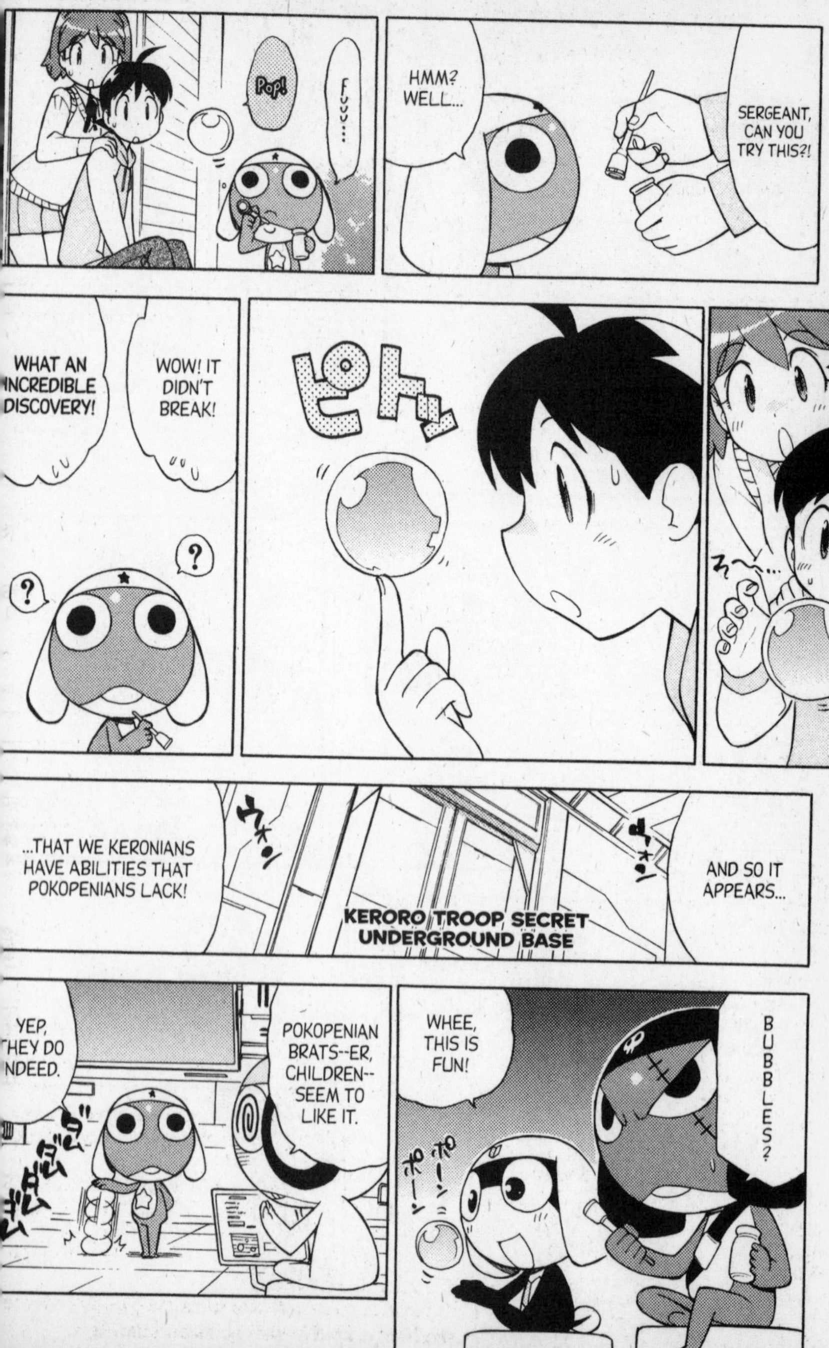
SERGEANT, CAN YOU TRY THIS?!
HMM? WELL...
FUUU...
Pop!
WOW! IT DIDN'T BREAK!
WHAT AN INCREDIBLE DISCOVERY!
?
?
AND SO IT APPEARS...
...THAT WE KERONIANS HAVE ABILITIES THAT POKOPENIANS LACK!
KERORO TROOP SECRET UNDERGROUND BASE
BUBBLES?
WHEE, THIS IS FUN!
POKOPENIAN BRATS--ER, CHILDREN-- SEEM TO LIKE IT.
YEP, THEY DO NDEED.

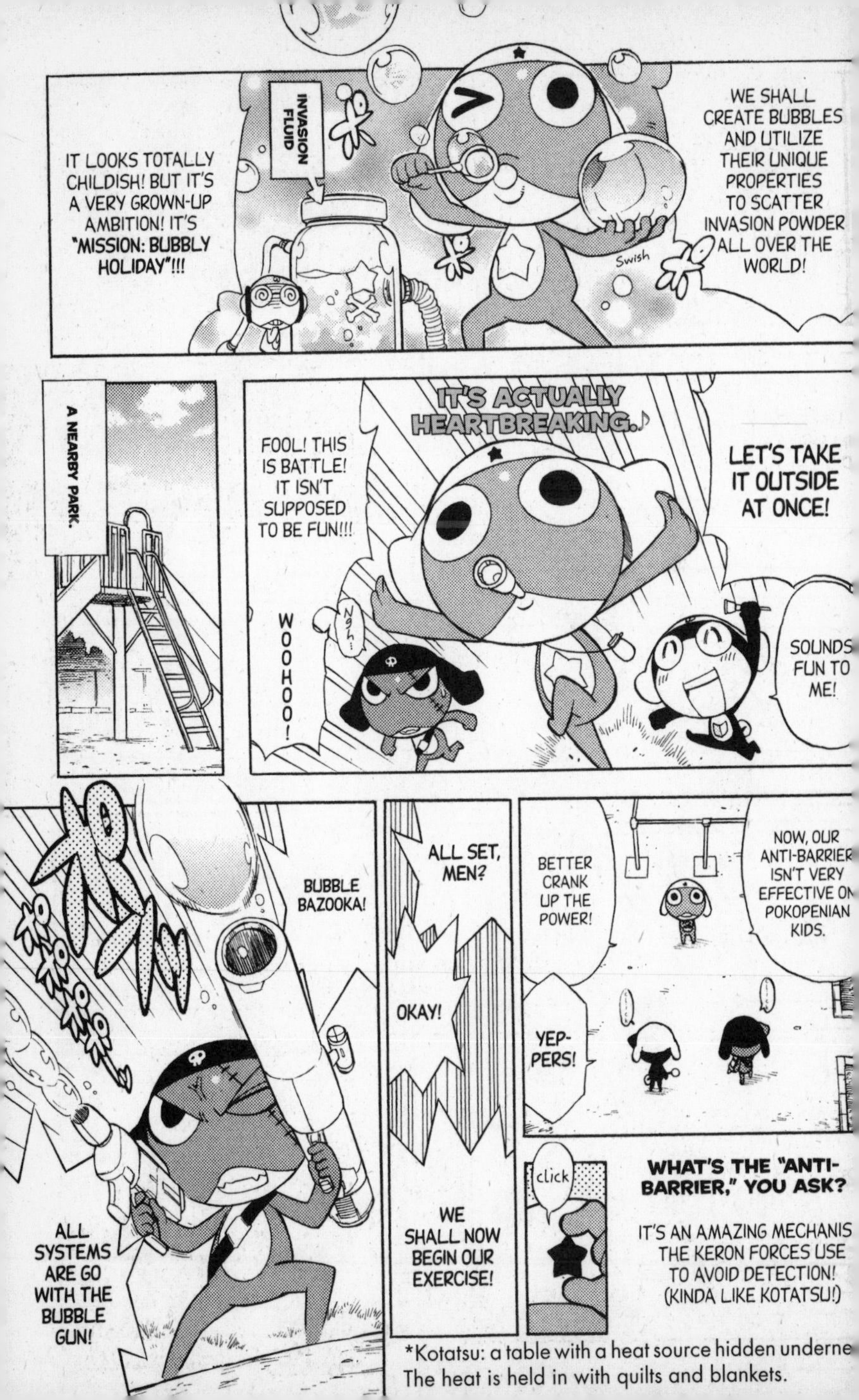
WE SHALL CREATE BUBBLES AND UTILIZE THEIR UNIQUE PROPERTIES TO SCATTER INVASION POWDER ALL OVER THE WORLD!
INVASION FLUID
IT LOOKS TOTALLY CHILDISH! BUT IT'S A VERY GROWN-UP AMBITION! IT'S "MISSION: BUBBLY HOLIDAY"!!!
Swish
LET'S TAKE IT OUTSIDE AT ONCE!
IT'S ACTUALLY HEARTBREAKING.♪
FOOL! THIS IS BATTLE! IT ISN'T SUPPOSED TO BE FUN!!!
SOUNDS FUN TO ME!
Ngh...
WOOHOO!
A NEARBY PARK.
NOW, OUR ANTI-BARRIER ISN'T VERY EFFECTIVE ON POKOPENIAN KIDS.
BETTER CRANK UP THE POWER!
YEP-PERS!
click
WHAT'S THE "ANTI-BARRIER," YOU ASK?
IT'S AN AMAZING MECHANIS THE KERON FORCES USE TO AVOID DETECTION! (KINDA LIKE KOTATSU!)
ALL SET, MEN?
OKAY!
WE SHALL NOW BEGIN OUR EXERCISE!
BUBBLE BAZOOKA!
ALL SYSTEMS ARE GO WITH THE BUBBLE GUN!

*Kotatsu: a table with a heat source hidden underne
The heat is held in with quilts and blankets.

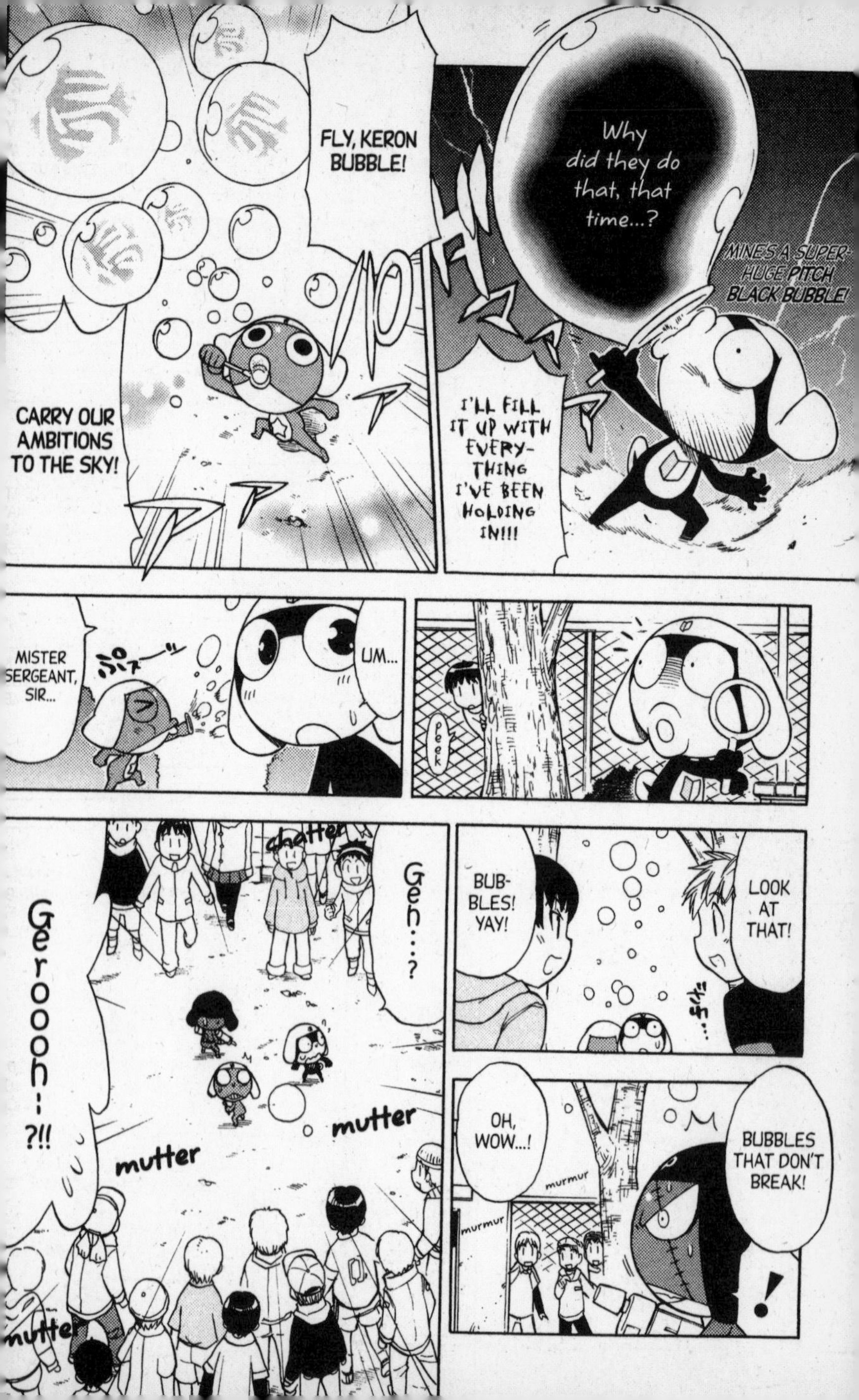
Why did they do that, that time...?
MINE'S A SUPER-HUGE PITCH BLACK BUBBLE!
I'LL FILL IT UP WITH EVERY-THING I'VE BEEN HOLDING IN!!!
FLY, KERON BUBBLE!
CARRY OUR AMBITIONS TO THE SKY!
peek
UM...
MISTER SERGEANT, SIR...
LOOK AT THAT!
BUBBLES! YAY!
BUBBLES THAT DON'T BREAK!
OH, WOW...!
murmur
murmur
!
chatter
Geh...?
Gerooooh!?!!
mutter
mutter
mutter

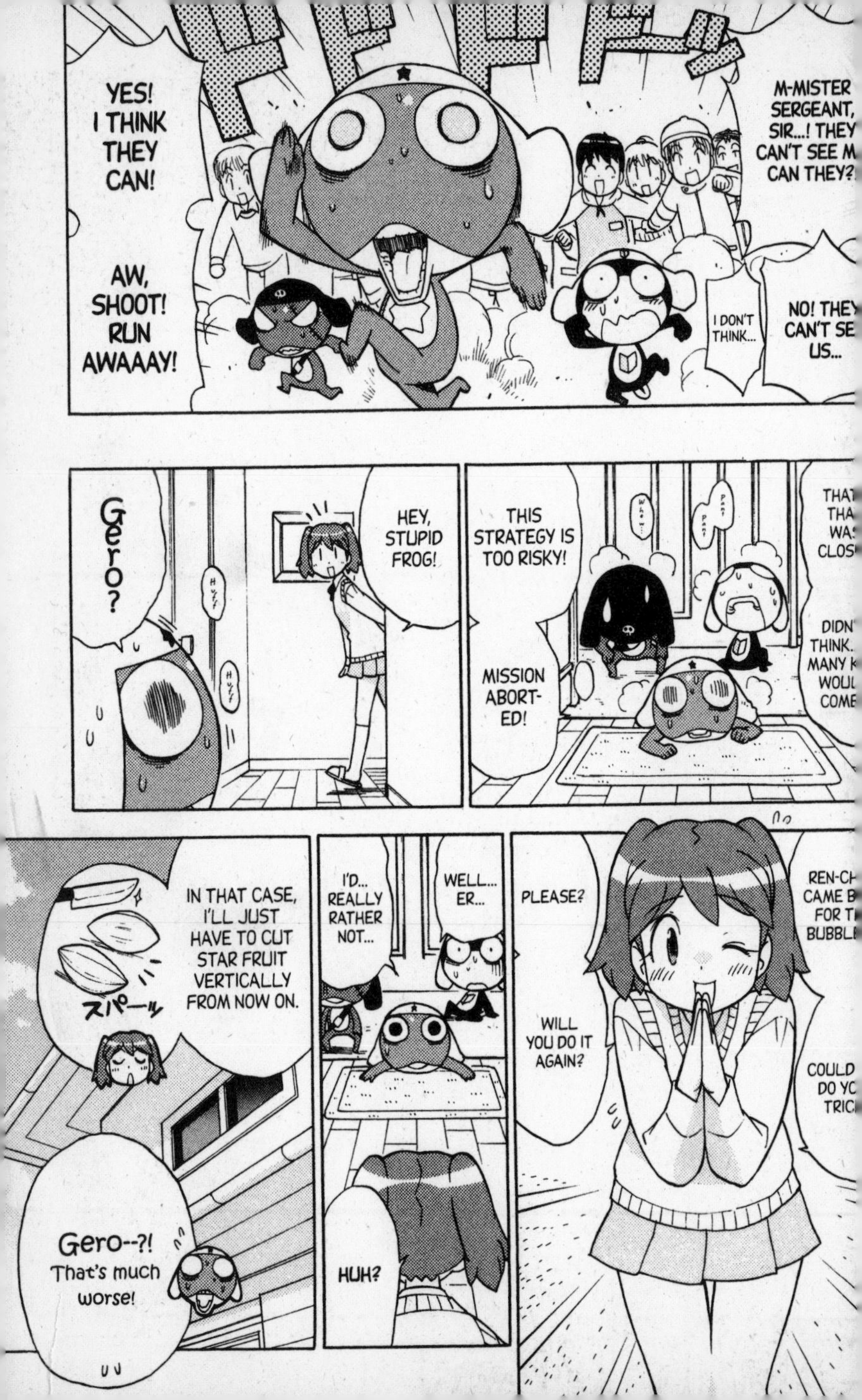
M-MISTER SERGEANT, SIR...! THEY CAN'T SEE M CAN THEY?
NO! THEY CAN'T SE US...
I DON'T THINK...
YES! I THINK THEY CAN!
AW, SHOOT! RUN AWAAAY!
THAT THA WAS CLOS
DIDN THINK. MANY K WOUL COME
THIS STRATEGY IS TOO RISKY!
MISSION ABORT-ED!
HEY, STUPID FROG!
Gero?
REN-CH CAME B FOR T BUBBL
COULD DO YO TRIC
PLEASE?
WILL YOU DO IT AGAIN?
WELL... ER...
I'D... REALLY RATHER NOT...
HUH?
IN THAT CASE, I'LL JUST HAVE TO CUT STAR FRUIT VERTICALLY FROM NOW ON.
スパーッ
Gero--?! That's much worse!

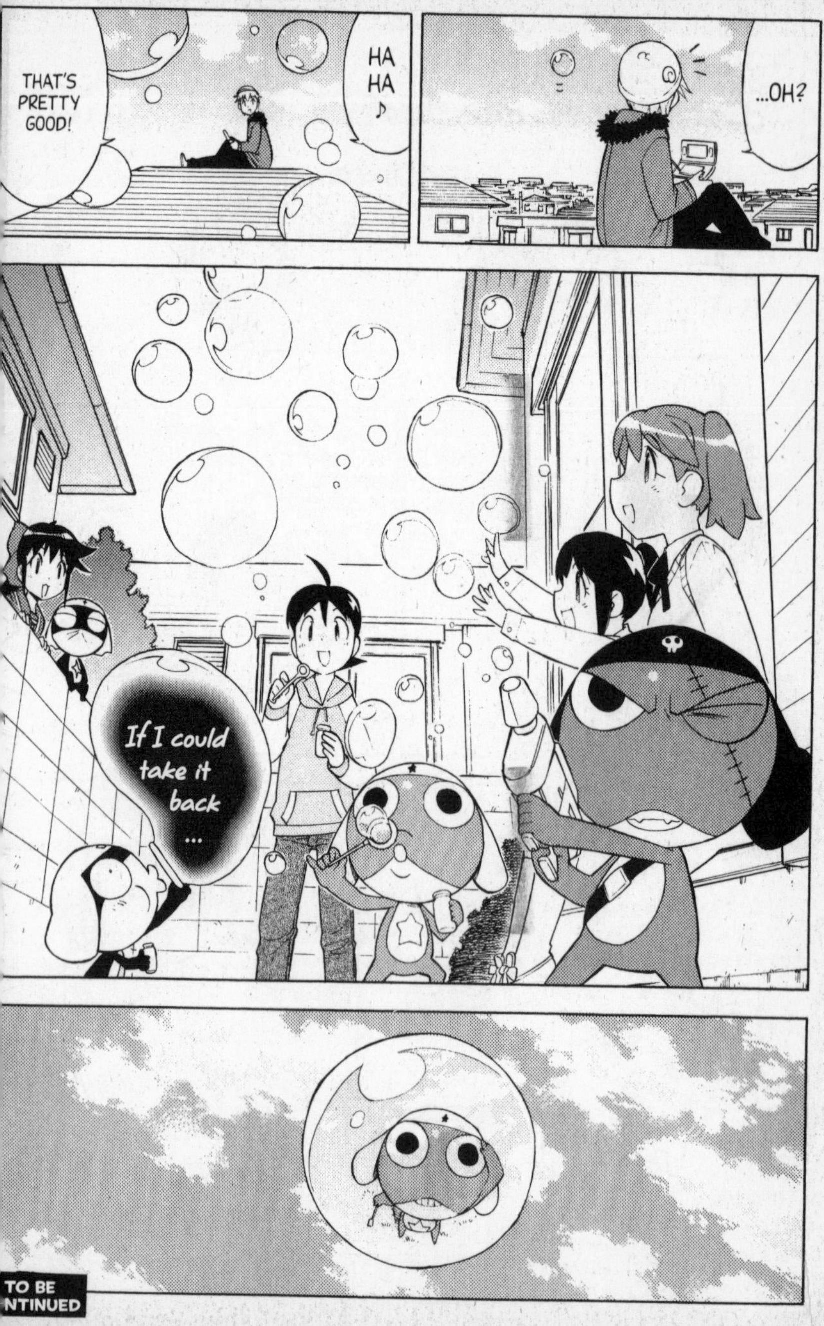

...OH?
HA HA ♪
THAT'S PRETTY GOOD!
If I could take it back ...
TO BE NTINUED

ENCOUNTER CLVII
A GALAXY-CLASS HOUSE SITTER!

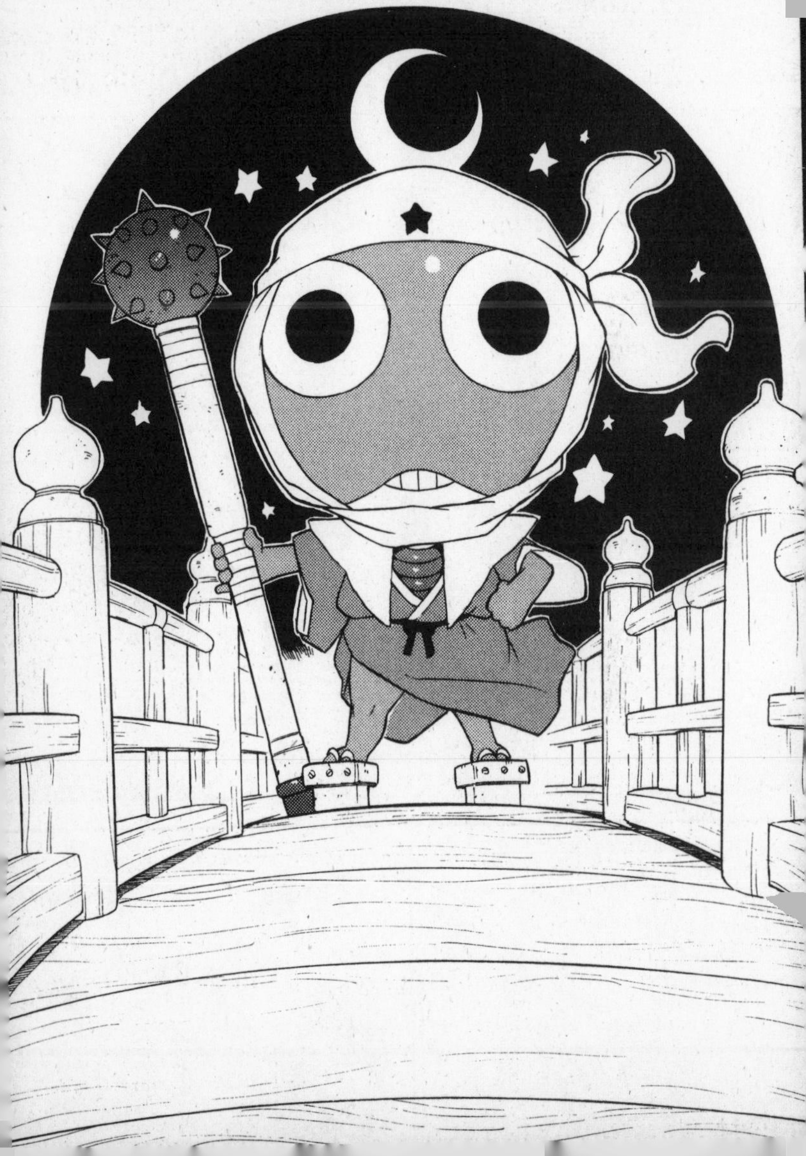

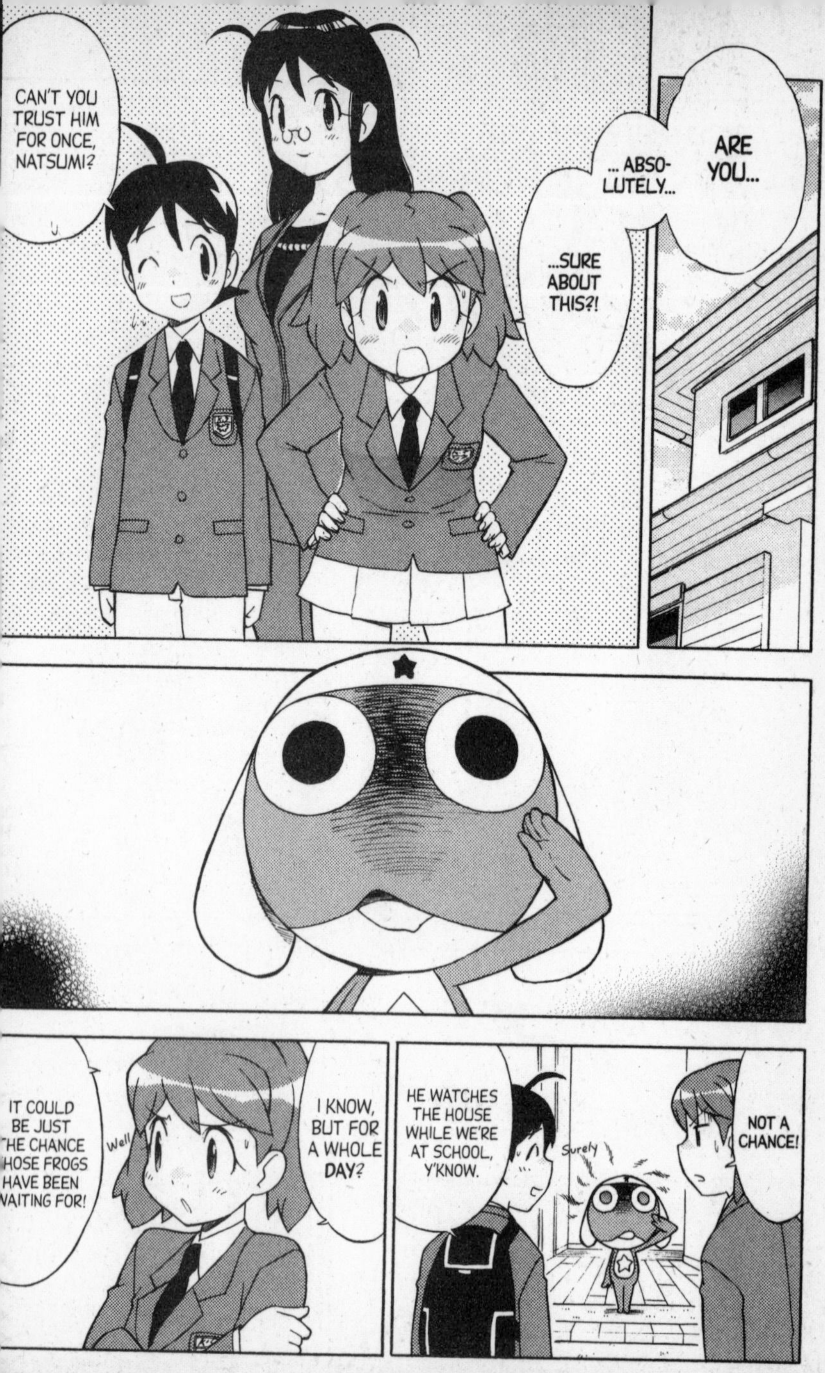
ARE YOU...
... ABSO-LUTELY...
...SURE ABOUT THIS?!
CAN'T YOU TRUST HIM FOR ONCE, NATSUMI?
NOT A CHANCE!
HE WATCHES THE HOUSE WHILE WE'RE AT SCHOOL, Y'KNOW.
Surely
I KNOW, BUT FOR A WHOLE DAY?
Well
IT COULD BE JUST THE CHANCE HOSE FROGS HAVE BEEN VAITING FOR!

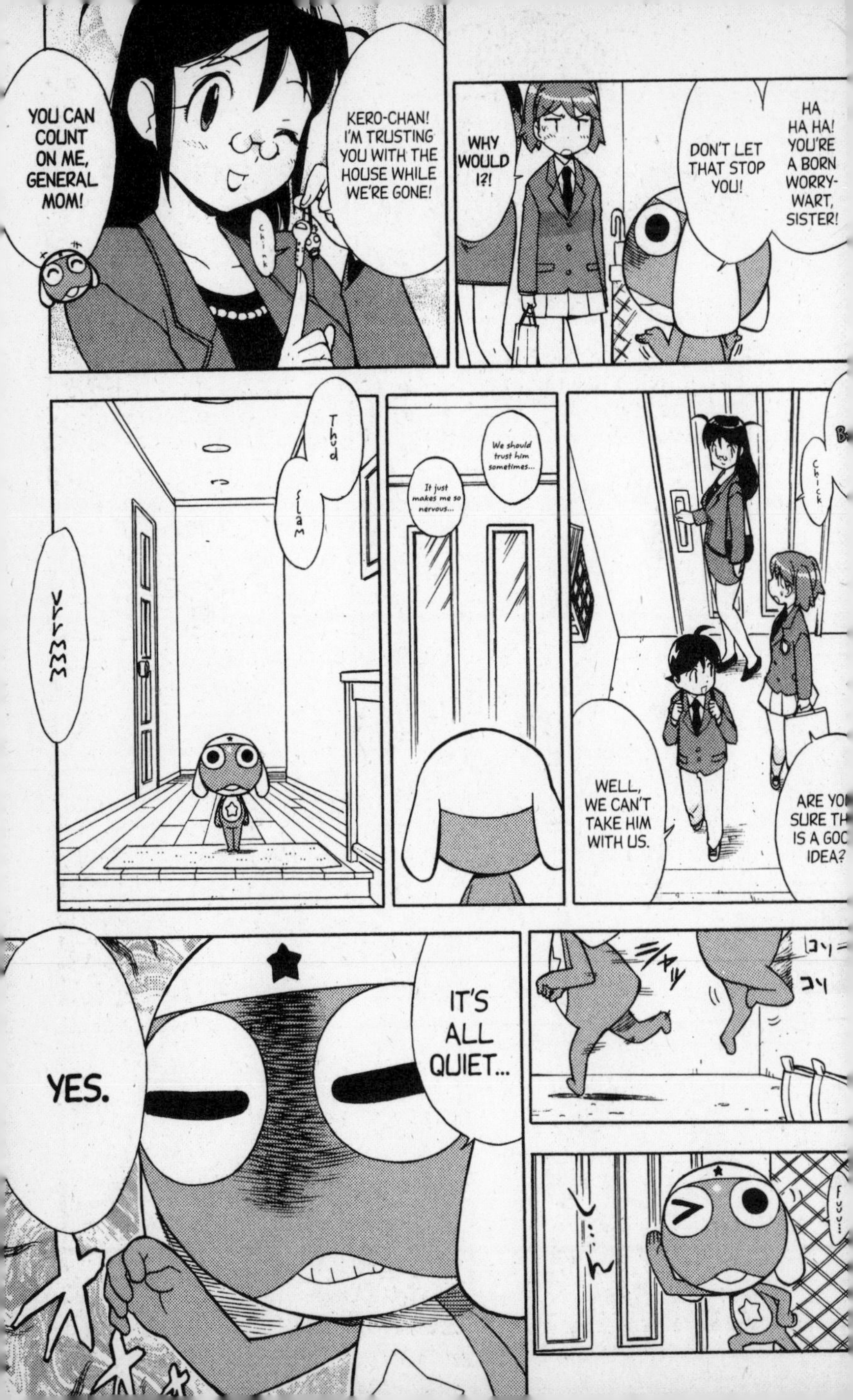
HA HA HA! YOU'RE A BORN WORRY-WART, SISTER!
DON'T LET THAT STOP YOU!
WHY WOULD I?!
KERO-CHAN! I'M TRUSTING YOU WITH THE HOUSE WHILE WE'RE GONE!
Chink
YOU CAN COUNT ON ME, GENERAL MOM!
Chick
ARE YO SURE TH IS A GOC IDEA?
WELL, WE CAN'T TAKE HIM WITH US.
We should trust him sometimes...
It just makes me so nervous...
Thud
Slam
Vrrmmm
Fuuu...
IT'S ALL QUIET...
YES.

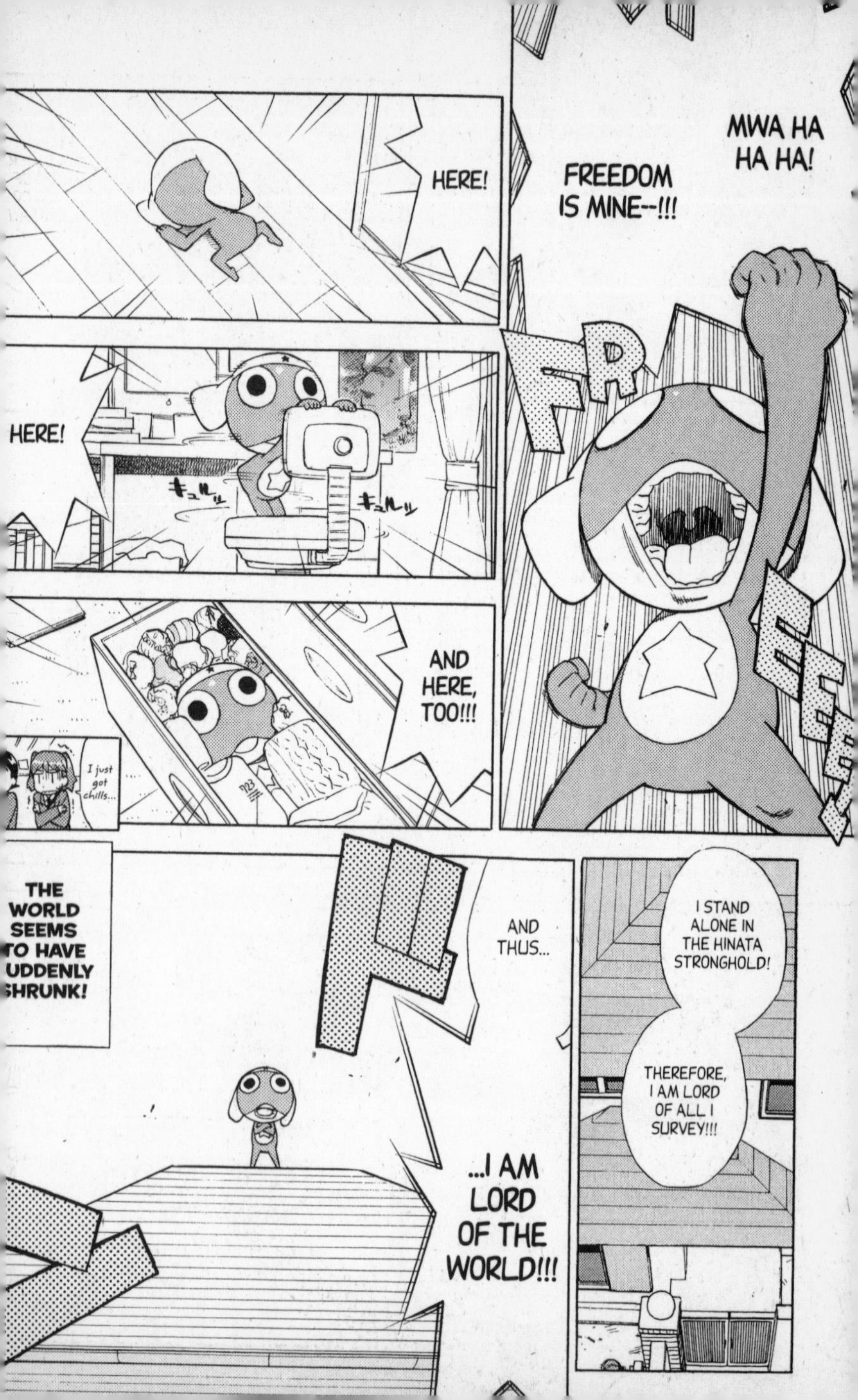
MWA HA HA HA!
FREEDOM IS MINE--!!!
FR
EEE
HERE!
HERE!
AND HERE, TOO!!!
I just got chills...
I STAND ALONE IN THE HINATA STRONGHOLD!
THEREFORE, I AM LORD OF ALL I SURVEY!!!
AND THUS...
...I AM LORD OF THE WORLD!!!
THE WORLD SEEMS TO HAVE UDDENLY HRUNK!

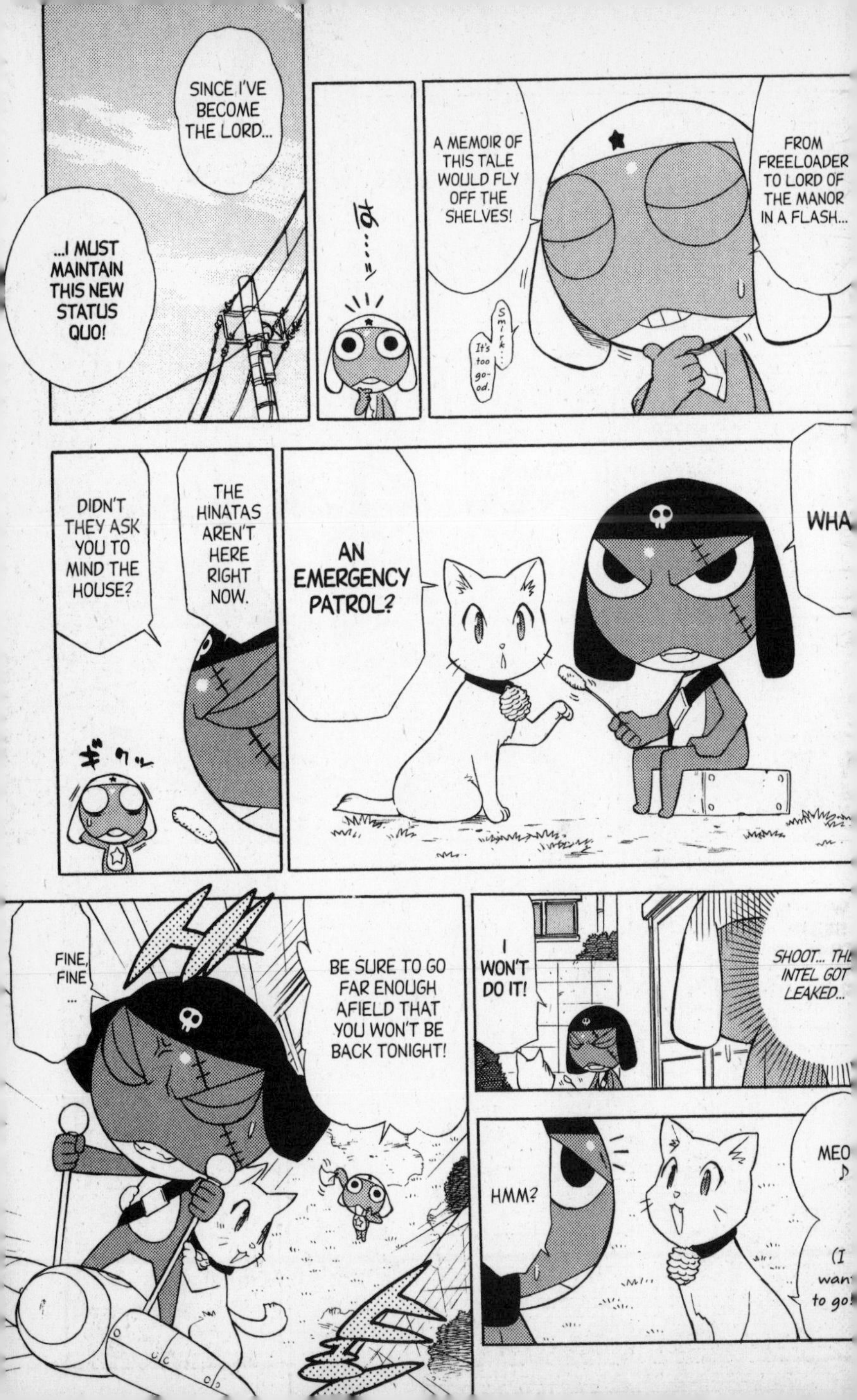
FROM FREELOADER TO LORD OF THE MANOR IN A FLASH...
A MEMOIR OF THIS TALE WOULD FLY OFF THE SHELVES!
Smirk...
It's too go-od.
SINCE I'VE BECOME THE LORD...
...I MUST MAINTAIN THIS NEW STATUS QUO!
WHA
AN EMERGENCY PATROL?
THE HINATAS AREN'T HERE RIGHT NOW.
DIDN'T THEY ASK YOU TO MIND THE HOUSE?
ギクッ
SHOOT... TH INTEL GOT LEAKED...
I WON'T DO IT!
MEO ♪
(I wan to go
HMM?
BE SURE TO GO FAR ENOUGH AFIELD THAT YOU WON'T BE BACK TONIGHT!
FINE, FINE ...

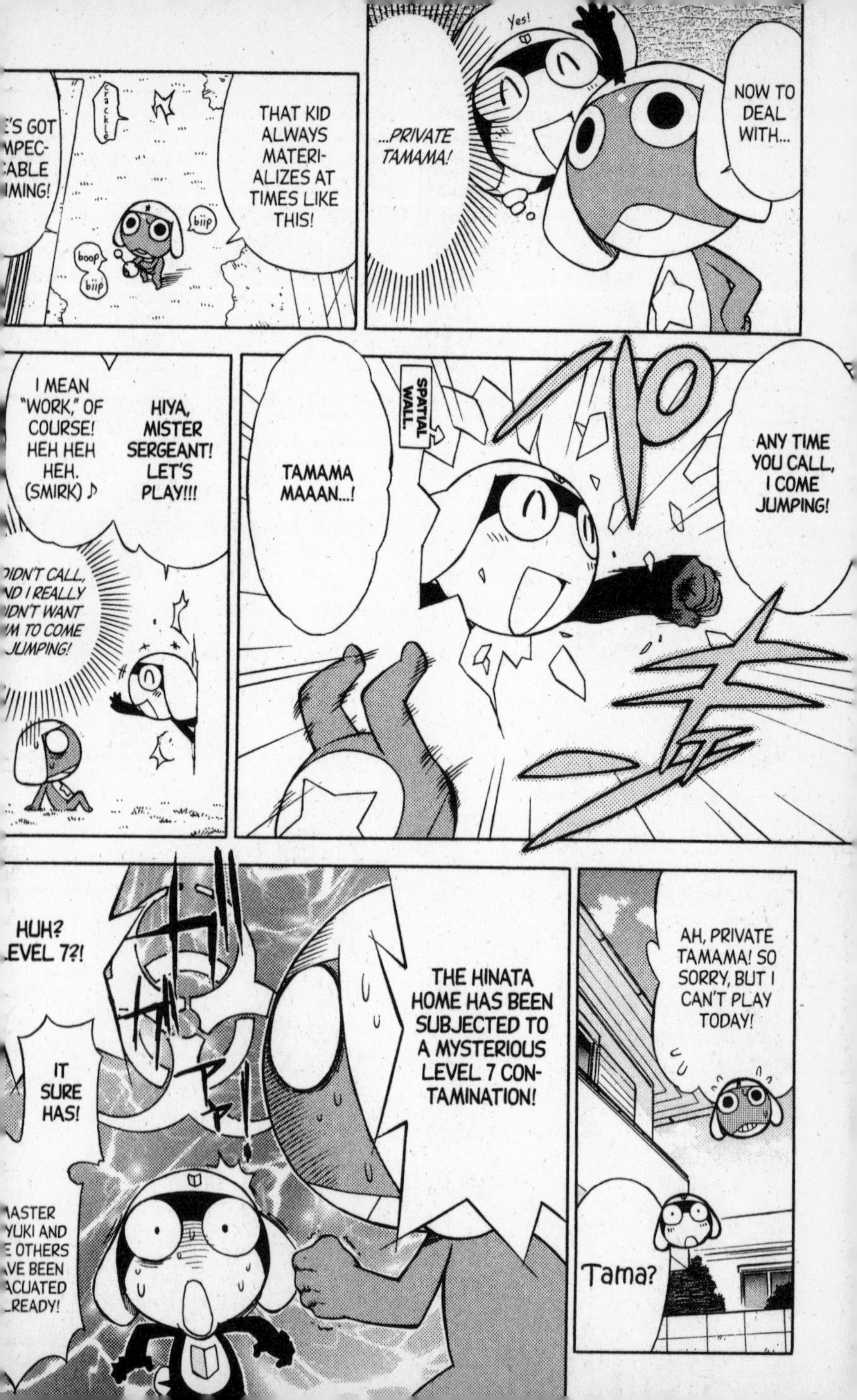
NOW TO DEAL WITH...
...PRIVATE TAMAMA!
Yes!
THAT KID ALWAYS MATERI-ALIZES AT TIMES LIKE THIS!
crackle
biip
boop
biip
'S GOT MPEC- ABLE IMING!
ANY TIME YOU CALL, I COME JUMPING!
SPATIAL WALL.
TAMAMA MAAAN...!
HIYA, MISTER SERGEANT! LET'S PLAY!!!
I MEAN "WORK," OF COURSE! HEH HEH HEH. (SMIRK) ♪
IDN'T CALL, ND I REALLY IDN'T WANT M TO COME JUMPING!
AH, PRIVATE TAMAMA! SO SORRY, BUT I CAN'T PLAY TODAY!
Tama?
THE HINATA HOME HAS BEEN SUBJECTED TO A MYSTERIOUS LEVEL 7 CON-TAMINATION!
HUH? EVEL 7?!
IT SURE HAS!
ASTER YUKI AND E OTHERS VE BEEN ACUATED READY!

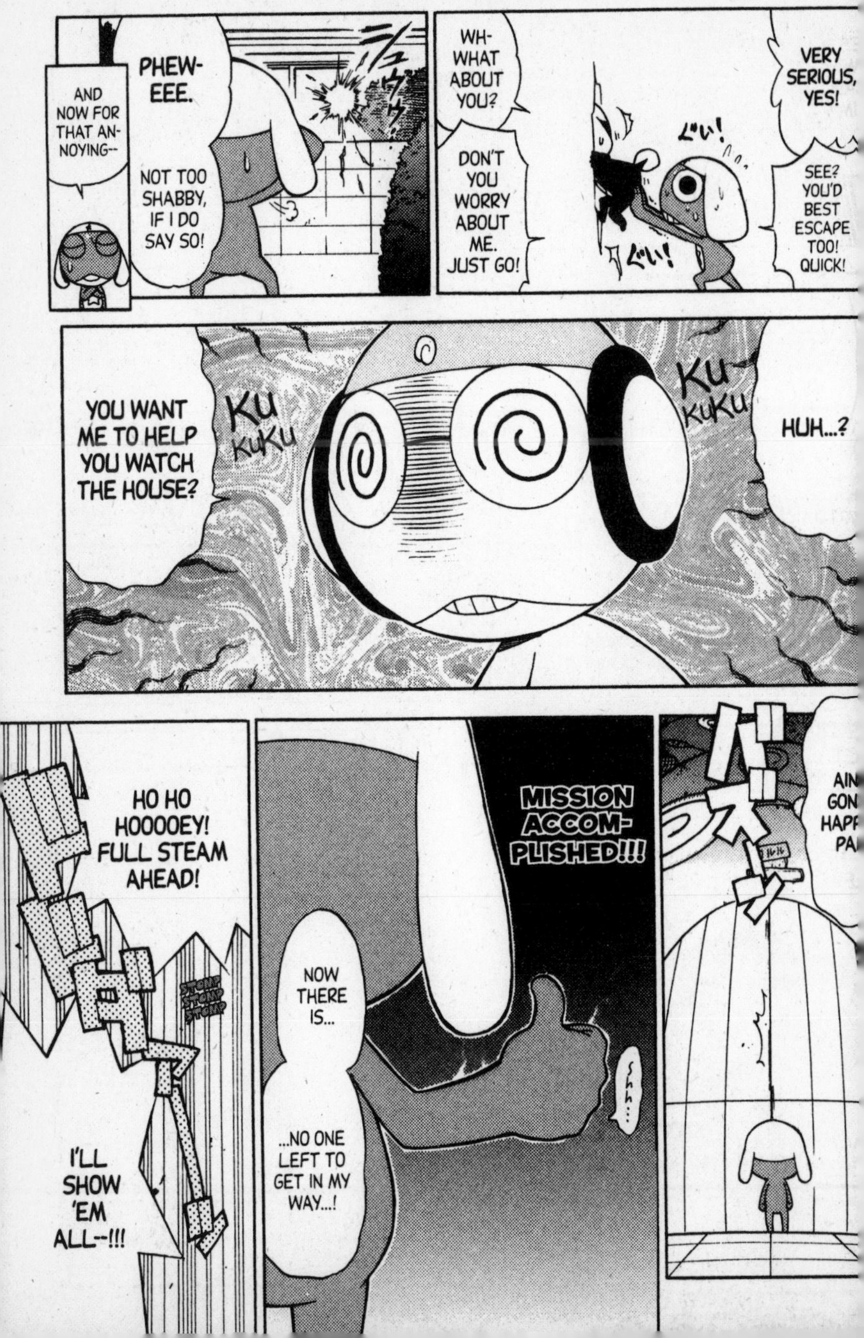
VERY SERIOUS, YES!
SEE? YOU'D BEST ESCAPE TOO! QUICK!
ぐい!
ぐい!
WH-WHAT ABOUT YOU?
DON'T YOU WORRY ABOUT ME. JUST GO!
PHEW-EEE.
NOT TOO SHABBY, IF I DO SAY SO!
AND NOW FOR THAT AN-NOYING--
HUH...?
KU KUKU
KU KUKU
YOU WANT ME TO HELP YOU WATCH THE HOUSE?
MISSION ACCOM-PLISHED!!!
NOW THERE IS...
...NO ONE LEFT TO GET IN MY WAY...!
shh...
HO HO HOOOOEY! FULL STEAM AHEAD!
STOMP STOMP STOMP
I'LL SHOW 'EM ALL--!!!

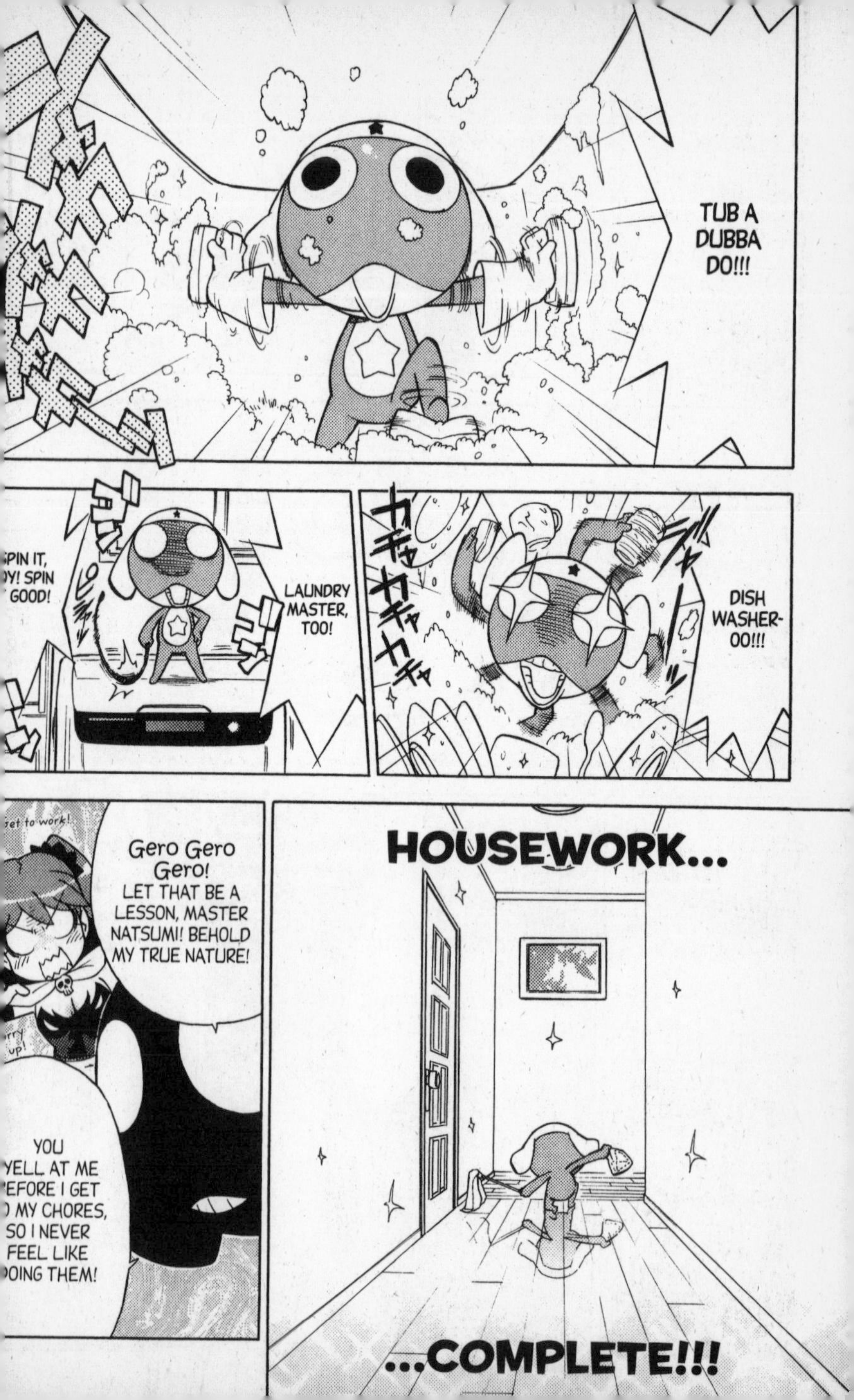
TUB A DUBBA DO!!!
DISH WASHER-OO!!!
LAUNDRY MASTER, TOO!
SPIN IT, OY! SPIN GOOD!
HOUSEWORK...
...COMPLETE!!!
Get to work!
Gero Gero Gero! LET THAT BE A LESSON, MASTER NATSUMI! BEHOLD MY TRUE NATURE!
rry up!
YOU YELL AT ME EFORE I GET O MY CHORES, SO I NEVER FEEL LIKE OING THEM!

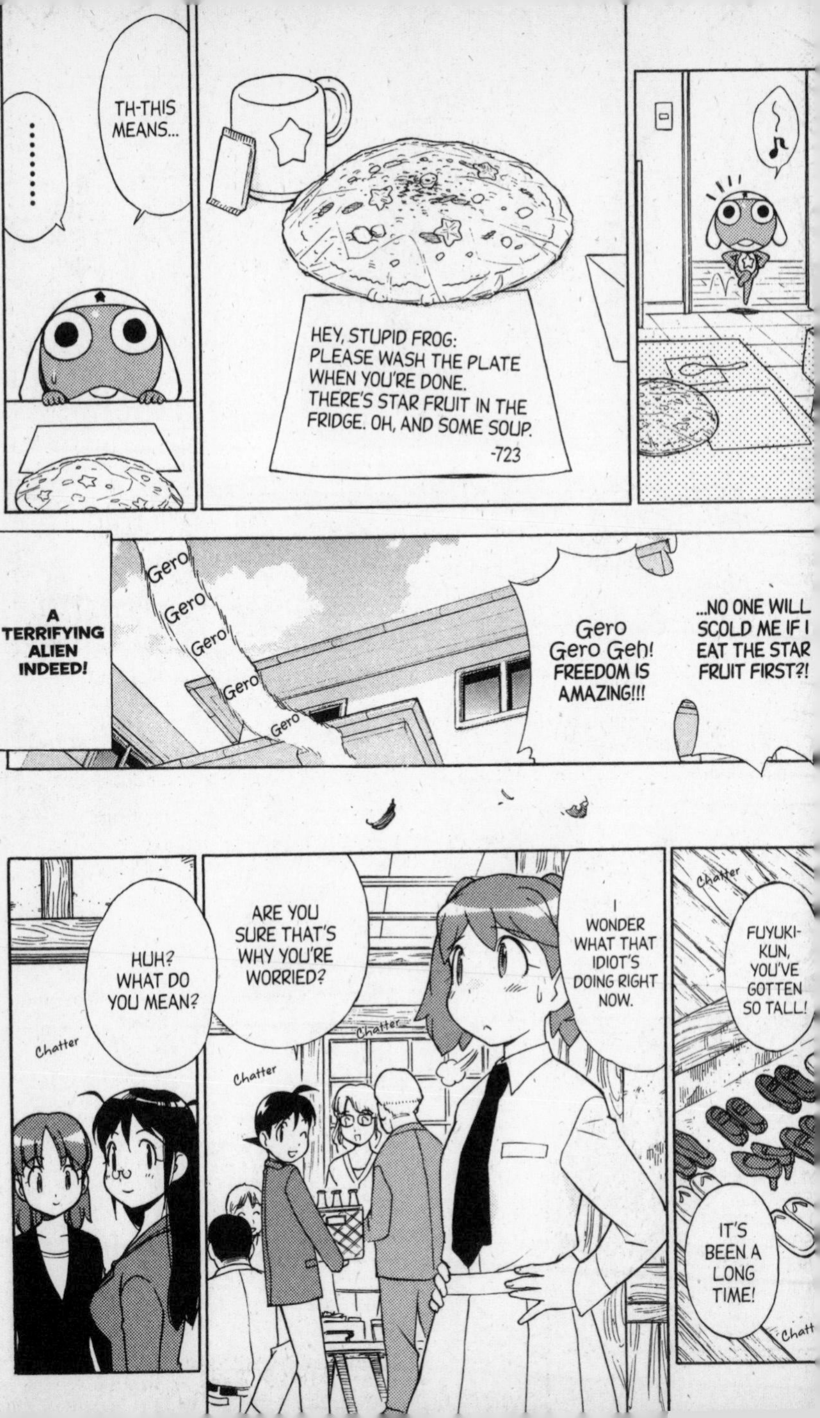
HEY, STUPID FROG:
PLEASE WASH THE PLATE
WHEN YOU'RE DONE.
THERE'S STAR FRUIT IN THE
FRIDGE. OH, AND SOME SOUP.
-723
TH-THIS MEANS...
....
...NO ONE WILL SCOLD ME IF I EAT THE STAR FRUIT FIRST?!
Gero Gero Geh! FREEDOM IS AMAZING!!!
Gero
Gero
Gero
Gero
Gero
A TERRIFYING ALIEN INDEED!
Chatter
FUYUKI-KUN, YOU'VE GOTTEN SO TALL!
IT'S BEEN A LONG TIME!
I WONDER WHAT THAT IDIOT'S DOING RIGHT NOW.
ARE YOU SURE THAT'S WHY YOU'RE WORRIED?
Chatter
Chatter
HUH? WHAT DO YOU MEAN?
Chatter

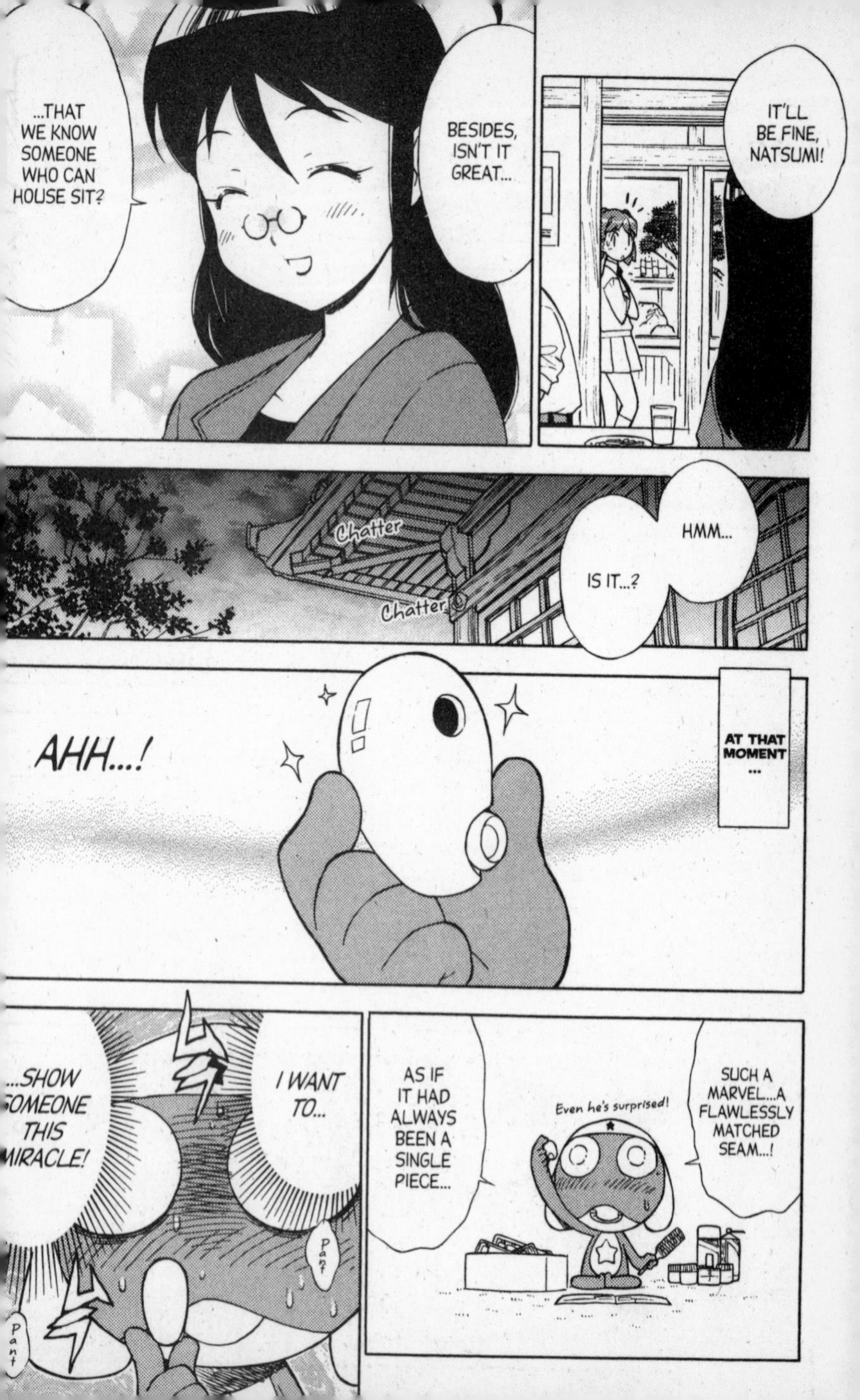
IT'LL BE FINE, NATSUMI!
BESIDES, ISN'T IT GREAT...
...THAT WE KNOW SOMEONE WHO CAN HOUSE SIT?
HMM...
IS IT...?
Chatter
Chatter
AT THAT MOMENT...
AHH...!
SUCH A MARVEL...A FLAWLESSLY MATCHED SEAM...!
Even he's surprised!
AS IF IT HAD ALWAYS BEEN A SINGLE PIECE...
I WANT TO...
...SHOW SOMEONE THIS MIRACLE!
Pant
Pant

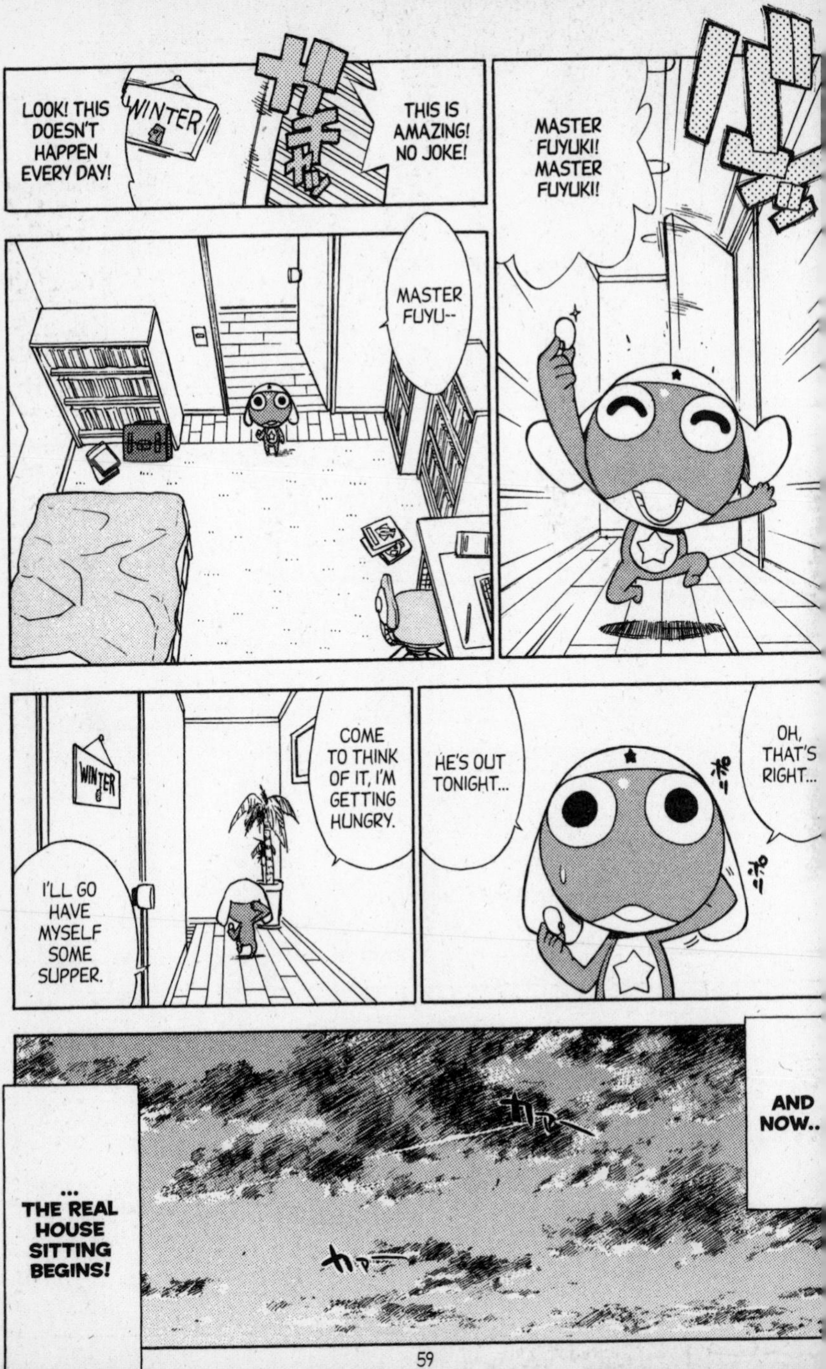
MASTER FUYUKI! MASTER FUYUKI!
THIS IS AMAZING! NO JOKE!
LOOK! THIS DOESN'T HAPPEN EVERY DAY!
WINTER
MASTER FUYU--
OH, THAT'S RIGHT...
HE'S OUT TONIGHT...
COME TO THINK OF IT, I'M GETTING HUNGRY.
WINTER
I'LL GO HAVE MYSELF SOME SUPPER.
AND NOW..
... THE REAL HOUSE SITTING BEGINS!

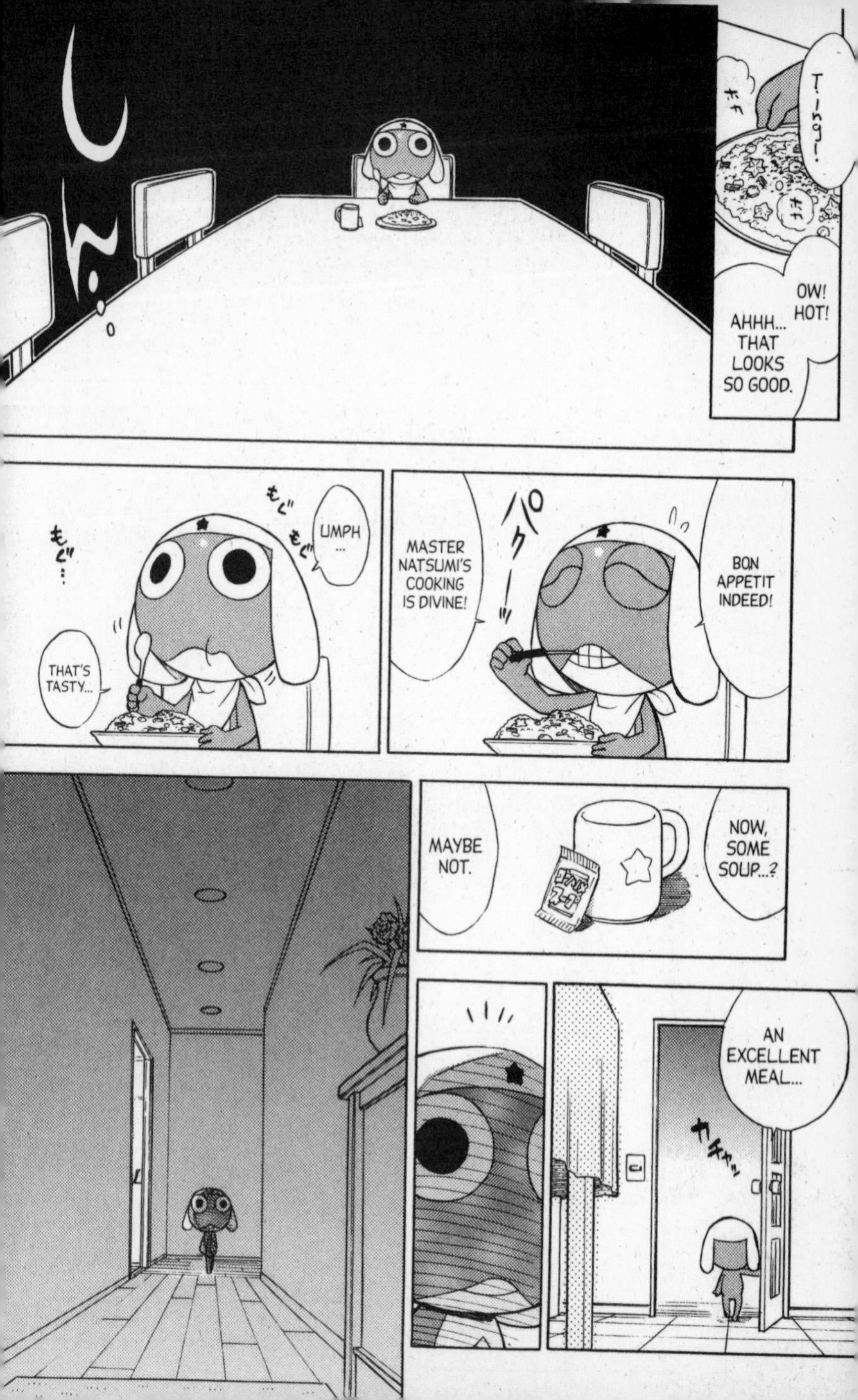

Ting!
OW! HOT!
AHHH... THAT LOOKS SO GOOD.
BON APPETIT INDEED!
MASTER NATSUMI'S COOKING IS DIVINE!
UMPH ...
THAT'S TASTY...
NOW, SOME SOUP...?
MAYBE NOT.
AN EXCELLENT MEAL...

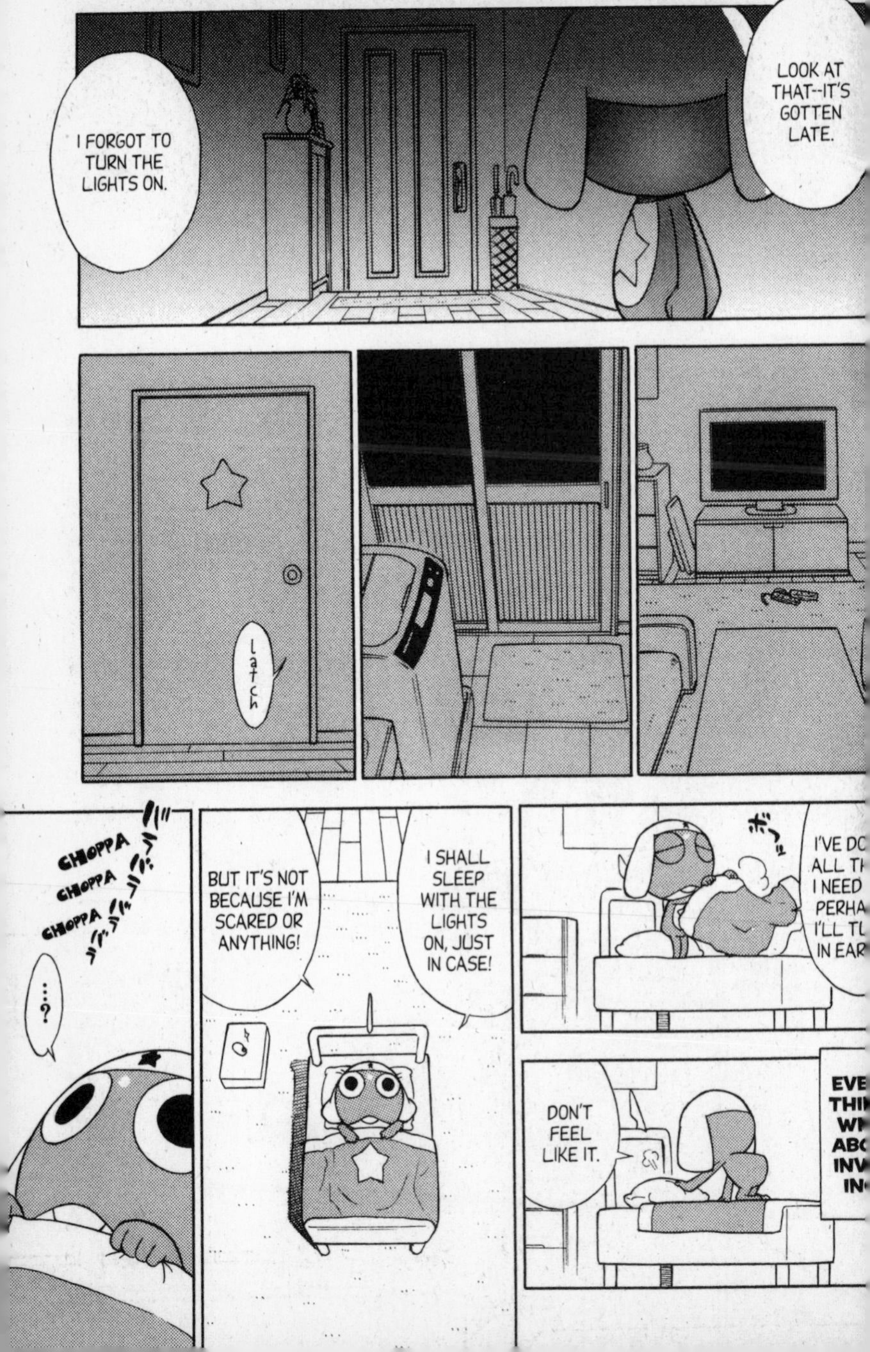
LOOK AT THAT--IT'S GOTTEN LATE.
I FORGOT TO TURN THE LIGHTS ON.
latch
I'VE DO ALL TH I NEED PERHA I'LL TU IN EAR
DON'T FEEL LIKE IT.
I SHALL SLEEP WITH THE LIGHTS ON, JUST IN CASE!
BUT IT'S NOT BECAUSE I'M SCARED OR ANYTHING!
CHOPPA CHOPPA CHOPPA
...?

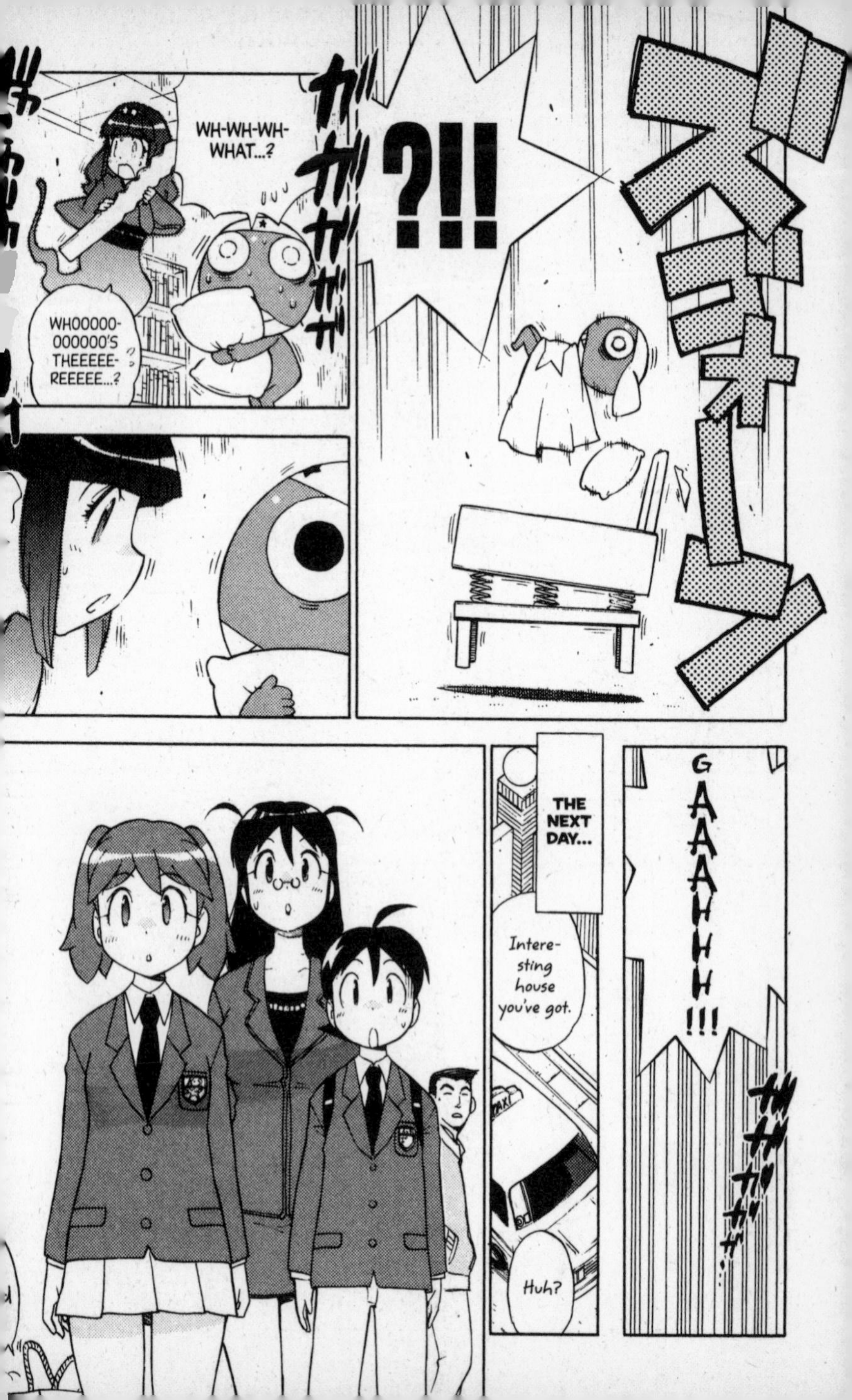
?!!
WH-WH-WH-WHAT...?
WHOOOOOO-OOOOOO'S THEEEEE-REEEEE...?
GAAAAHHH!!!
THE NEXT DAY...
Interesting house you've got.
Huh?

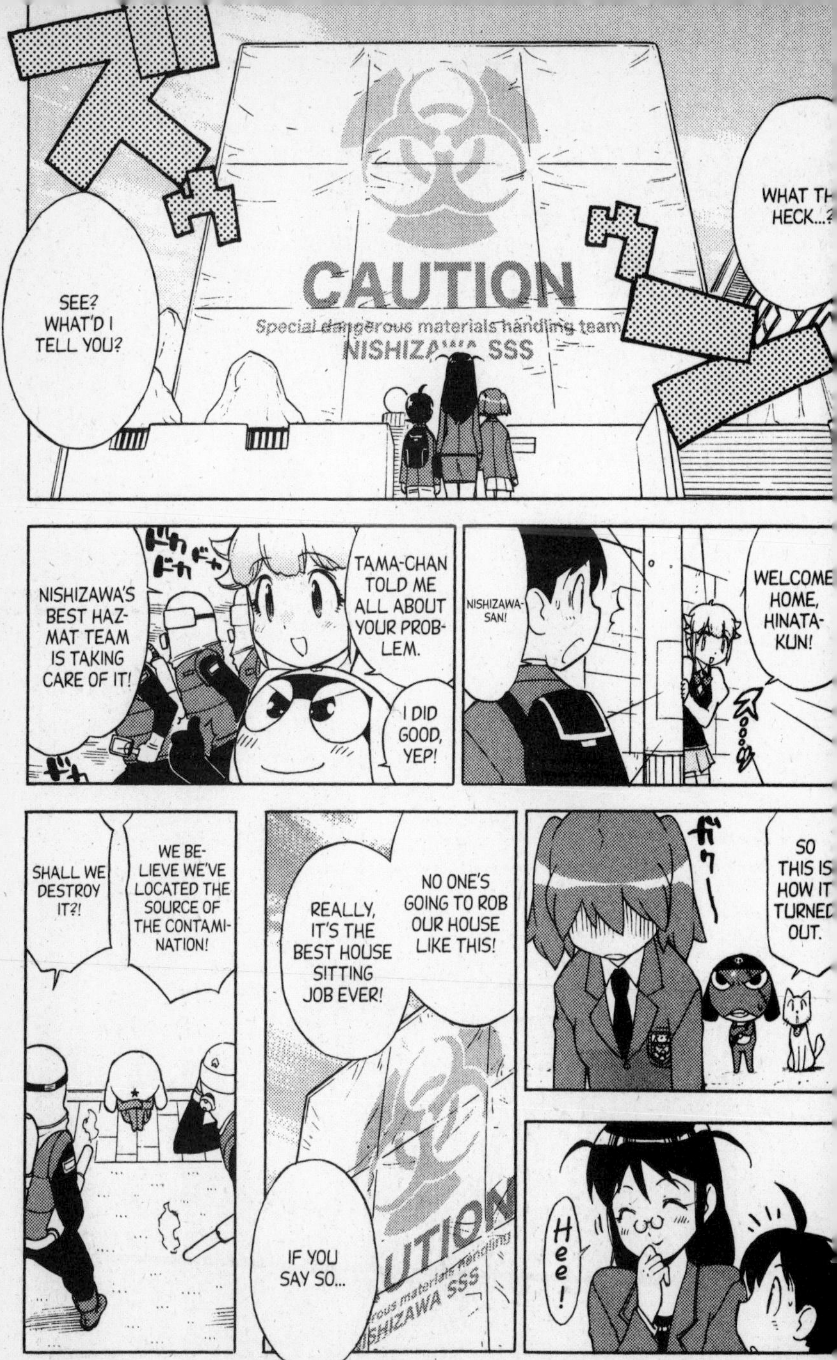
WHAT TH HECK...?
CAUTION
Special dangerous materials handling team
NISHIZAWA SSS
SEE? WHAT'D I TELL YOU?
WELCOME HOME, HINATA-KUN!
NISHIZAWA-SAN!
TAMA-CHAN TOLD ME ALL ABOUT YOUR PROB-LEM.
I DID GOOD, YEP!
NISHIZAWA'S BEST HAZ-MAT TEAM IS TAKING CARE OF IT!
SO THIS IS HOW IT TURNED OUT.
Hee!
NO ONE'S GOING TO ROB OUR HOUSE LIKE THIS!
REALLY, IT'S THE BEST HOUSE SITTING JOB EVER!
IF YOU SAY SO...
WE BE-LIEVE WE'VE LOCATED THE SOURCE OF THE CONTAMI-NATION!
SHALL WE DESTROY IT?!

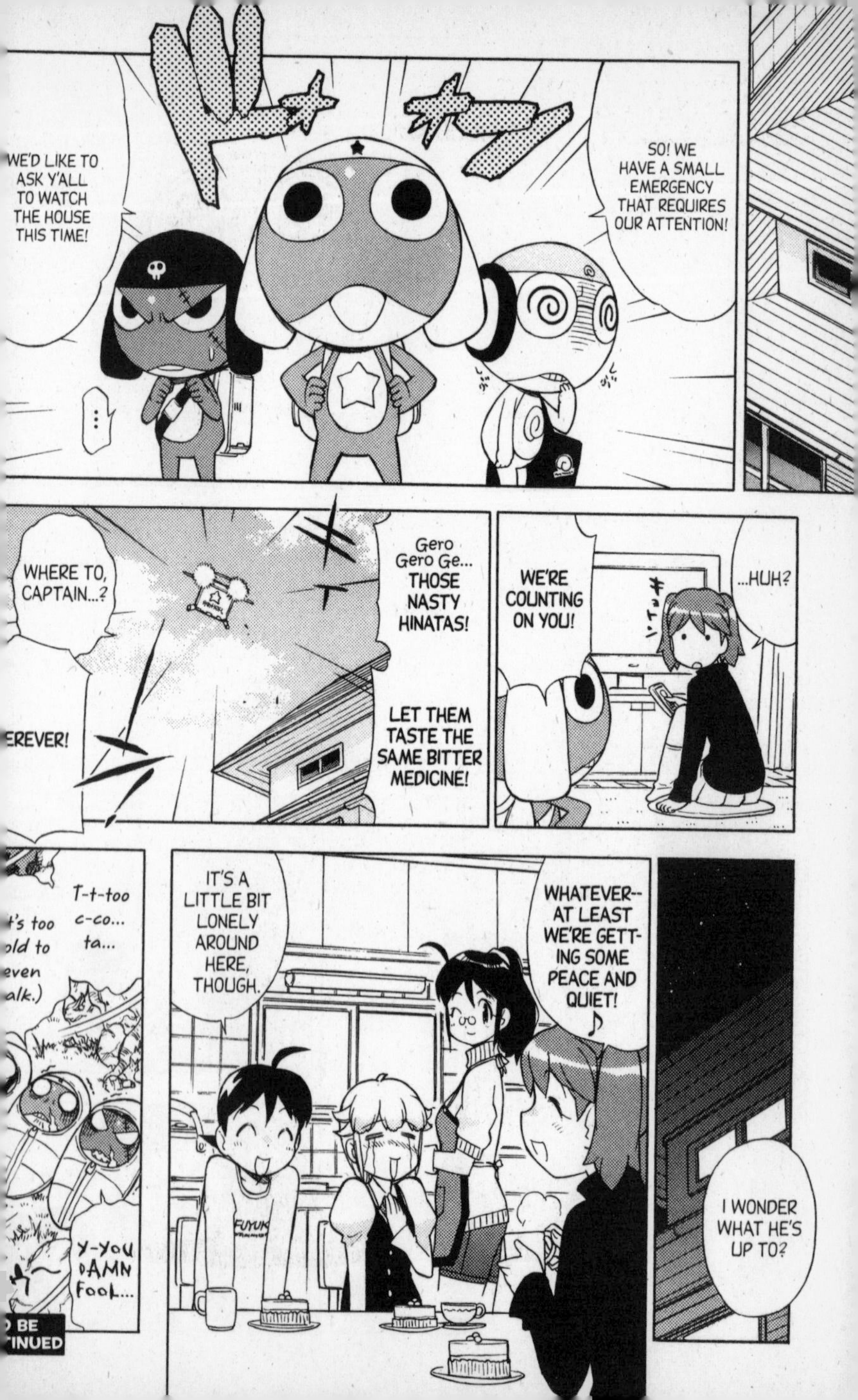
SO! WE HAVE A SMALL EMERGENCY THAT REQUIRES OUR ATTENTION!
WE'D LIKE TO ASK Y'ALL TO WATCH THE HOUSE THIS TIME!
...
...HUH?
キョトン
WE'RE COUNTING ON YOU!
Gero Gero Ge... THOSE NASTY HINATAS!
LET THEM TASTE THE SAME BITTER MEDICINE!
WHERE TO, CAPTAIN...?
EREVER!
I WONDER WHAT HE'S UP TO?
WHATEVER-- AT LEAST WE'RE GETT- ING SOME PEACE AND QUIET! ♪
IT'S A LITTLE BIT LONELY AROUND HERE, THOUGH.
FUYUK
T-t-too c-co... ta...
t's too old to even alk.)
Y-YOU DAMN FOOL...
D BE TINUED

ENCOUNTER CLVIII
IN-ALIEN-ABLE PUNISHMENT!

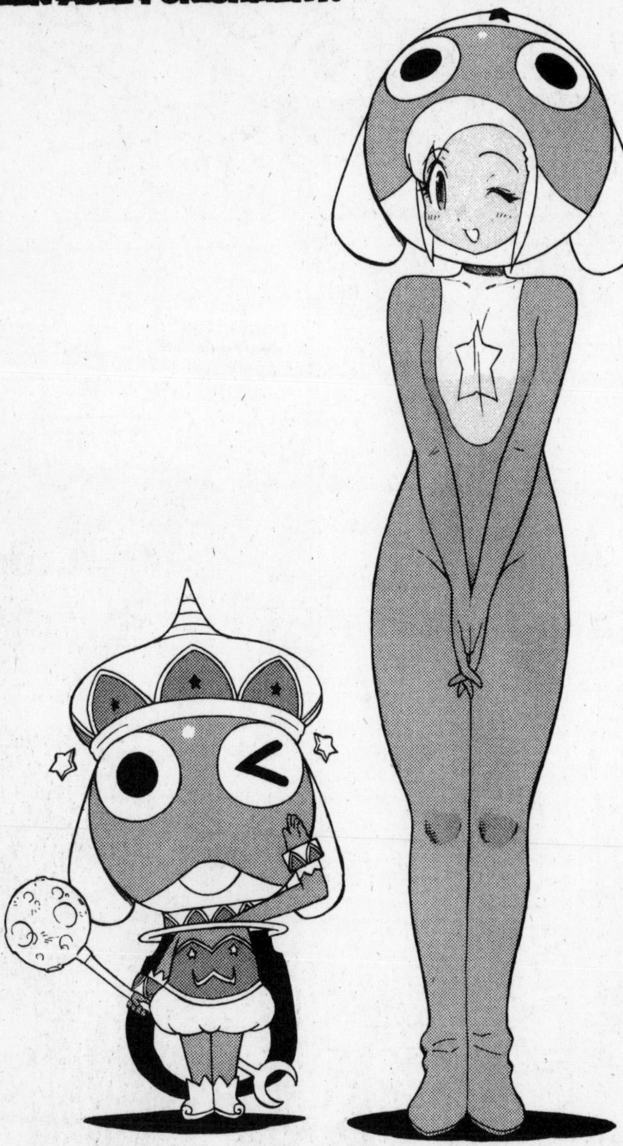

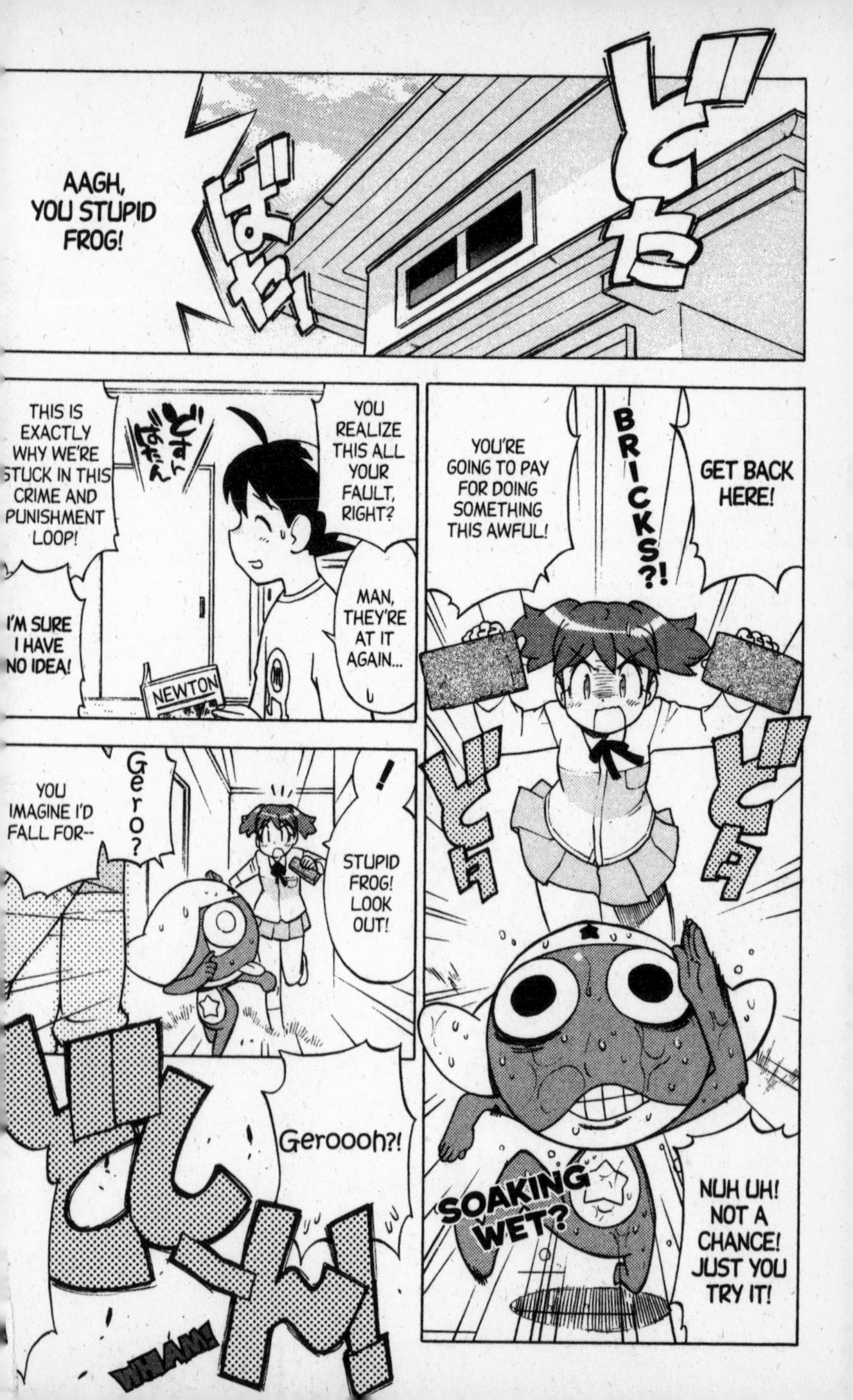
どた
ばた
AAGH, YOU STUPID FROG!
GET BACK HERE!
BRICKS?!
YOU'RE GOING TO PAY FOR DOING SOMETHING THIS AWFUL!
NUH UH! NOT A CHANCE! JUST YOU TRY IT!
SOAKING WET?
YOU REALIZE THIS ALL YOUR FAULT, RIGHT?
THIS IS EXACTLY WHY WE'RE STUCK IN THIS CRIME AND PUNISHMENT LOOP!
どすん ばたん
I'M SURE I HAVE NO IDEA!
MAN, THEY'RE AT IT AGAIN...
NEWTON
!
STUPID FROG! LOOK OUT!
Gero?
YOU IMAGINE I'D FALL FOR--
Geroooh?!
WHAM!

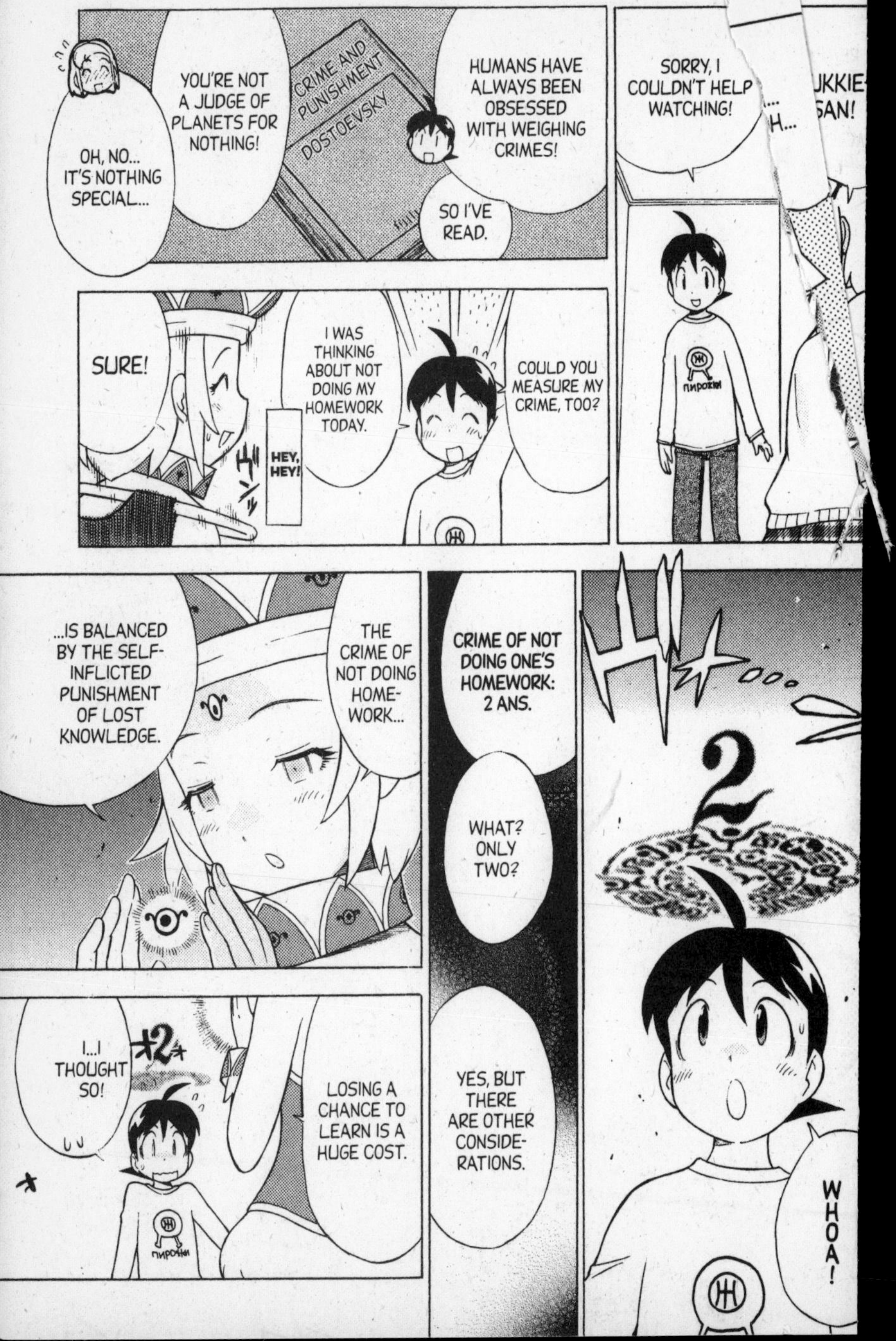

UKKIE-SAN!
...H...
SORRY, I COULDN'T HELP WATCHING!
HUMANS HAVE ALWAYS BEEN OBSESSED WITH WEIGHING CRIMES!
SO I'VE READ.
CRIME AND PUNISHMENT
DOSTOEVSKY
YOU'RE NOT A JUDGE OF PLANETS FOR NOTHING!
OH, NO... IT'S NOTHING SPECIAL...
COULD YOU MEASURE MY CRIME, TOO?
I WAS THINKING ABOUT NOT DOING MY HOMEWORK TODAY.
HEY, HEY!
SURE!
2
WHOA!
CRIME OF NOT DOING ONE'S HOMEWORK: 2 ANS.
WHAT? ONLY TWO?
YES, BUT THERE ARE OTHER CONSIDE-RATIONS.
THE CRIME OF NOT DOING HOME-WORK...
...IS BALANCED BY THE SELF-INFLICTED PUNISHMENT OF LOST KNOWLEDGE.
LOSING A CHANCE TO LEARN IS A HUGE COST.
I...I THOUGHT SO!

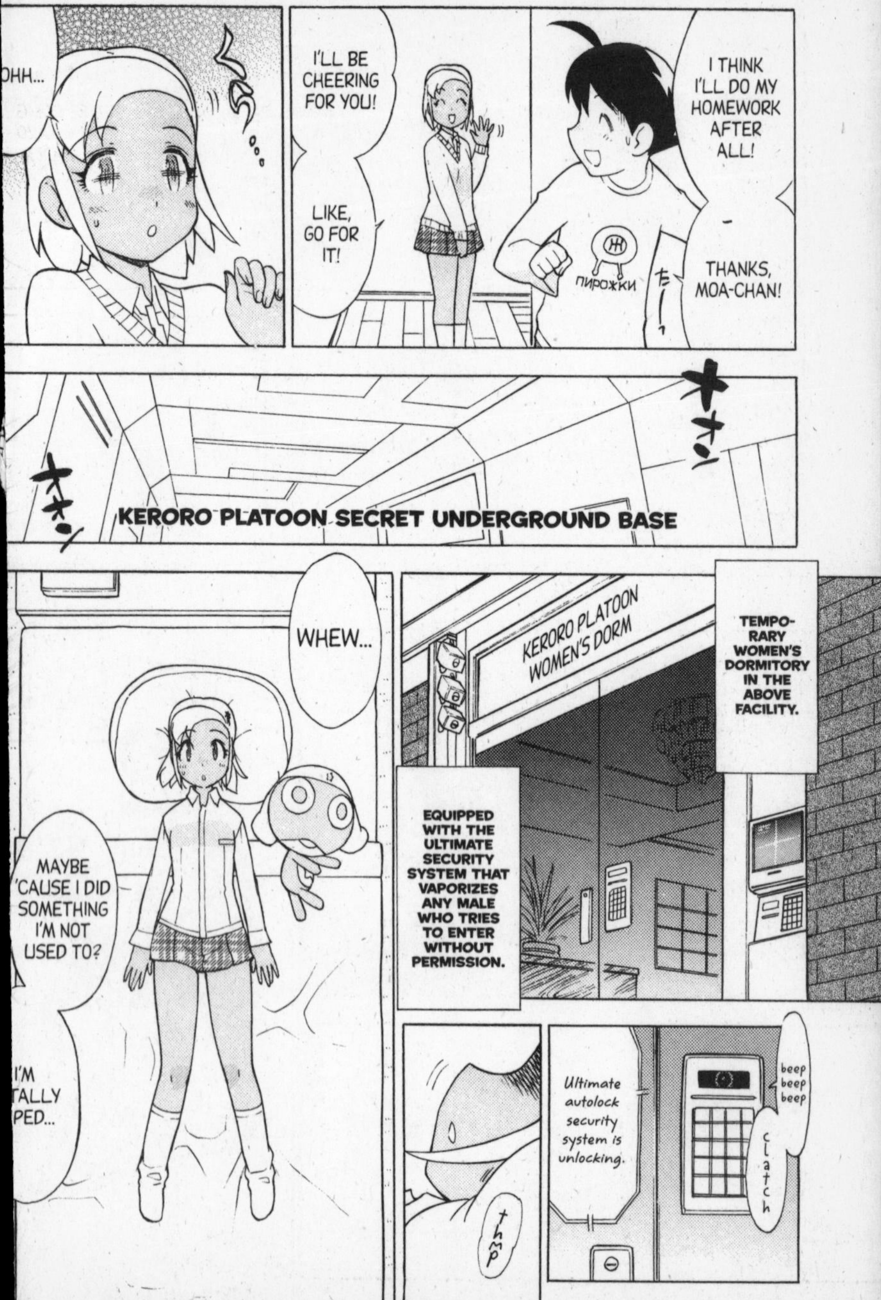
I THINK I'LL DO MY HOMEWORK AFTER ALL!
THANKS, MOA-CHAN!
ПИРОЖКИ
I'LL BE CHEERING FOR YOU!
LIKE, GO FOR IT!
OHH...
KERORO PLATOON SECRET UNDERGROUND BASE
TEMPORARY WOMEN'S DORMITORY IN THE ABOVE FACILITY.
KERORO PLATOON WOMEN'S DORM
EQUIPPED WITH THE ULTIMATE SECURITY SYSTEM THAT VAPORIZES ANY MALE WHO TRIES TO ENTER WITHOUT PERMISSION.
beep beep beep
Ultimate autolock security system is unlocking.
clatch
thmp
WHEW...
MAYBE 'CAUSE I DID SOMETHING I'M NOT USED TO?
I'M
TALLY
PED...

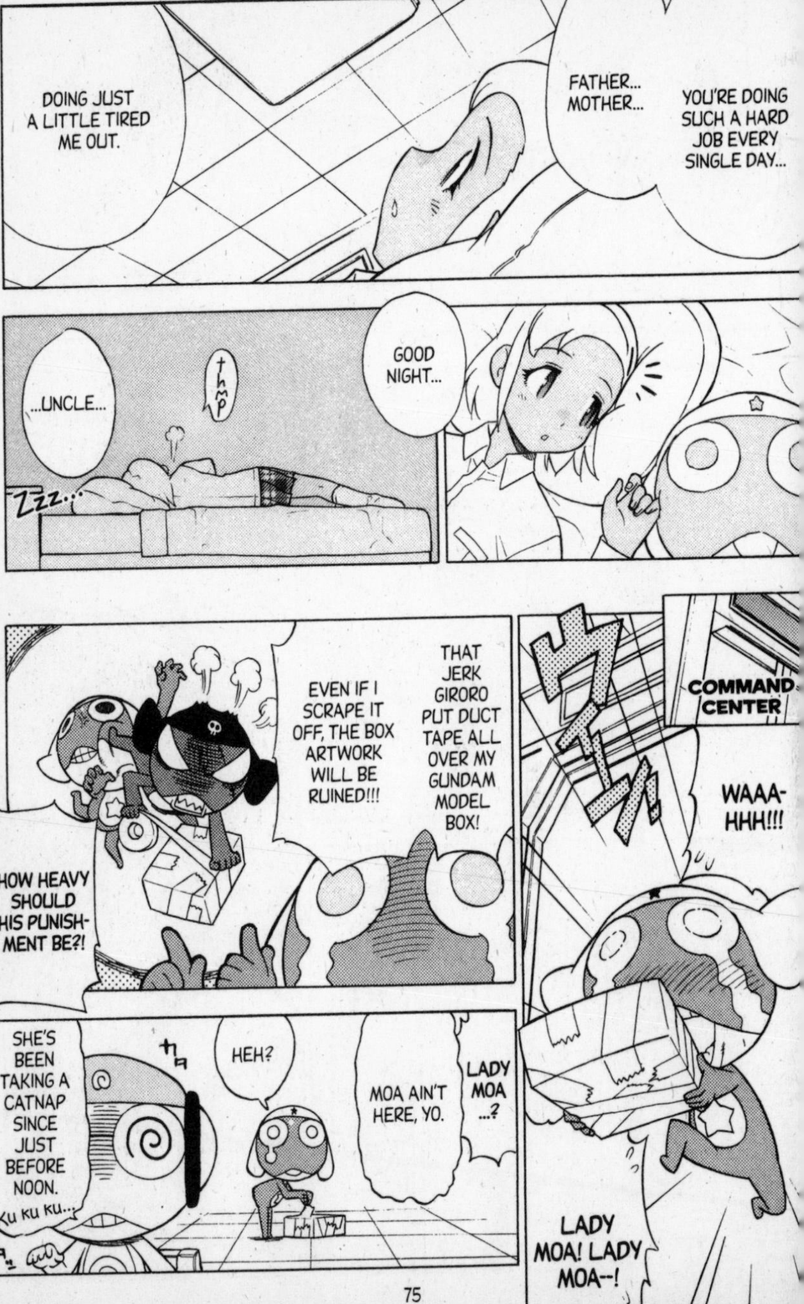

YOU'RE DOING SUCH A HARD JOB EVERY SINGLE DAY...
FATHER... MOTHER...
DOING JUST A LITTLE TIRED ME OUT.
GOOD NIGHT...
thmp
...UNCLE...
Zzz...
COMMAND CENTER
WAAA-HHH!!!
LADY MOA! LADY MOA--!
THAT JERK GIRORO PUT DUCT TAPE ALL OVER MY GUNDAM MODEL BOX!
EVEN IF I SCRAPE IT OFF, THE BOX ARTWORK WILL BE RUINED!!!
HOW HEAVY SHOULD HIS PUNISHMENT BE?!
LADY MOA ...?
MOA AIN'T HERE, YO.
HEH?
SHE'S BEEN TAKING A CATNAP SINCE JUST BEFORE NOON.
Ku ku ku...

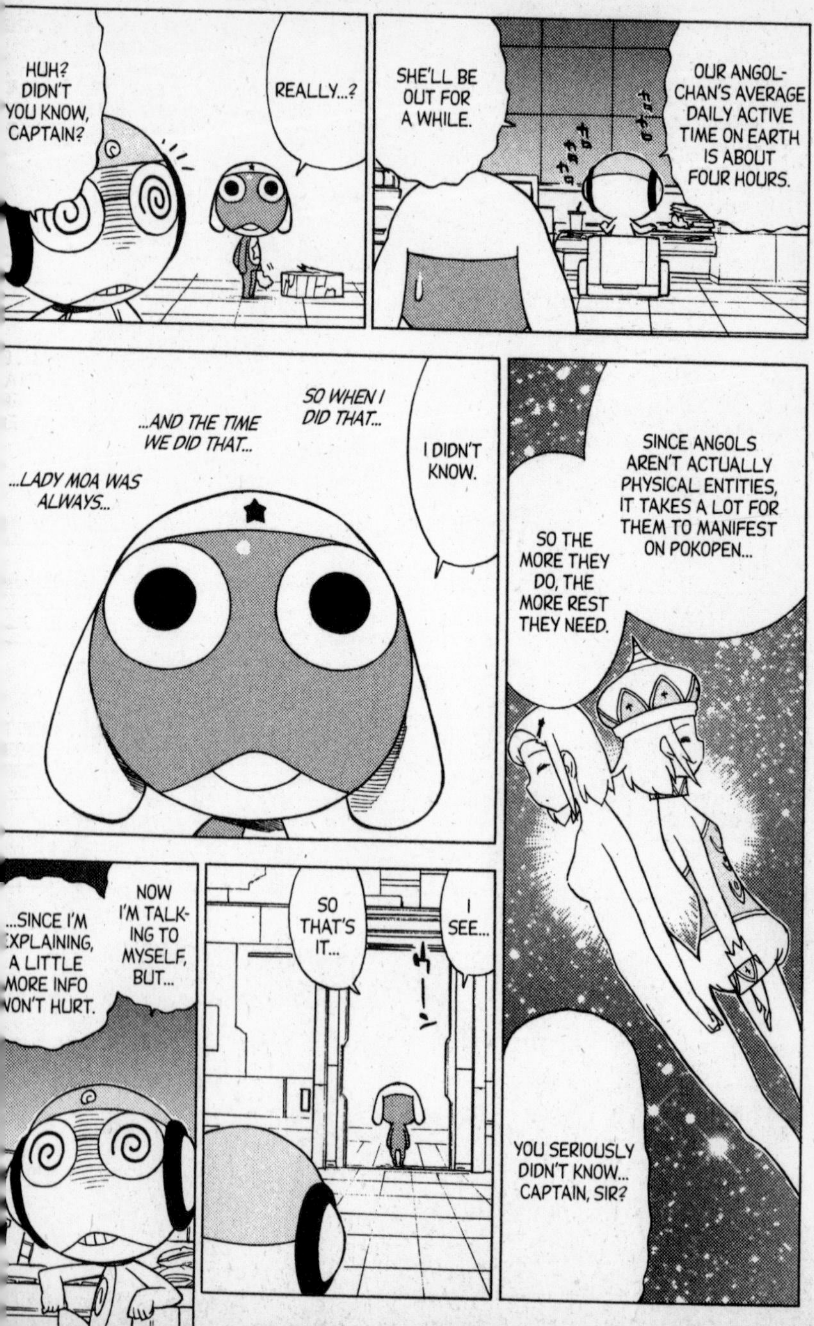
OUR ANGOL-CHAN'S AVERAGE DAILY ACTIVE TIME ON EARTH IS ABOUT FOUR HOURS.
SHE'LL BE OUT FOR A WHILE.
REALLY...?
HUH? DIDN'T YOU KNOW, CAPTAIN?
SINCE ANGOLS AREN'T ACTUALLY PHYSICAL ENTITIES, IT TAKES A LOT FOR THEM TO MANIFEST ON POKOPEN...
SO THE MORE THEY DO, THE MORE REST THEY NEED.
YOU SERIOUSLY DIDN'T KNOW... CAPTAIN, SIR?
I DIDN'T KNOW.
SO WHEN I DID THAT...
...AND THE TIME WE DID THAT...
...LADY MOA WAS ALWAYS...
I SEE...
SO THAT'S IT...
NOW I'M TALKING TO MYSELF, BUT...
...SINCE I'M EXPLAINING, A LITTLE MORE INFO WON'T HURT.

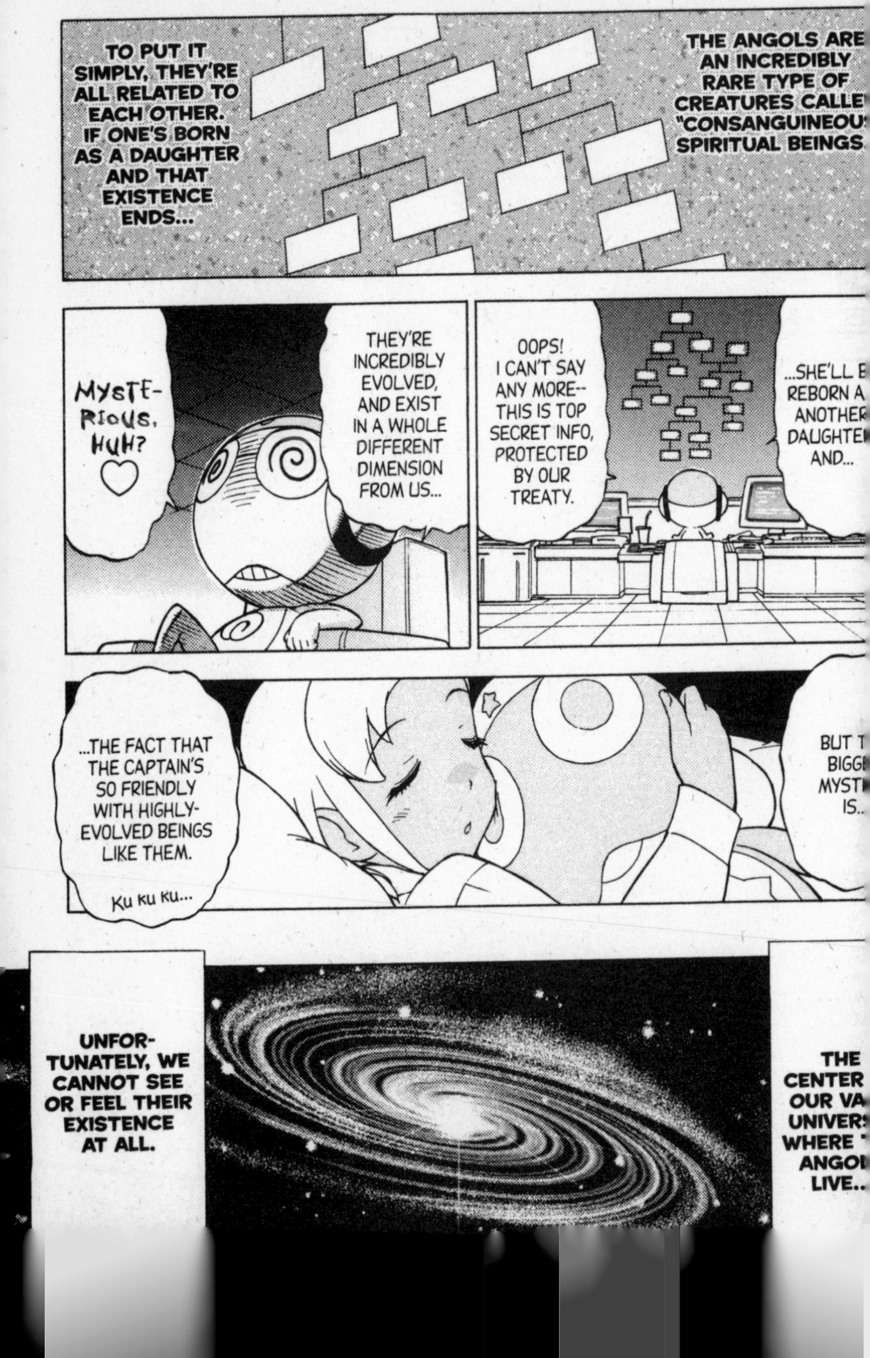
THE ANGOLS ARE AN INCREDIBLY RARE TYPE OF CREATURES CALLE "CONSANGUINEOU SPIRITUAL BEINGS.
TO PUT IT SIMPLY, THEY'RE ALL RELATED TO EACH OTHER. IF ONE'S BORN AS A DAUGHTER AND THAT EXISTENCE ENDS...
...SHE'LL B REBORN A ANOTHER DAUGHTE AND...
OOPS! I CAN'T SAY ANY MORE-- THIS IS TOP SECRET INFO, PROTECTED BY OUR TREATY.
THEY'RE INCREDIBLY EVOLVED, AND EXIST IN A WHOLE DIFFERENT DIMENSION FROM US...
MYSTE-RIOUS, HUH? ♡
BUT T BIGG MYST IS..
...THE FACT THAT THE CAPTAIN'S SO FRIENDLY WITH HIGHLY-EVOLVED BEINGS LIKE THEM.
Ku ku ku...
THE CENTER OUR VA UNIVERS WHERE T ANGOI LIVE..
UNFOR-TUNATELY, WE CANNOT SEE OR FEEL THEIR EXISTENCE AT ALL.

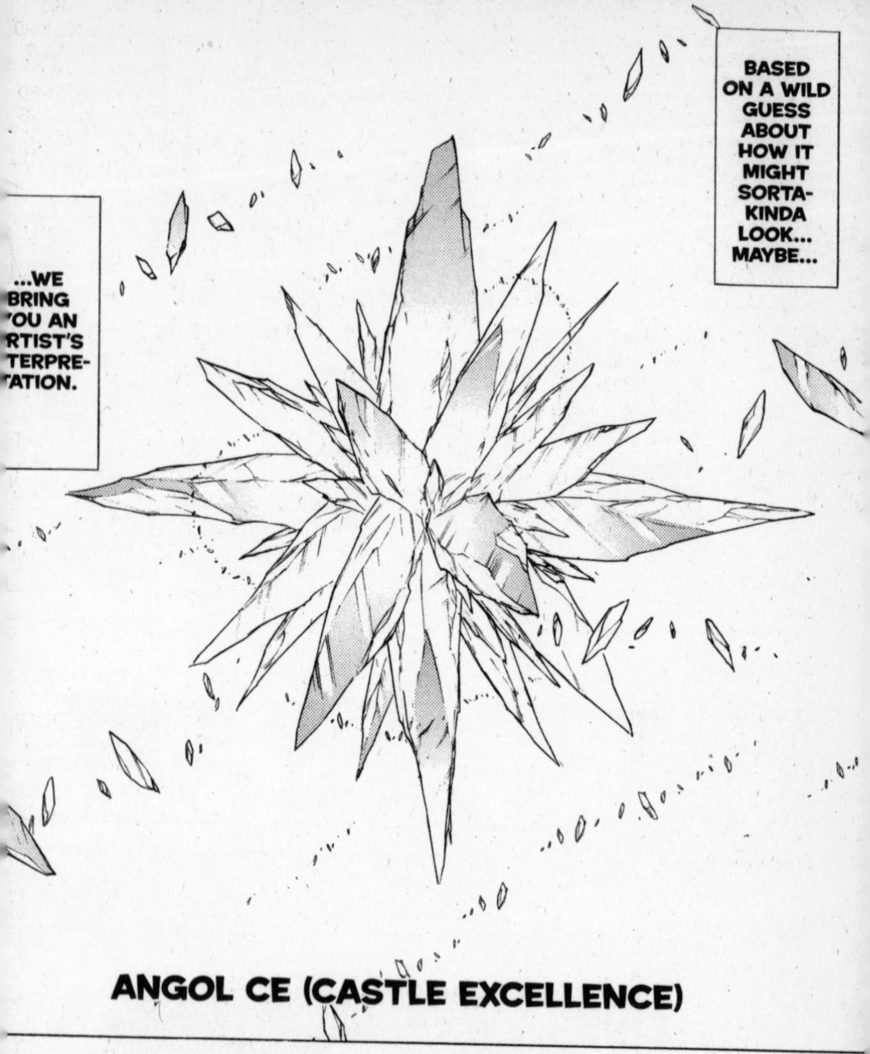
BASED ON A WILD GUESS ABOUT HOW IT MIGHT SORTA-KINDA LOOK... MAYBE...
...WE BRING OU AN RTIST'S TERPRE-ATION.
ANGOL CE (CASTLE EXCELLENCE)

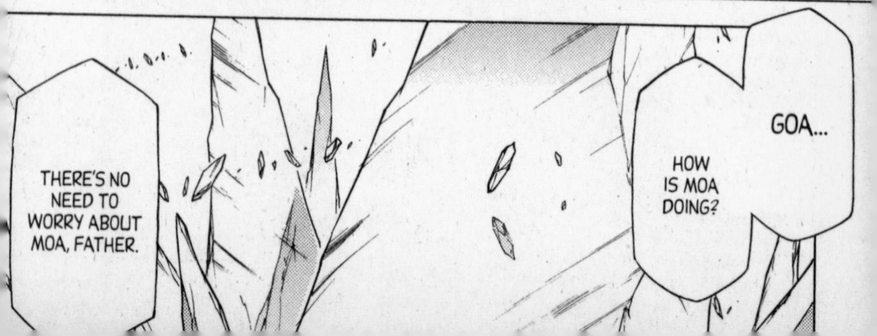
GOA...
HOW IS MOA DOING?
THERE'S NO NEED TO WORRY ABOUT MOA, FATHER.

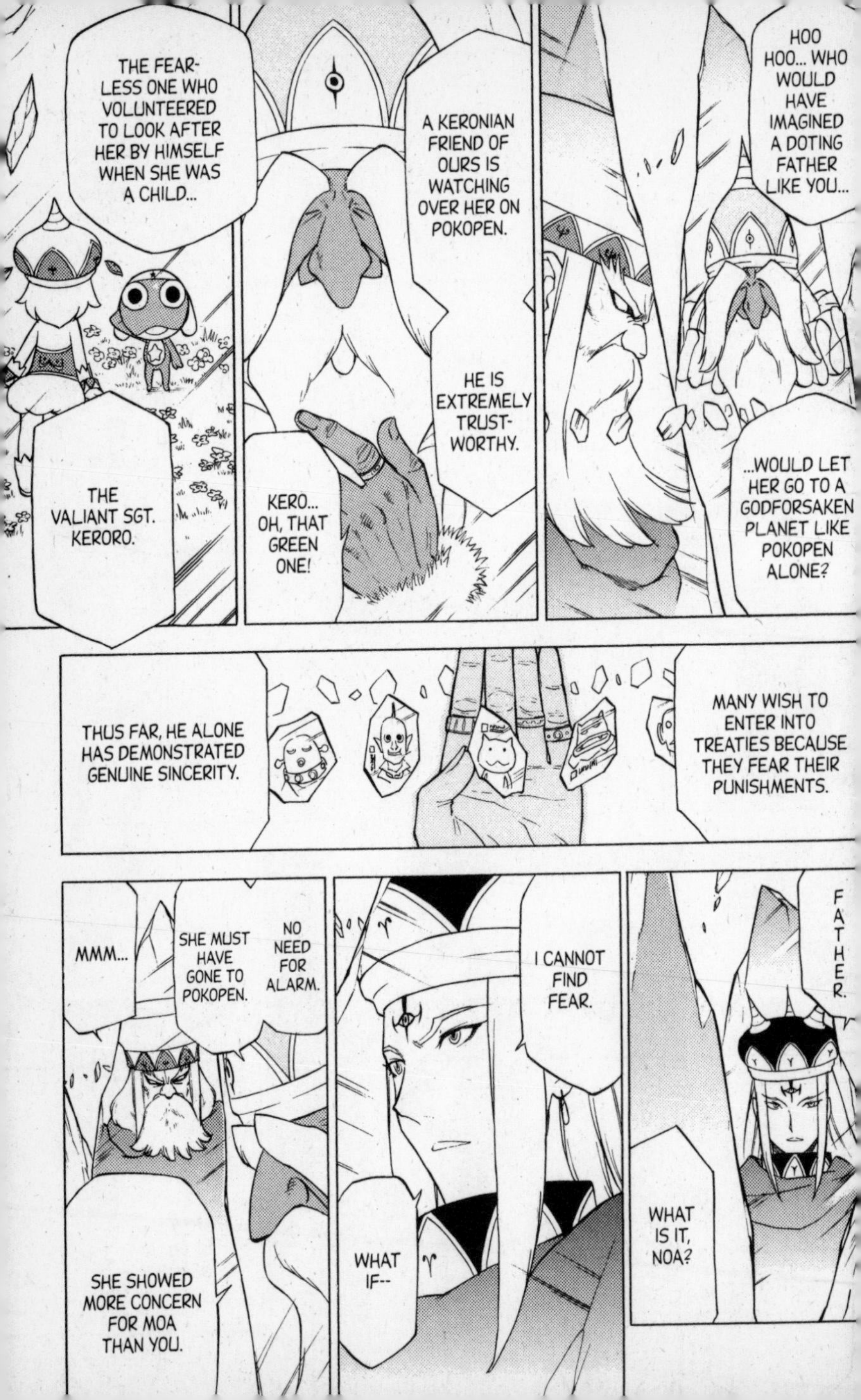
HOO HOO... WHO WOULD HAVE IMAGINED A DOTING FATHER LIKE YOU...
...WOULD LET HER GO TO A GODFORSAKEN PLANET LIKE POKOPEN ALONE?
A KERONIAN FRIEND OF OURS IS WATCHING OVER HER ON POKOPEN.
HE IS EXTREMELY TRUST-WORTHY.
KERO... OH, THAT GREEN ONE!
THE FEAR-LESS ONE WHO VOLUNTEERED TO LOOK AFTER HER BY HIMSELF WHEN SHE WAS A CHILD...
THE VALIANT SGT. KERORO.
MANY WISH TO ENTER INTO TREATIES BECAUSE THEY FEAR THEIR PUNISHMENTS.
THUS FAR, HE ALONE HAS DEMONSTRATED GENUINE SINCERITY.
FATHER.
WHAT IS IT, NOA?
I CANNOT FIND FEAR.
WHAT IF--
NO NEED FOR ALARM.
SHE MUST HAVE GONE TO POKOPEN.
MMM...
SHE SHOWED MORE CONCERN FOR MOA THAN YOU.

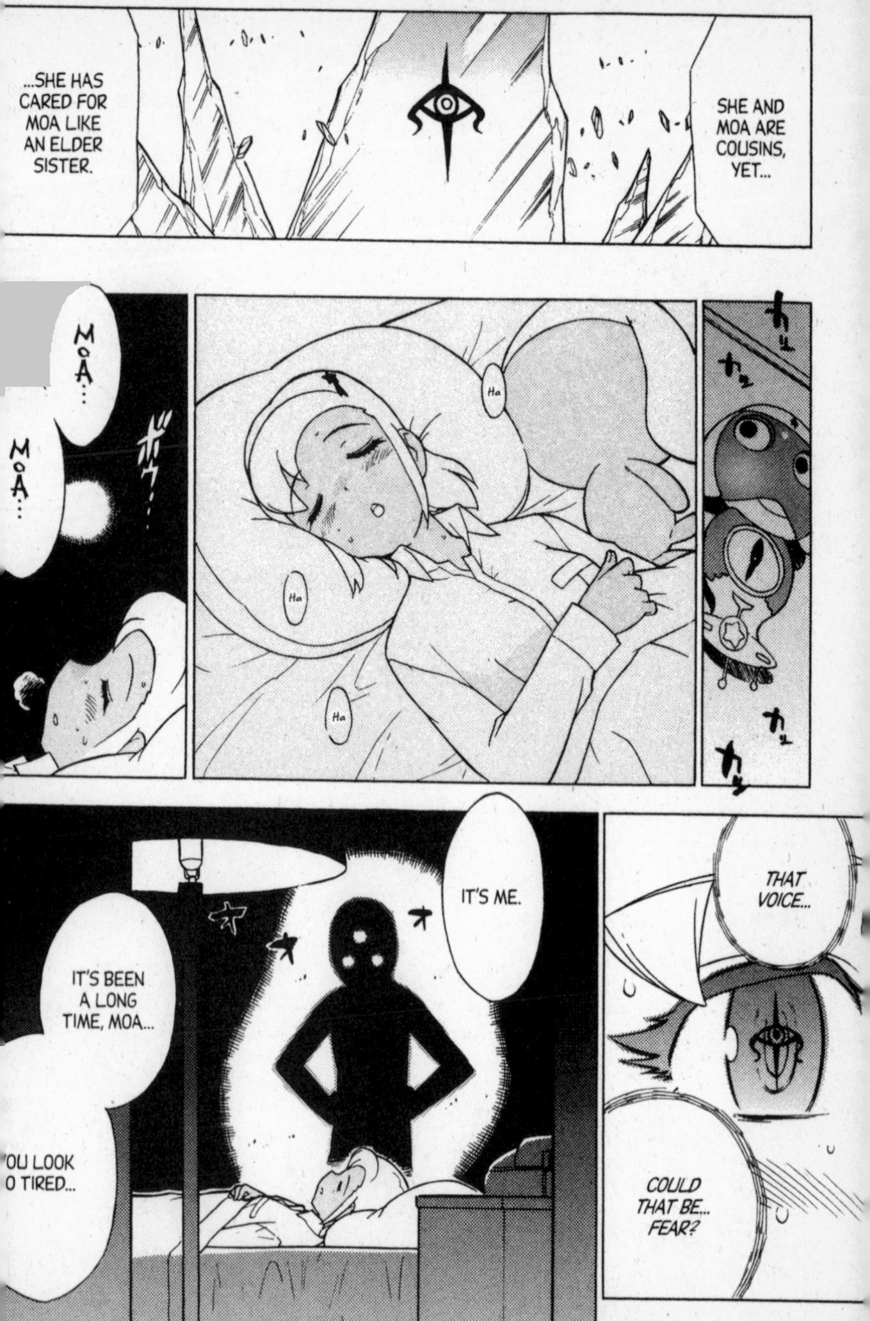
SHE AND MOA ARE COUSINS, YET...
...SHE HAS CARED FOR MOA LIKE AN ELDER SISTER.
Ha
Ha
Ha
MOA...
MOA...
THAT VOICE...
COULD THAT BE... FEAR?
IT'S ME.
IT'S BEEN A LONG TIME, MOA...
OU LOOK O TIRED...

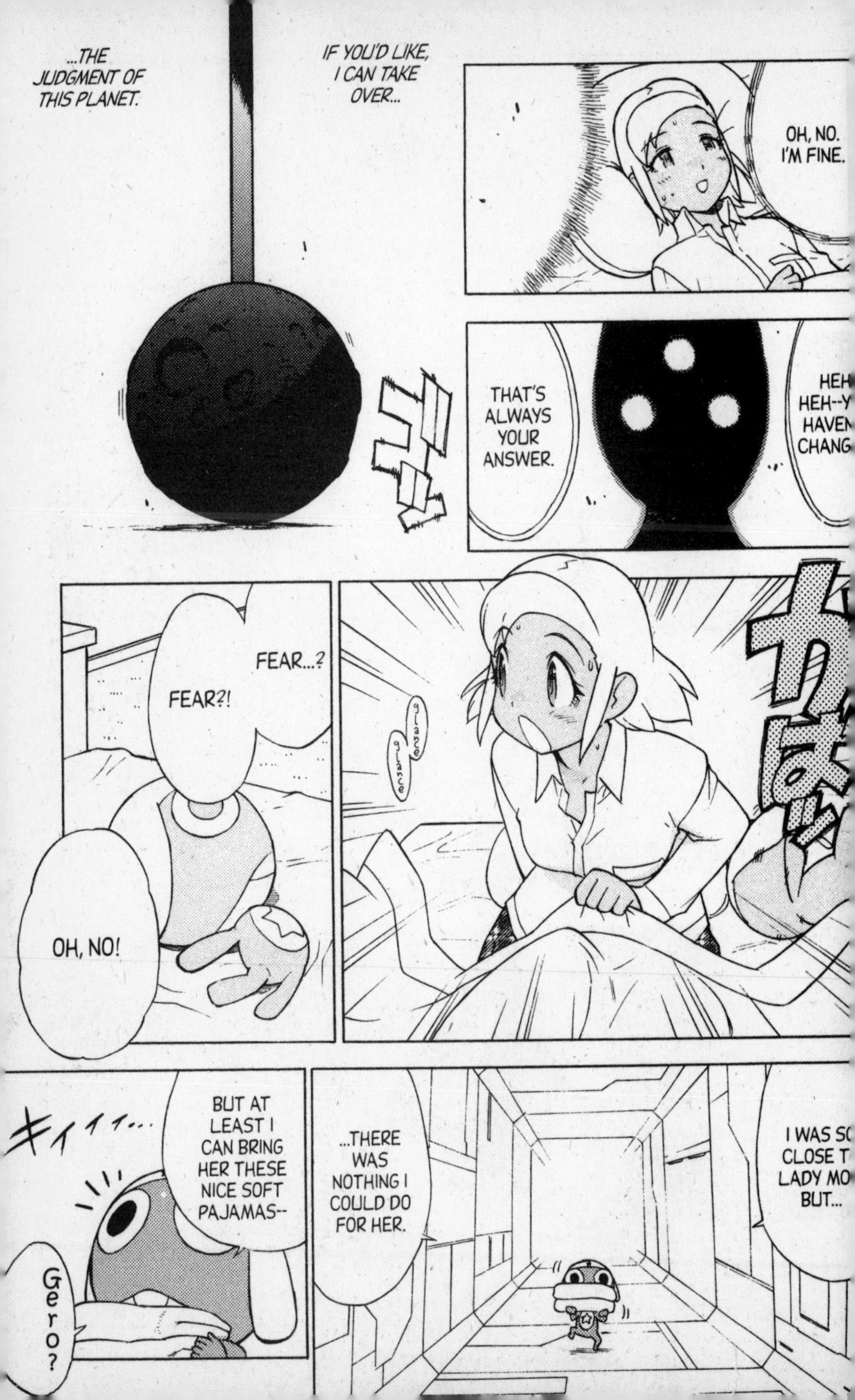
OH, NO. I'M FINE.
HEH HEH--Y HAVEN CHANG
THAT'S ALWAYS YOUR ANSWER.
IF YOU'D LIKE, I CAN TAKE OVER...
...THE JUDGMENT OF THIS PLANET.
glance glance
FEAR...?
FEAR?!
OH, NO!
I WAS SO CLOSE T LADY MO BUT...
...THERE WAS NOTHING I COULD DO FOR HER.
BUT AT LEAST I CAN BRING HER THESE NICE SOFT PAJAMAS--
キィィィ...
Gero?

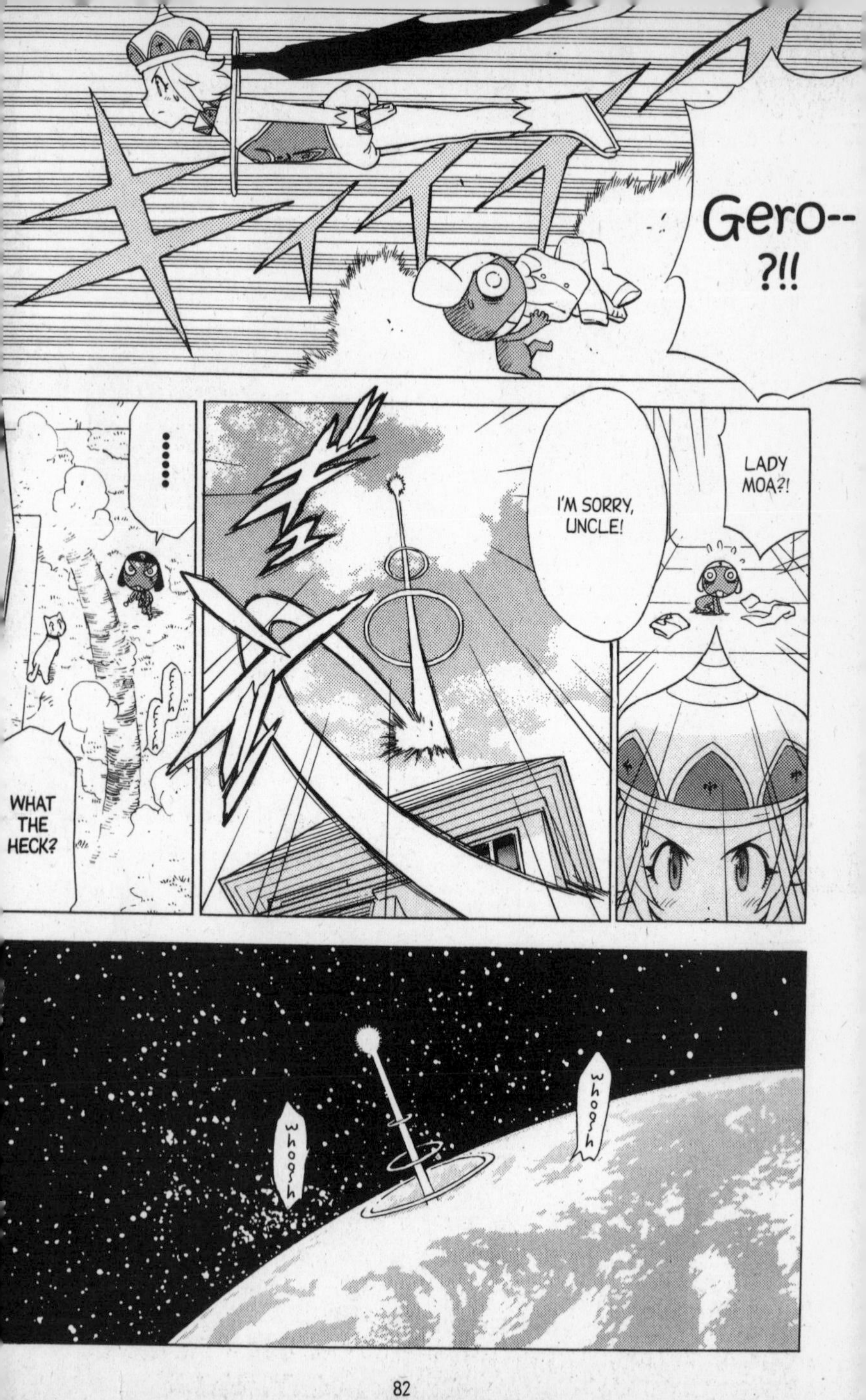
Gero-- ?!!
LADY MOA?!
I'M SORRY, UNCLE!
......
WHAT THE HECK?
whoosh
whoosh

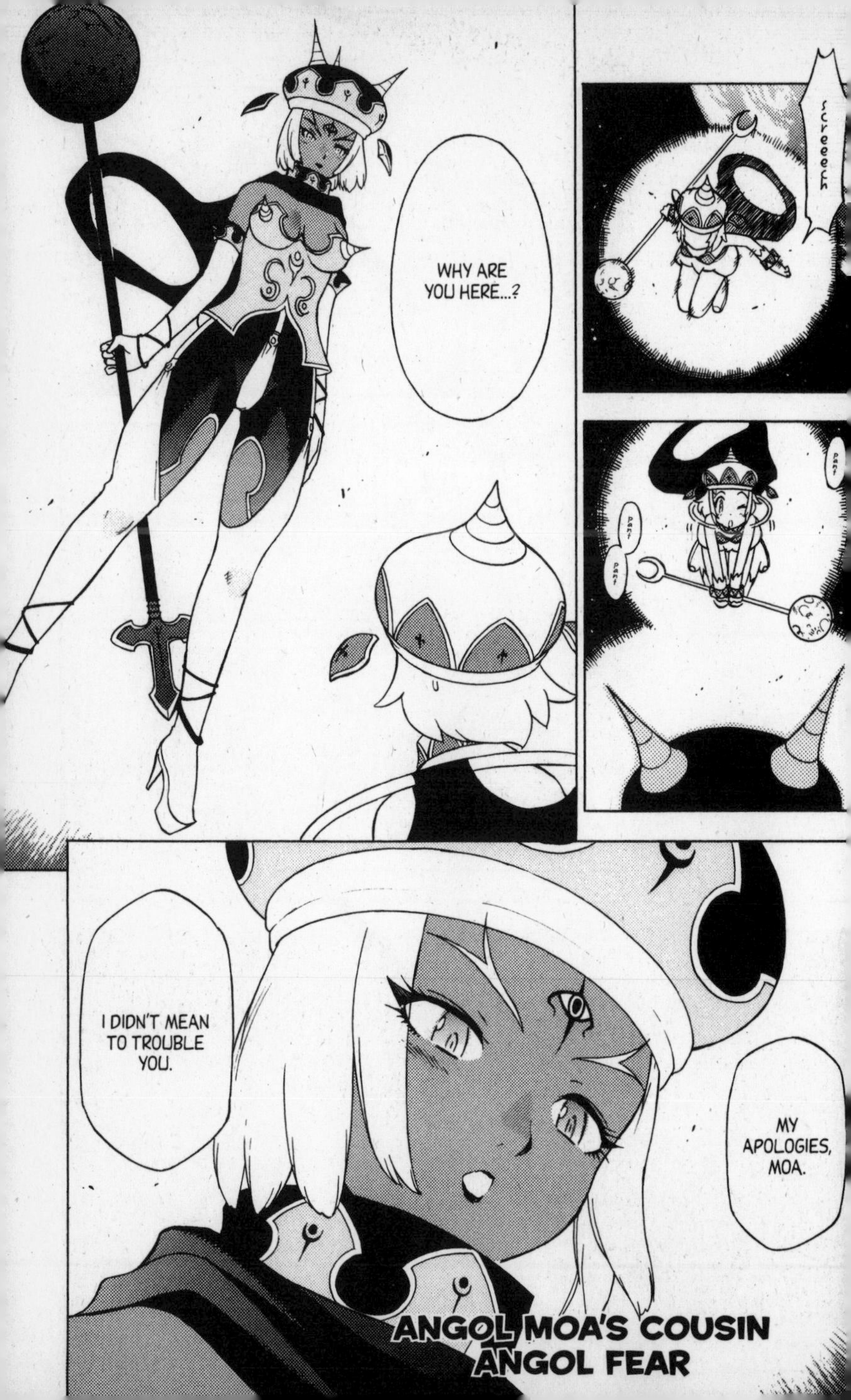
screeech
pant
pant
pant
WHY ARE YOU HERE...?
MY APOLOGIES, MOA.
I DIDN'T MEAN TO TROUBLE YOU.
ANGOL MOA'S COUSIN
ANGOL FEAR

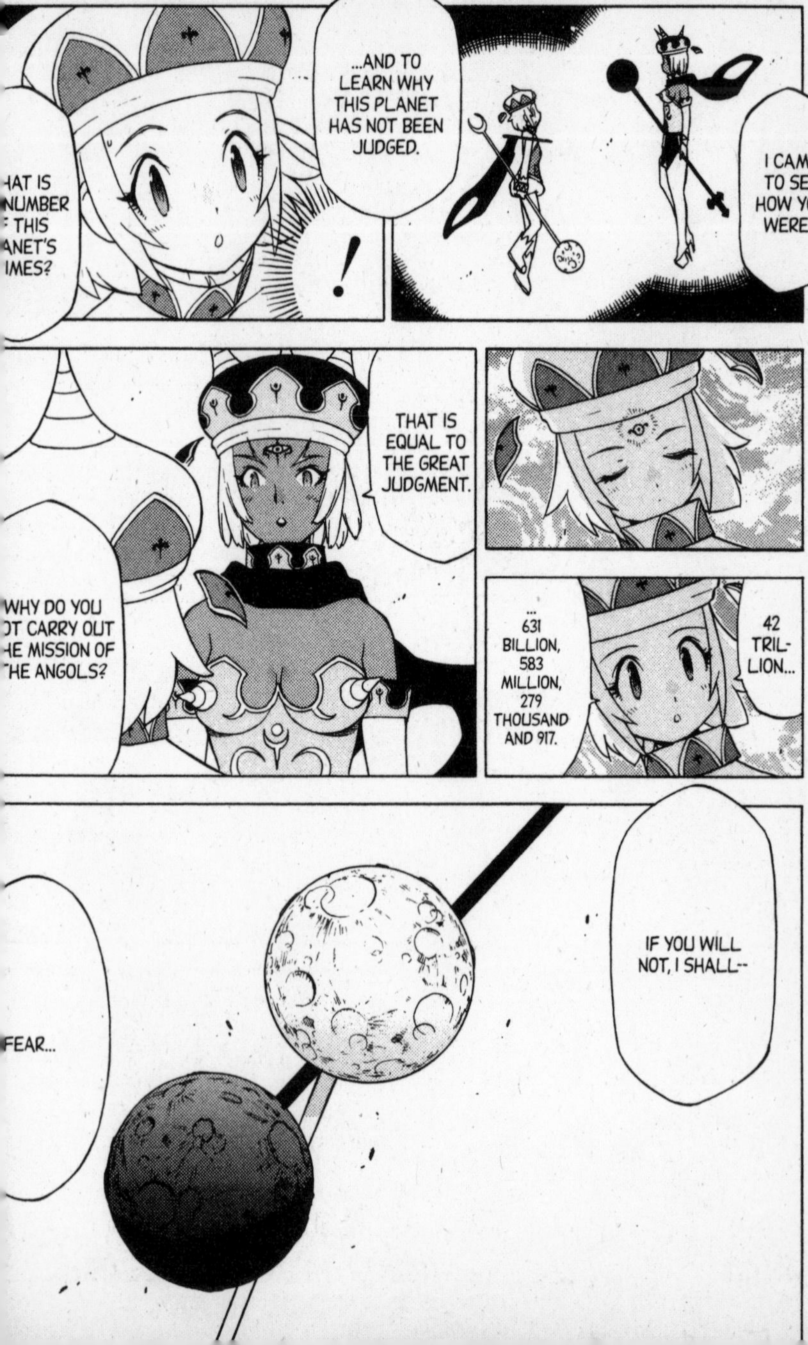
I CAME TO SEE HOW YOU WERE...
...AND TO LEARN WHY THIS PLANET HAS NOT BEEN JUDGED.
!
HAT IS NUMBER F THIS ANET'S IMES?
42 TRIL-LION...
... 631 BILLION, 583 MILLION, 279 THOUSAND AND 917.
THAT IS EQUAL TO THE GREAT JUDGMENT.
WHY DO YOU OT CARRY OUT HE MISSION OF THE ANGOLS?
IF YOU WILL NOT, I SHALL--
FEAR...

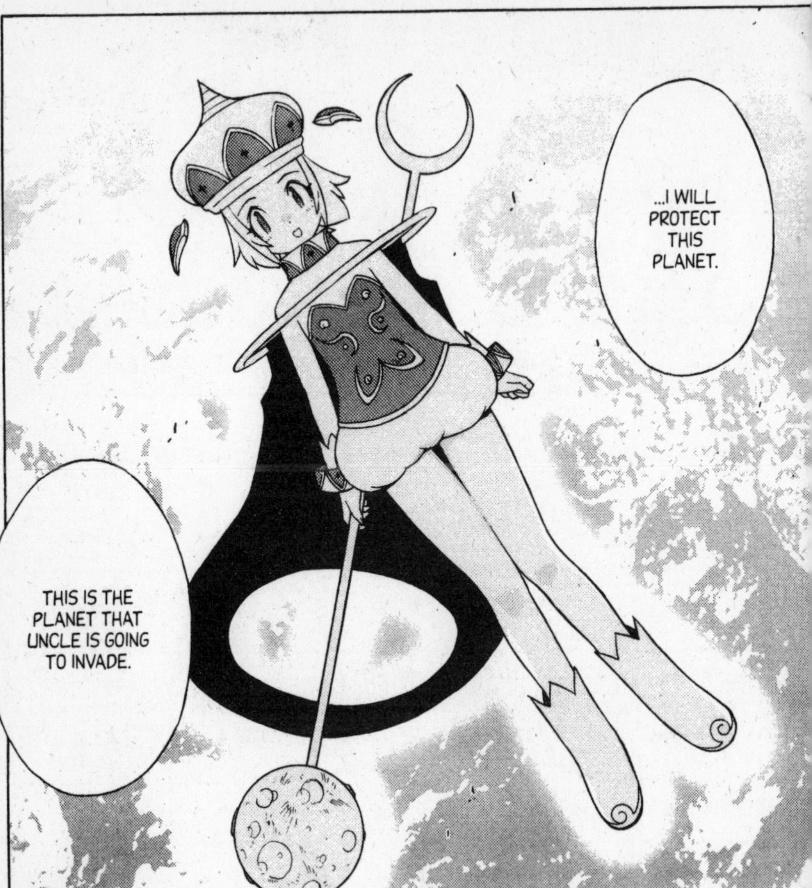
...I WILL PROTECT THIS PLANET.
THIS IS THE PLANET THAT UNCLE IS GOING TO INVADE.
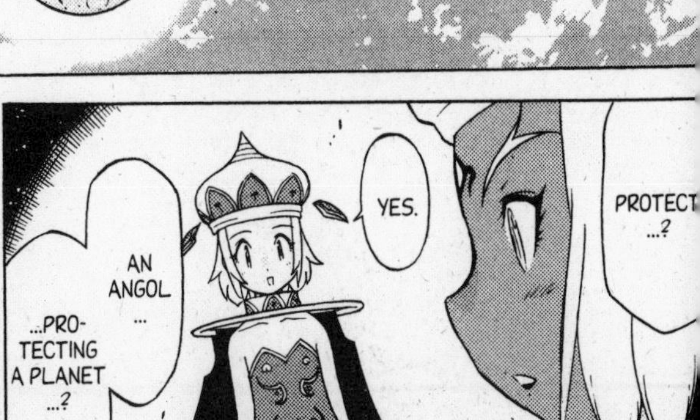
PROTECT ...?
YES.
AN ANGOL ...
...PRO-TECTING A PLANET ...?
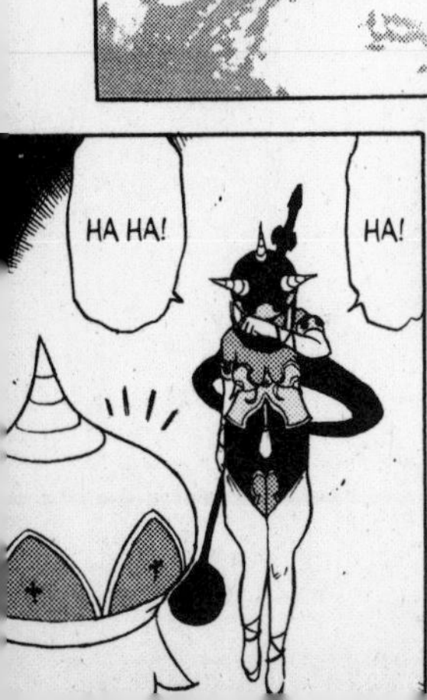
HA!
HA HA!

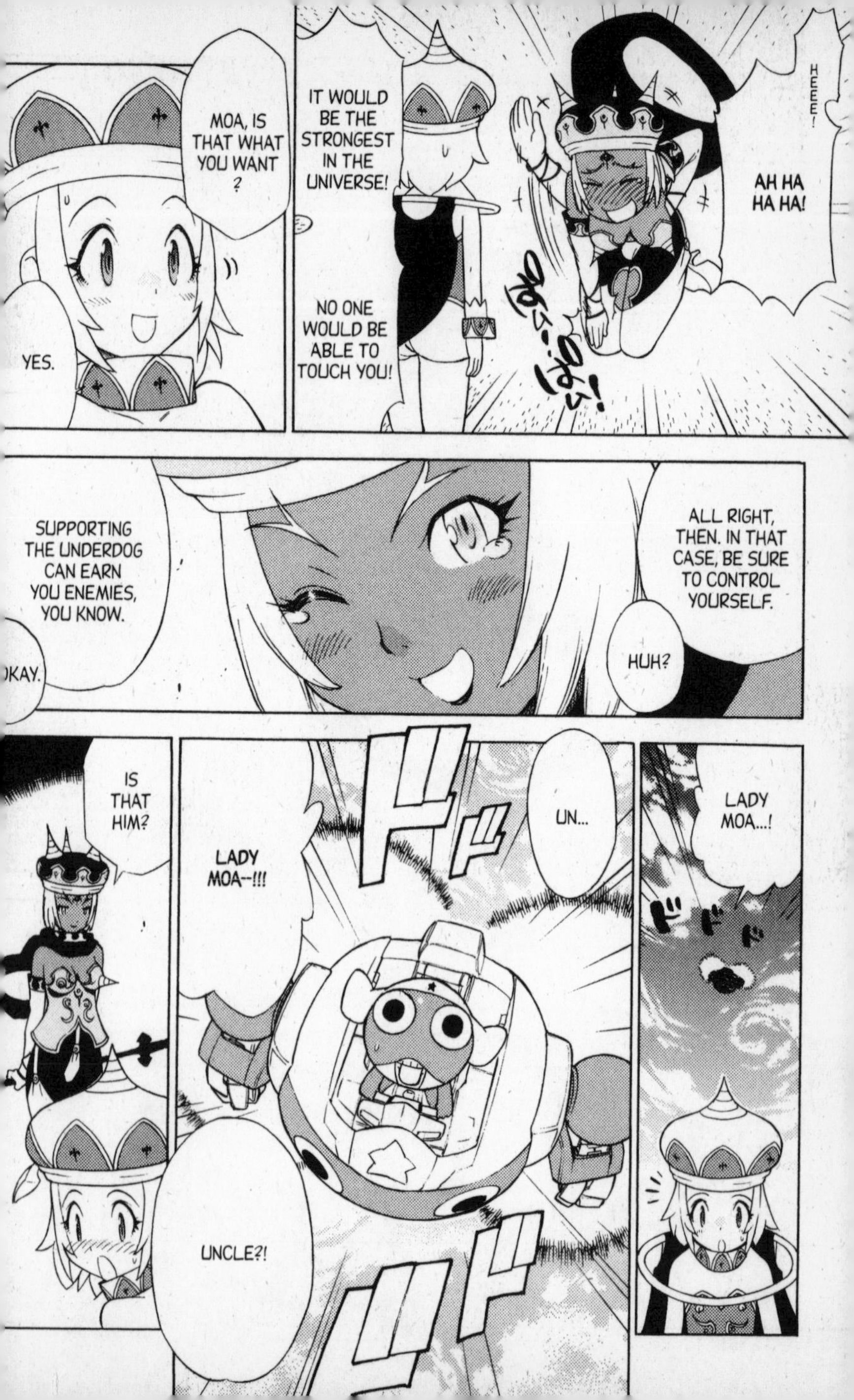
HEEEE!
AH HA HA HA!
IT WOULD BE THE STRONGEST IN THE UNIVERSE!
NO ONE WOULD BE ABLE TO TOUCH YOU!
MOA, IS THAT WHAT YOU WANT?
YES.
ALL RIGHT, THEN. IN THAT CASE, BE SURE TO CONTROL YOURSELF.
HUH?
SUPPORTING THE UNDERDOG CAN EARN YOU ENEMIES, YOU KNOW.
KAY.
LADY MOA...!
ドドド
UN...
LADY MOA--!!!
UNCLE?!
IS THAT HIM?

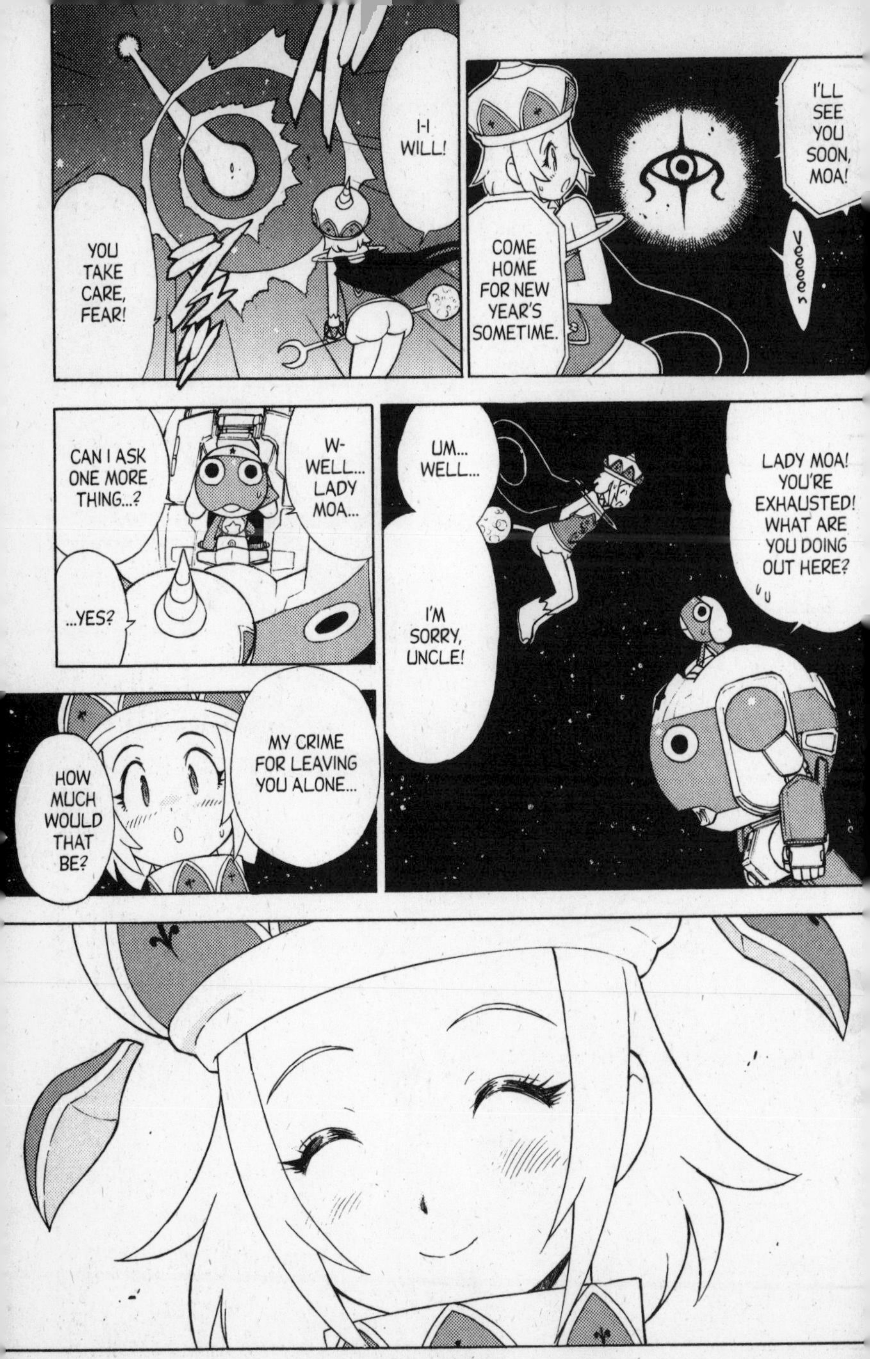
I'LL SEE YOU SOON, MOA!
Veeeen
COME HOME FOR NEW YEAR'S SOMETIME.
I-I WILL!
YOU TAKE CARE, FEAR!
LADY MOA! YOU'RE EXHAUSTED! WHAT ARE YOU DOING OUT HERE?
UM... WELL...
I'M SORRY, UNCLE!
W-WELL... LADY MOA...
CAN I ASK ONE MORE THING...?
...YES?
MY CRIME FOR LEAVING YOU ALONE...
HOW MUCH WOULD THAT BE?

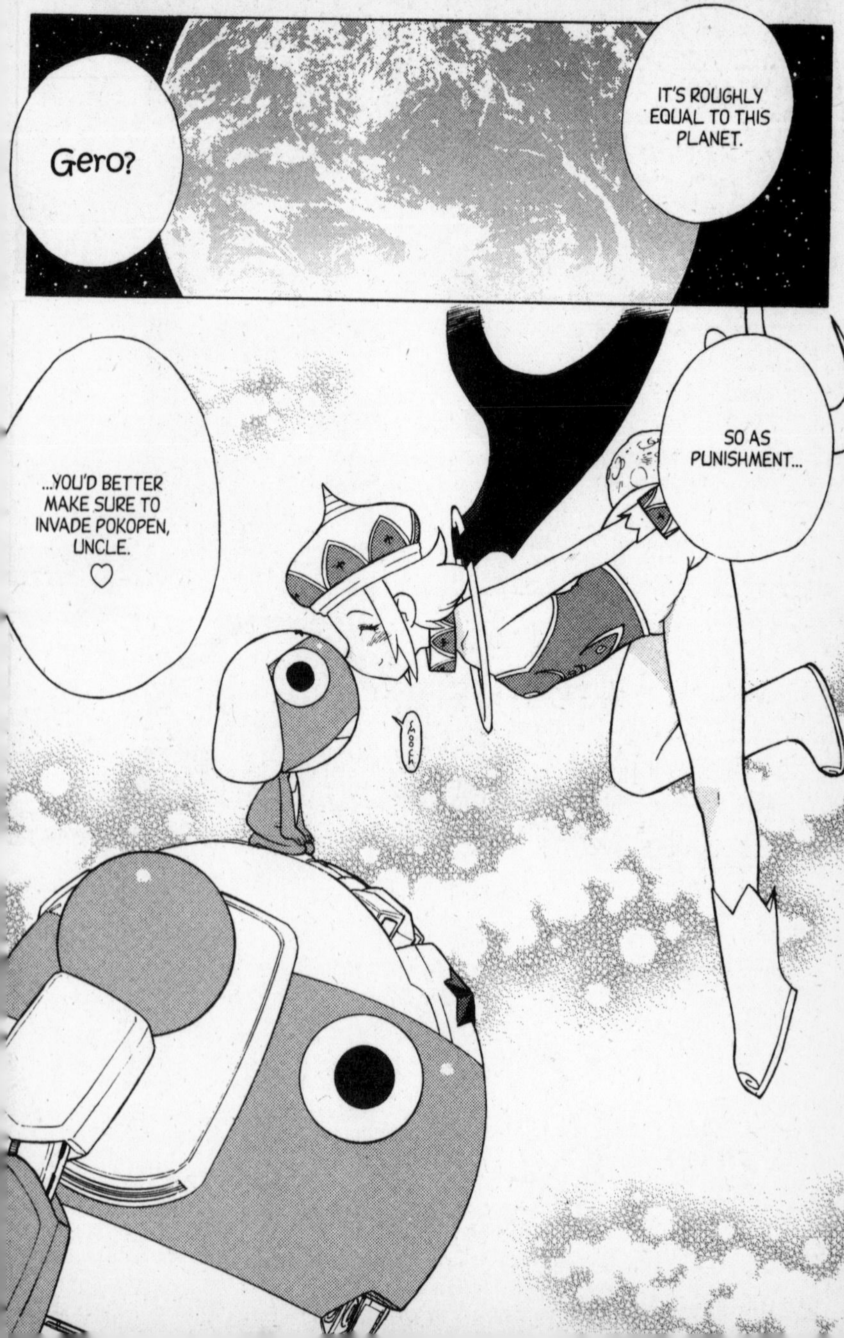
IT'S ROUGHLY EQUAL TO THIS PLANET.
Gero?
SO AS PUNISHMENT...
...YOU'D BETTER MAKE SURE TO INVADE POKOPEN, UNCLE. ♡
smooch

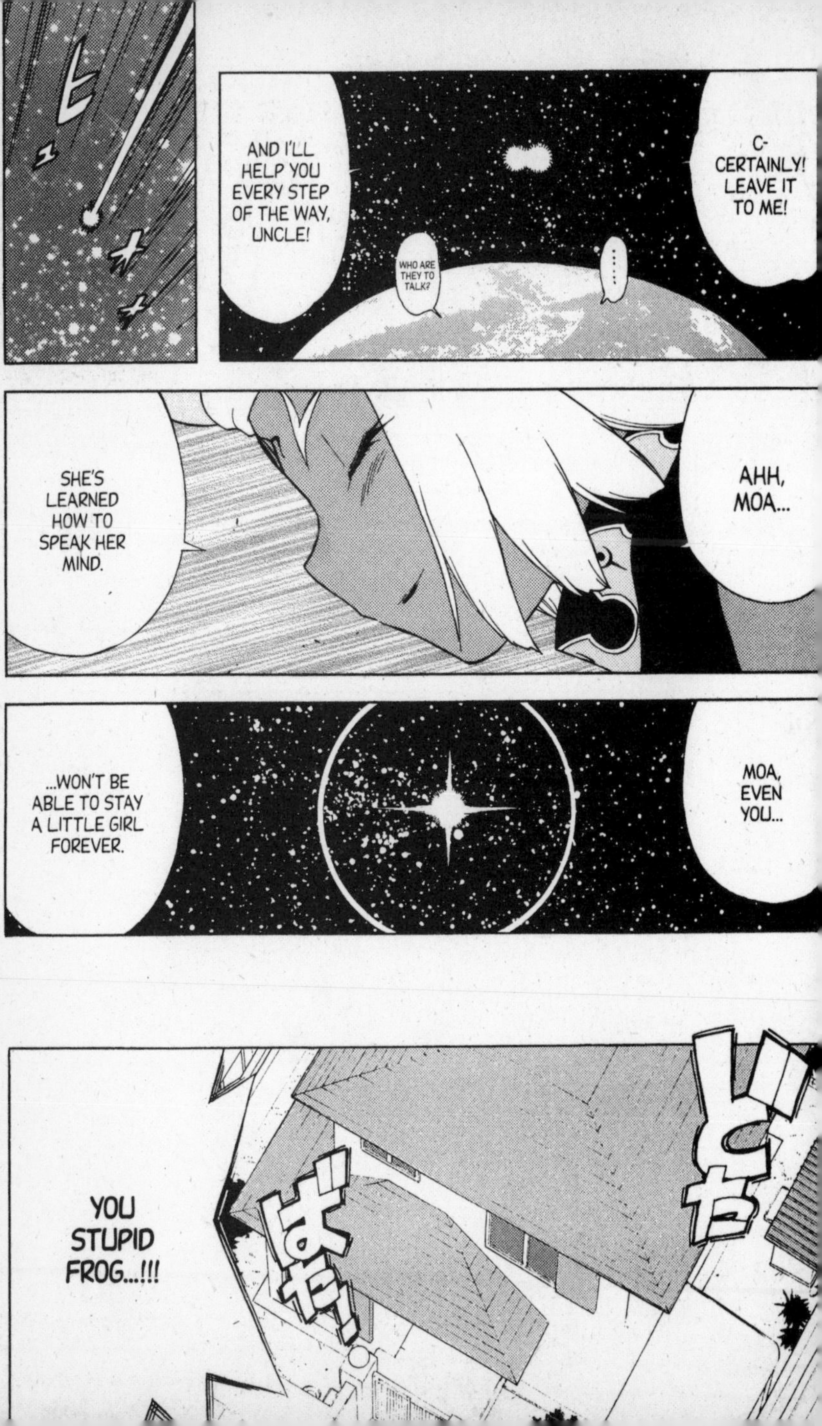
C-CERTAINLY! LEAVE IT TO ME!
......
WHO ARE THEY TO TALK?
AND I'LL HELP YOU EVERY STEP OF THE WAY, UNCLE!
AHH, MOA...
SHE'S LEARNED HOW TO SPEAK HER MIND.
MOA, EVEN YOU...
...WON'T BE ABLE TO STAY A LITTLE GIRL FOREVER.
YOU STUPID FROG...!!!

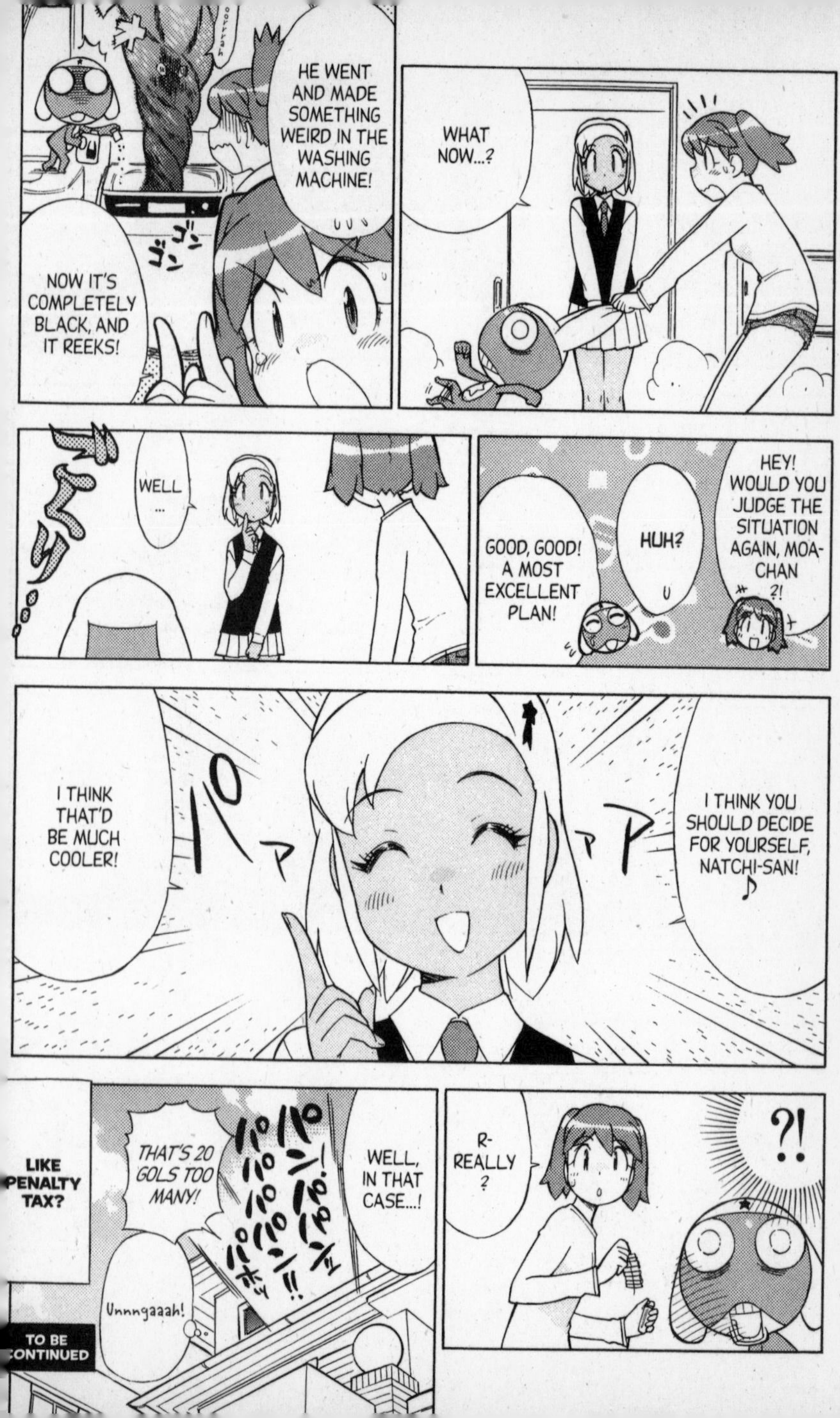
WHAT NOW...?
HE WENT AND MADE SOMETHING WEIRD IN THE WASHING MACHINE!
NOW IT'S COMPLETELY BLACK, AND IT REEKS!
HEY! WOULD YOU JUDGE THE SITUATION AGAIN, MOA-CHAN ?!
HUH?
GOOD, GOOD! A MOST EXCELLENT PLAN!
WELL ...
I THINK YOU SHOULD DECIDE FOR YOURSELF, NATCHI-SAN! ♪
I THINK THAT'D BE MUCH COOLER!
?!
R-REALLY?
WELL, IN THAT CASE...!
THAT'S 20 GOLS TOO MANY!
Unnngaaah!
LIKE PENALTY TAX?
TO BE CONTINUED

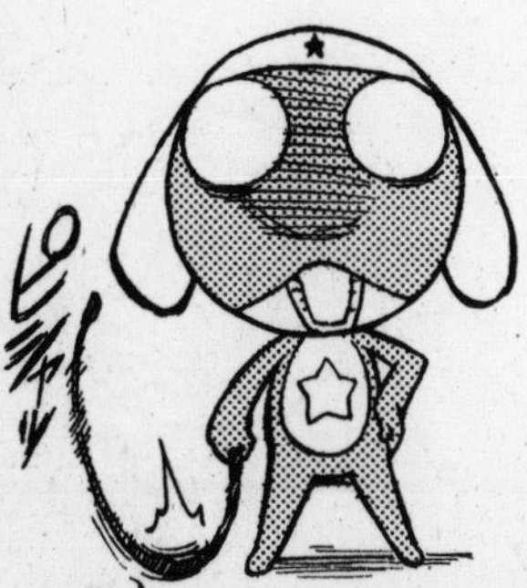

ピシャッ

ENCOUNTER CLIX
PLAN RC: REMOTE-CONTROLLED EARTHLINGS

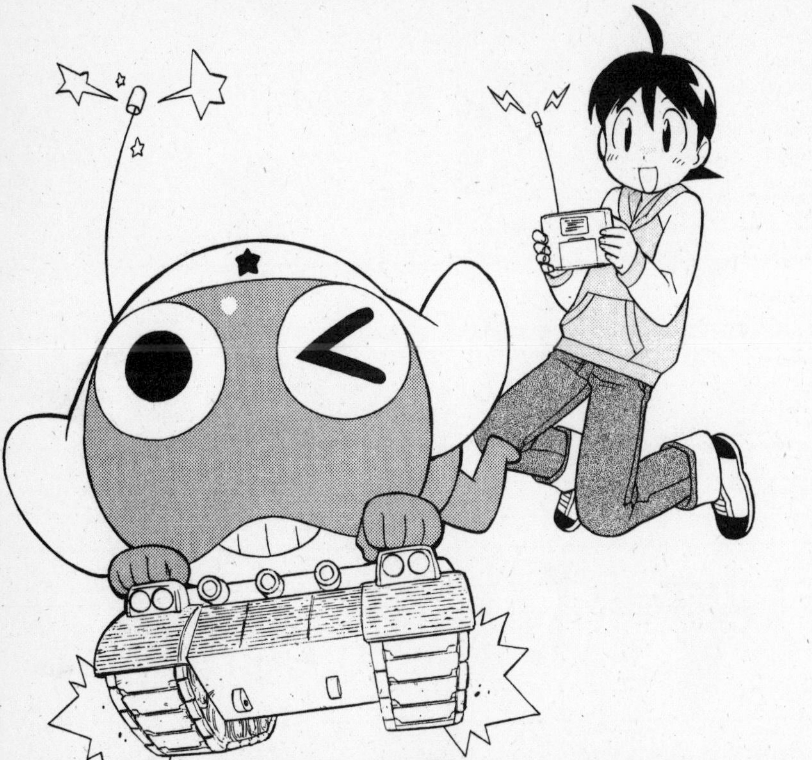

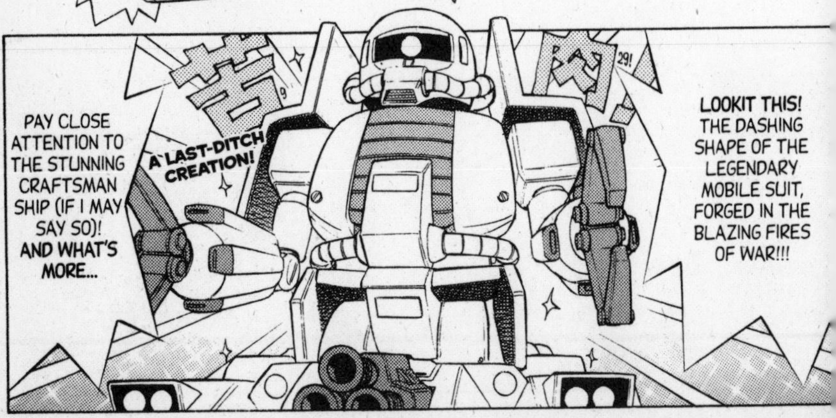
LOOKIT THIS! THE DASHING SHAPE OF THE LEGENDARY MOBILE SUIT, FORGED IN THE BLAZING FIRES OF WAR!!!
苦肉
A LAST-DITCH CREATION!
PAY CLOSE ATTENTION TO THE STUNNING CRAFTSMAN SHIP (IF I MAY SAY SO)! AND WHAT'S MORE...

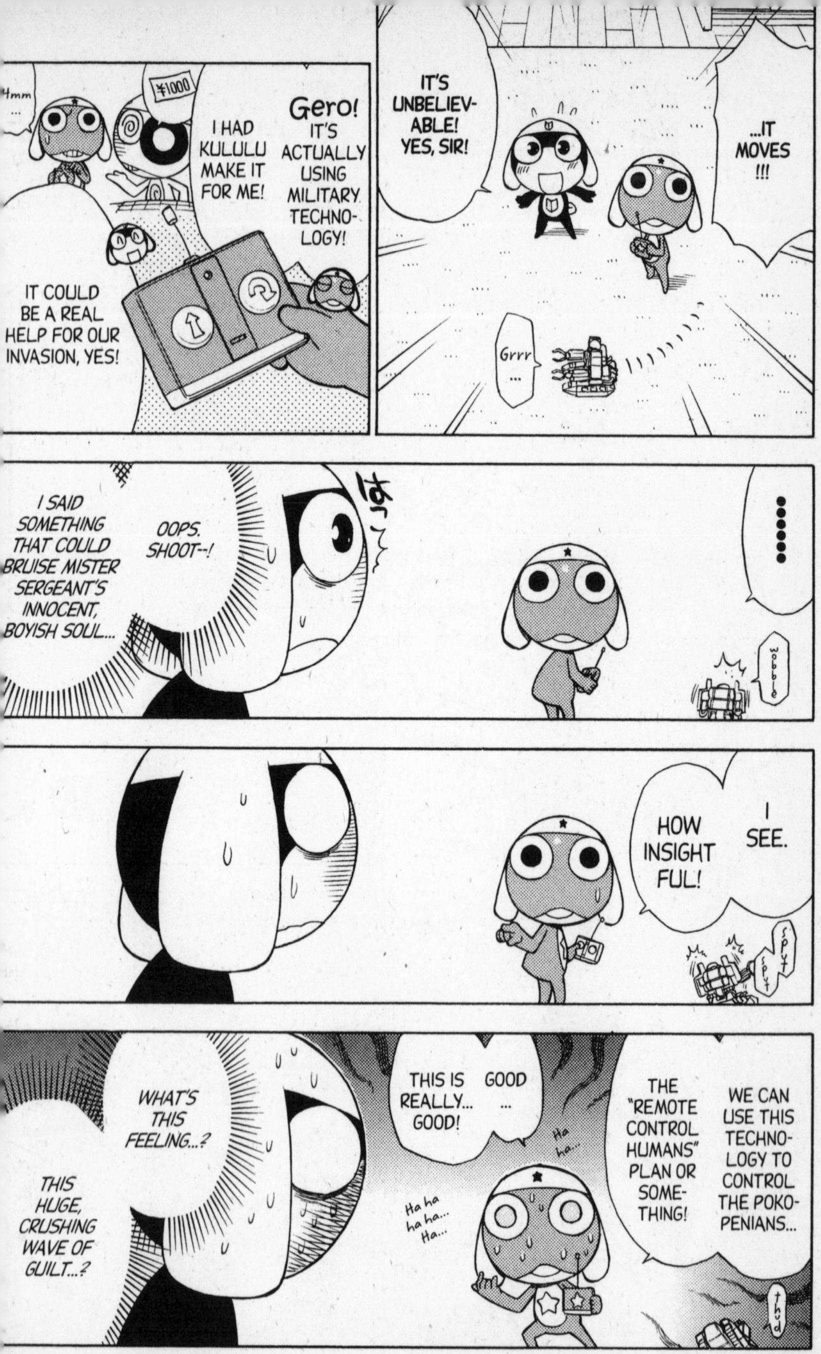
...IT MOVES !!!
IT'S UNBELIEVABLE! YES, SIR!
Grrr ...
Gero! IT'S ACTUALLY USING MILITARY TECHNOLOGY!
I HAD KULULU MAKE IT FOR ME!
¥1000
mm ...
IT COULD BE A REAL HELP FOR OUR INVASION, YES!
••••••
wobble
OOPS. SHOOT--!
I SAID SOMETHING THAT COULD BRUISE MISTER SERGEANT'S INNOCENT, BOYISH SOUL...
I SEE.
HOW INSIGHTFUL!
spyt spyt
WE CAN USE THIS TECHNOLOGY TO CONTROL THE POKOPENIANS...
THE "REMOTE CONTROL HUMANS" PLAN OR SOMETHING!
GOOD ...
THIS IS REALLY... GOOD!
Ha ha...
Ha ha ha ha... Ha...
thud
WHAT'S THIS FEELING...?
THIS HUGE, CRUSHING WAVE OF GUILT...?

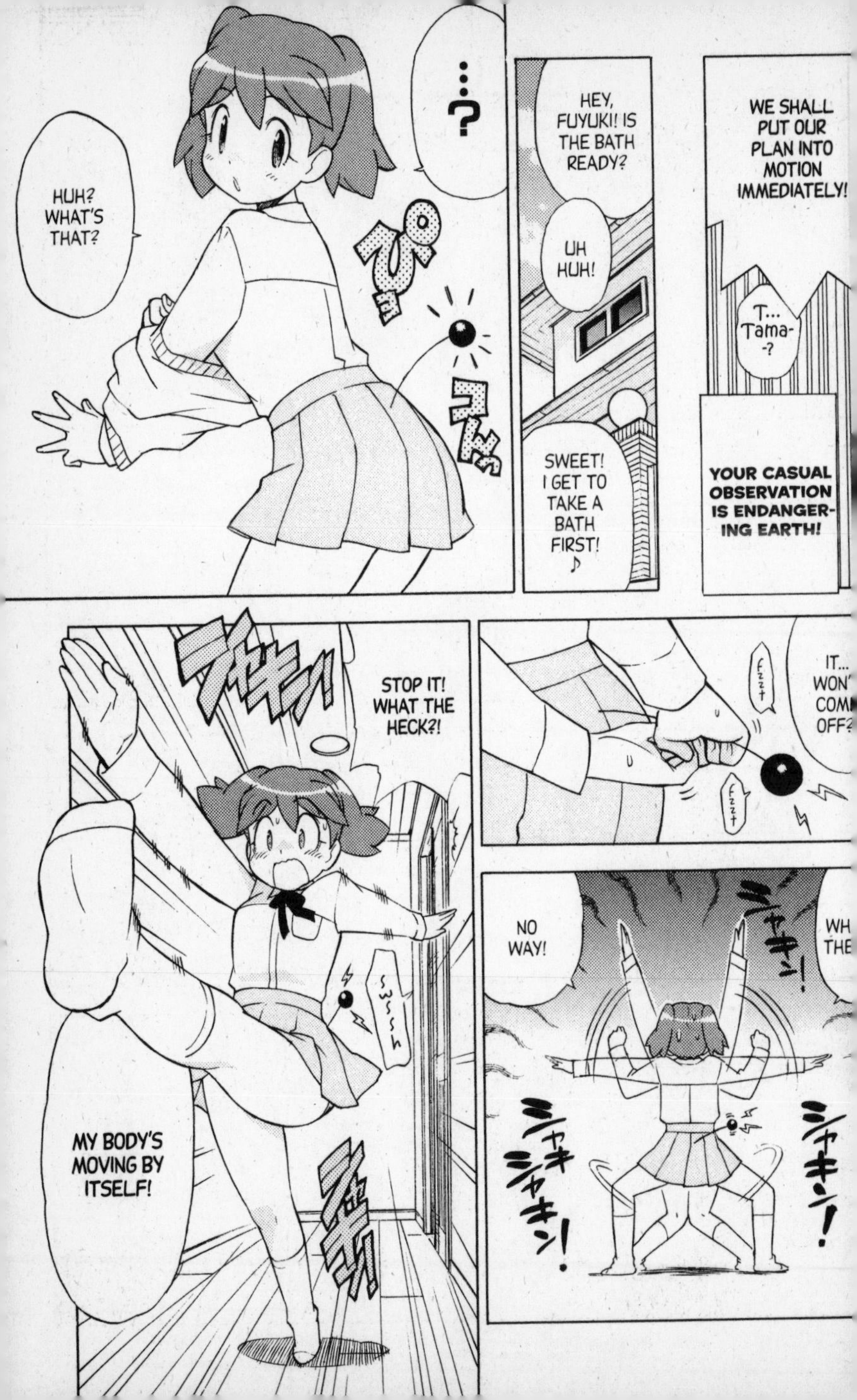
WE SHALL PUT OUR PLAN INTO MOTION IMMEDIATELY!
T... Tama-?
YOUR CASUAL OBSERVATION IS ENDANGERING EARTH!
HEY, FUYUKI! IS THE BATH READY?
UH HUH!
SWEET! I GET TO TAKE A BATH FIRST! ♪
...?
ぴょ
こん
HUH? WHAT'S THAT?
IT... WON' COM OFF?
fzzt
fzzt
WH THE
NO WAY!
シャキン!
シャキ シャキン!
シャキン!
ジャキン!!
STOP IT! WHAT THE HECK?!
swssh
MY BODY'S MOVING BY ITSELF!

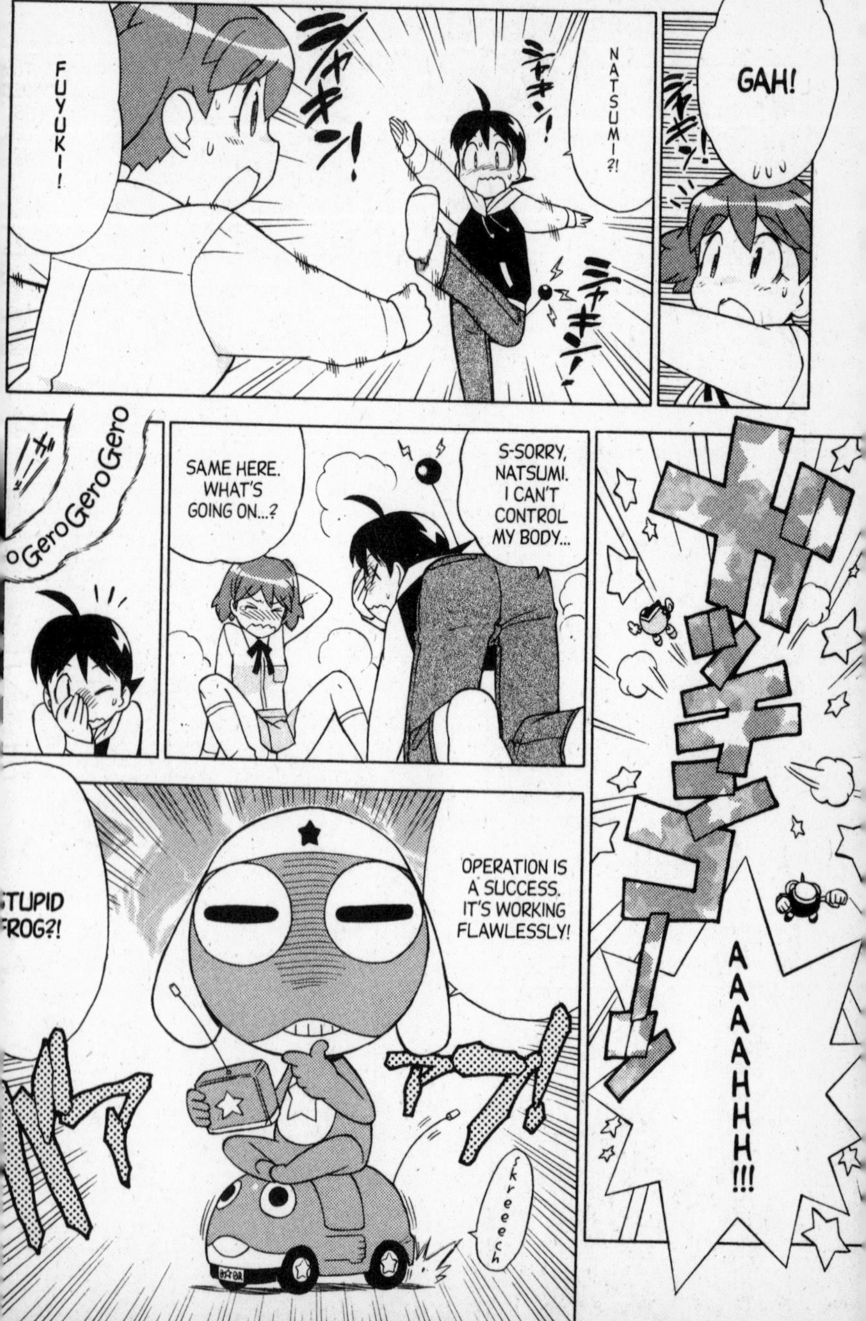

GAH!
NATSUMI?!
シャキン!
シャキン!
FUYUKI!
シャキン!
AAAAAHHHH!!!
S-SORRY, NATSUMI. I CAN'T CONTROL MY BODY...
SAME HERE. WHAT'S GOING ON...?
GeroGeroGero
OPERATION IS A SUCCESS. IT'S WORKING FLAWLESSLY!
STUPID FROG?!
skreeeech

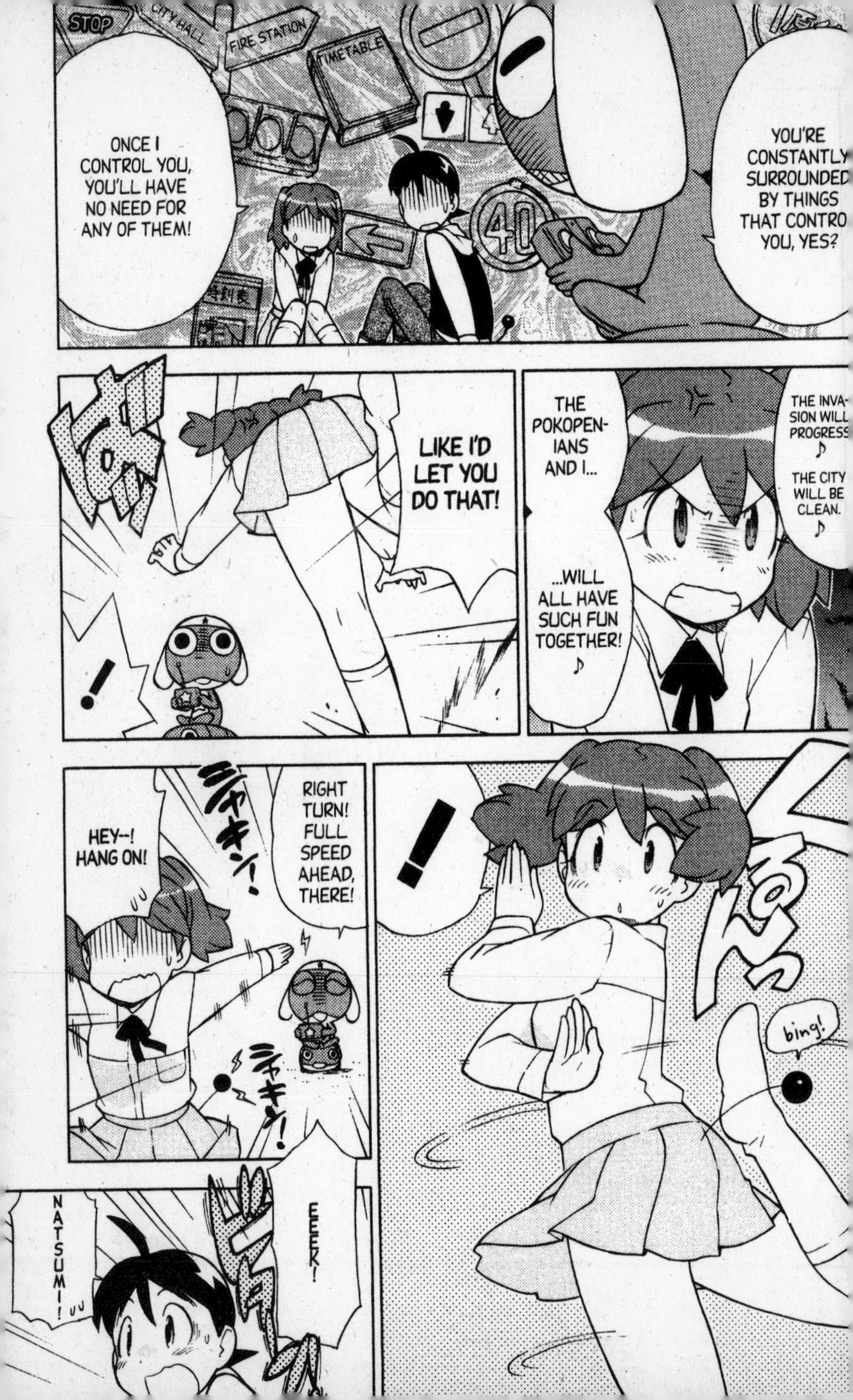
STOP
CITY HALL
FIRE STATION
TIMETABLE
40
YOU'RE CONSTANTLY SURROUNDED BY THINGS THAT CONTRO YOU, YES?
ONCE I CONTROL YOU, YOU'LL HAVE NO NEED FOR ANY OF THEM!
THE INVA-SION WILL PROGRESS ♪
THE CITY WILL BE CLEAN. ♪
THE POKOPEN-IANS AND I...
...WILL ALL HAVE SUCH FUN TOGETHER! ♪
LIKE I'D LET YOU DO THAT!
bing!
RIGHT TURN! FULL SPEED AHEAD, THERE!
HEY--! HANG ON!
EEEK!
NATSUMI!

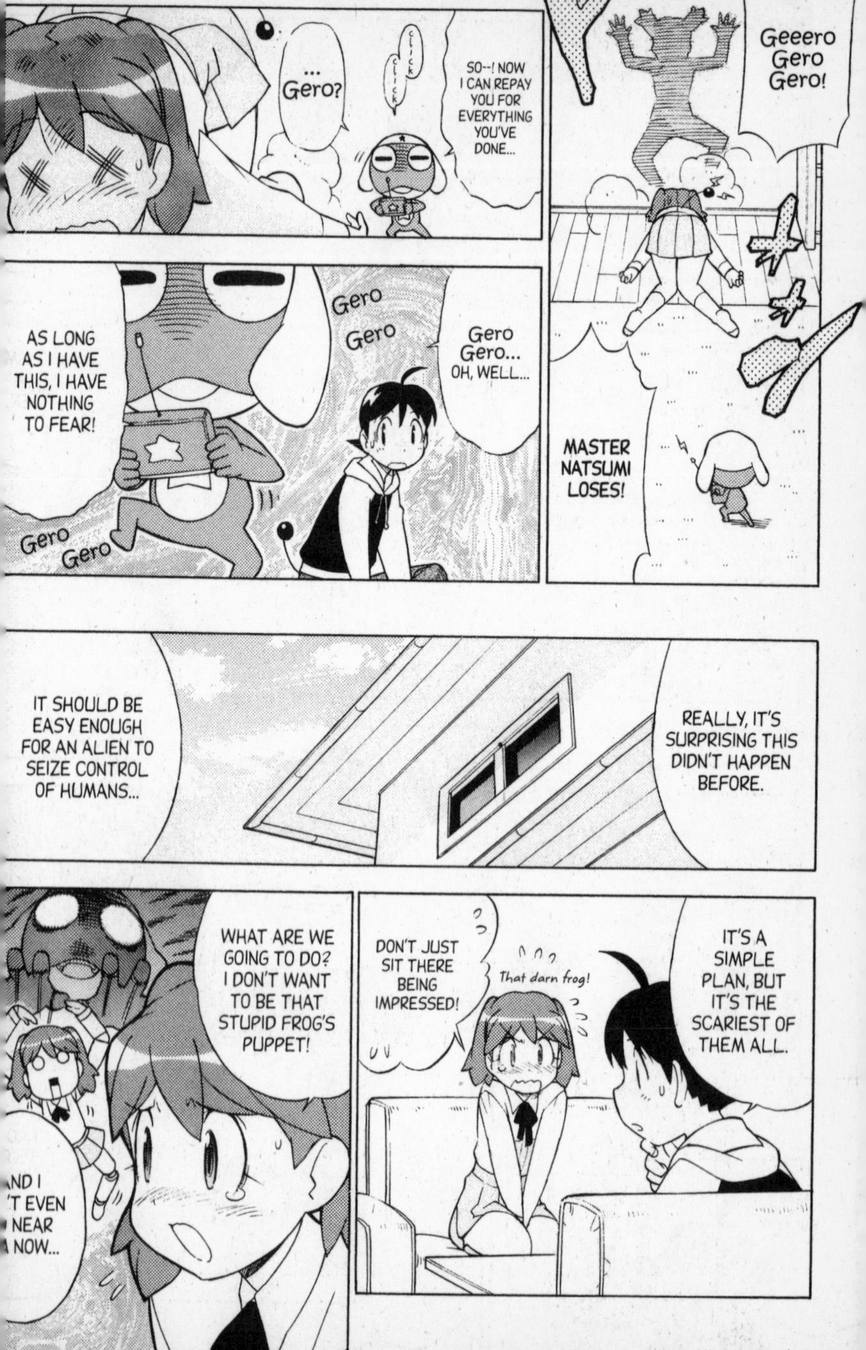
Geeero Gero Gero!
...
MASTER NATSUMI LOSES!
SO--! NOW I CAN REPAY YOU FOR EVERYTHING YOU'VE DONE...
click click
... Gero?
Gero Gero... OH, WELL...
Gero Gero
AS LONG AS I HAVE THIS, I HAVE NOTHING TO FEAR!
Gero Gero
REALLY, IT'S SURPRISING THIS DIDN'T HAPPEN BEFORE.
IT SHOULD BE EASY ENOUGH FOR AN ALIEN TO SEIZE CONTROL OF HUMANS...
IT'S A SIMPLE PLAN, BUT IT'S THE SCARIEST OF THEM ALL.
That darn frog!
DON'T JUST SIT THERE BEING IMPRESSED!
WHAT ARE WE GOING TO DO? I DON'T WANT TO BE THAT STUPID FROG'S PUPPET!
ND I 'T EVEN NEAR NOW...

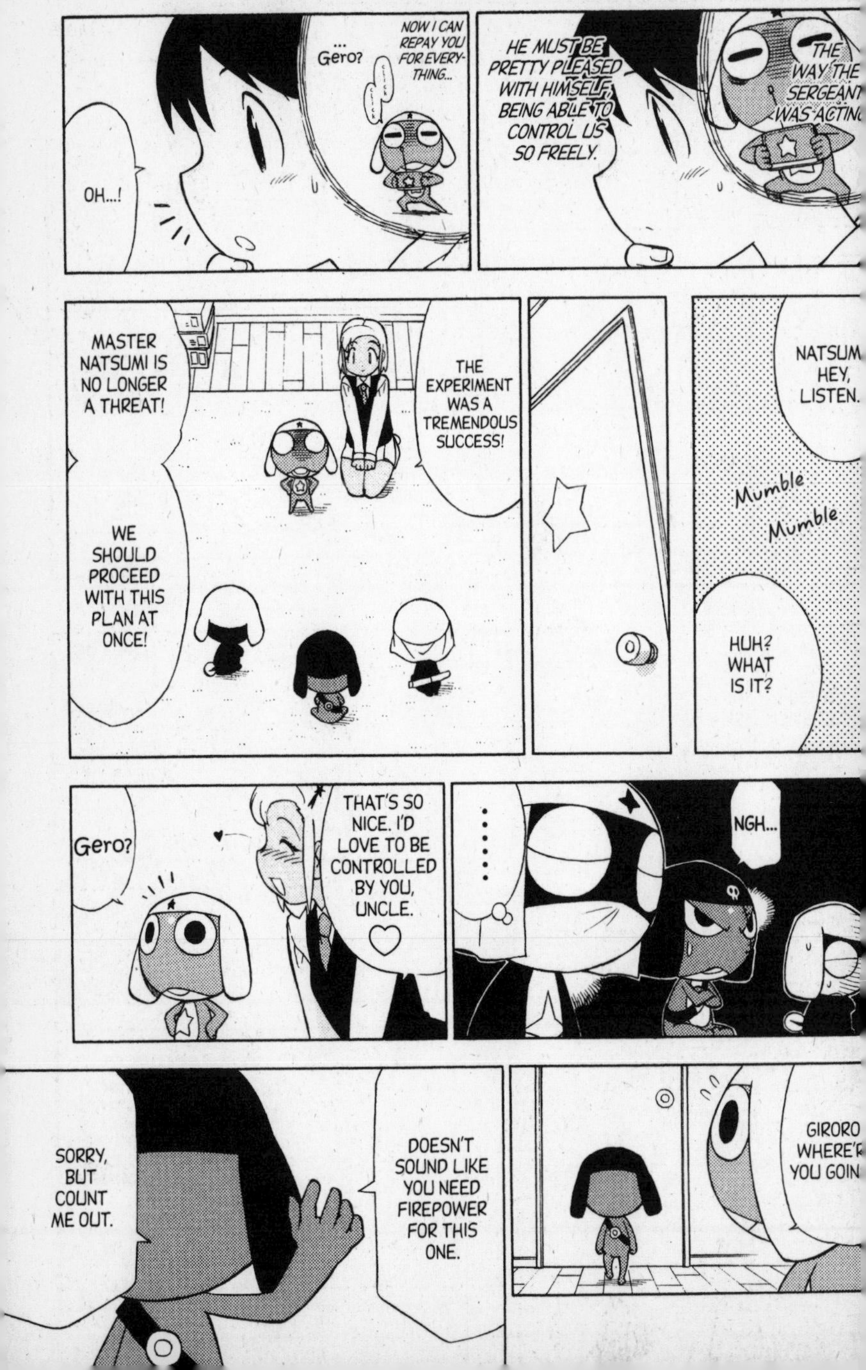
THE WAY THE SERGEAN WAS ACTIN
HE MUST BE PRETTY PLEASED WITH HIMSELF, BEING ABLE TO CONTROL US SO FREELY.
NOW I CAN REPAY YOU FOR EVERY-THING...
... Gero?
CLICK CLICK
OH...!
NATSUM HEY, LISTEN.
Mumble Mumble
HUH? WHAT IS IT?
THE EXPERIMENT WAS A TREMENDOUS SUCCESS!
MASTER NATSUMI IS NO LONGER A THREAT!
WE SHOULD PROCEED WITH THIS PLAN AT ONCE!
NGH...
......
THAT'S SO NICE. I'D LOVE TO BE CONTROLLED BY YOU, UNCLE.
Gero?
GIRORO WHERE'R YOU GOIN
DOESN'T SOUND LIKE YOU NEED FIREPOWER FOR THIS ONE.
SORRY, BUT COUNT ME OUT.

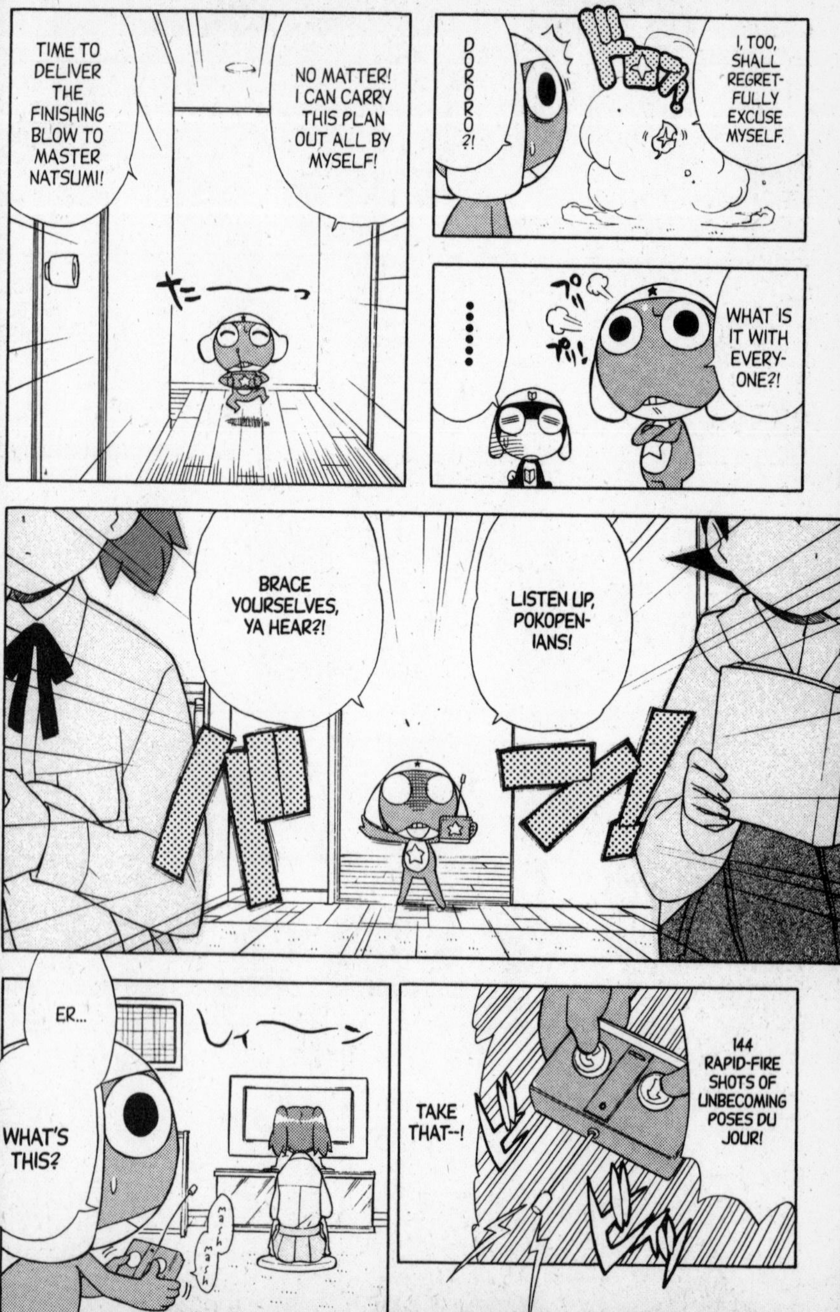
I, TOO, SHALL REGRETFULLY EXCUSE MYSELF.
DORORO?!
WHAT IS IT WITH EVERYONE?!
......
NO MATTER! I CAN CARRY THIS PLAN OUT ALL BY MYSELF!
TIME TO DELIVER THE FINISHING BLOW TO MASTER NATSUMI!
LISTEN UP, POKOPENIANS!
BRACE YOURSELVES, YA HEAR?!
144 RAPID-FIRE SHOTS OF UNBECOMING POSES DU JOUR!
TAKE THAT--!
ER...
WHAT'S THIS?
Mash Mash

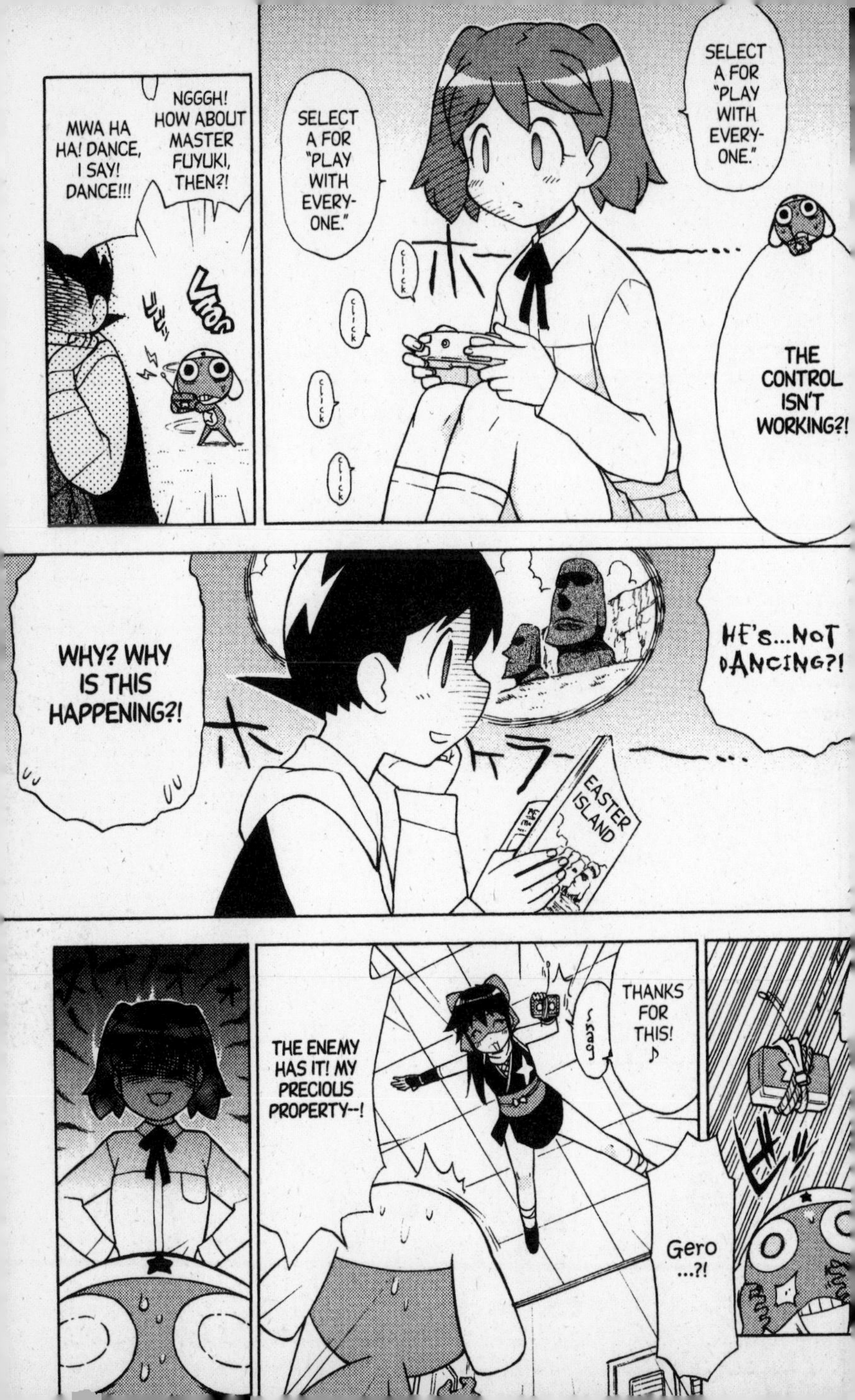
SELECT A FOR "PLAY WITH EVERY-ONE."
THE CONTROL ISN'T WORKING?!
SELECT A FOR "PLAY WITH EVERY-ONE."
click
click
click
click
NGGGH! HOW ABOUT MASTER FUYUKI, THEN?!
MWA HA HA! DANCE, I SAY! DANCE!!!
HE'S...NOT DANCING?!
EASTER ISLAND
WHY? WHY IS THIS HAPPENING?!
THANKS FOR THIS! ♪
Gero ...?!
THE ENEMY HAS IT! MY PRECIOUS PROPERTY--!

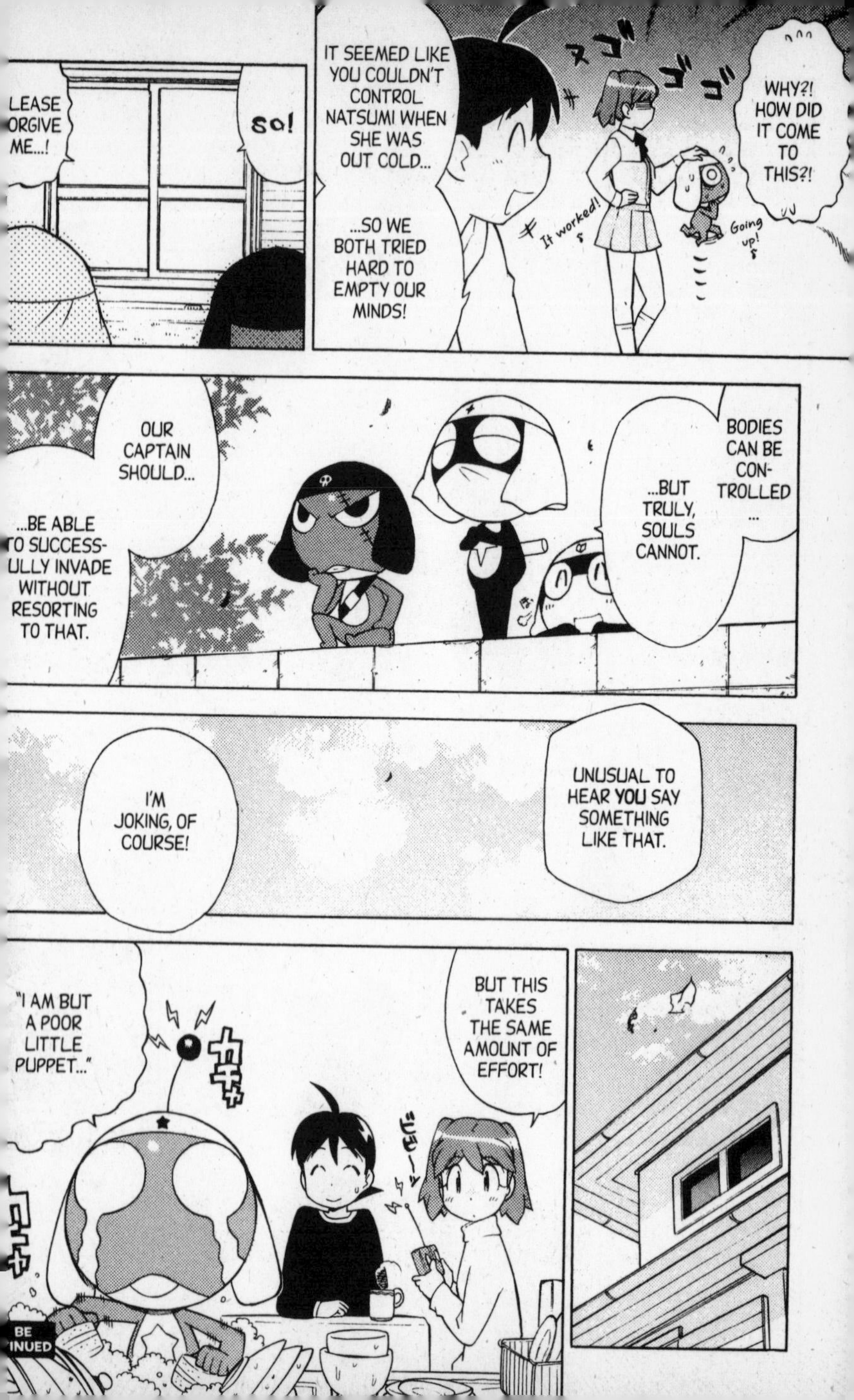
WHY?! HOW DID IT COME TO THIS?!
Going up!
It worked!
IT SEEMED LIKE YOU COULDN'T CONTROL NATSUMI WHEN SHE WAS OUT COLD...
...SO WE BOTH TRIED HARD TO EMPTY OUR MINDS!
SO!
LEASE ORGIVE ME...!
BODIES CAN BE CON-TROLLED ...
...BUT TRULY, SOULS CANNOT.
OUR CAPTAIN SHOULD...
...BE ABLE TO SUCCESS-ULLY INVADE WITHOUT RESORTING TO THAT.
UNUSUAL TO HEAR YOU SAY SOMETHING LIKE THAT.
I'M JOKING, OF COURSE!
BUT THIS TAKES THE SAME AMOUNT OF EFFORT!
"I AM BUT A POOR LITTLE PUPPET..."
BE INUED

ENCOUNTER CLX
KERON-MAN: THE ORIGIN STORY

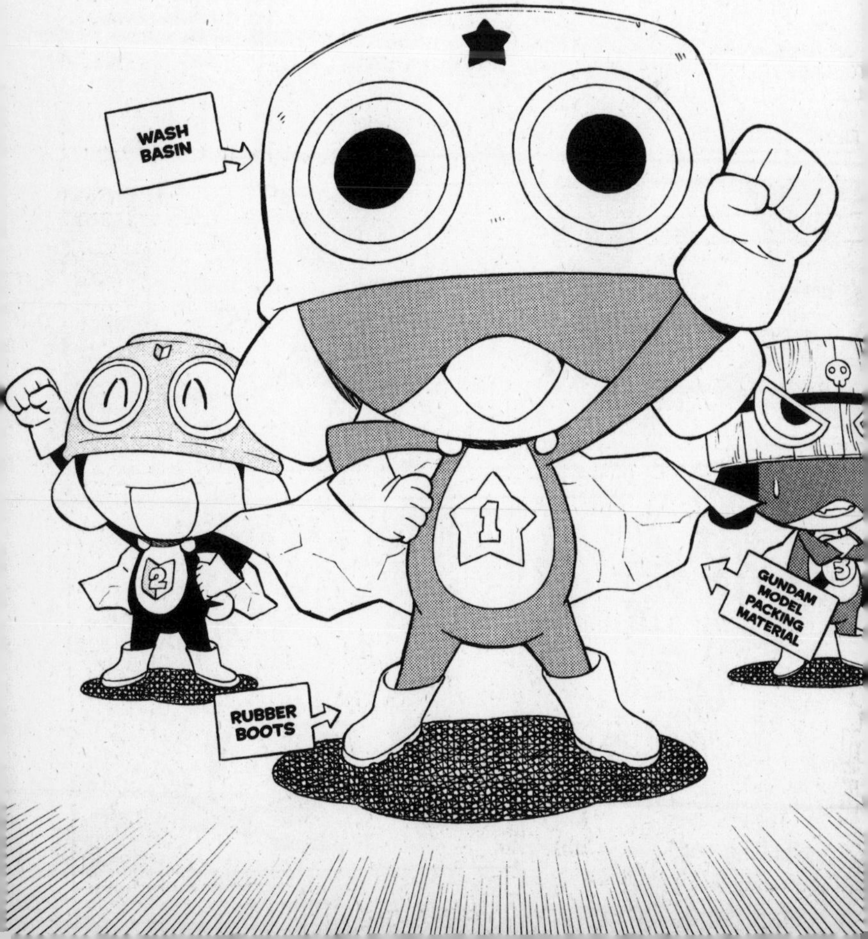
WASH BASIN
GUNDAM MODEL PACKING MATERIAL
RUBBER BOOTS

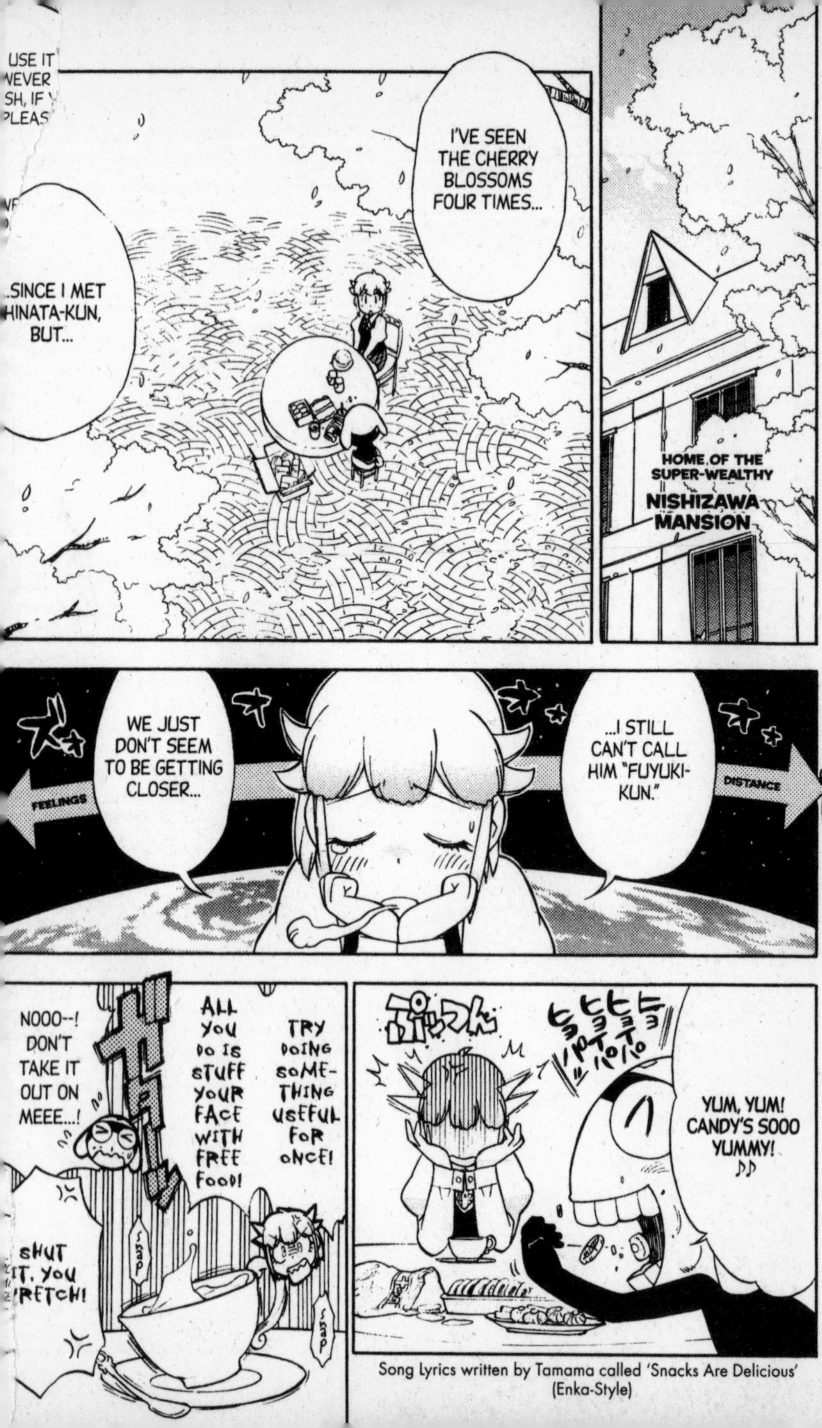
HOME OF THE SUPER-WEALTHY
NISHIZAWA MANSION
I'VE SEEN THE CHERRY BLOSSOMS FOUR TIMES...
...SINCE I MET HINATA-KUN, BUT...
...I STILL CAN'T CALL HIM "FUYUKI-KUN."
DISTANCE
WE JUST DON'T SEEM TO BE GETTING CLOSER...
FEELINGS
ぷっつん
YUM, YUM! CANDY'S SOOO YUMMY! ♪♪
TRY DOING SOME-THING USEFUL FOR ONCE!
ALL YOU DO IS STUFF YOUR FACE WITH FREE FOOD!
NOOO--! DON'T TAKE IT OUT ON MEEE...!
SHUT IT, YOU WRETCH!

Song Lyrics written by Tamama called 'Snacks Are Delicious' (Enka-Style)

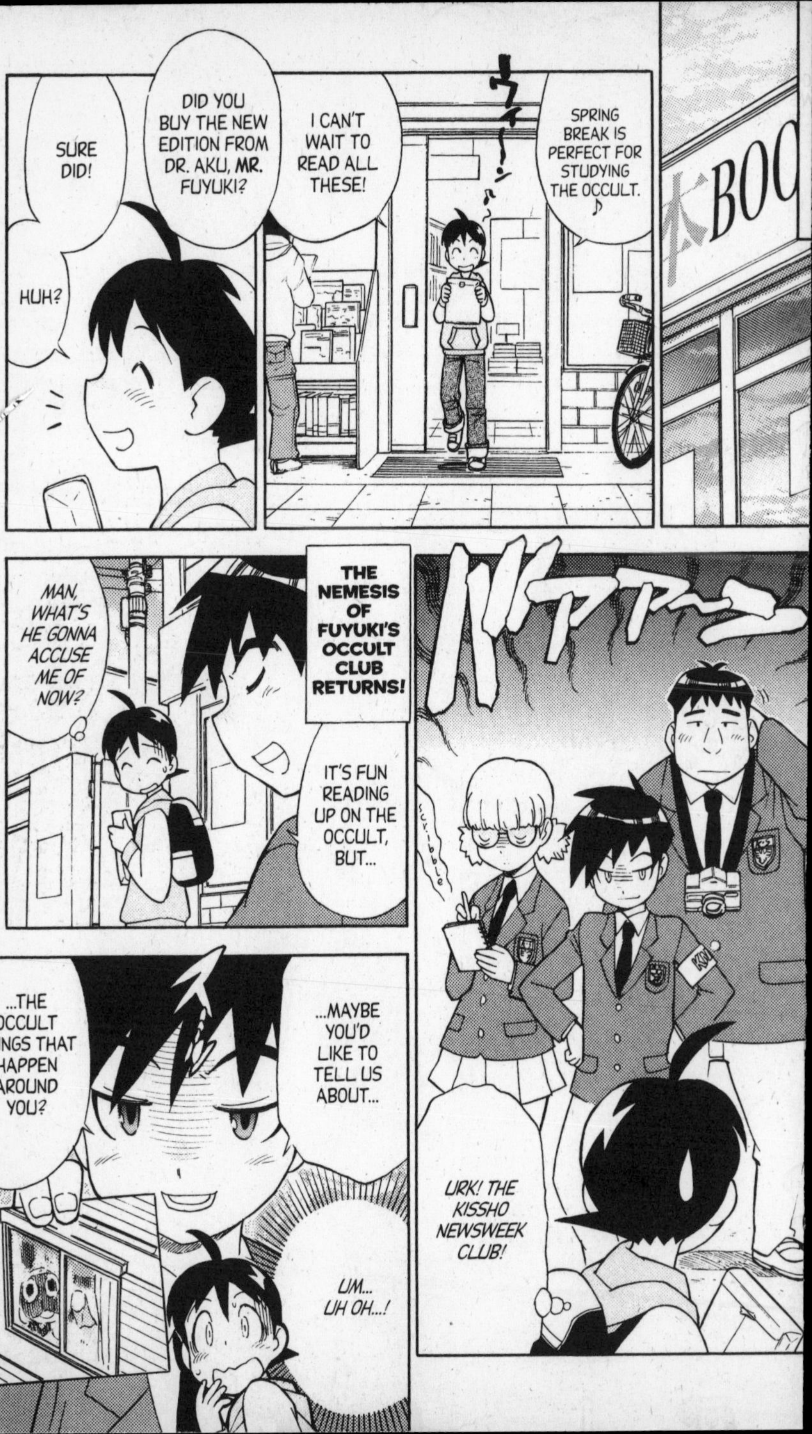
SPRING BREAK IS PERFECT FOR STUDYING THE OCCULT. ♪
I CAN'T WAIT TO READ ALL THESE!
DID YOU BUY THE NEW EDITION FROM DR. AKU, MR. FUYUKI?
SURE DID!
HUH?
THE NEMESIS OF FUYUKI'S OCCULT CLUB RETURNS!
scribble
URK! THE KISSHO NEWSWEEK CLUB!
IT'S FUN READING UP ON THE OCCULT, BUT...
MAN, WHAT'S HE GONNA ACCUSE ME OF NOW?
...MAYBE YOU'D LIKE TO TELL US ABOUT...
...THE OCCULT THINGS THAT HAPPEN AROUND YOU?
UM... UH OH...!

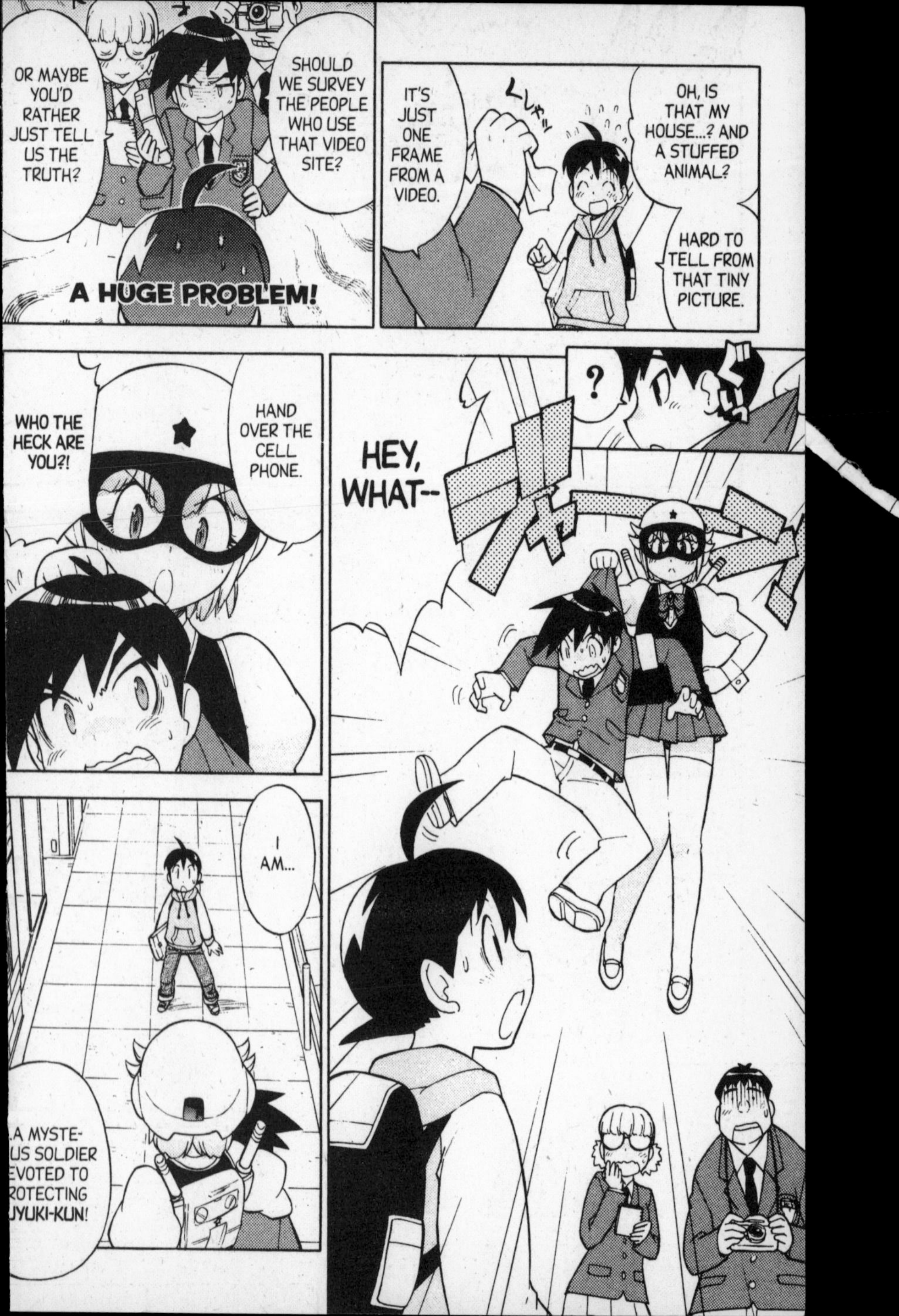
OH, IS THAT MY HOUSE...? AND A STUFFED ANIMAL?
IT'S JUST ONE FRAME FROM A VIDEO.
HARD TO TELL FROM THAT TINY PICTURE.
SHOULD WE SURVEY THE PEOPLE WHO USE THAT VIDEO SITE?
OR MAYBE YOU'D RATHER JUST TELL US THE TRUTH?
A HUGE PROBLEM!
?
HEY, WHAT--
HAND OVER THE CELL PHONE.
WHO THE HECK ARE YOU?!
I AM...
.A MYSTE- US SOLDIER EVOTED TO ROTECTING UYUKI-KUN!

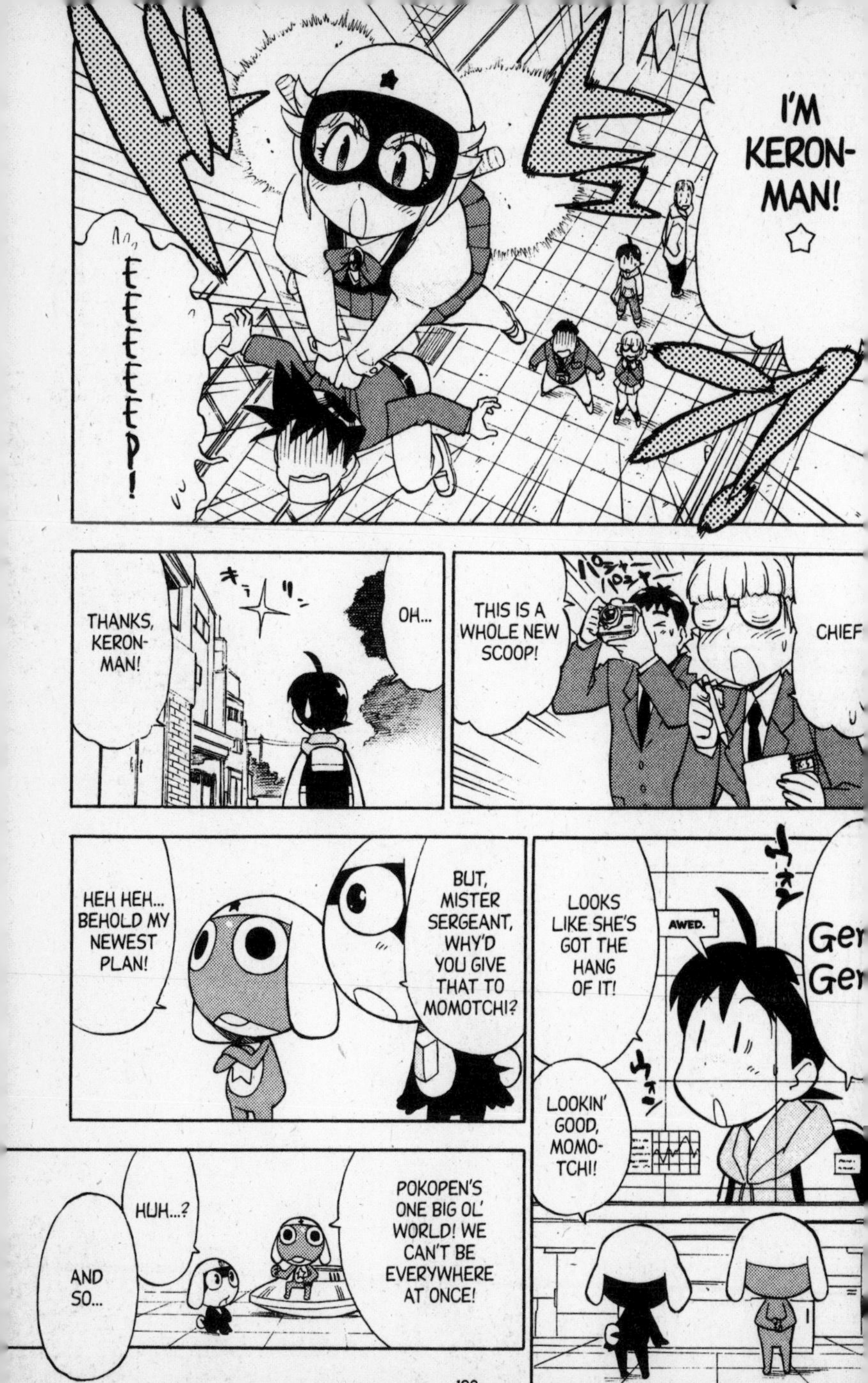
I'M KERON-MAN! ☆
EEEEEEEP!
CHIEF
THIS IS A WHOLE NEW SCOOP!
OH...
THANKS, KERON-MAN!
AWED.
LOOKS LIKE SHE'S GOT THE HANG OF IT!
LOOKIN' GOOD, MOMO-TCHI!
BUT, MISTER SERGEANT, WHY'D YOU GIVE THAT TO MOMOTCHI?
HEH HEH... BEHOLD MY NEWEST PLAN!
POKOPEN'S ONE BIG OL' WORLD! WE CAN'T BE EVERYWHERE AT ONCE!
HUH...?
AND SO...

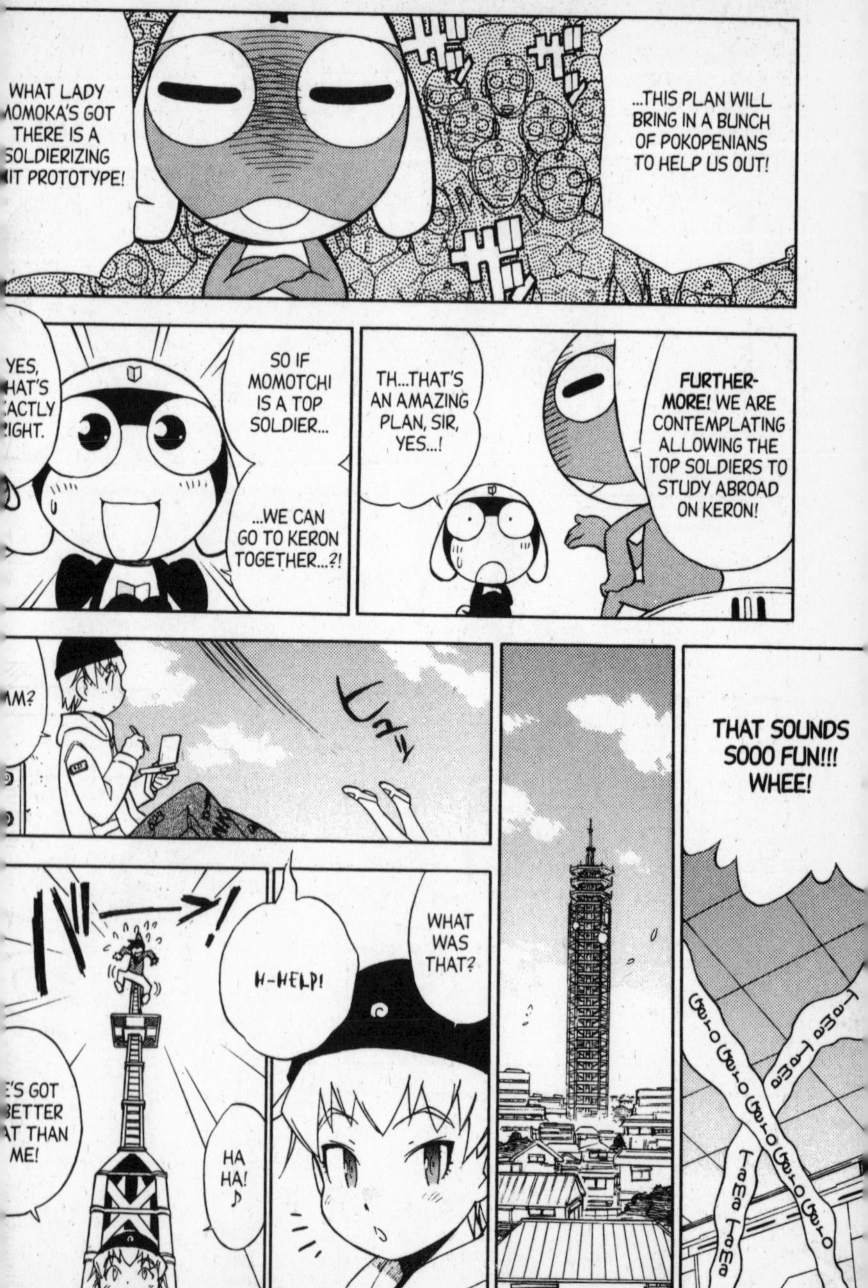
...THIS PLAN WILL BRING IN A BUNCH OF POKOPENIANS TO HELP US OUT!
WHAT LADY OMOKA'S GOT THERE IS A OLDIERIZING IT PROTOTYPE!
FURTHERMORE! WE ARE CONTEMPLATING ALLOWING THE TOP SOLDIERS TO STUDY ABROAD ON KERON!
TH...THAT'S AN AMAZING PLAN, SIR, YES...!
SO IF MOMOTCHI IS A TOP SOLDIER...
...WE CAN GO TO KERON TOGETHER...?!
YES, HAT'S ACTLY IGHT.
THAT SOUNDS SOOO FUN!!! WHEE!
Gero Gero Gero Gero Gero Gero
Tama Tama Tama Tama
AM?
WHAT WAS THAT?
H-HELP!
HA HA! ♪
E'S GOT BETTER AT THAN ME!

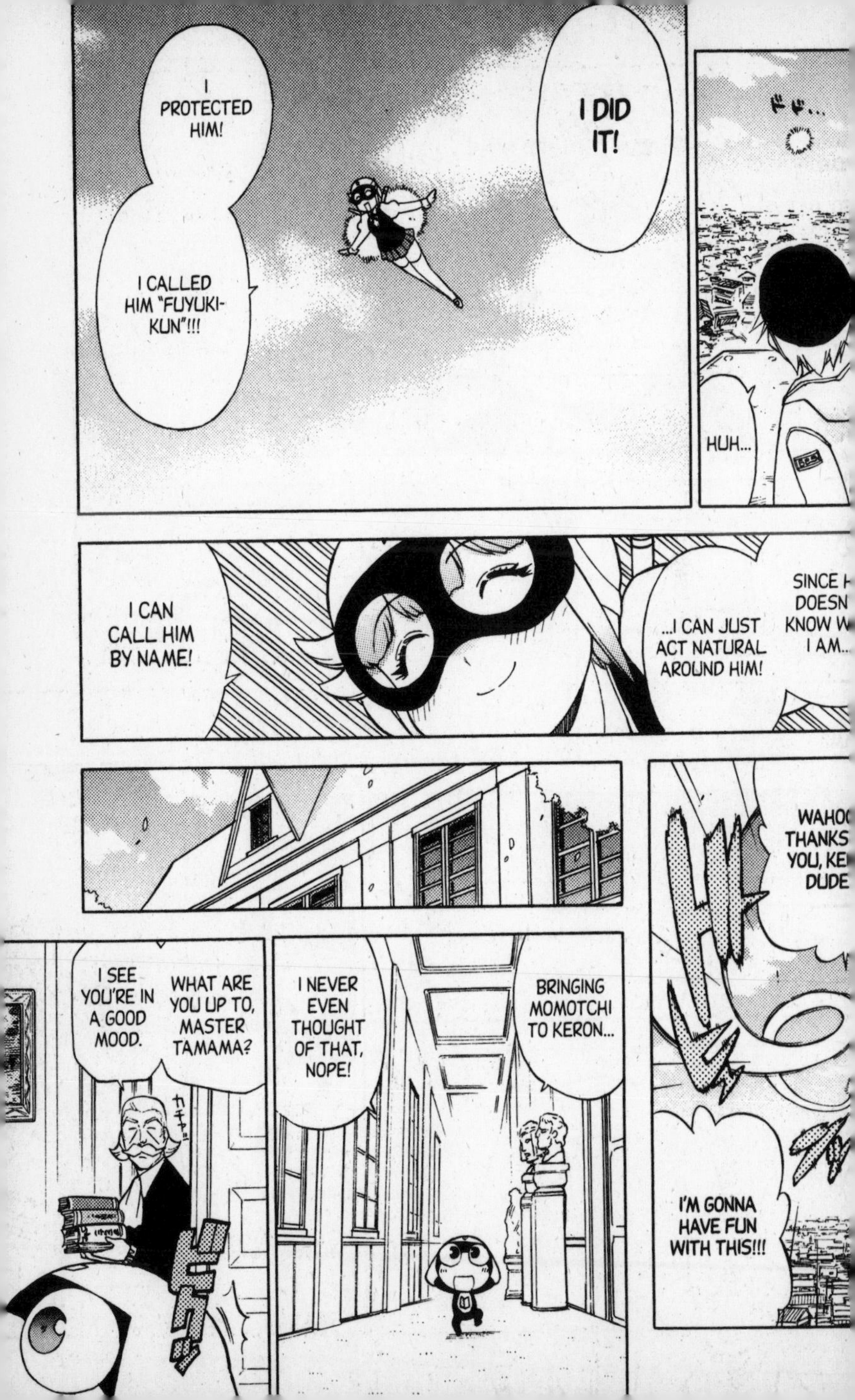
ドド…
HUH...
I DID IT!
I PROTECTED HIM!
I CALLED HIM "FUYUKI-KUN"!!!
SINCE H DOESN KNOW W I AM...
...I CAN JUST ACT NATURAL AROUND HIM!
I CAN CALL HIM BY NAME!
WAHO THANKS YOU, KE DUDE
I'M GONNA HAVE FUN WITH THIS!!!
BRINGING MOMOTCHI TO KERON...
I NEVER EVEN THOUGHT OF THAT, NOPE!
WHAT ARE YOU UP TO, MASTER TAMAMA?
I SEE YOU'RE IN A GOOD MOOD.
カチャ

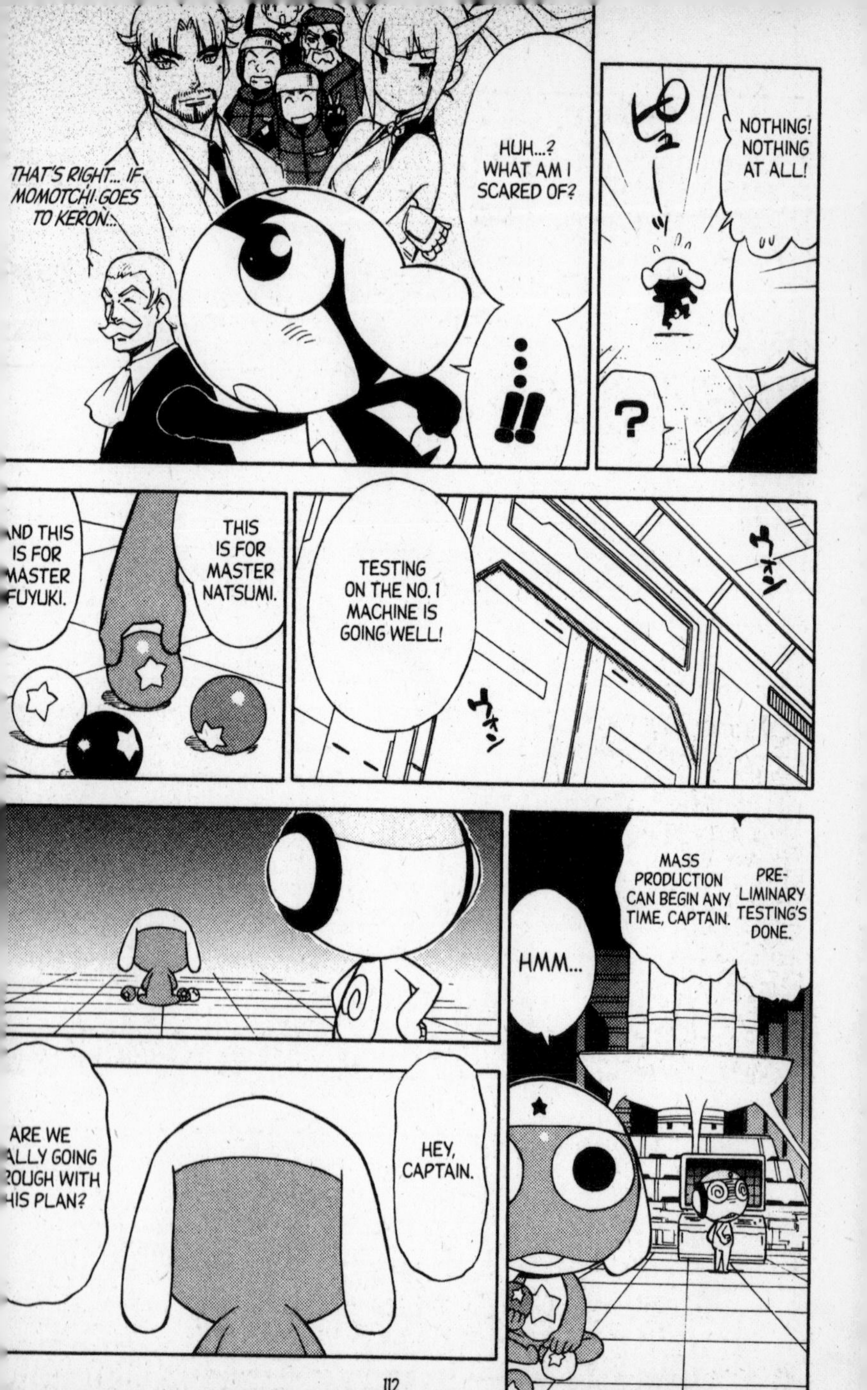
NOTHING! NOTHING AT ALL!
ピュ
ッ
?
HUH...? WHAT AM I SCARED OF?
...!!
THAT'S RIGHT... IF MOMOTCHI GOES TO KERON...
TESTING ON THE NO. 1 MACHINE IS GOING WELL!
ウォン
ウォン
THIS IS FOR MASTER NATSUMI.
ND THIS IS FOR MASTER FUYUKI.
PRE-LIMINARY TESTING'S DONE.
MASS PRODUCTION CAN BEGIN ANY TIME, CAPTAIN.
HMM...
HEY, CAPTAIN.
ARE WE ALLY GOING ROUGH WITH HIS PLAN?

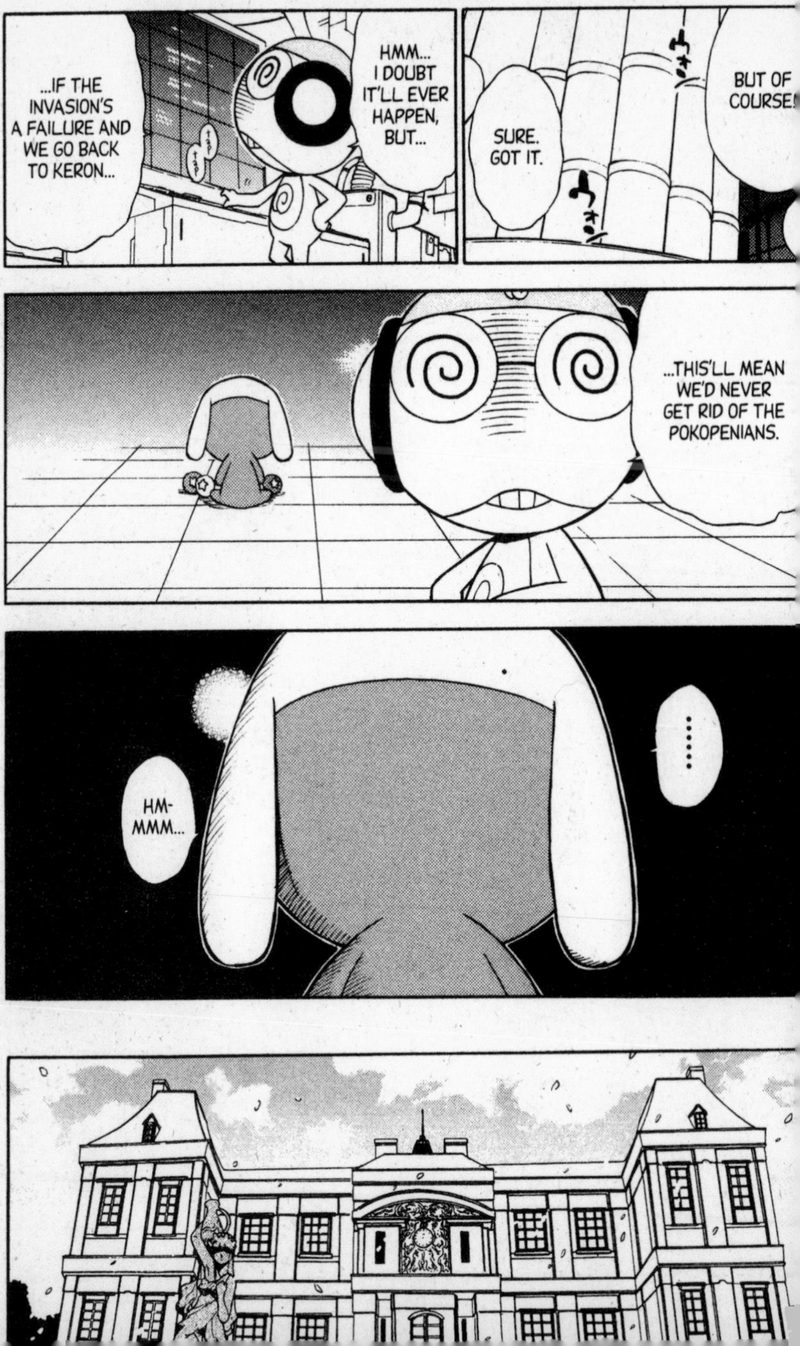
BUT OF COURSE!
SURE. GOT IT.
HMM... I DOUBT IT'LL EVER HAPPEN, BUT...
...IF THE INVASION'S A FAILURE AND WE GO BACK TO KERON...
...THIS'LL MEAN WE'D NEVER GET RID OF THE POKOPENIANS.
......
HM-MMM...

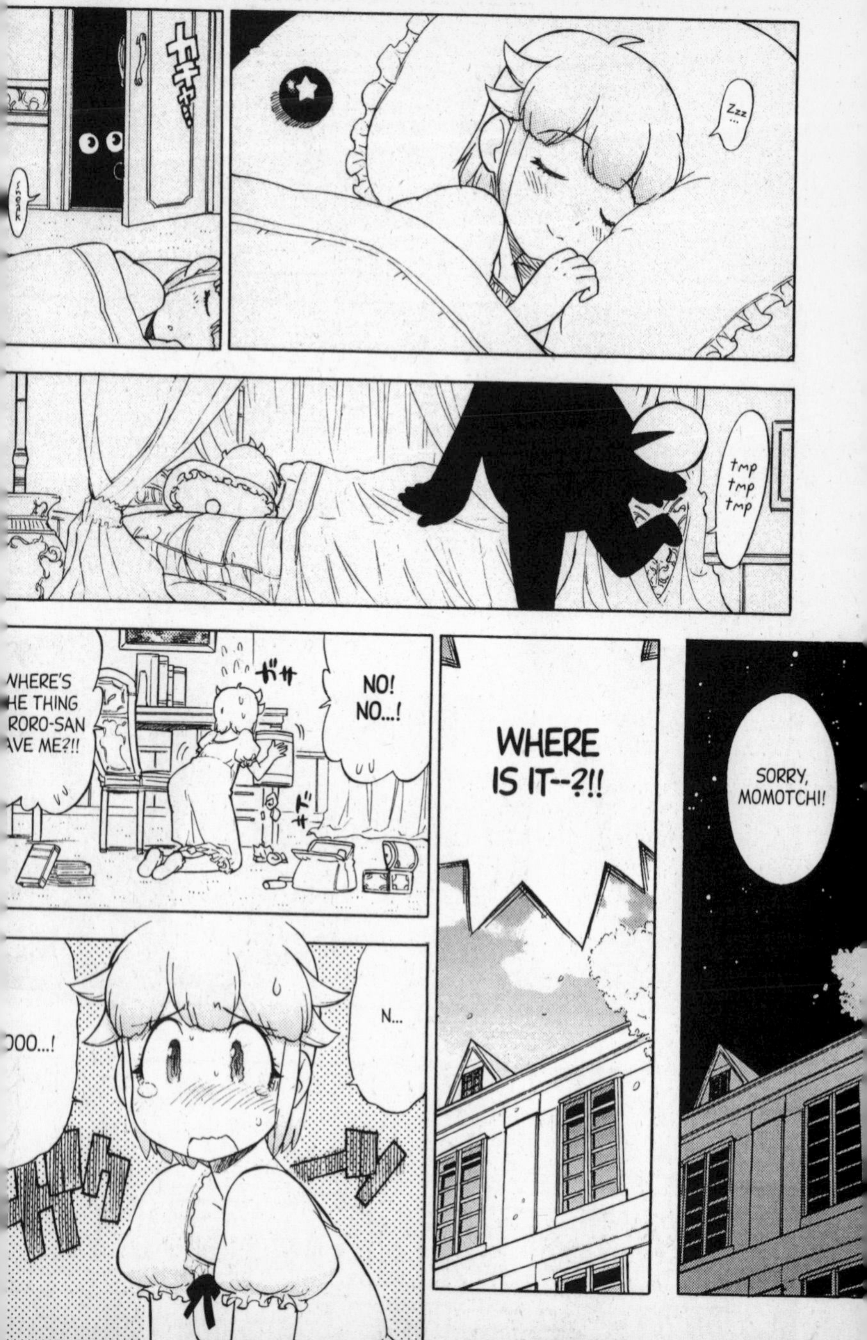
Zzz...
creak
tmp tmp tmp
SORRY, MOMOTCHI!
WHERE IS IT--?!!
NO! NO...!
WHERE'S
HE THING
RORO-SAN
AVE ME?!!
N...
OOO...!

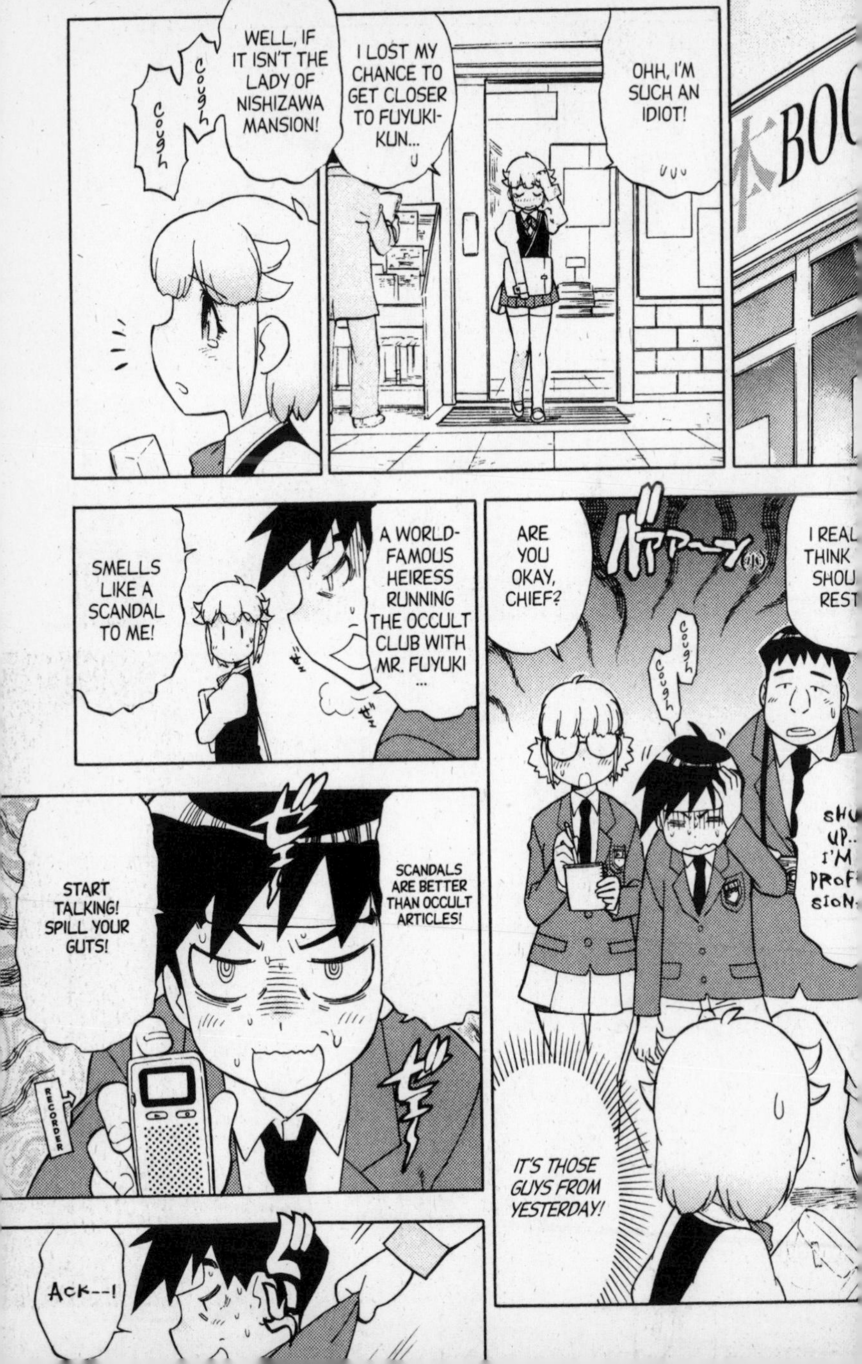

BOO
OHH, I'M SUCH AN IDIOT!
I LOST MY CHANCE TO GET CLOSER TO FUYUKI-KUN...
WELL, IF IT ISN'T THE LADY OF NISHIZAWA MANSION!
Cough Cough
I REAL THINK SHOU REST
ARE YOU OKAY, CHIEF?
Cough Cough
SHU UP.. I'M PROF SION..
IT'S THOSE GUYS FROM YESTERDAY!
A WORLD-FAMOUS HEIRESS RUNNING THE OCCULT CLUB WITH MR. FUYUKI ...
SMELLS LIKE A SCANDAL TO ME!
SCANDALS ARE BETTER THAN OCCULT ARTICLES!
START TALKING! SPILL YOUR GUTS!
RECORDER
ACK--!

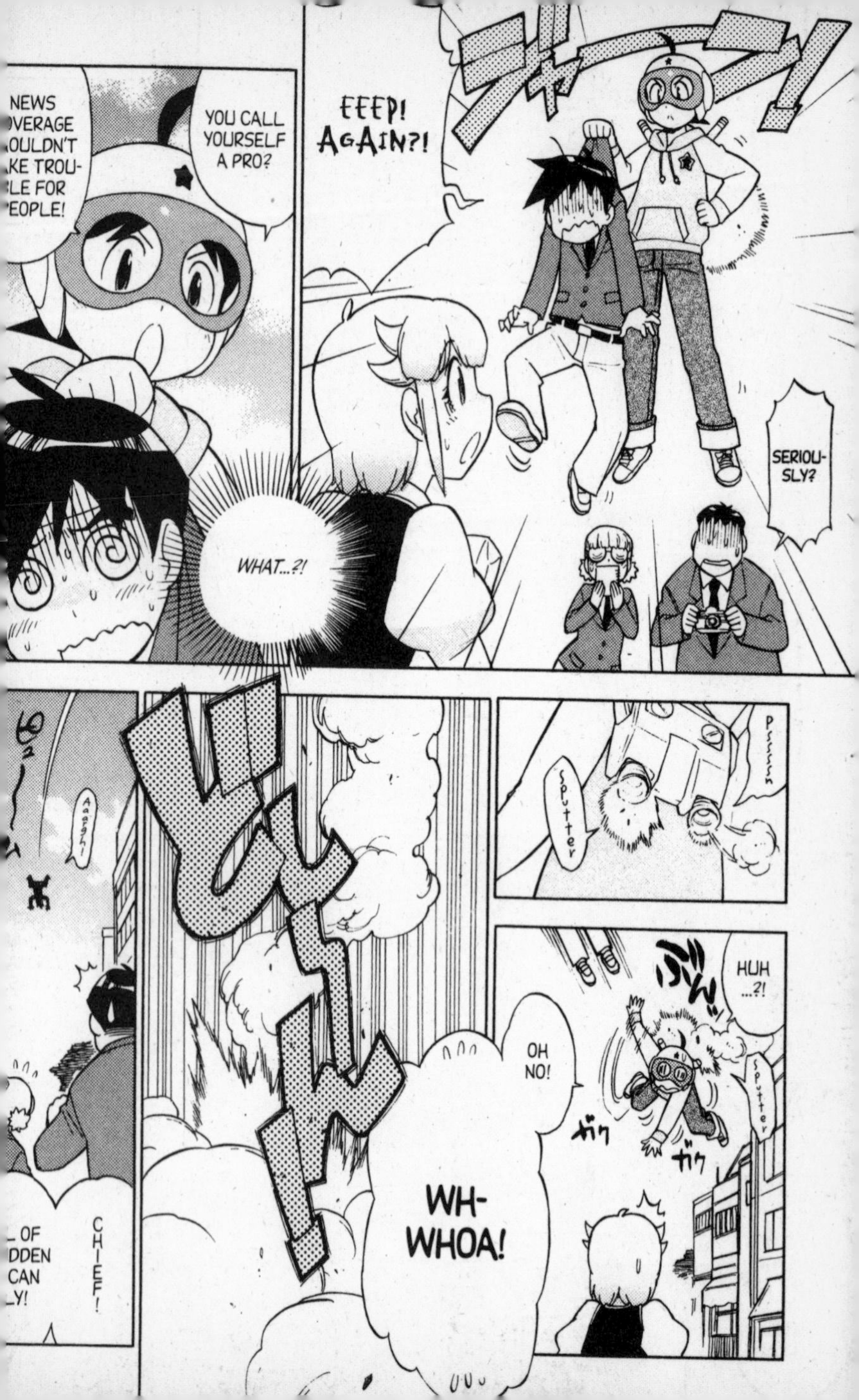
EEEP! AGAIN?!
SERIOU-SLY?
WHAT...?!
YOU CALL YOURSELF A PRO?
NEWS
OVERAGE
OULDN'T
KE TROU-
LE FOR
EOPLE!
Psssssn
Sputter
HUH ...?!
Sputter
OH NO!
WH-WHOA!
Aaagh!
CHIEF!
L OF
DDEN
CAN
LY!

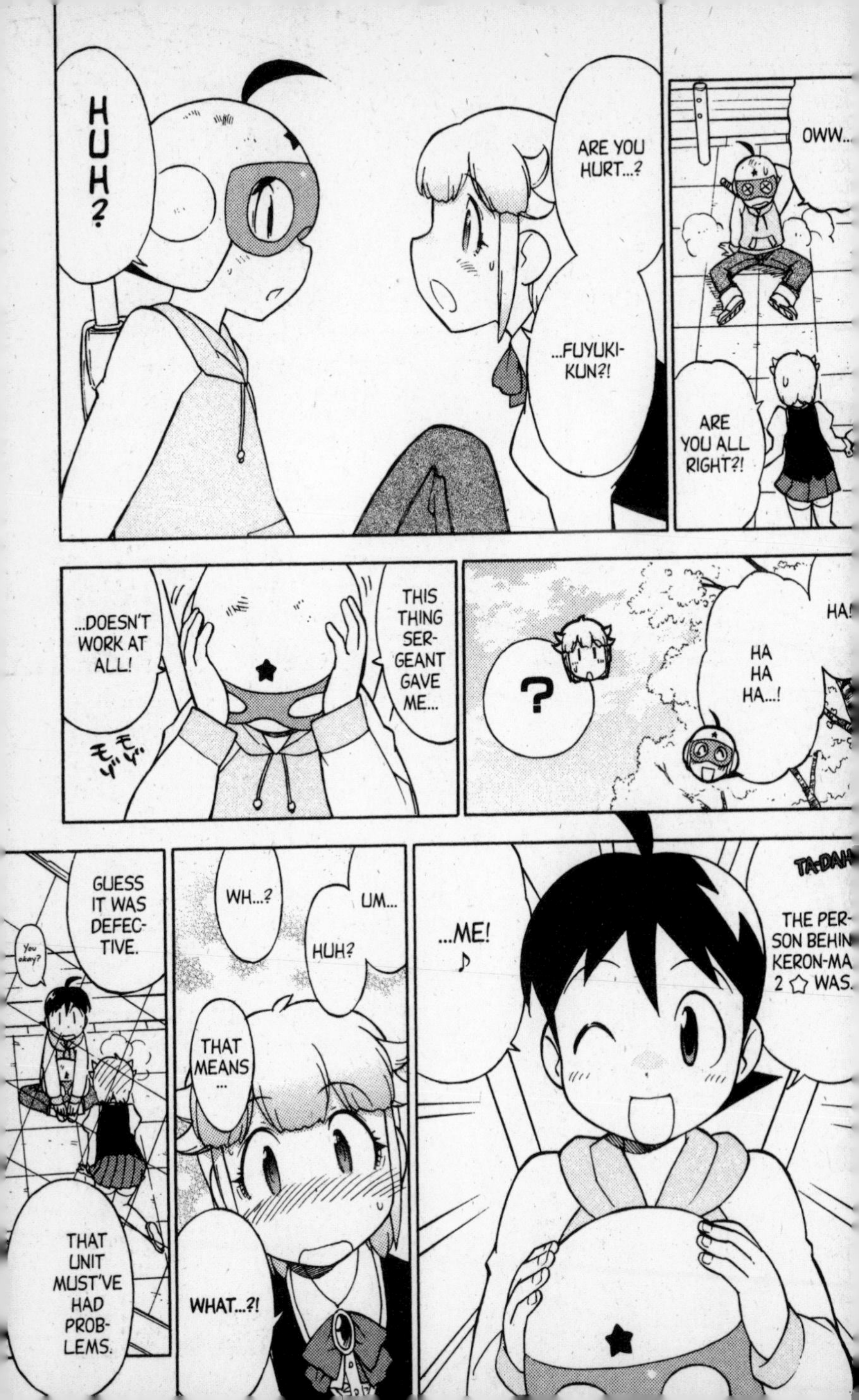
OWW...
ARE YOU ALL RIGHT?!
ARE YOU HURT...?
...FUYUKI-KUN?!
HUH?
HA!
HA HA HA...!
?
THIS THING SERGEANT GAVE ME...
...DOESN'T WORK AT ALL!
モゾ モゾ
TA-DAH
THE PERSON BEHIN KERON-MA 2 ☆ WAS.
...ME! ♪
UM...
WH...?
HUH?
THAT MEANS...
WHAT...?!
GUESS IT WAS DEFECTIVE.
You okay?
THAT UNIT MUST'VE HAD PROBLEMS.

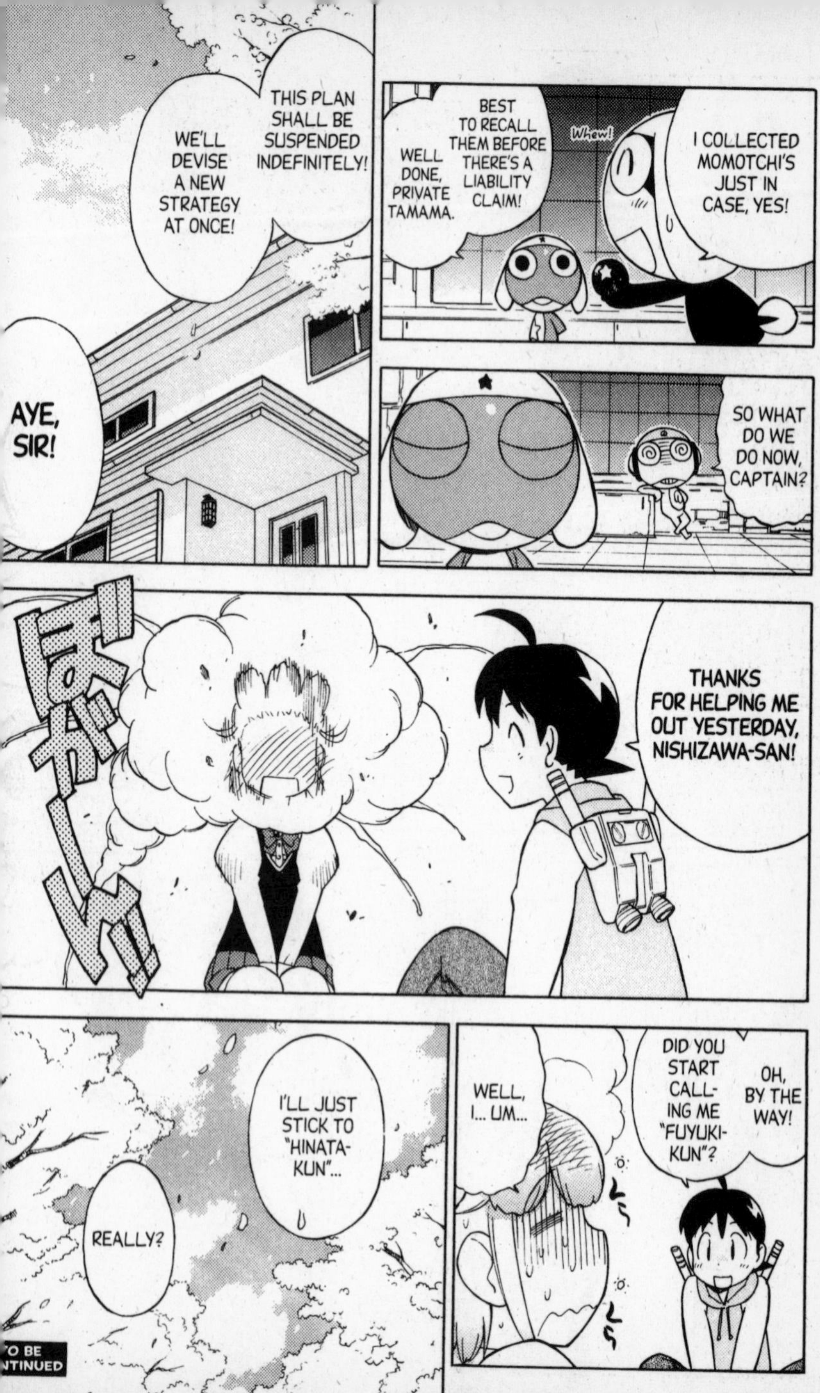
I COLLECTED MOMOTCHI'S JUST IN CASE, YES!
Whew!
BEST TO RECALL THEM BEFORE THERE'S A LIABILITY CLAIM!
WELL DONE, PRIVATE TAMAMA.
SO WHAT DO WE DO NOW, CAPTAIN?
THIS PLAN SHALL BE SUSPENDED INDEFINITELY!
WE'LL DEVISE A NEW STRATEGY AT ONCE!
AYE, SIR!
THANKS FOR HELPING ME OUT YESTERDAY, NISHIZAWA-SAN!
OH, BY THE WAY!
DID YOU START CALL-ING ME "FUYUKI-KUN"?
WELL, I... UM...
I'LL JUST STICK TO "HINATA-KUN"...
REALLY?
O BE NTINUED

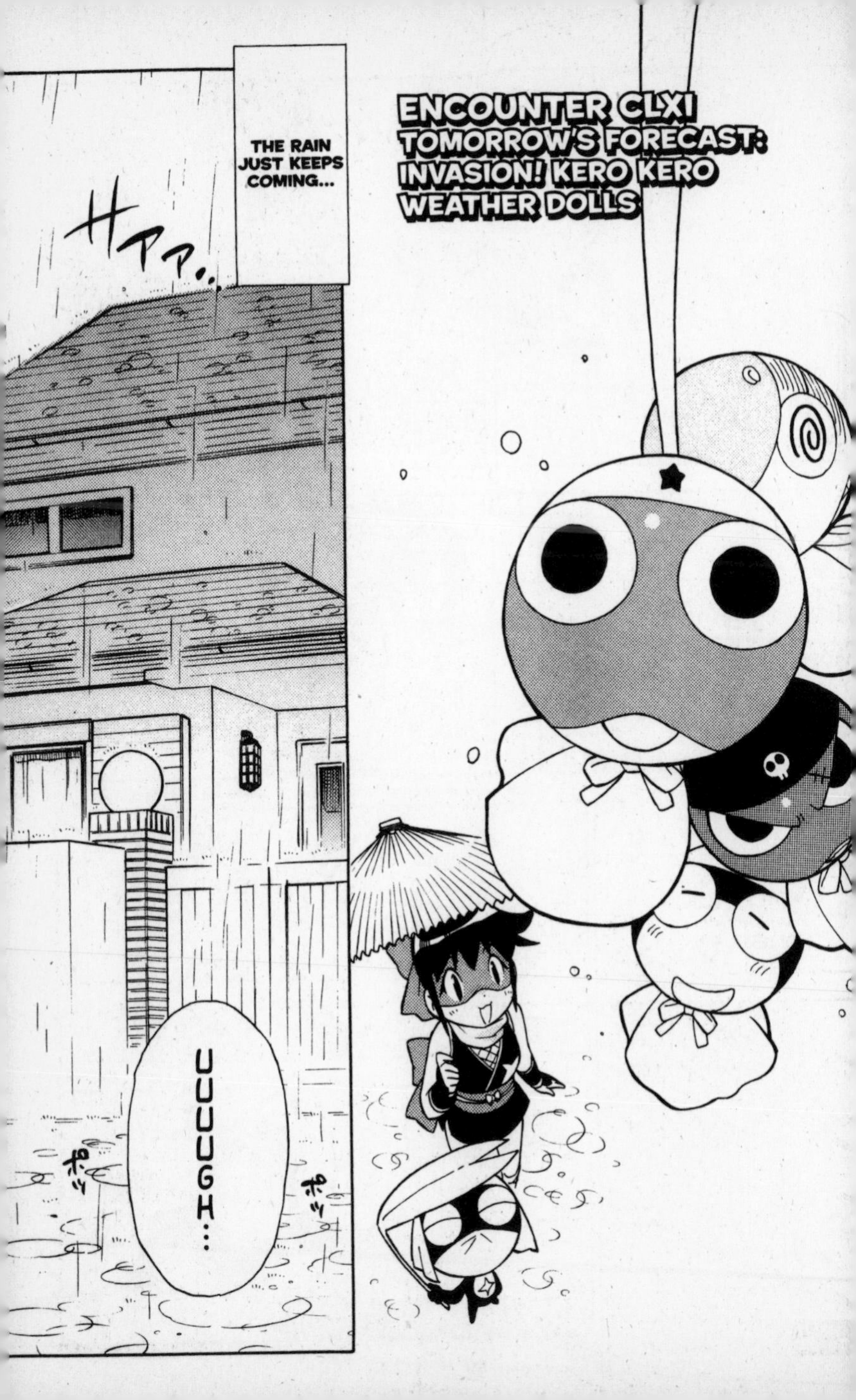
ENCOUNTER CLXI
TOMORROW'S FORECAST: INVASION! KERO KERO WEATHER DOLLS
THE RAIN JUST KEEPS COMING...
UUUUGH...
ポツ
ポツ

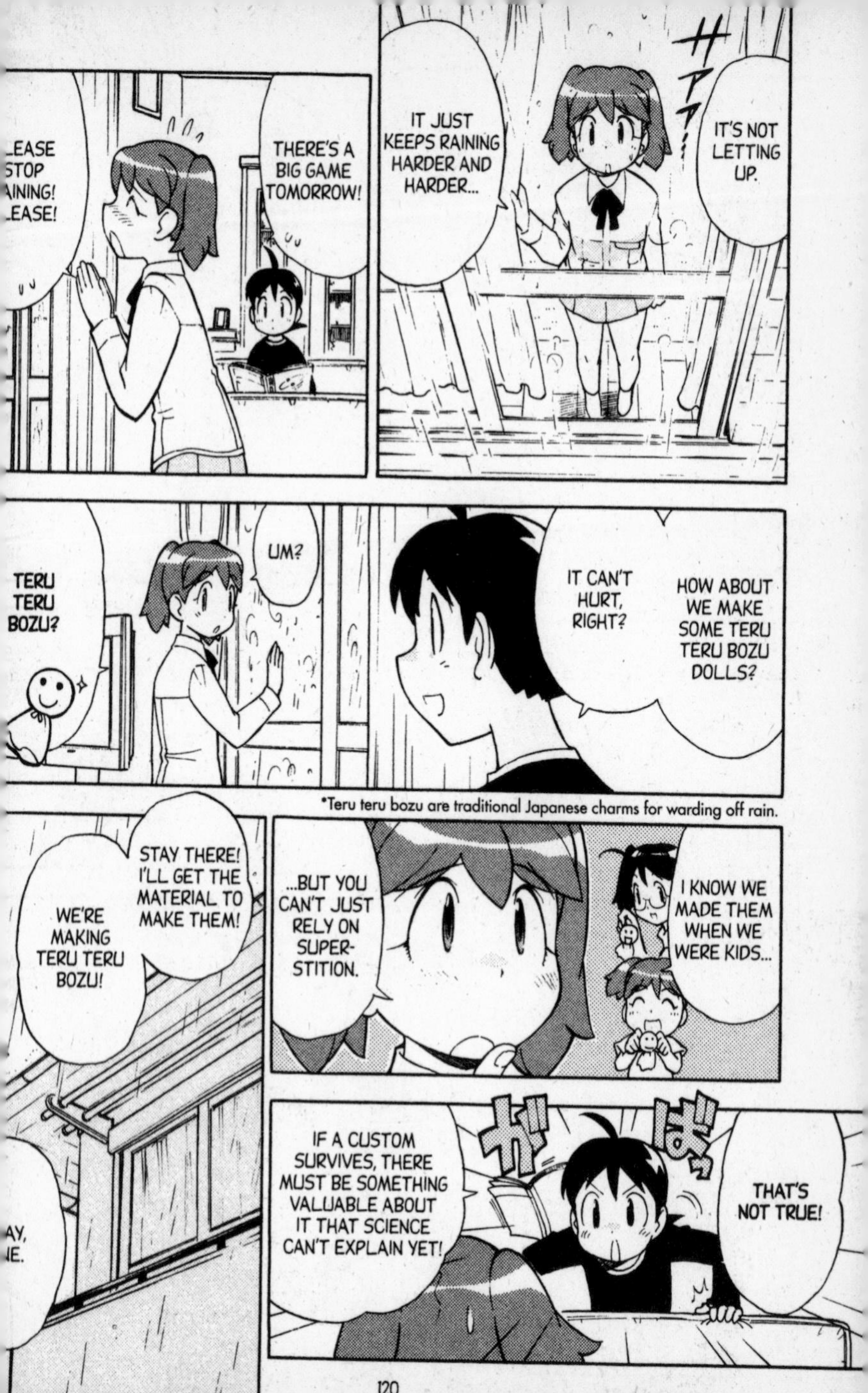
IT'S NOT LETTING UP.
IT JUST KEEPS RAINING HARDER AND HARDER...
THERE'S A BIG GAME TOMORROW!
LEASE STOP AINING! LEASE!
HOW ABOUT WE MAKE SOME TERU TERU BOZU DOLLS?
IT CAN'T HURT, RIGHT?
UM?
TERU TERU BOZU?
I KNOW WE MADE THEM WHEN WE WERE KIDS...
...BUT YOU CAN'T JUST RELY ON SUPER-STITION.
がば
THAT'S NOT TRUE!
IF A CUSTOM SURVIVES, THERE MUST BE SOMETHING VALUABLE ABOUT IT THAT SCIENCE CAN'T EXPLAIN YET!
STAY THERE! I'LL GET THE MATERIAL TO MAKE THEM!
WE'RE MAKING TERU TERU BOZU!
AY, NE.

*Teru teru bozu are traditional Japanese charms for warding off rain.

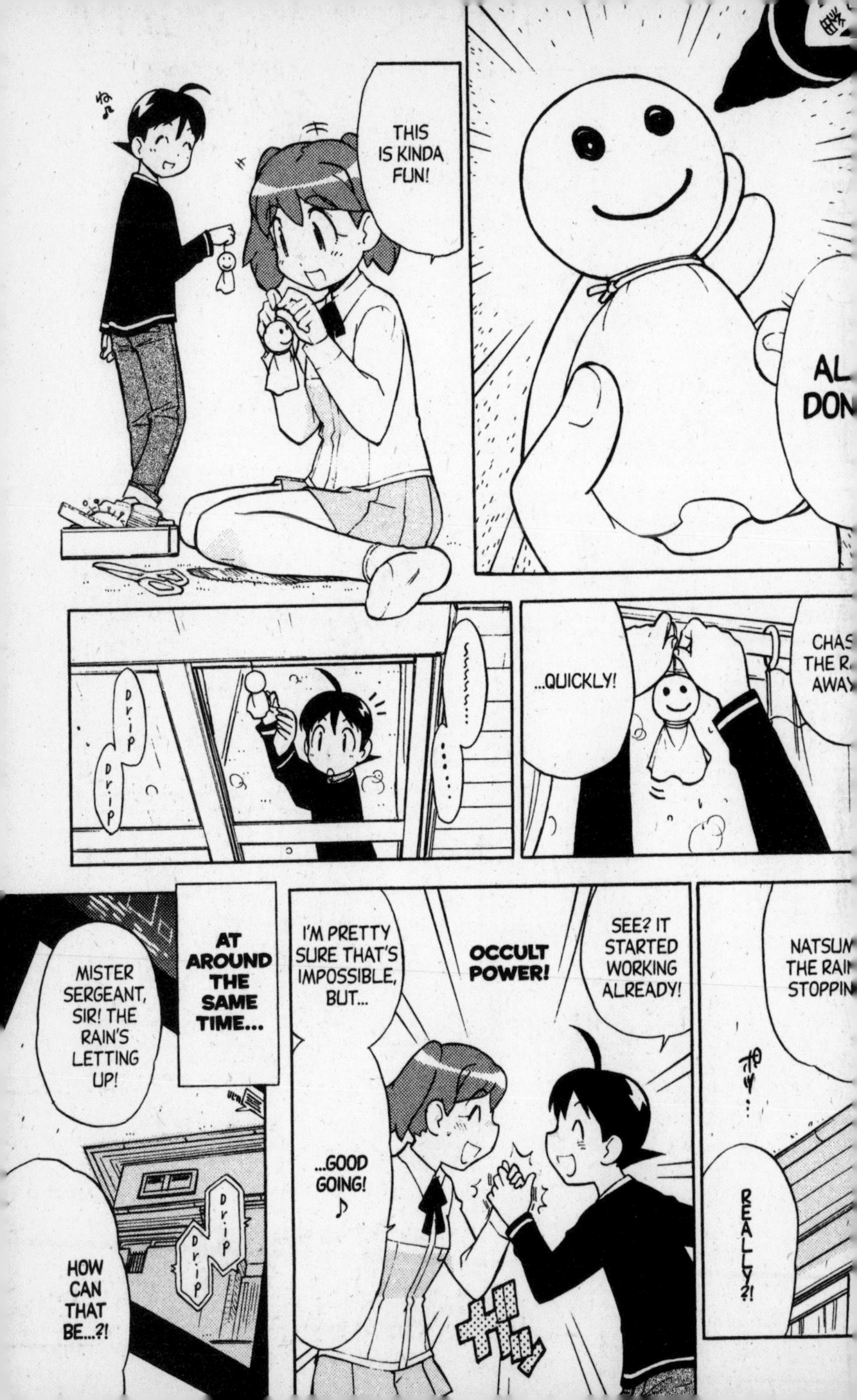
AL
DON
THIS IS KINDA FUN!
CHAS
THE RA
AWAY
...QUICKLY!
......
......
Drip
Drip
NATSUM
THE RAI
STOPPIN
REALLY?!
SEE? IT STARTED WORKING ALREADY!
OCCULT POWER!
I'M PRETTY SURE THAT'S IMPOSSIBLE, BUT...
...GOOD GOING! ♪
AT AROUND THE SAME TIME...
MISTER SERGEANT, SIR! THE RAIN'S LETTING UP!
Drip
Drip
HOW CAN THAT BE...?!

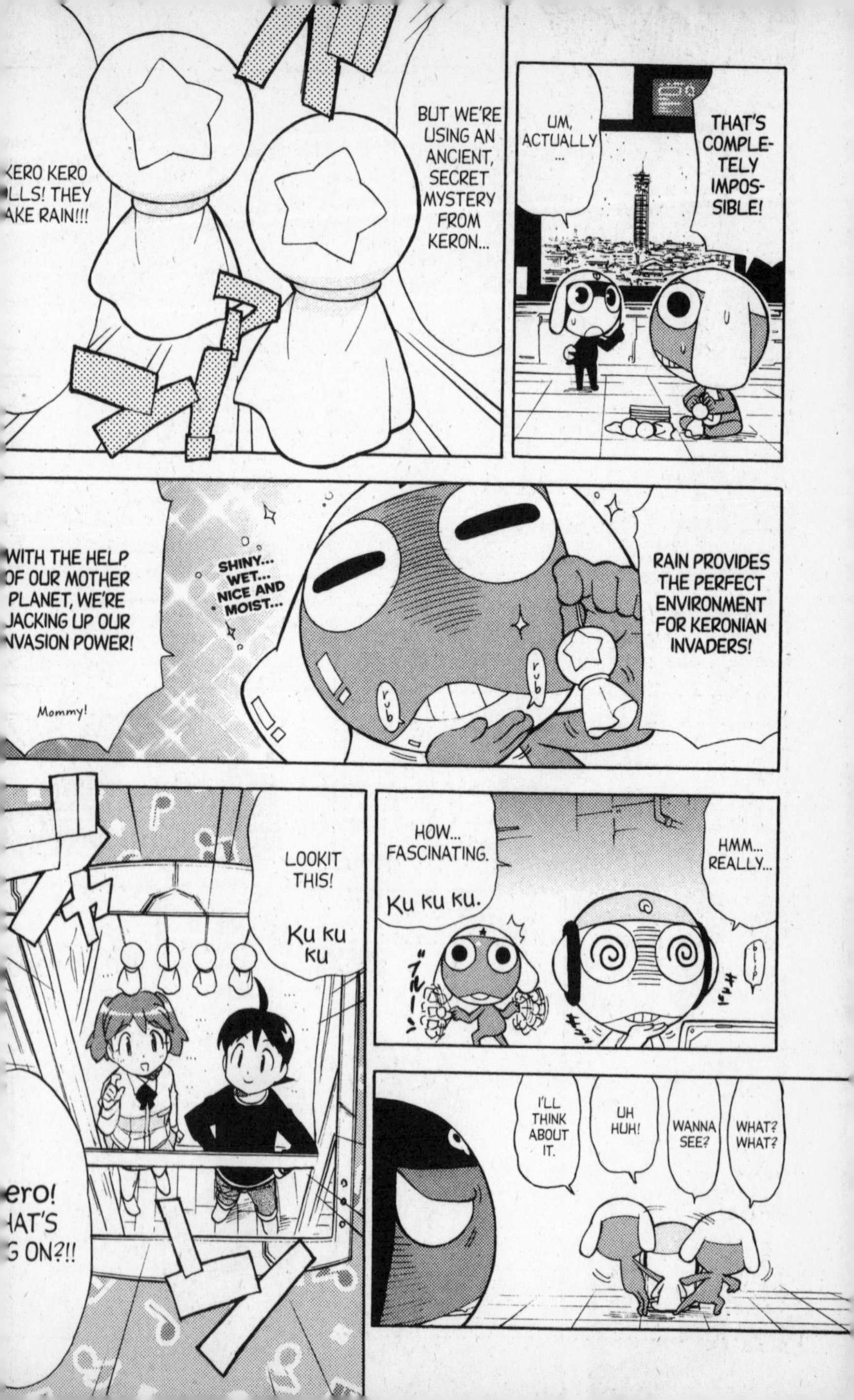
THAT'S COMPLETELY IMPOSSIBLE!
UM, ACTUALLY ...
BUT WE'RE USING AN ANCIENT, SECRET MYSTERY FROM KERON...
KERO KERO
LLS! THEY
AKE RAIN!!!
RAIN PROVIDES THE PERFECT ENVIRONMENT FOR KERONIAN INVADERS!
rub
rub
SHINY... WET... NICE AND MOIST...
WITH THE HELP
OF OUR MOTHER
PLANET, WE'RE
JACKING UP OUR
NVASION POWER!
Mommy!
HMM... REALLY...
blip
HOW... FASCINATING.
Ku ku ku.
WHAT? WHAT?
WANNA SEE?
UH HUH!
I'LL THINK ABOUT IT.
LOOKIT THIS!
Ku ku ku
ero!
HAT'S
G ON?!!

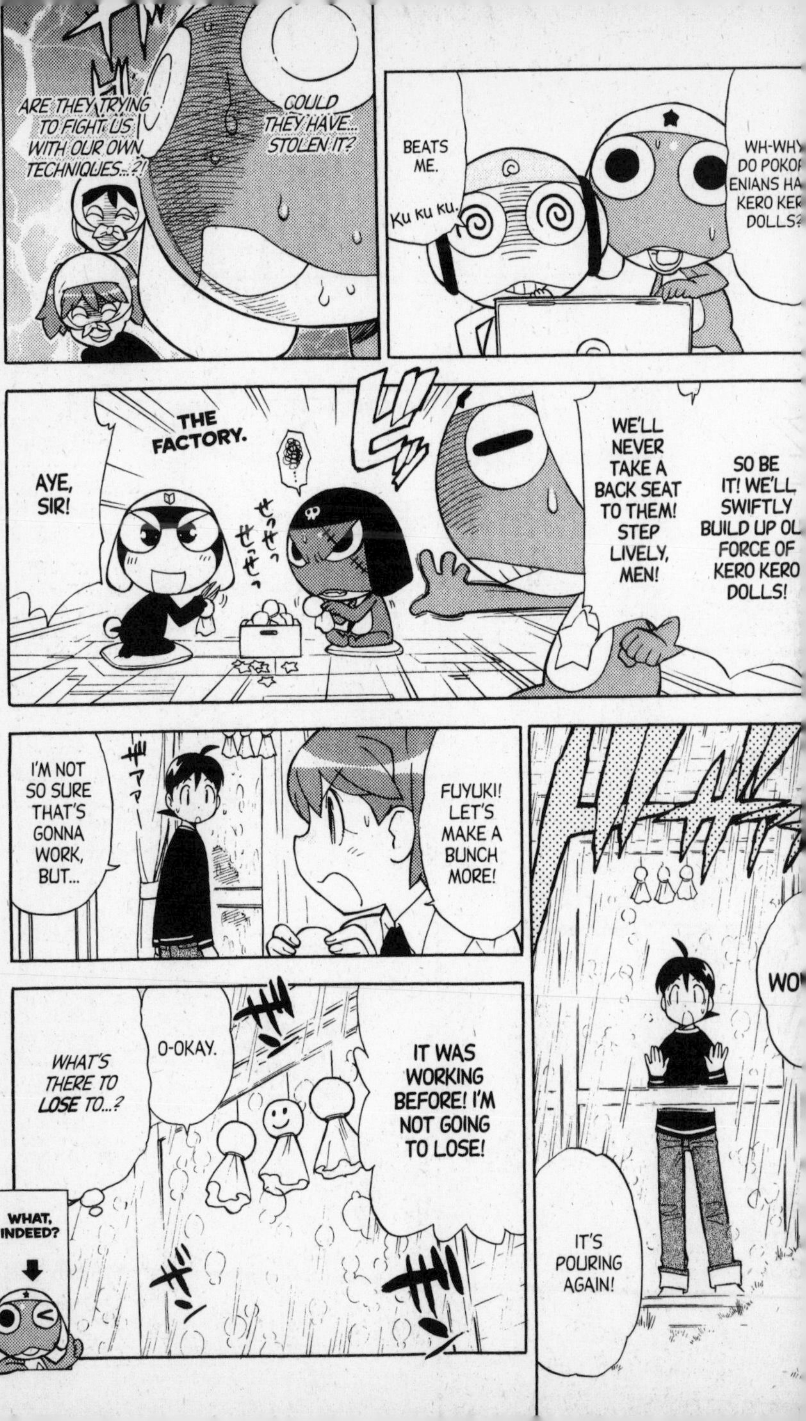

WH-WHY DO POKOP ENIANS HA KERO KER DOLLS?
BEATS ME.
Ku ku ku.
COULD THEY HAVE... STOLEN IT?
ARE THEY TRYING TO FIGHT US WITH OUR OWN TECHNIQUES...?!
SO BE IT! WE'LL SWIFTLY BUILD UP OU FORCE OF KERO KERO DOLLS!
WE'LL NEVER TAKE A BACK SEAT TO THEM! STEP LIVELY, MEN!
THE FACTORY.
せっせっせっせっ
AYE, SIR!
WO
IT'S POURING AGAIN!
FUYUKI! LET'S MAKE A BUNCH MORE!
I'M NOT SO SURE THAT'S GONNA WORK, BUT...
IT WAS WORKING BEFORE! I'M NOT GOING TO LOSE!
O-OKAY.
WHAT'S THERE TO LOSE TO...?
WHAT, INDEED?

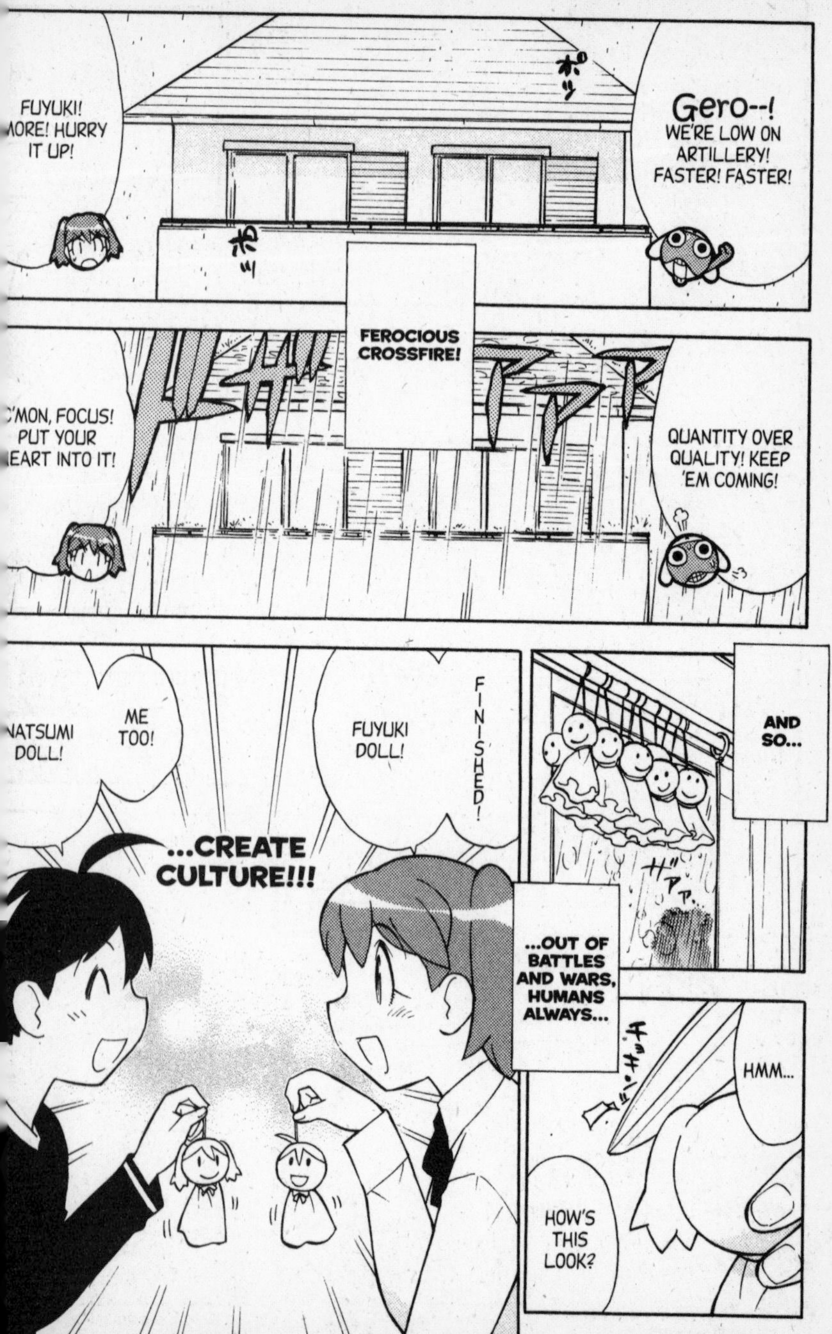
Gero--! WE'RE LOW ON ARTILLERY! FASTER! FASTER!
FUYUKI! MORE! HURRY IT UP!
FEROCIOUS CROSSFIRE!
QUANTITY OVER QUALITY! KEEP 'EM COMING!
C'MON, FOCUS! PUT YOUR HEART INTO IT!
AND SO...
...OUT OF BATTLES AND WARS, HUMANS ALWAYS...
HMM...
HOW'S THIS LOOK?
FINISHED!
FUYUKI DOLL!
ME TOO!
NATSUMI DOLL!
...CREATE CULTURE!!!

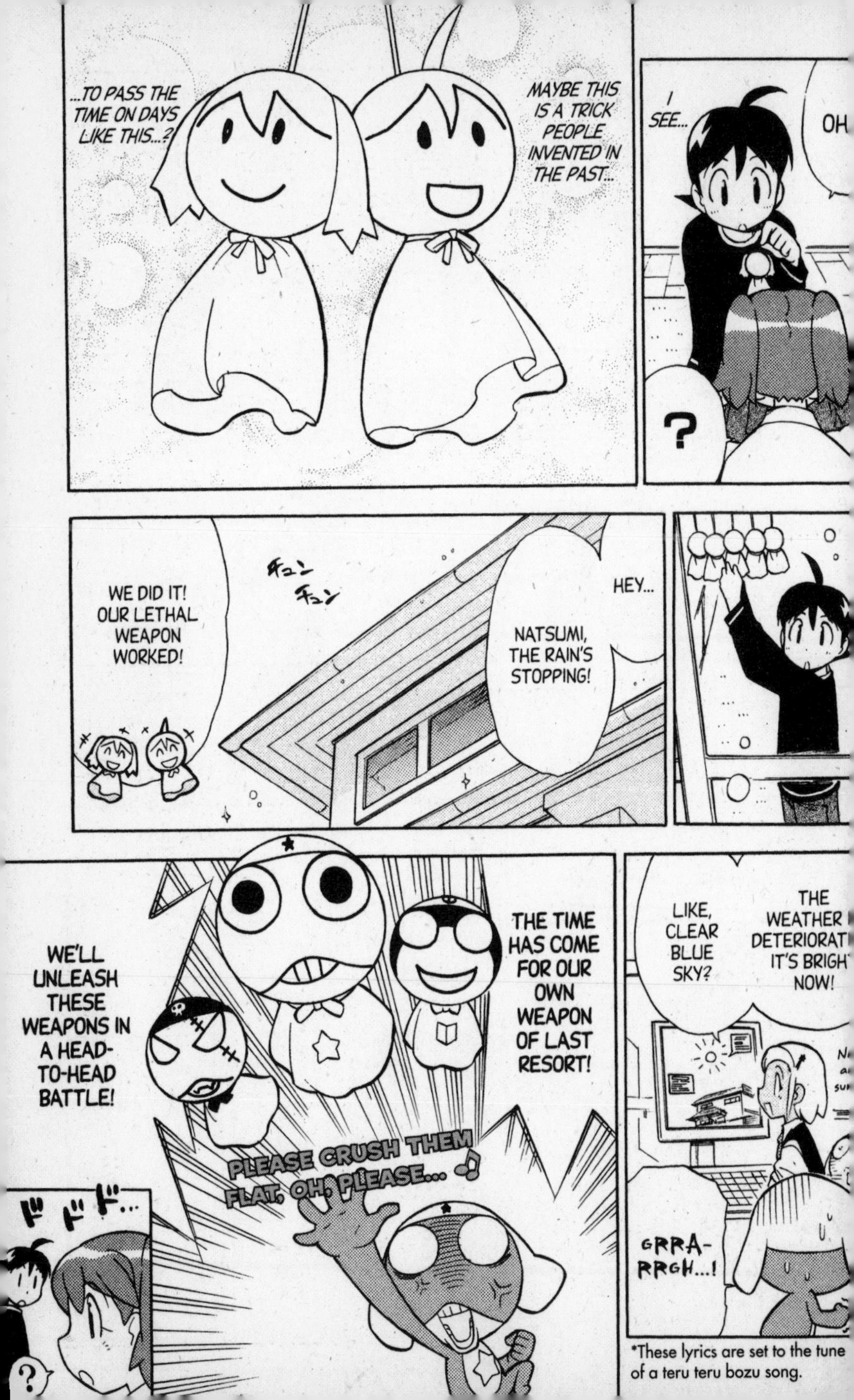
OH
I SEE...
?
MAYBE THIS IS A TRICK PEOPLE INVENTED IN THE PAST...
...TO PASS THE TIME ON DAYS LIKE THIS...?
HEY...
NATSUMI, THE RAIN'S STOPPING!
チュン チュン
WE DID IT! OUR LETHAL WEAPON WORKED!
THE WEATHER DETERIORAT IT'S BRIGH NOW!
LIKE, CLEAR BLUE SKY?
GRRA-RRGH...!
THE TIME HAS COME FOR OUR OWN WEAPON OF LAST RESORT!
WE'LL UNLEASH THESE WEAPONS IN A HEAD-TO-HEAD BATTLE!
PLEASE CRUSH THEM FLAT, OH, PLEASE... ♪
ドドド...
?

*These lyrics are set to the tune of a teru teru bozu song.

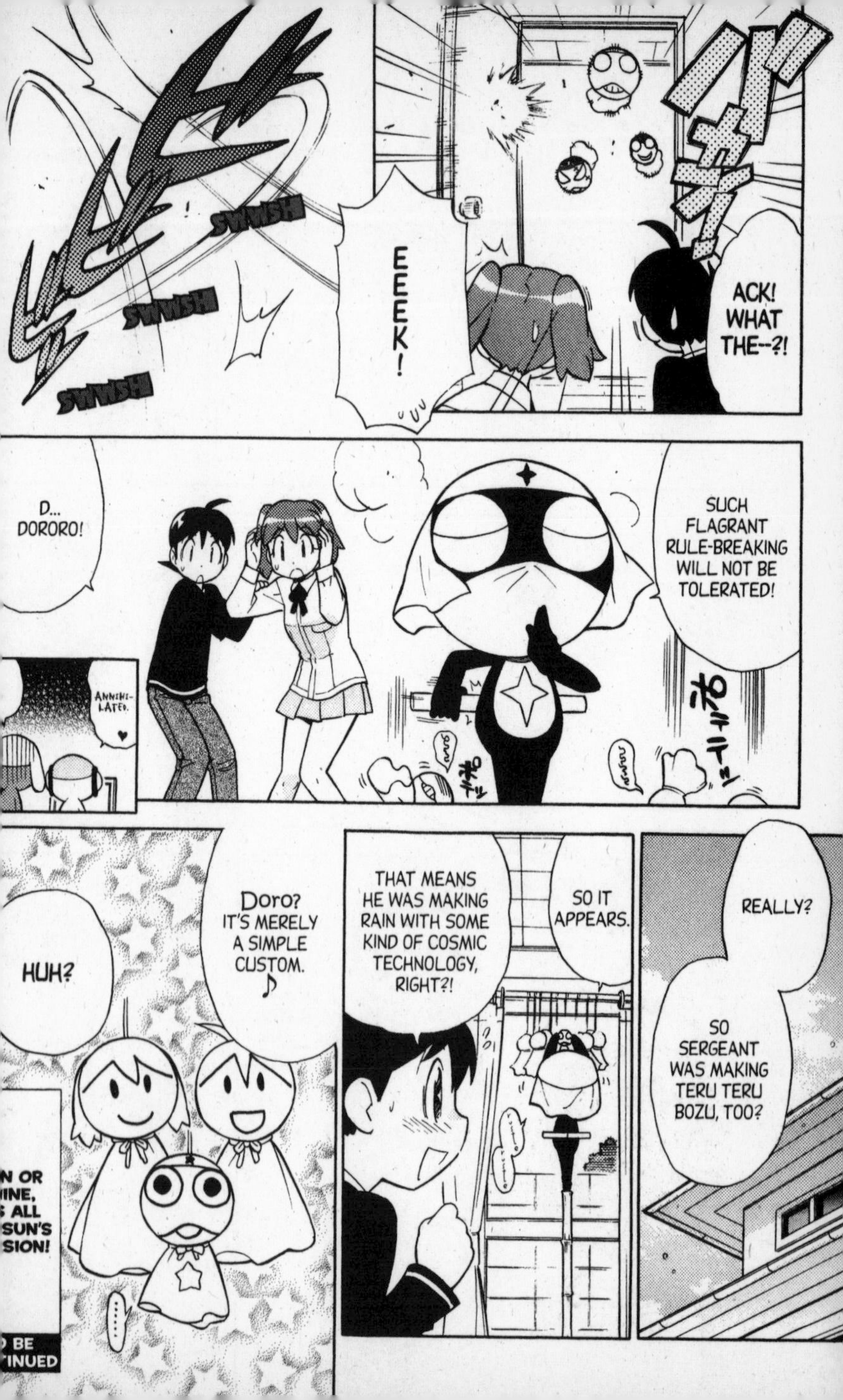
ACK! WHAT THE--?!
EEEK!
SWISH
SWISH
SWISH
SUCH FLAGRANT RULE-BREAKING WILL NOT BE TOLERATED!
D... DORORO!
ANNIHI-LATED. ♥
REALLY?
SO SERGEANT WAS MAKING TERU TERU BOZU, TOO?
SO IT APPEARS.
THAT MEANS HE WAS MAKING RAIN WITH SOME KIND OF COSMIC TECHNOLOGY, RIGHT?!
Doro? IT'S MERELY A SIMPLE CUSTOM. ♪
HUH?
......
N OR INE, S ALL SUN'S SION!
D BE TINUED

ENCOUNTER CLXII
GETTING THE RIGHT SHOT: THE TRAINING OF A FRONT-LINE REPORTER

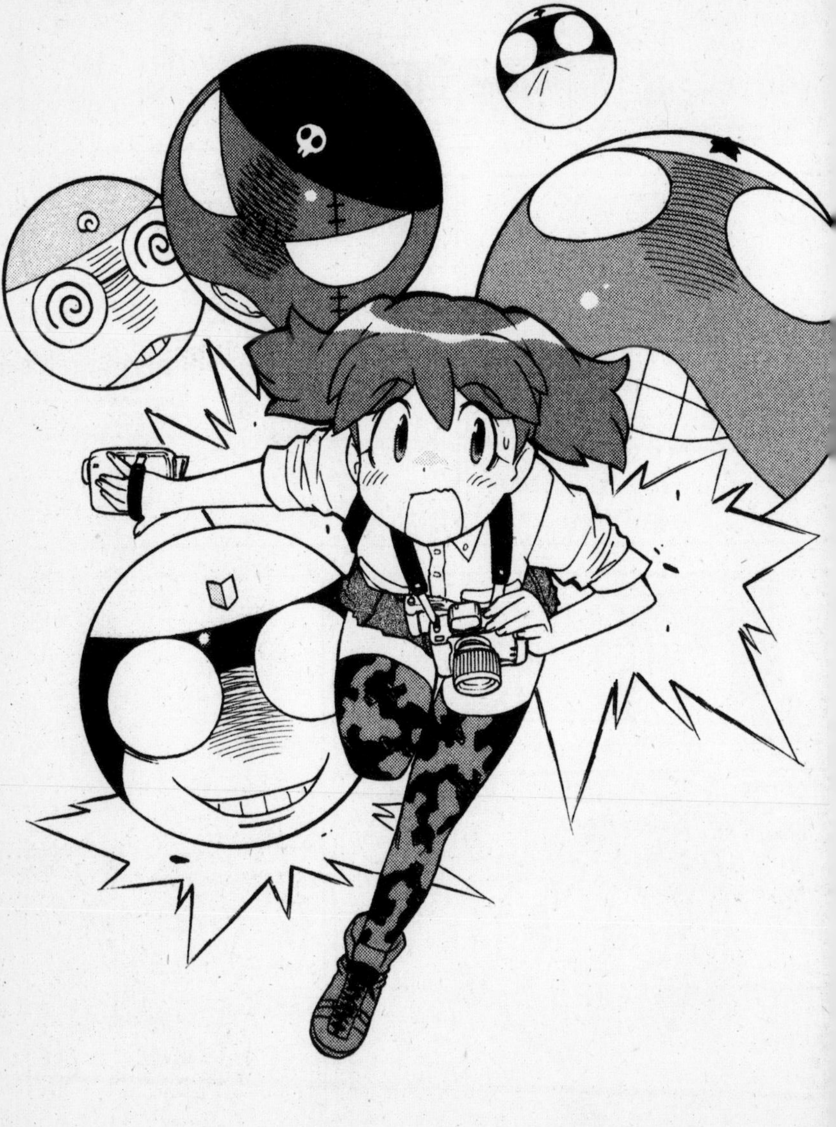

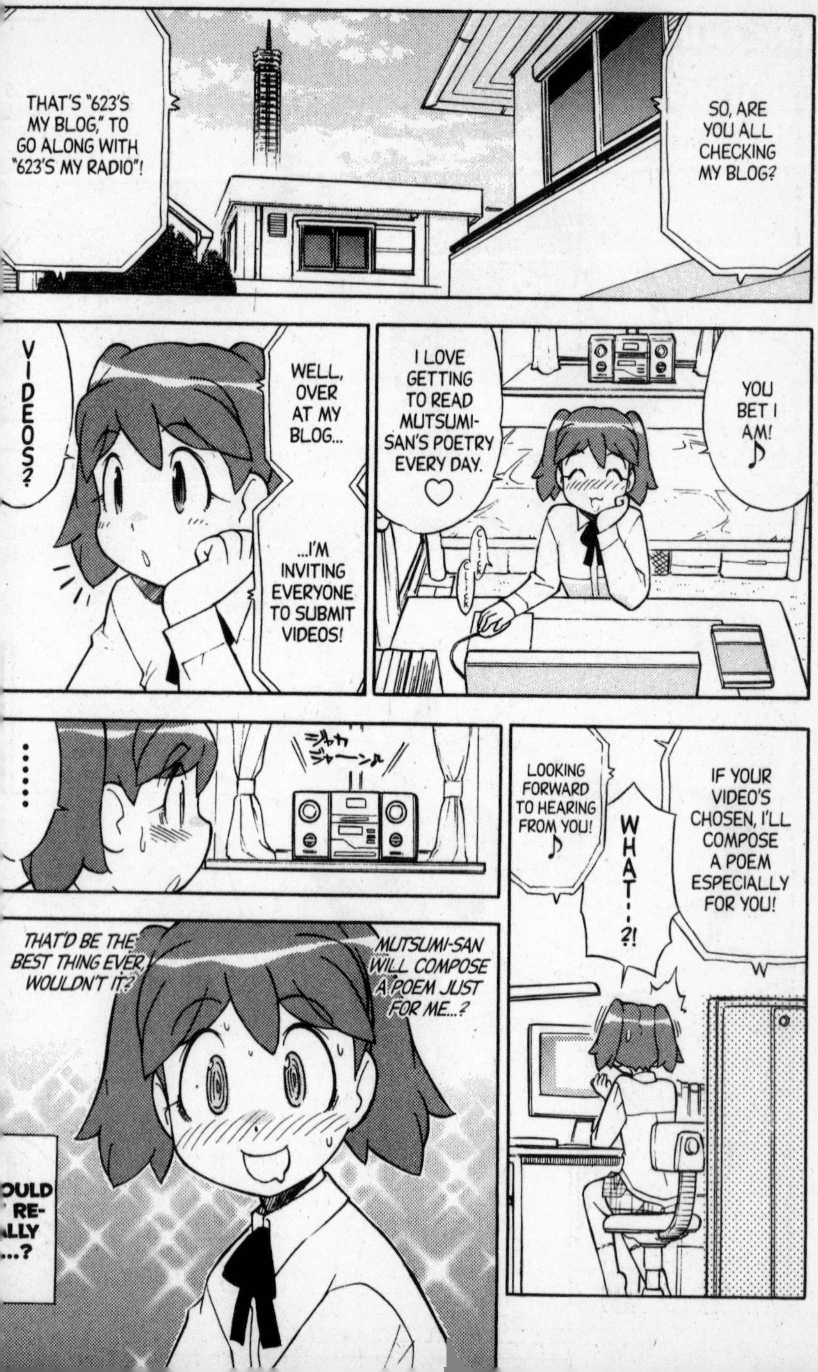
SO, ARE YOU ALL CHECKING MY BLOG?
THAT'S "623'S MY BLOG," TO GO ALONG WITH "623'S MY RADIO"!
YOU BET I AM! ♪
I LOVE GETTING TO READ MUTSUMI-SAN'S POETRY EVERY DAY. ♥
CLICK CLICK
WELL, OVER AT MY BLOG...
...I'M INVITING EVERYONE TO SUBMIT VIDEOS!
VIDEOS?
IF YOUR VIDEO'S CHOSEN, I'LL COMPOSE A POEM ESPECIALLY FOR YOU!
WHAT...?!
LOOKING FORWARD TO HEARING FROM YOU! ♪
ジャカ ジャーン♪
......
MUTSUMI-SAN WILL COMPOSE A POEM JUST FOR ME...?
THAT'D BE THE BEST THING EVER, WOULDN'T IT?
OULD RE- LLY ...?

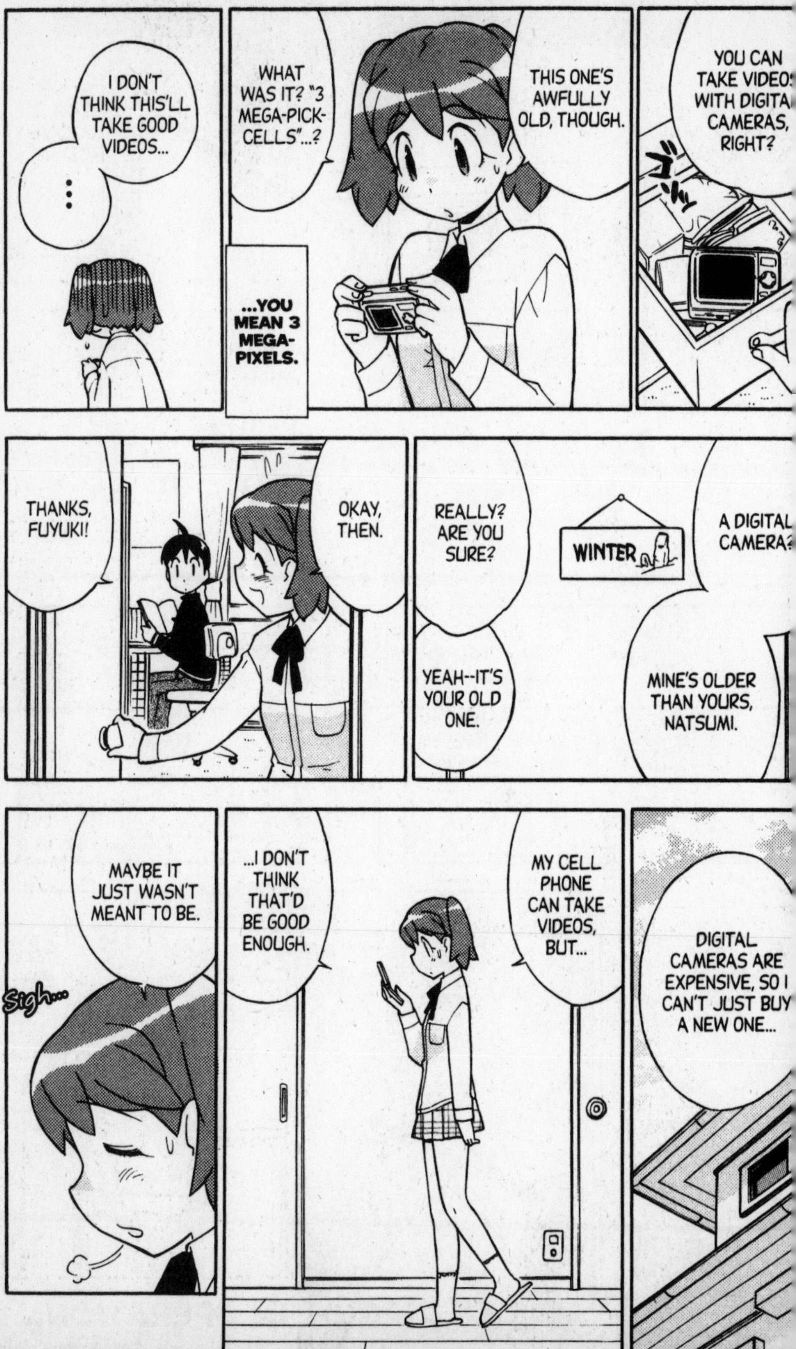
YOU CAN TAKE VIDEO WITH DIGITA CAMERAS, RIGHT?
THIS ONE'S AWFULLY OLD, THOUGH.
WHAT WAS IT? "3 MEGA-PICK-CELLS"...?
...YOU MEAN 3 MEGA-PIXELS.
I DON'T THINK THIS'LL TAKE GOOD VIDEOS...
...
A DIGITAL CAMERA?
WINTER
REALLY? ARE YOU SURE?
MINE'S OLDER THAN YOURS, NATSUMI.
YEAH--IT'S YOUR OLD ONE.
OKAY, THEN.
THANKS, FUYUKI!
DIGITAL CAMERAS ARE EXPENSIVE, SO I CAN'T JUST BUY A NEW ONE...
MY CELL PHONE CAN TAKE VIDEOS, BUT...
...I DON'T THINK THAT'D BE GOOD ENOUGH.
MAYBE IT JUST WASN'T MEANT TO BE.
Sigh...

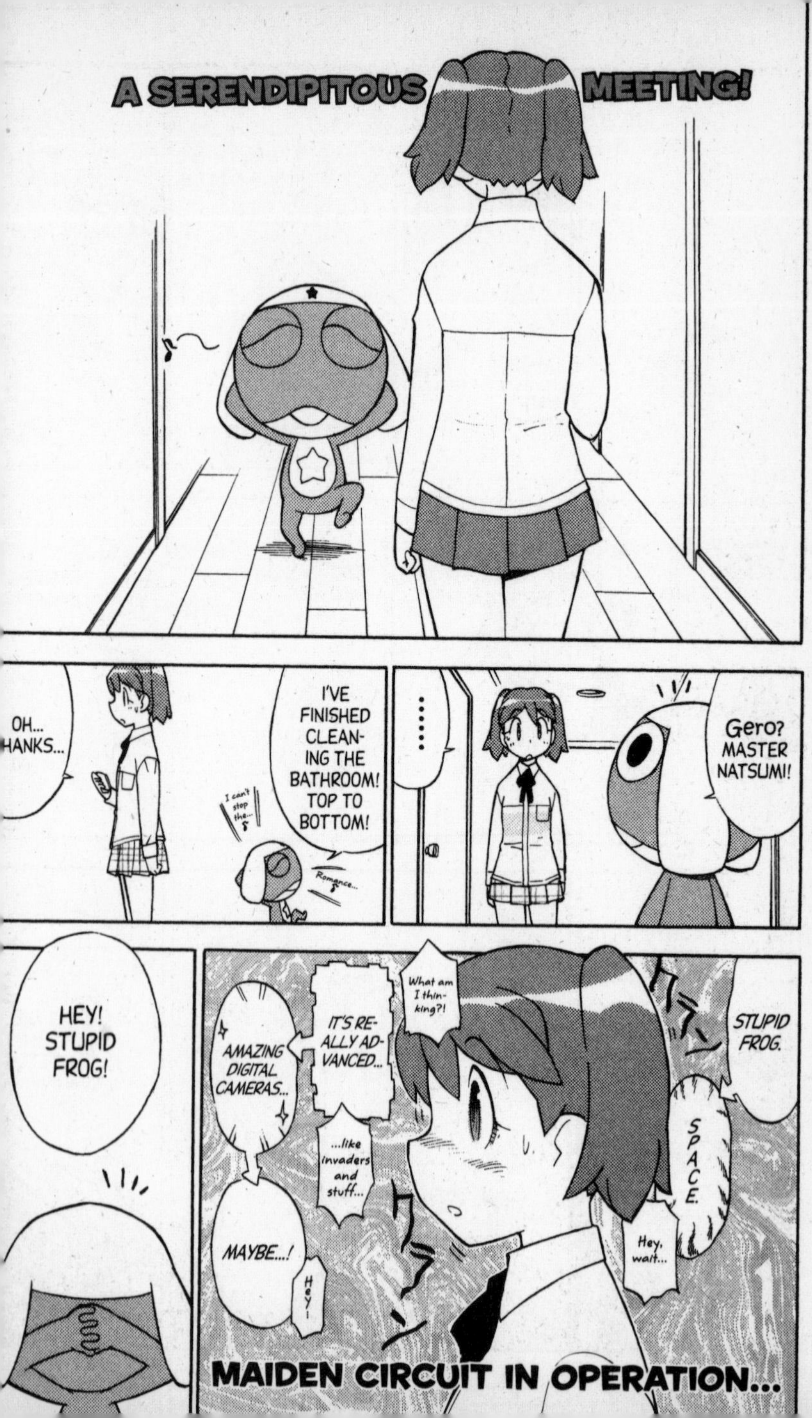
A SERENDIPITOUS MEETING!
Gero? MASTER NATSUMI!
......
I'VE FINISHED CLEAN-ING THE BATHROOM! TOP TO BOTTOM!
I can't stop the...
Romance...
OH... HANKS...
STUPID FROG.
SPACE.
Hey, wait...
What am I thin-king?!
IT'S RE-ALLY AD-VANCED...
AMAZING DIGITAL CAMERAS...
...like invaders and stuff...
MAYBE...!
Hey!
MAIDEN CIRCUIT IN OPERATION...
HEY! STUPID FROG!

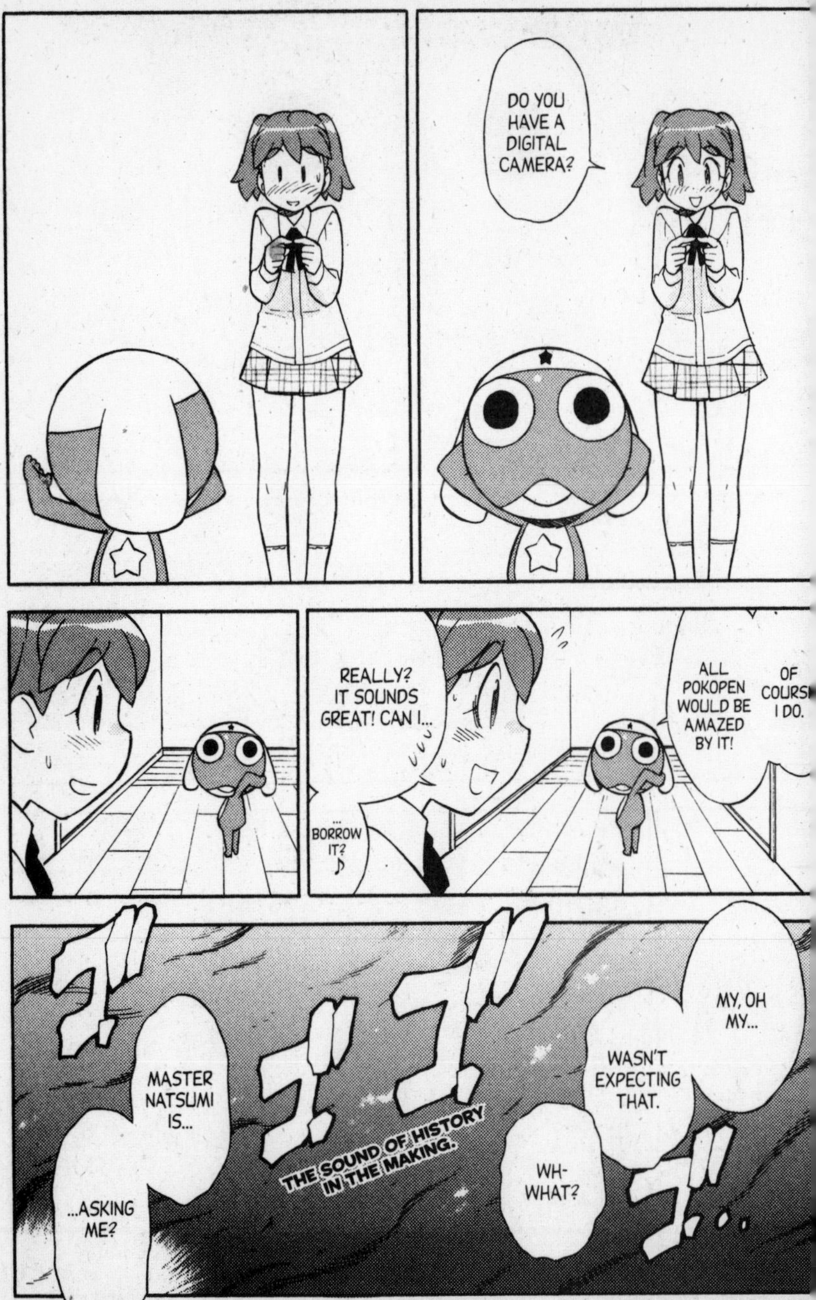
DO YOU HAVE A DIGITAL CAMERA?
OF COURS I DO.
ALL POKOPEN WOULD BE AMAZED BY IT!
REALLY? IT SOUNDS GREAT! CAN I...
... BORROW IT? ♪
MY, OH MY...
WASN'T EXPECTING THAT.
WH-WHAT?
ゴゴゴゴ...
THE SOUND OF HISTORY IN THE MAKING.
MASTER NATSUMI IS...
...ASKING ME?

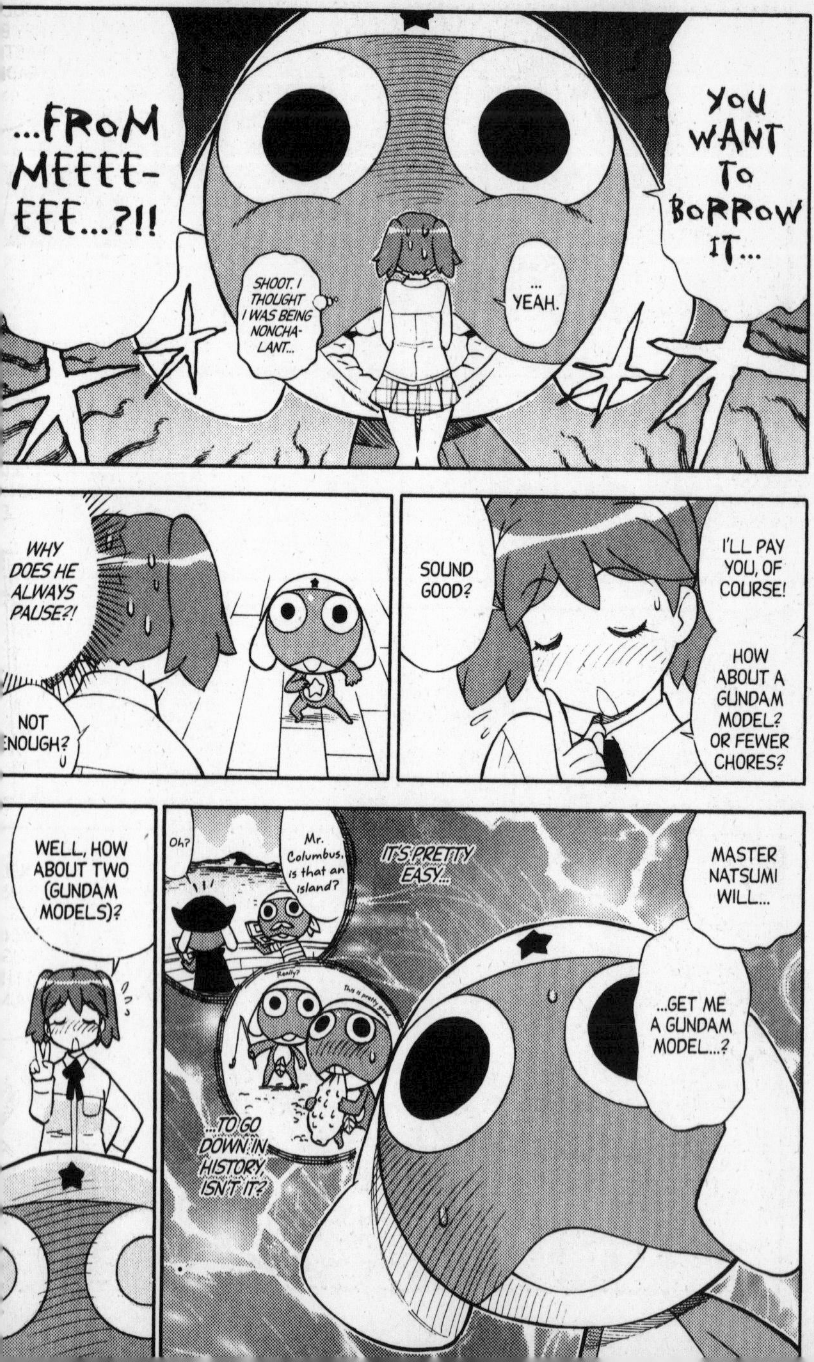
YOU WANT TO BORROW IT...
...YEAH.
SHOOT. I THOUGHT I WAS BEING NONCHALANT...
...FROM MEEEE-EEE...?!!
I'LL PAY YOU, OF COURSE!
HOW ABOUT A GUNDAM MODEL? OR FEWER CHORES?
SOUND GOOD?
WHY DOES HE ALWAYS PAUSE?!
NOT ENOUGH?
MASTER NATSUMI WILL...
...GET ME A GUNDAM MODEL...?
IT'S PRETTY EASY...
Mr. Columbus, is that an island?
Oh?
Really?
This is pretty good
...TO GO DOWN IN HISTORY, ISN'T IT?
WELL, HOW ABOUT TWO (GUNDAM MODELS)?

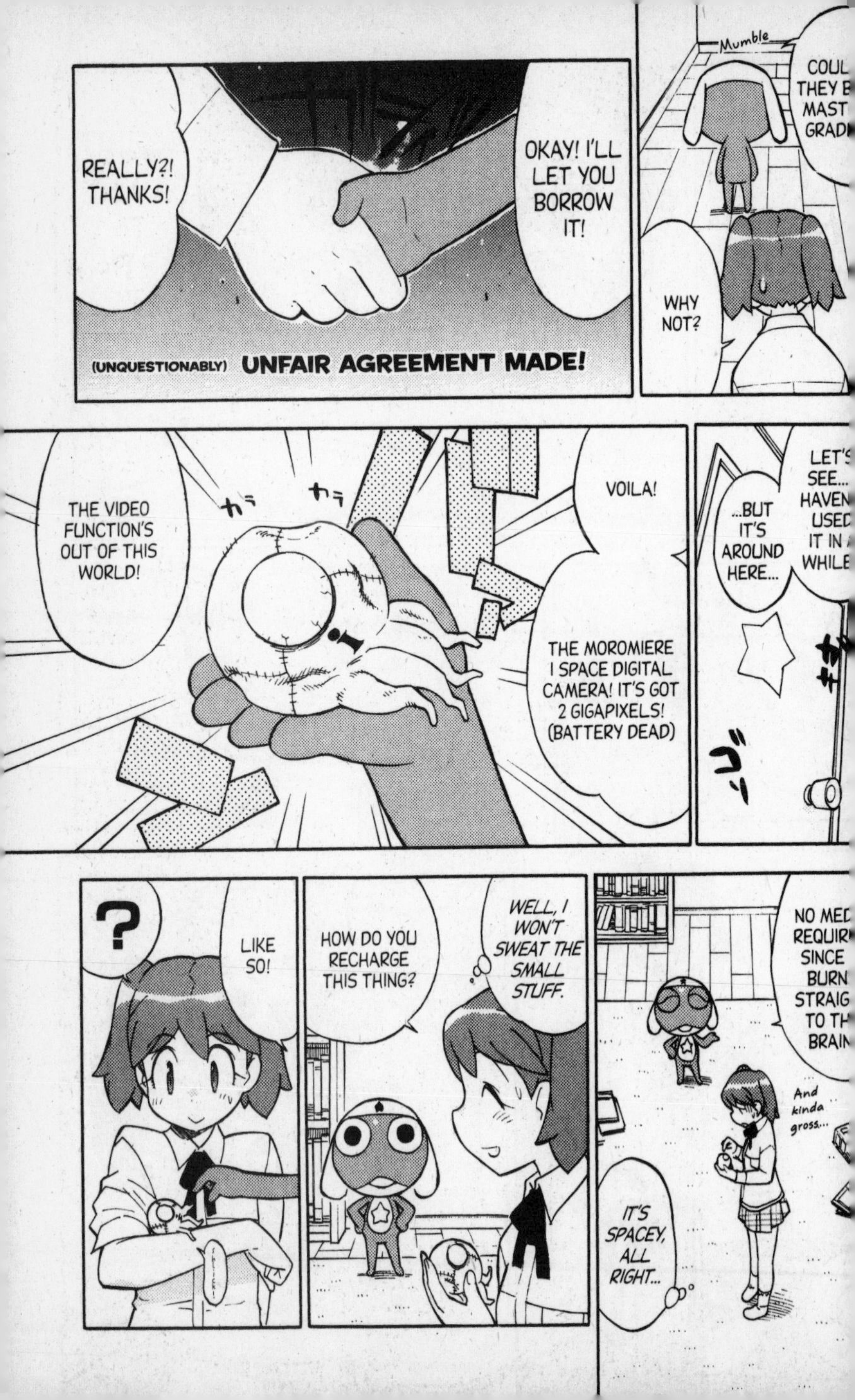
Mumble
COUL THEY B MAST GRAD
WHY NOT?
OKAY! I'LL LET YOU BORROW IT!
REALLY?! THANKS!
(UNQUESTIONABLY) UNFAIR AGREEMENT MADE!
LET'S SEE... HAVEN USED IT IN A WHILE
...BUT IT'S AROUND HERE...
VOILA!
THE MOROMIERE I SPACE DIGITAL CAMERA! IT'S GOT 2 GIGAPIXELS! (BATTERY DEAD)
THE VIDEO FUNCTION'S OUT OF THIS WORLD!
NO MED REQUIR SINCE BURN STRAIG TO TH BRAIN
And kinda gross...
IT'S SPACEY, ALL RIGHT...
WELL, I WON'T SWEAT THE SMALL STUFF.
HOW DO YOU RECHARGE THIS THING?
LIKE SO!
?

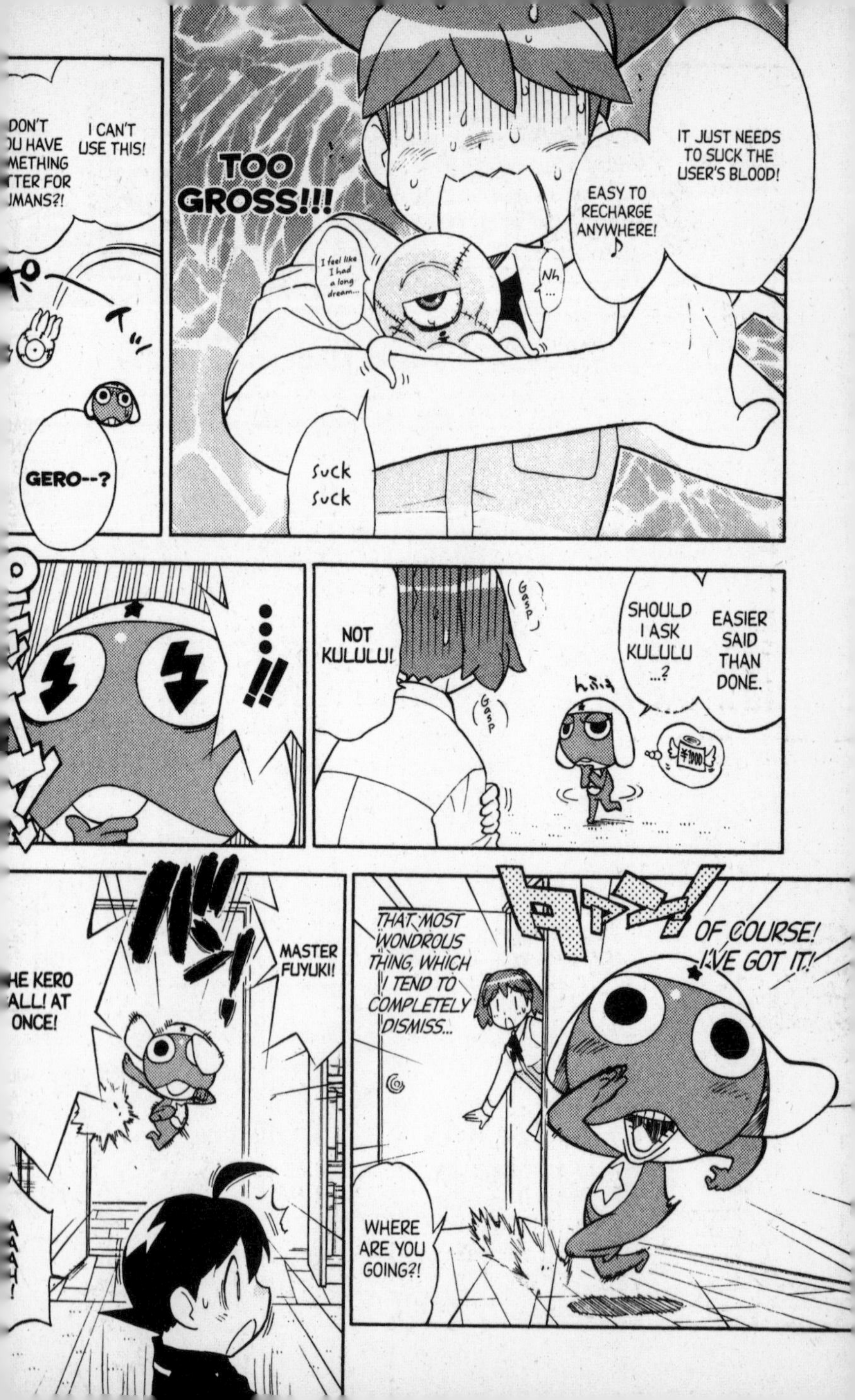
IT JUST NEEDS TO SUCK THE USER'S BLOOD!
EASY TO RECHARGE ANYWHERE! ♪
Nh...
I feel like I had a long dream...
TOO GROSS!!!
suck suck
I CAN'T USE THIS!
DON'T OU HAVE METHING TTER FOR UMANS?!
GERO--?
SHOULD I ASK KULULU ...?
EASIER SAID THAN DONE.
Gasp
NOT KULULU!
Gasp
...!!
OF COURSE! I'VE GOT IT!
THAT MOST WONDROUS THING, WHICH I TEND TO COMPLETELY DISMISS...
WHERE ARE YOU GOING?!
MASTER FUYUKI!
HE KERO ALL! AT ONCE!
AAAT!

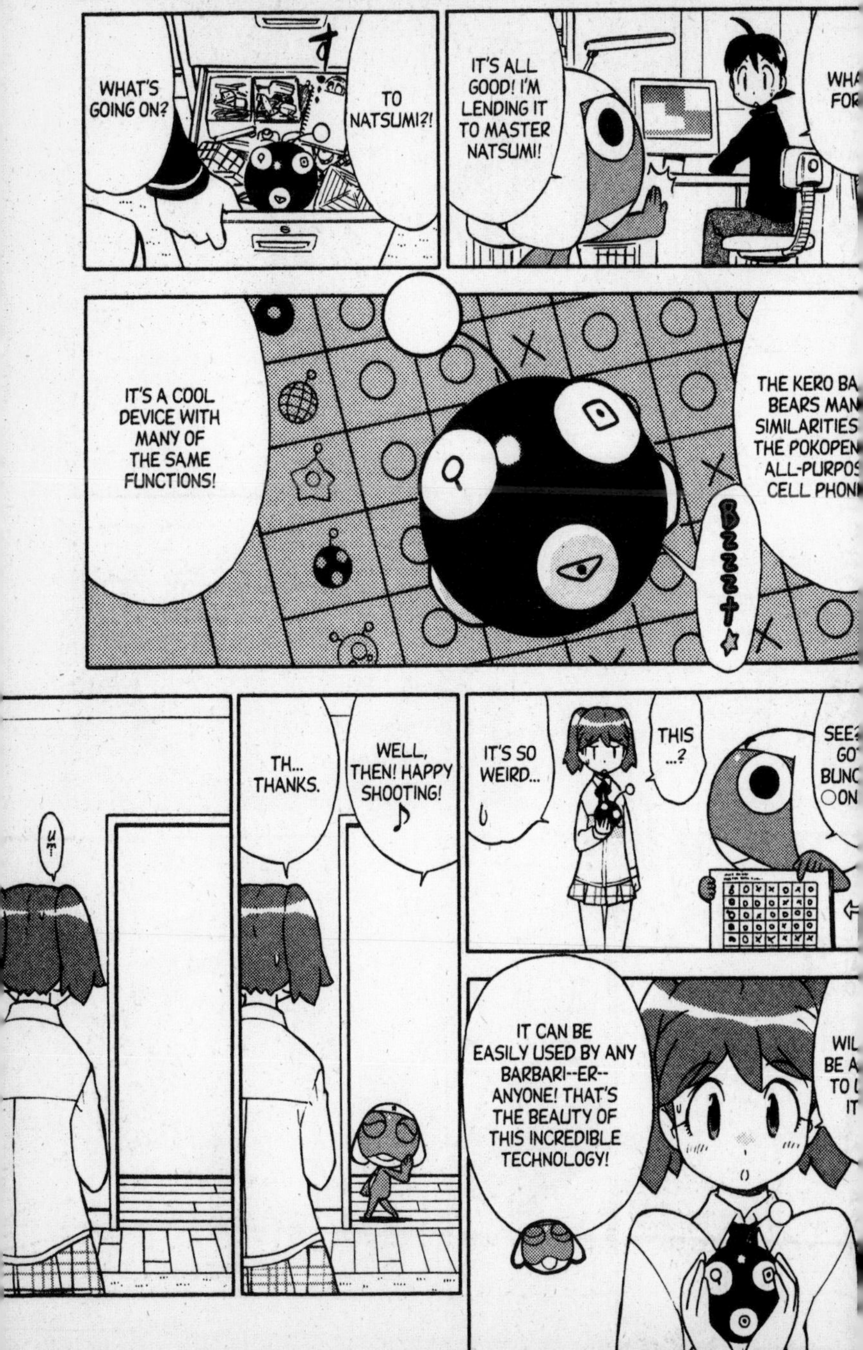
WHA FOR
IT'S ALL GOOD! I'M LENDING IT TO MASTER NATSUMI!
TO NATSUMI?!
WHAT'S GOING ON?
THE KERO BA BEARS MAN SIMILARITIES THE POKOPEN ALL-PURPOS CELL PHON
BZZZT☆
IT'S A COOL DEVICE WITH MANY OF THE SAME FUNCTIONS!
SEE? GO BUNC ○ON
THIS ...?
IT'S SO WEIRD...
WIL BE A TO U IT
IT CAN BE EASILY USED BY ANY BARBARI--ER-- ANYONE! THAT'S THE BEAUTY OF THIS INCREDIBLE TECHNOLOGY!
WELL, THEN! HAPPY SHOOTING! ♪
TH... THANKS.

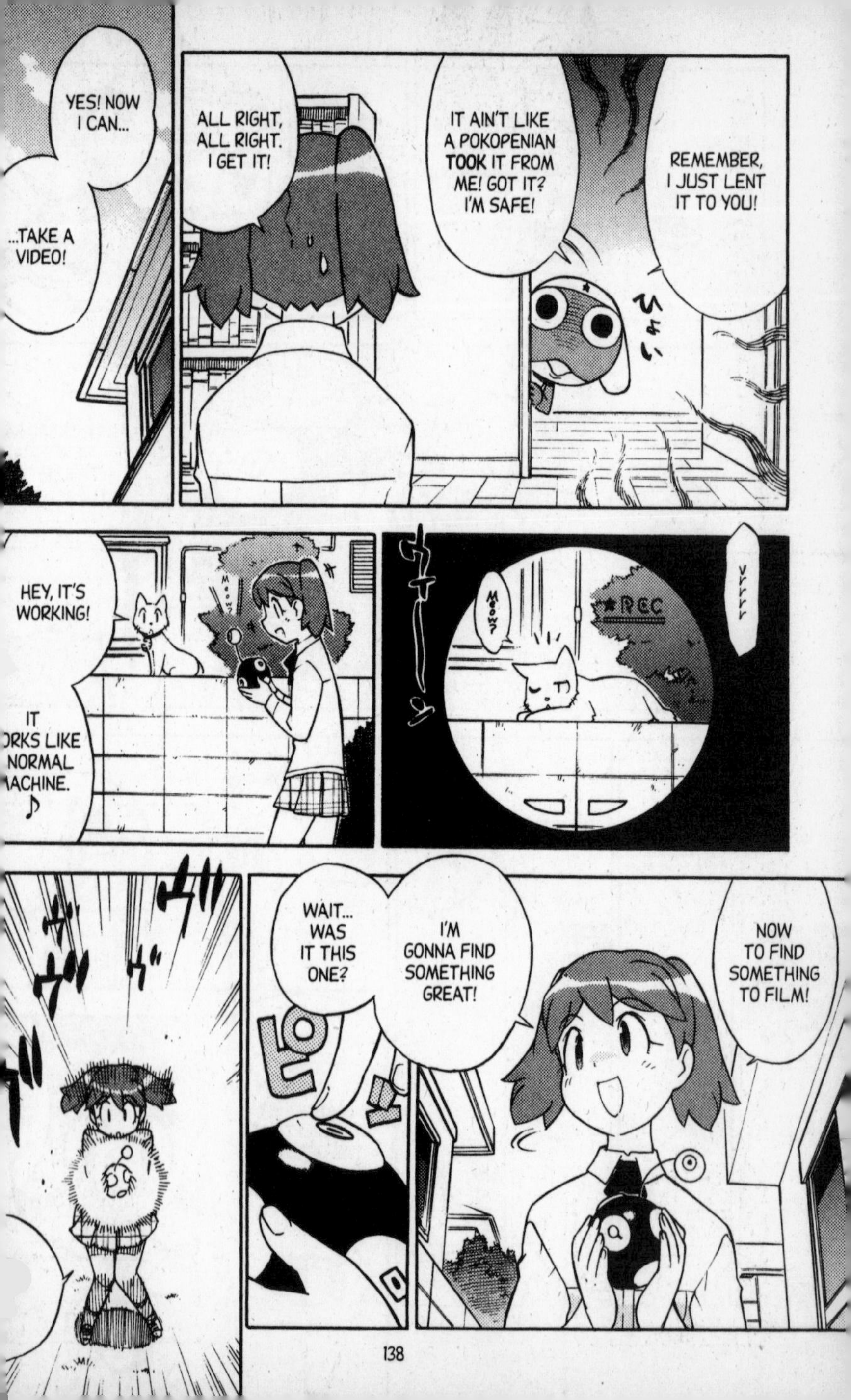
REMEMBER, I JUST LENT IT TO YOU!
ひょい
IT AIN'T LIKE A POKOPENIAN TOOK IT FROM ME! GOT IT? I'M SAFE!
ALL RIGHT, ALL RIGHT. I GET IT!
YES! NOW I CAN...
...TAKE A VIDEO!
Vrrrr
Meow?
REC
Meow
HEY, IT'S WORKING!
IT ORKS LIKE NORMAL ACHINE. ♪
NOW TO FIND SOMETHING TO FILM!
I'M GONNA FIND SOMETHING GREAT!
WAIT... WAS IT THIS ONE?

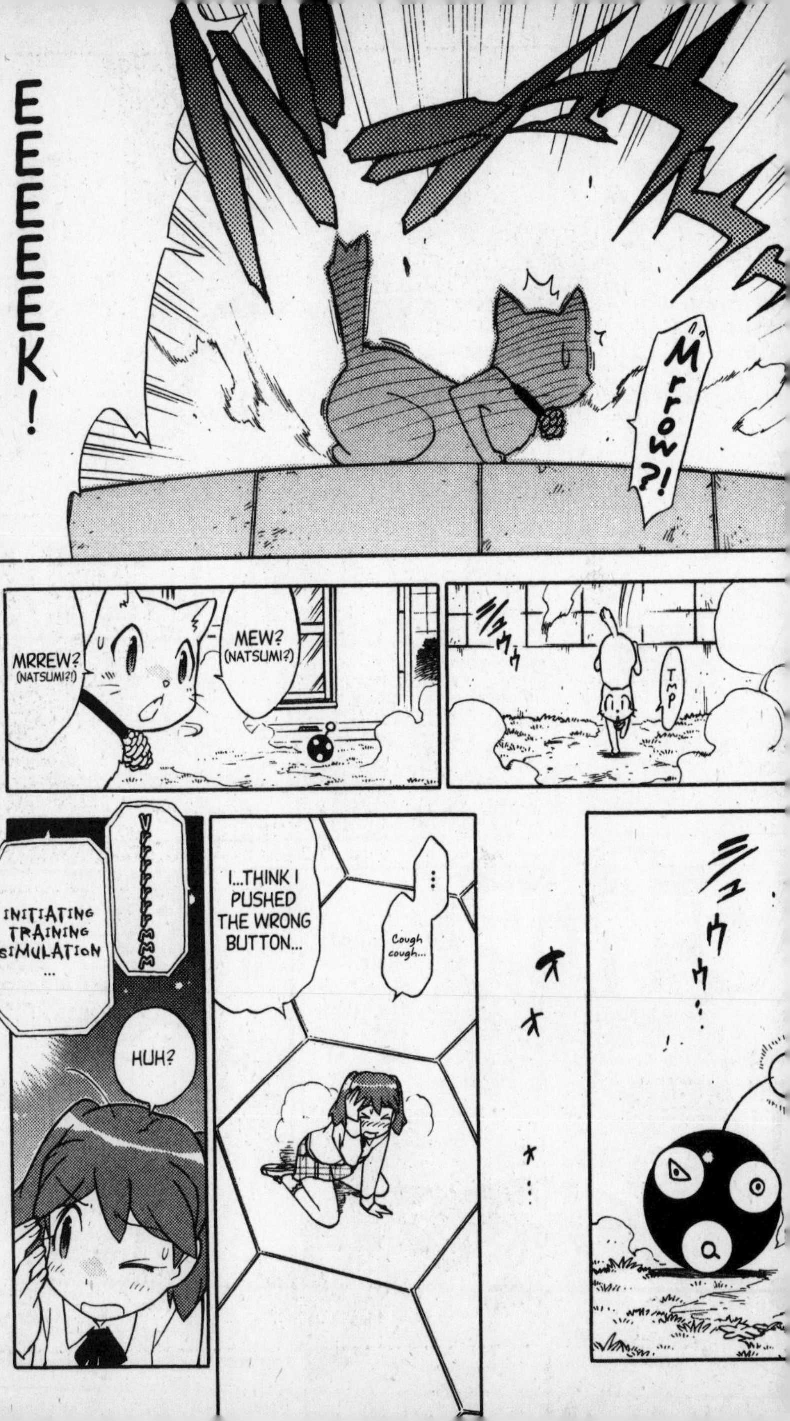
Mrrow?!
EEEEEEK!
TMP
MEW? (NATSUMI?)
MRREW? (NATSUMI?!)
...
Cough cough...
I...THINK I PUSHED THE WRONG BUTTON...
VRRRRRRRRRMMM
INITIATING TRAINING SIMULATION ...
HUH?

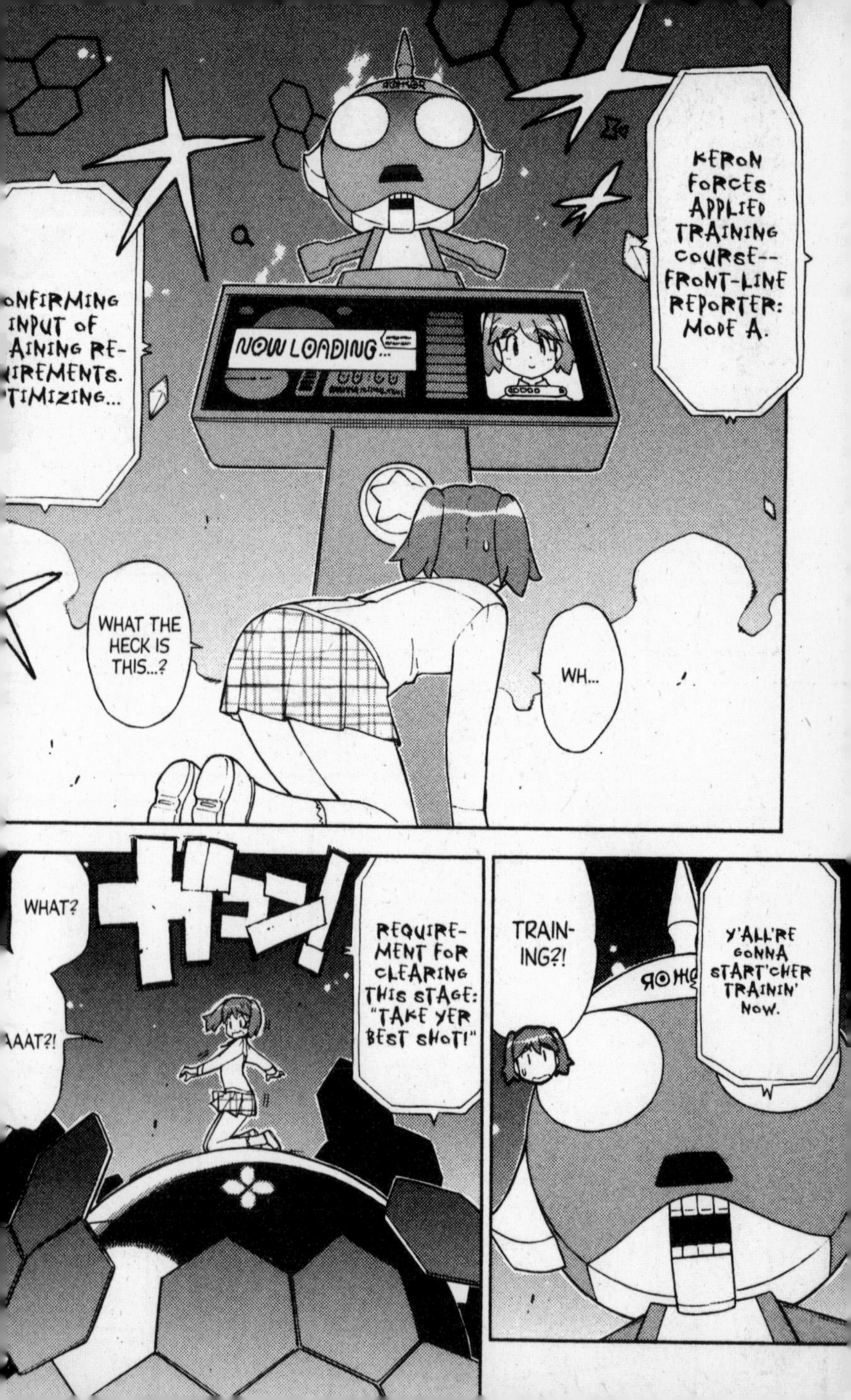
KERON FORCES APPLIED TRAINING COURSE-- FRONT-LINE REPORTER: MODE A.
NOW LOADING...
ONFIRMING INPUT OF AINING RE- IREMENTS. TIMIZING...
WH...
WHAT THE HECK IS THIS...?
Y'ALL'RE GONNA START'CHER TRAININ' NOW.
TRAIN-ING?!
REQUIRE-MENT FOR CLEARING THIS STAGE: "TAKE YER BEST SHOT!"
WHAT?
AAAT?!

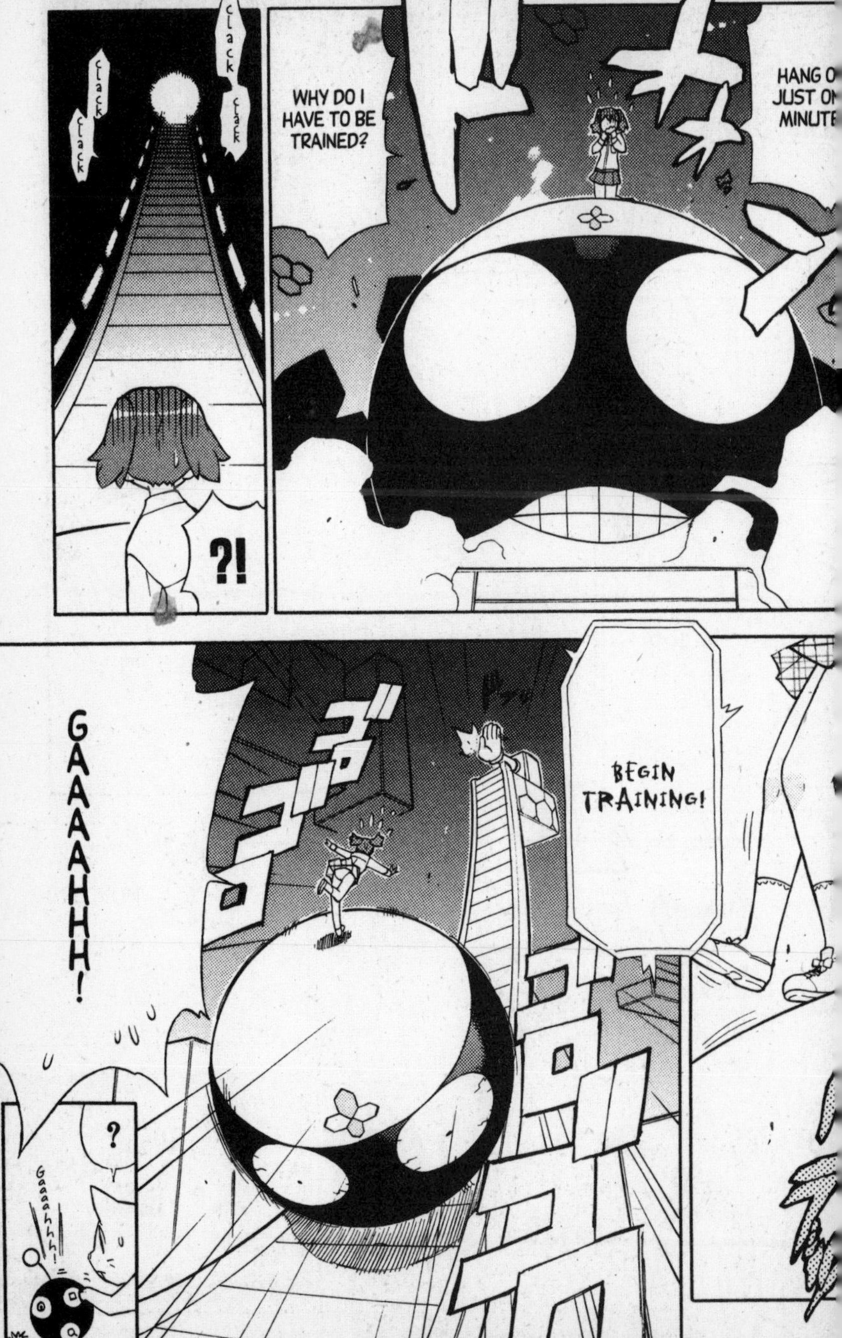

HANG O JUST ON MINUTE
WHY DO I HAVE TO BE TRAINED?
Clack clack
Clack clack
?!
BEGIN TRAINING!
GAAAAAHHHH!
?
Gaaaahhh!

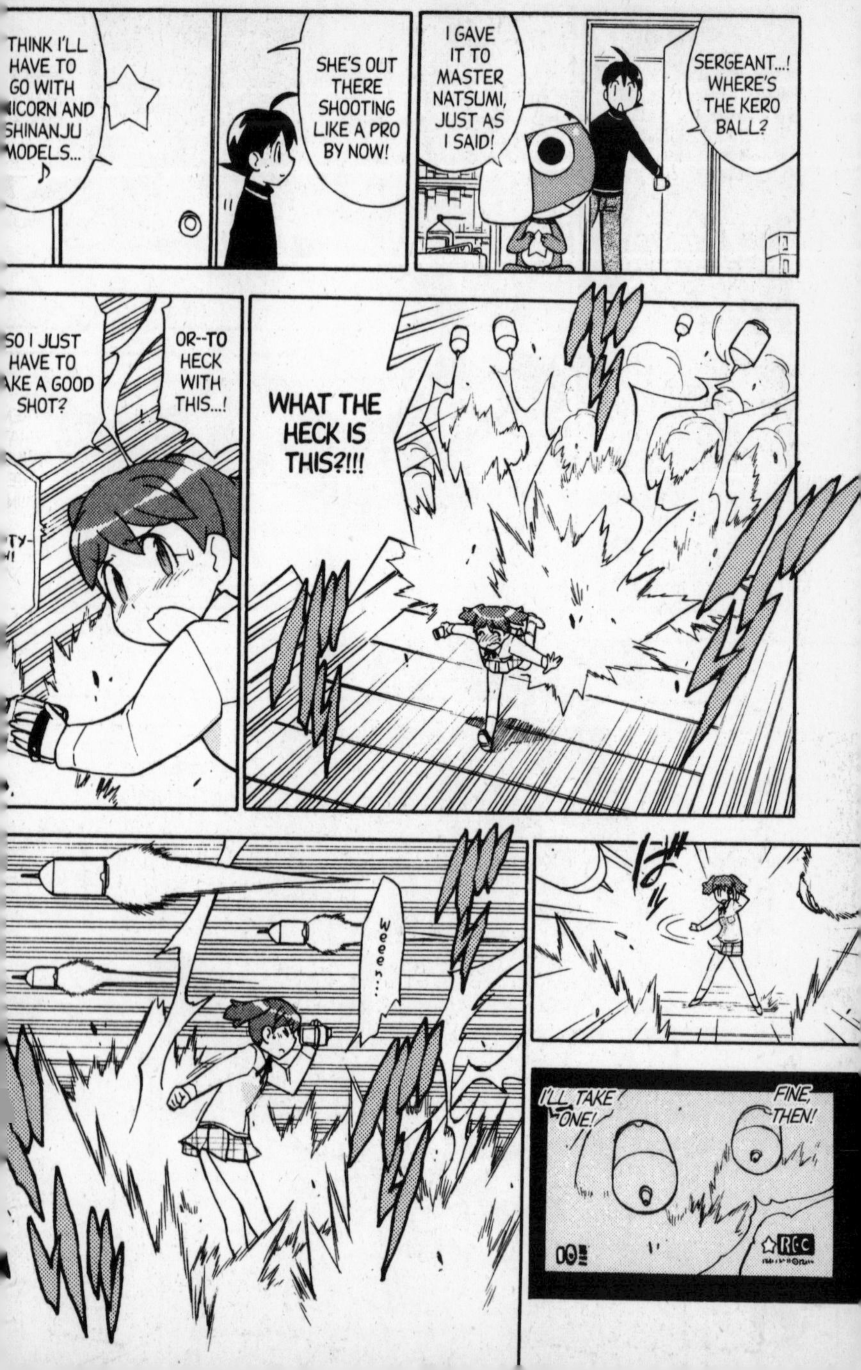
SERGEANT...! WHERE'S THE KERO BALL?
I GAVE IT TO MASTER NATSUMI, JUST AS I SAID!
SHE'S OUT THERE SHOOTING LIKE A PRO BY NOW!
THINK I'LL HAVE TO GO WITH ICORN AND SHINANJU MODELS... ♪
WHAT THE HECK IS THIS?!!!
OR--TO HECK WITH THIS...!
SO I JUST HAVE TO AKE A GOOD SHOT?
ば
FINE, THEN!
I'LL TAKE ONE!
REC
Weeen...

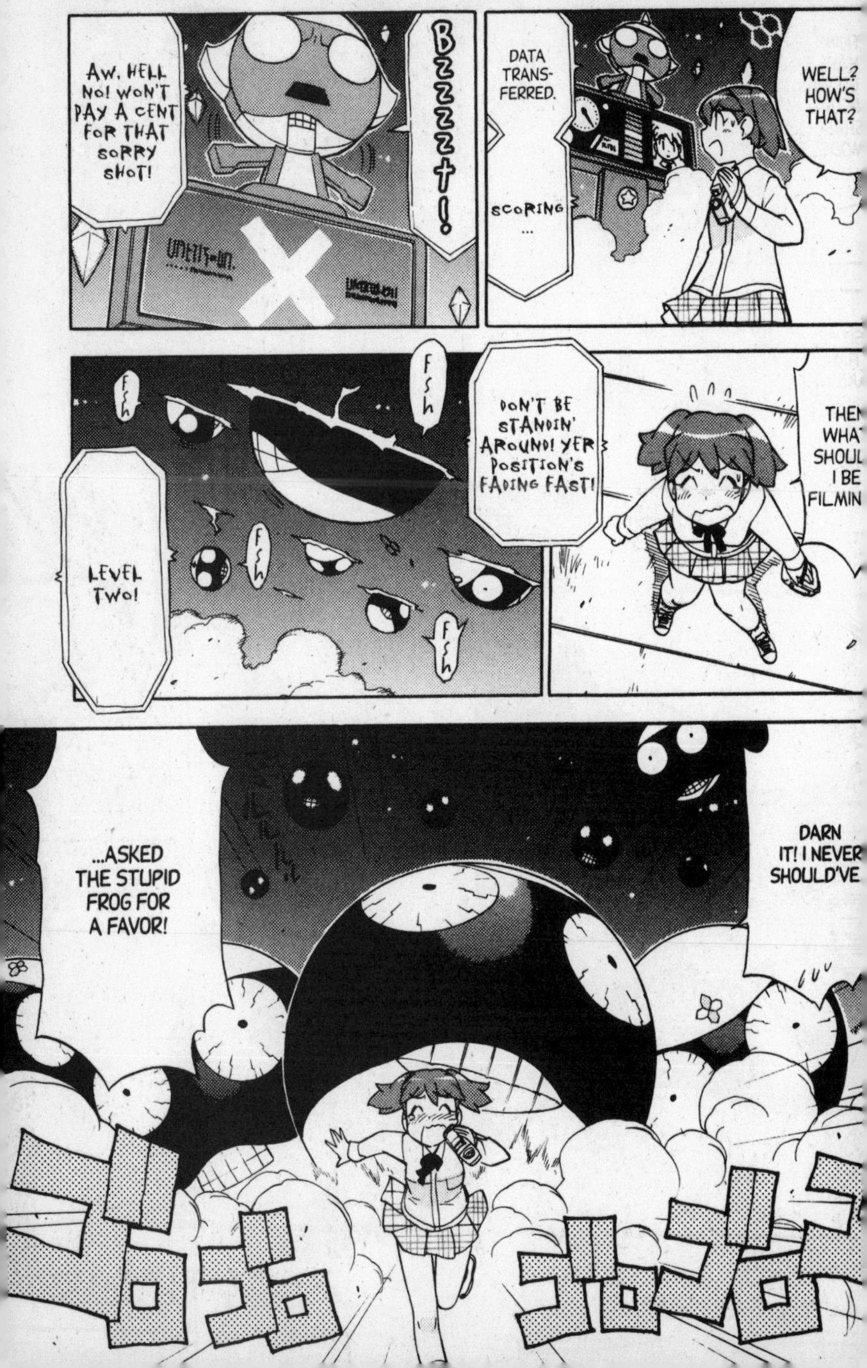
WELL? HOW'S THAT?
DATA TRANSFERRED.
SCORING ...
BZZZZT!
AW, HELL NO! WON'T PAY A CENT FOR THAT SORRY SHOT!
THEN WHAT SHOUL I BE FILMIN
DON'T BE STANDIN' AROUND! YER POSITION'S FADING FAST!
Fsh
Fsh
LEVEL TWO!
Fsh
Fsh
DARN IT! I NEVER SHOULD'VE
...ASKED THE STUPID FROG FOR A FAVOR!
ゴロゴロ
ゴロゴロ

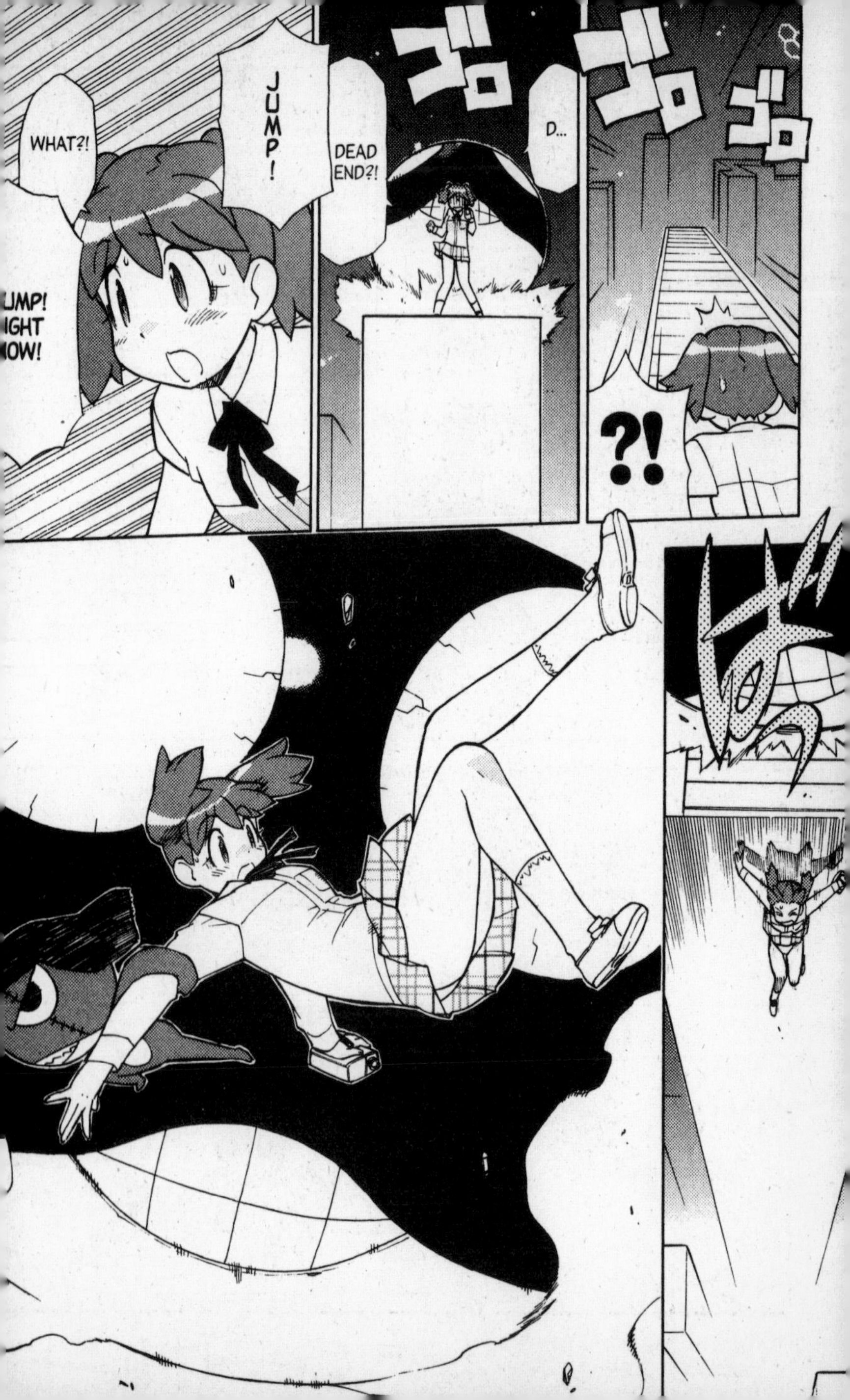
ゴロ
ゴロ
?!
ゴロ
D...
DEAD END?!
JUMP!
WHAT?!
UMP! IGHT OW!

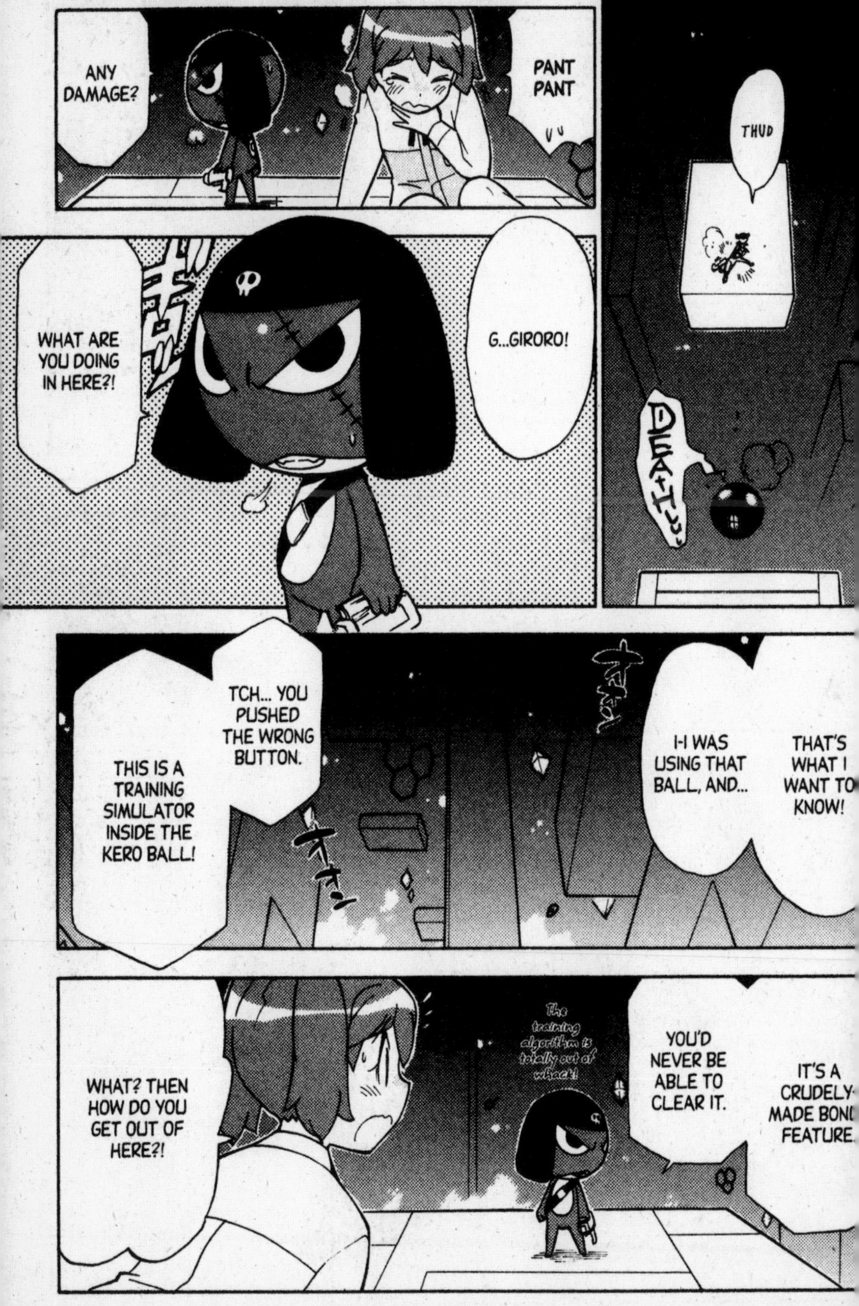
THUD
DEATH
PANT PANT
ANY DAMAGE?
G...GIRORO!
WHAT ARE YOU DOING IN HERE?!
THAT'S WHAT I WANT TO KNOW!
I-I WAS USING THAT BALL, AND...
TCH... YOU PUSHED THE WRONG BUTTON.
THIS IS A TRAINING SIMULATOR INSIDE THE KERO BALL!
IT'S A CRUDELY-MADE BON FEATURE.
YOU'D NEVER BE ABLE TO CLEAR IT.
The training algorithm is totally out of whack!
WHAT? THEN HOW DO YOU GET OUT OF HERE?!

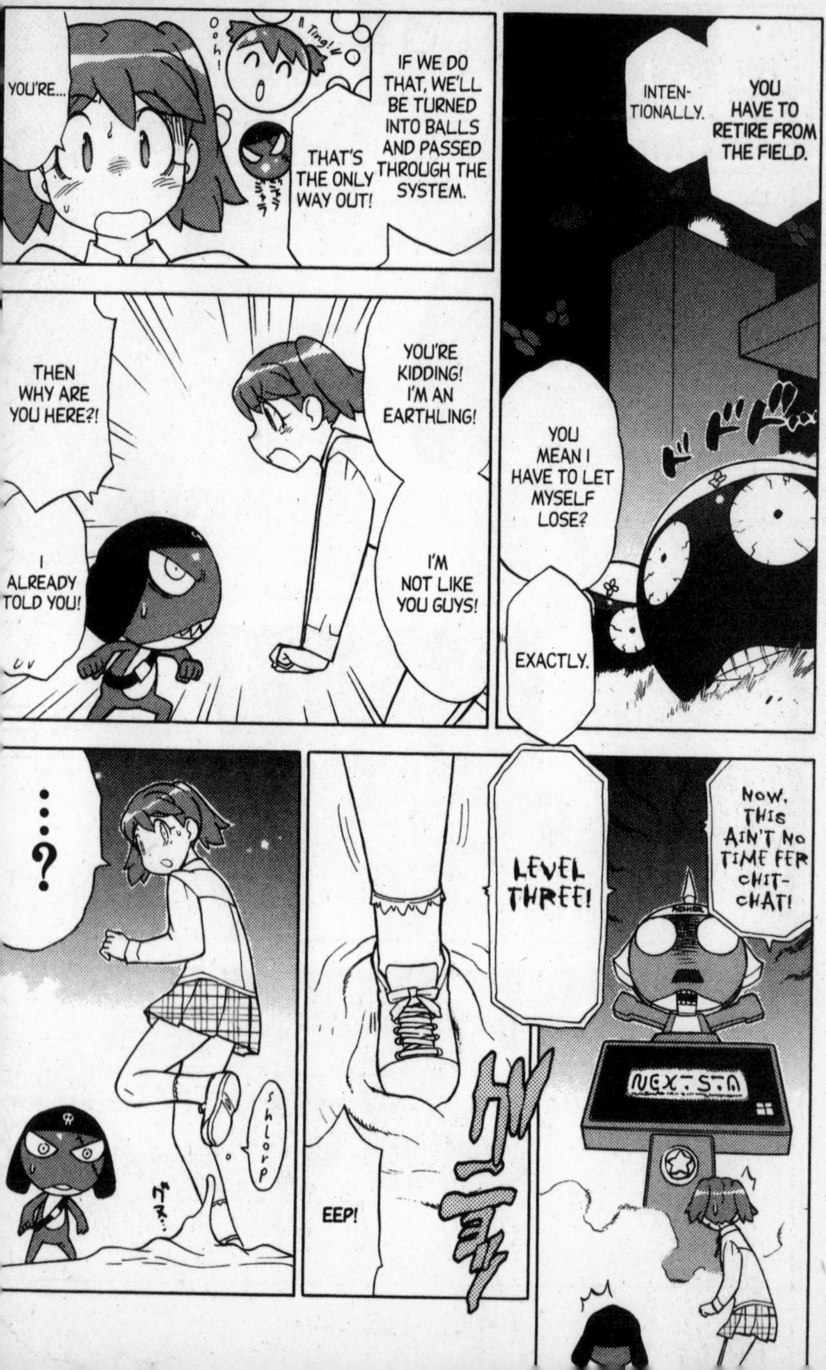
INTEN-TIONALLY.
YOU HAVE TO RETIRE FROM THE FIELD.
YOU MEAN I HAVE TO LET MYSELF LOSE?
EXACTLY.
IF WE DO THAT, WE'LL BE TURNED INTO BALLS AND PASSED THROUGH THE SYSTEM.
THAT'S THE ONLY WAY OUT!
Ting!
Ooh!
YOU'RE...
YOU'RE KIDDING! I'M AN EARTHLING!
I'M NOT LIKE YOU GUYS!
THEN WHY ARE YOU HERE?!
I ALREADY TOLD YOU!
NOW, THIS AIN'T NO TIME FER CHIT-CHAT!
LEVEL THREE!
NEXT STA
EEP!
...?
shlorp

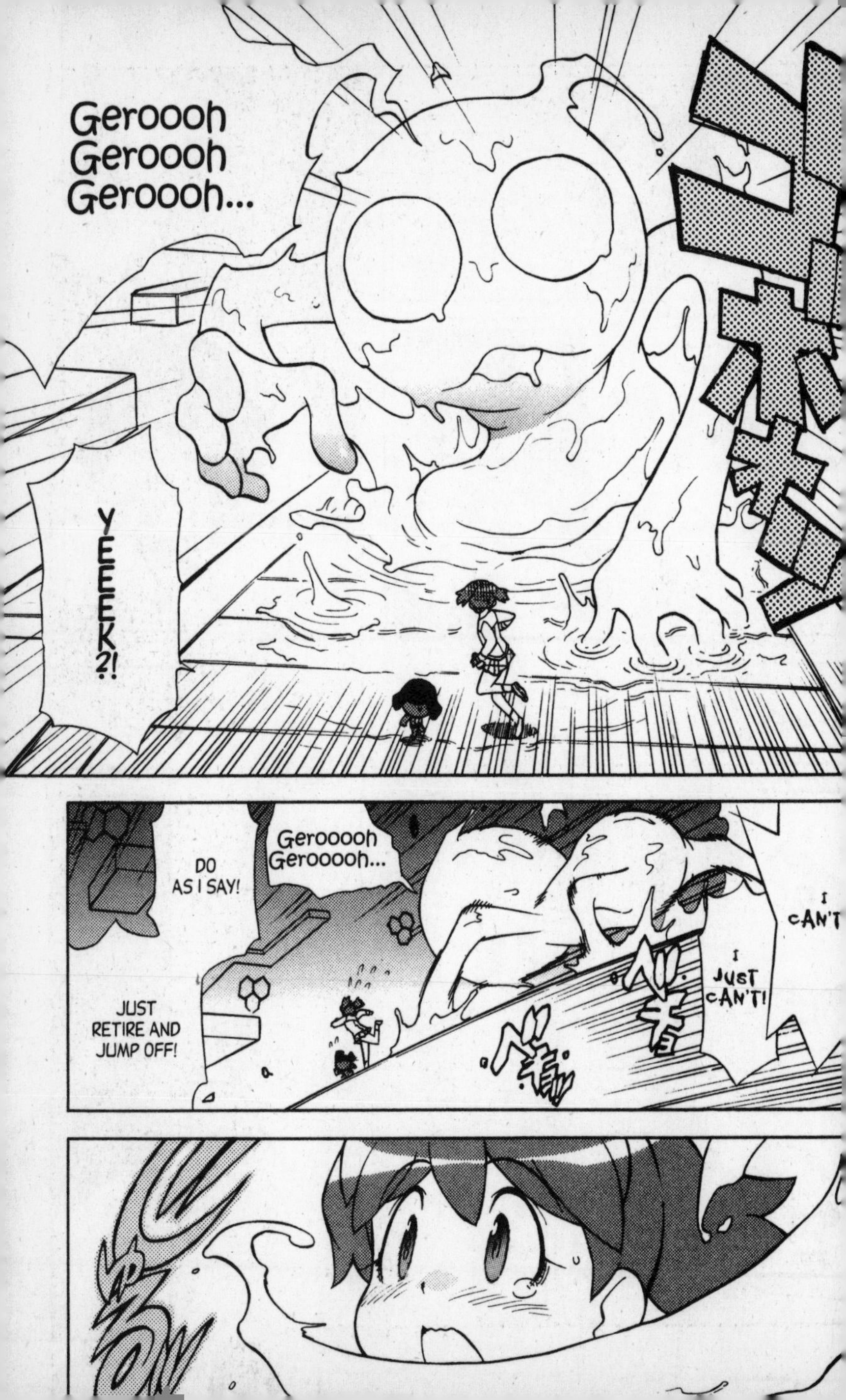
Geroooh
Geroooh
Geroooh...
YEEEK?!
I CAN'T
I JUST CAN'T!
Gerooooh Gerooooh...
DO AS I SAY!
JUST RETIRE AND JUMP OFF!

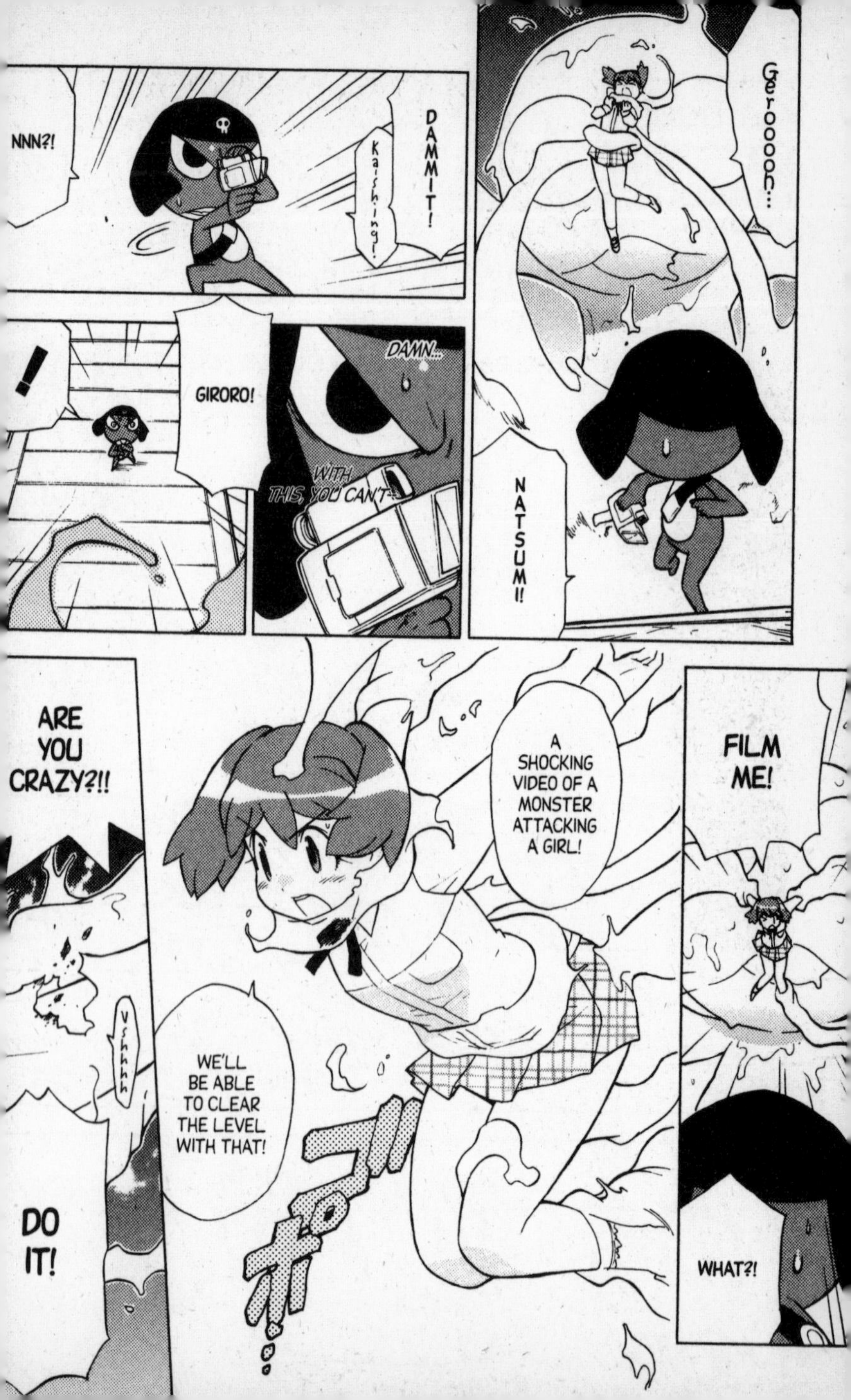
Geroooooh...
NATSUMI!
DAMMIT!
Kaishing!
NNN?!
DAMN...
WITH THIS, YOU CAN'T-
GIRORO!
!
FILM ME!
WHAT?!
A SHOCKING VIDEO OF A MONSTER ATTACKING A GIRL!
WE'LL BE ABLE TO CLEAR THE LEVEL WITH THAT!
ARE YOU CRAZY?!!
Vshhhh
DO IT!

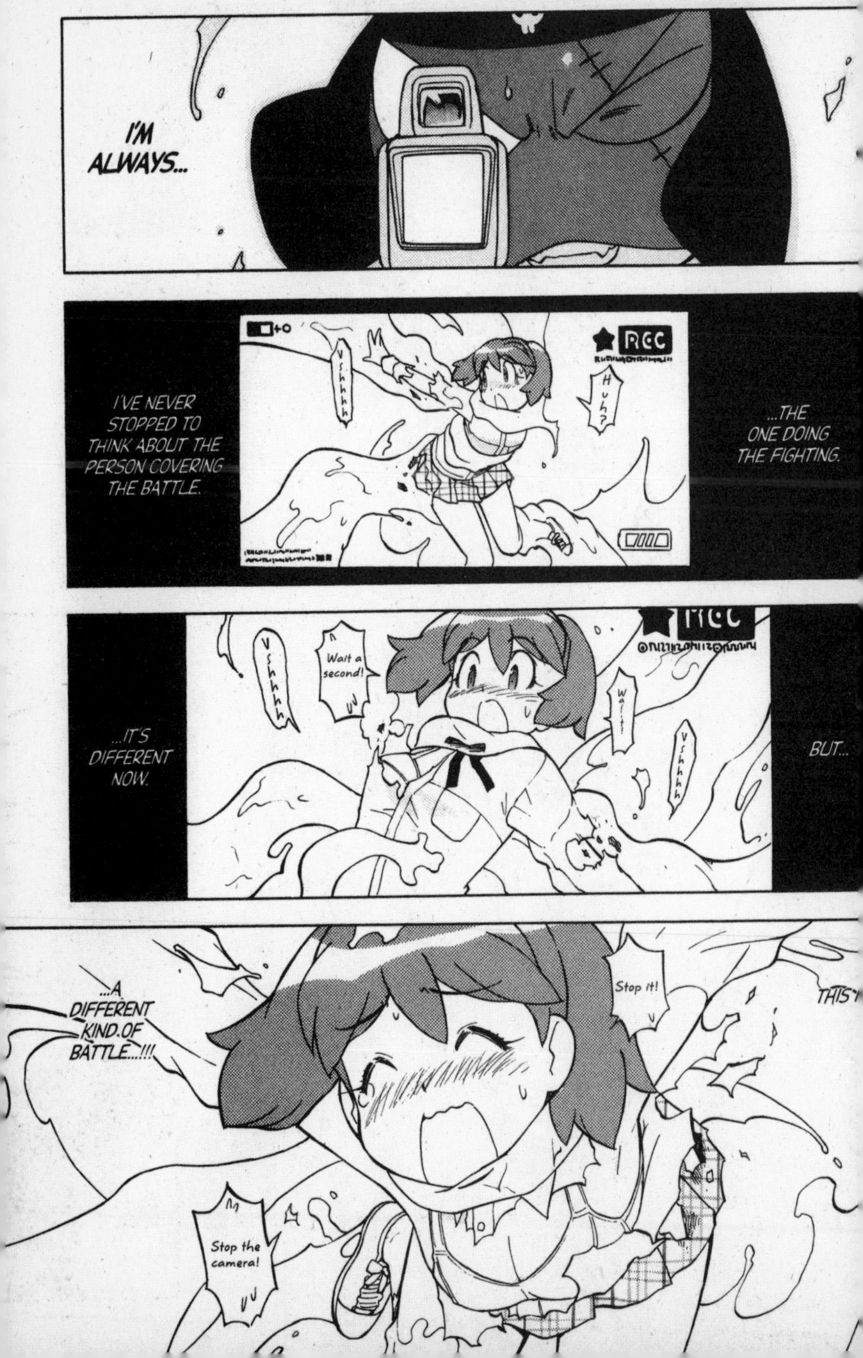
I'M ALWAYS...
...THE ONE DOING THE FIGHTING.
Huh?
Vshhhh
I'VE NEVER STOPPED TO THINK ABOUT THE PERSON COVERING THE BATTLE.
REC
BUT...
REC
Vshhhh
Wait!
Wait a second!
Vshhhh
...IT'S DIFFERENT NOW.
THIS
Stop it!
Stop the camera!
...A DIFFERENT KIND OF BATTLE...!!!

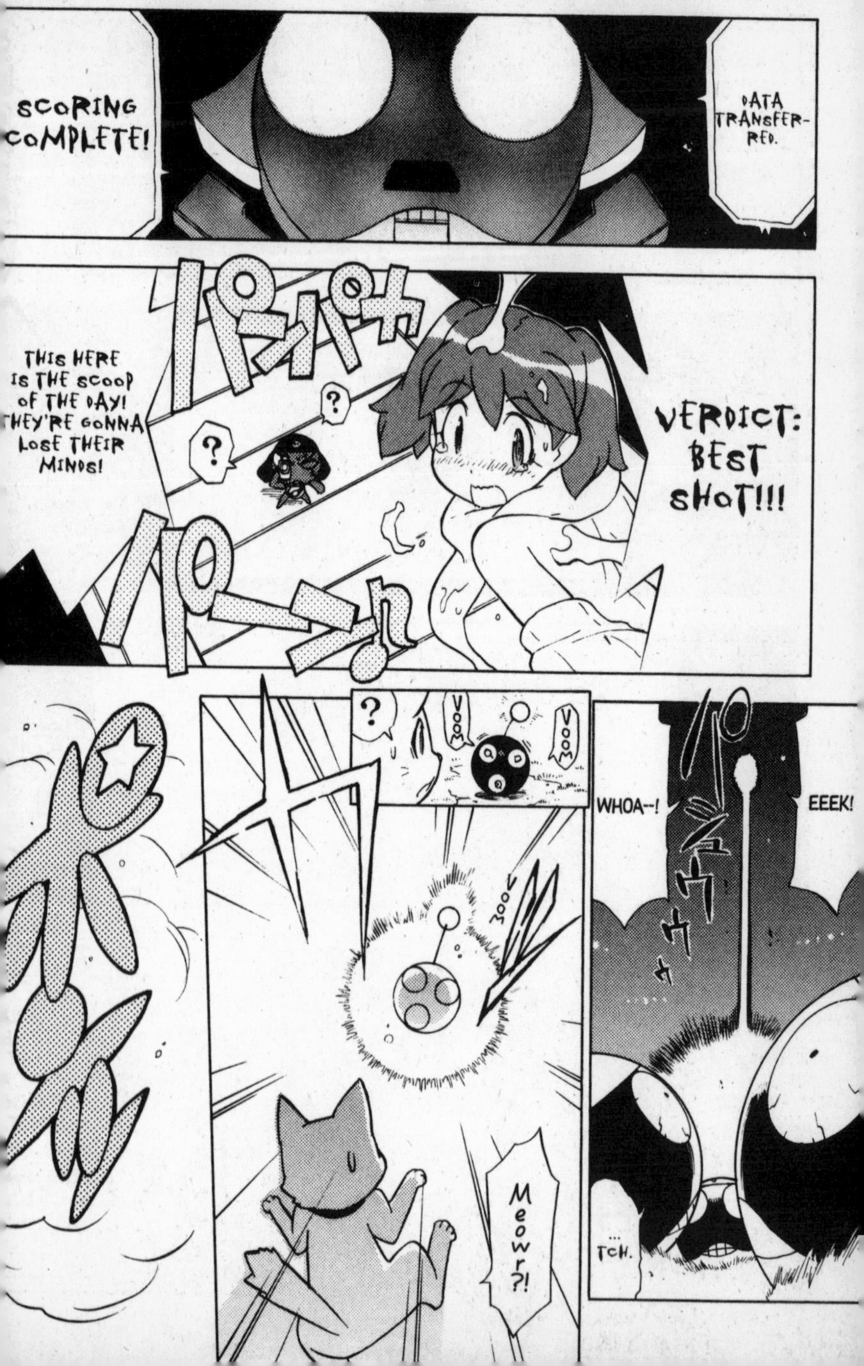
DATA TRANSFER-RED.
SCORING COMPLETE!
VERDICT: BEST SHOT!!!
?
?
THIS HERE IS THE SCOOP OF THE DAY! THEY'RE GONNA LOSE THEIR MINDS!
パッパカ
パーン
EEEK!
WHOA--!
... TCH.
VOOM
VOOM
?
VOOM
Meowr?!

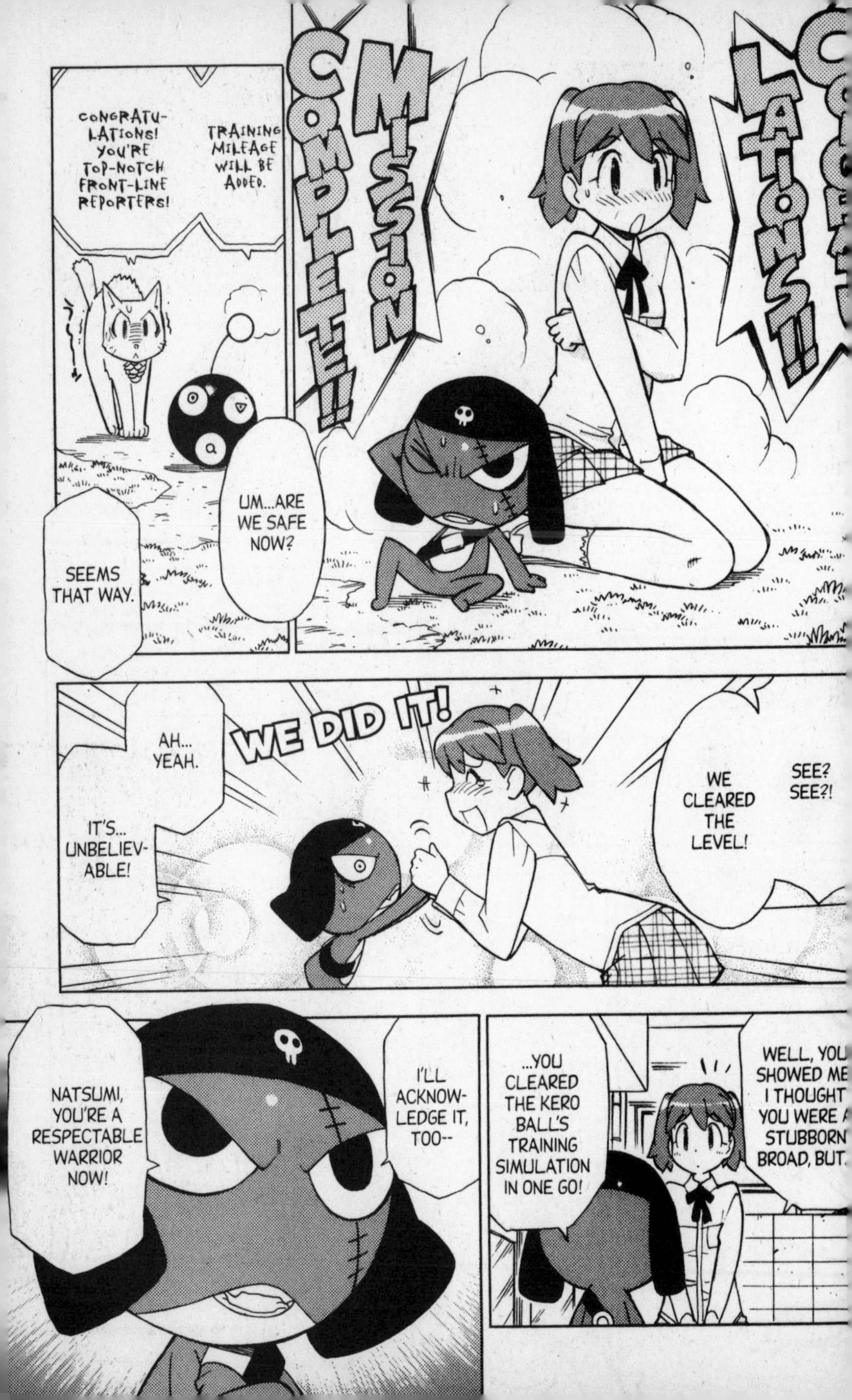
LATIONS!!
MISSION COMPLETE!!
UM...ARE WE SAFE NOW?
TRAINING MILEAGE WILL BE ADDED.
CONGRATU-LATIONS! YOU'RE TOP-NOTCH FRONT-LINE REPORTERS!
SEEMS THAT WAY.
SEE? SEE?!
WE CLEARED THE LEVEL!
WE DID IT!
AH... YEAH.
IT'S... UNBELIEV-ABLE!
WELL, YOU SHOWED ME I THOUGHT YOU WERE A STUBBORN BROAD, BUT
...YOU CLEARED THE KERO BALL'S TRAINING SIMULATION IN ONE GO!
I'LL ACKNOW-LEDGE IT, TOO--
NATSUMI, YOU'RE A RESPECTABLE WARRIOR NOW!

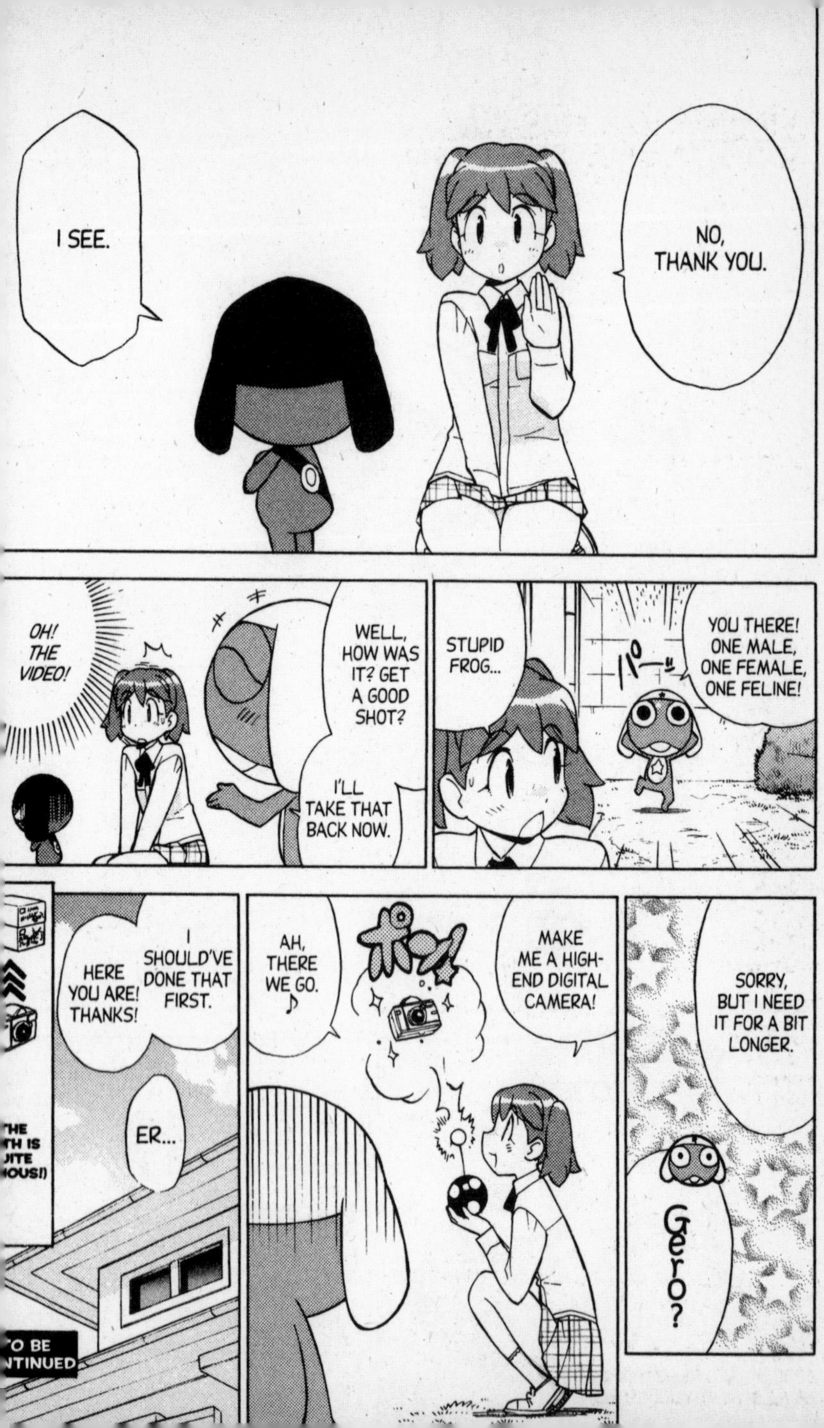
NO, THANK YOU.
I SEE.
YOU THERE! ONE MALE, ONE FEMALE, ONE FELINE!
STUPID FROG...
WELL, HOW WAS IT? GET A GOOD SHOT?
I'LL TAKE THAT BACK NOW.
OH! THE VIDEO!
SORRY, BUT I NEED IT FOR A BIT LONGER.
Gero?
MAKE ME A HIGH-END DIGITAL CAMERA!
AH, THERE WE GO. ♪
I SHOULD'VE DONE THAT FIRST.
HERE YOU ARE! THANKS!
ER...
O BE NTINUED

ENCOUNTER CLXIII
FAREWELL, KEROROROBOT!

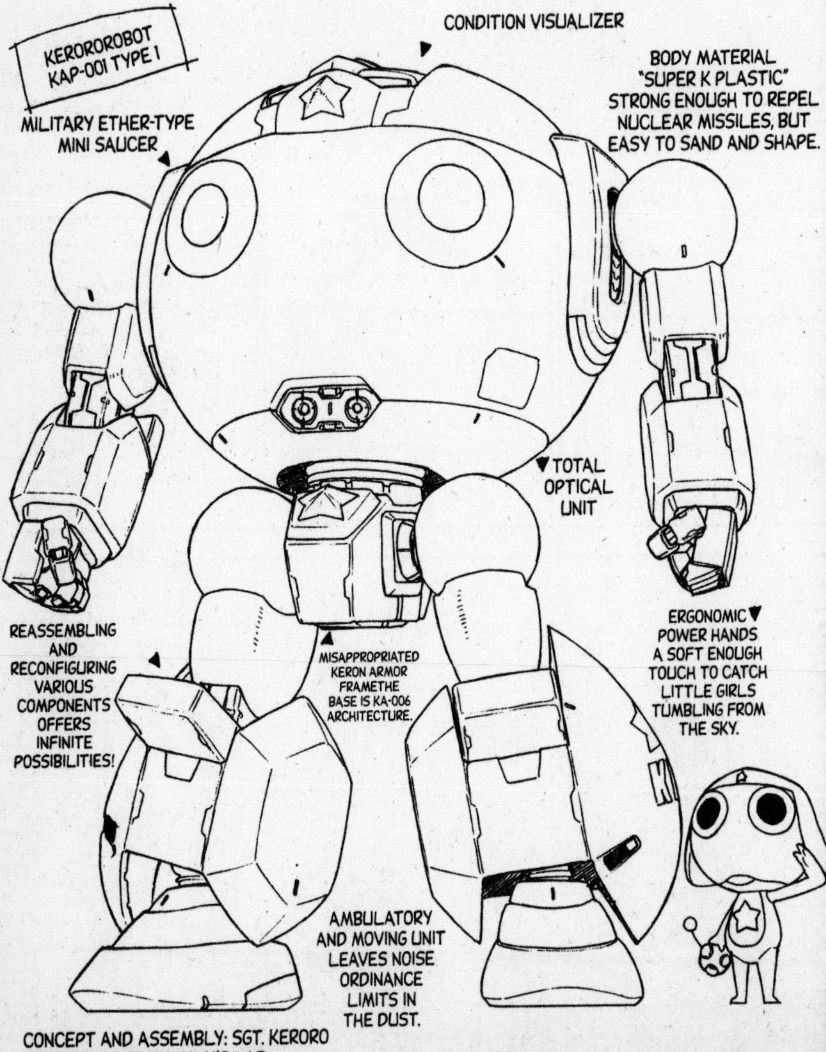
KEROROROBOT
KAP-001 TYPE 1
CONDITION VISUALIZER
BODY MATERIAL "SUPER K PLASTIC" STRONG ENOUGH TO REPEL NUCLEAR MISSILES, BUT EASY TO SAND AND SHAPE.
MILITARY ETHER-TYPE MINI SAUCER
TOTAL OPTICAL UNIT
ERGONOMIC POWER HANDS A SOFT ENOUGH TOUCH TO CATCH LITTLE GIRLS TUMBLING FROM THE SKY.
MISAPPROPRIATED KERON ARMOR FRAMETHE BASE IS KA-006 ARCHITECTURE.
REASSEMBLING AND RECONFIGURING VARIOUS COMPONENTS OFFERS INFINITE POSSIBILITIES!
AMBULATORY AND MOVING UNIT LEAVES NOISE ORDINANCE LIMITS IN THE DUST.

CONCEPT AND ASSEMBLY: SGT. KERORO
DEVELOPMENT: KULULU'S LAB

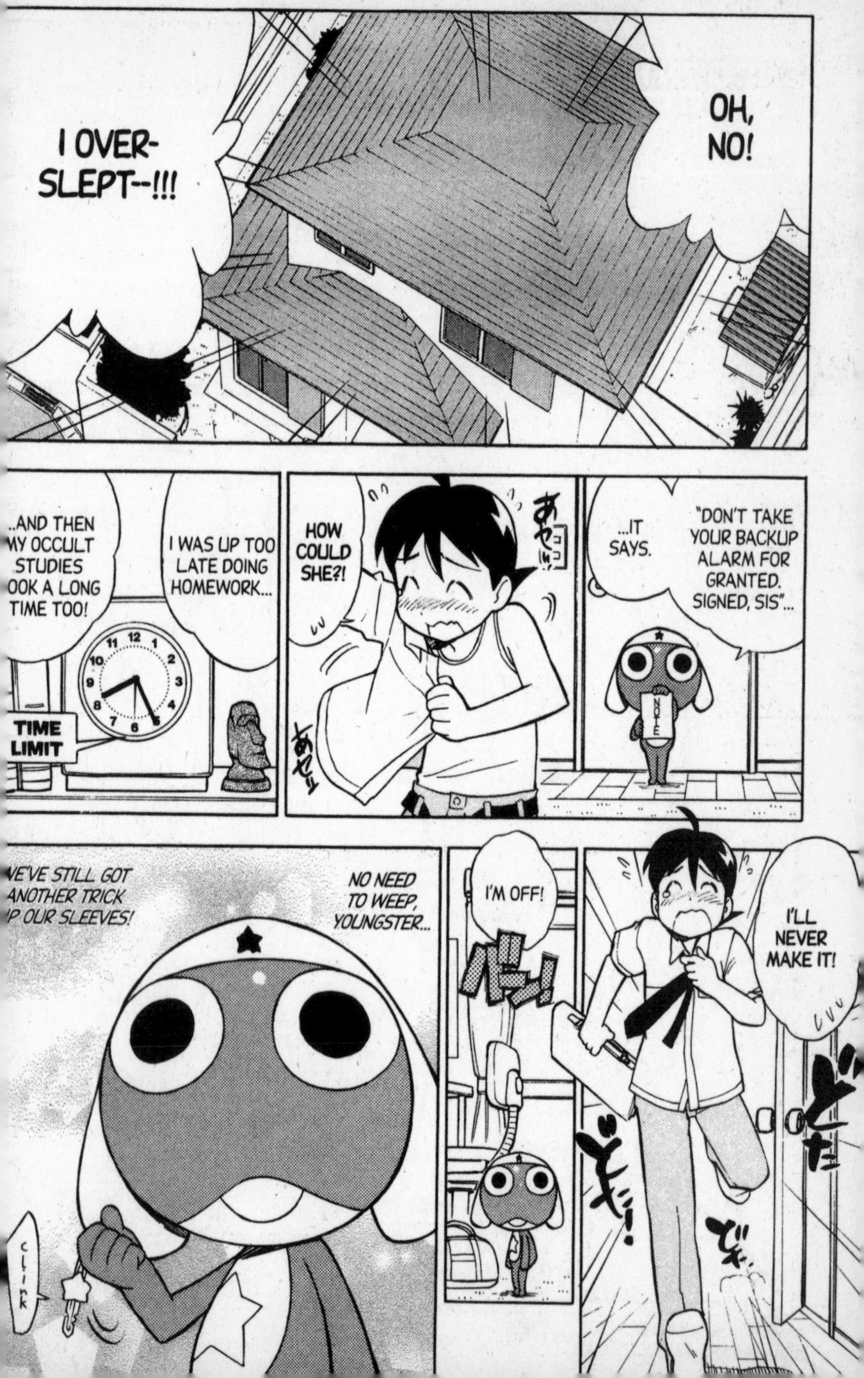
OH, NO!
I OVER-SLEPT--!!!
"DON'T TAKE YOUR BACKUP ALARM FOR GRANTED. SIGNED, SIS"...
...IT SAYS.
HOW COULD SHE?!
I WAS UP TOO LATE DOING HOMEWORK...
..AND THEN MY OCCULT STUDIES OOK A LONG TIME TOO!
TIME LIMIT
NOTE
I'LL NEVER MAKE IT!
I'M OFF!
NO NEED TO WEEP, YOUNGSTER...
VE'VE STILL GOT ANOTHER TRICK P OUR SLEEVES!
clink

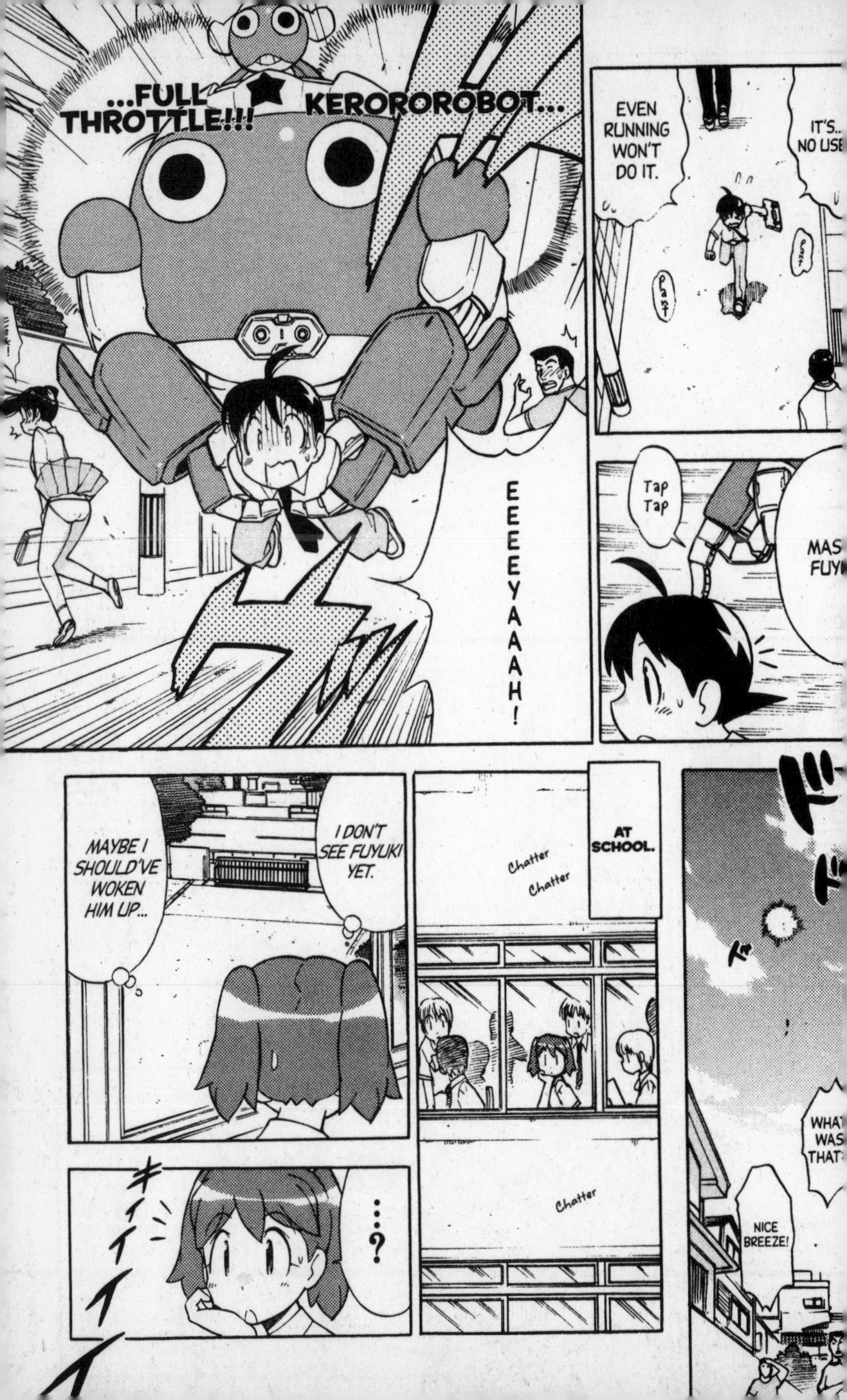
IT'S.. NO USE
EVEN RUNNING WON'T DO IT.
Pant
Pant
MAS- FUY
Tap Tap
KERORORORBOT...
...FULL THROTTLE!!!
EEEEYAAAAH!
ドドド
WHAT WAS THAT
NICE BREEZE!
AT SCHOOL.
Chatter
Chatter
Chatter
I DON'T SEE FUYUKI YET.
MAYBE I SHOULD'VE WOKEN HIM UP...
キィィィ
...?

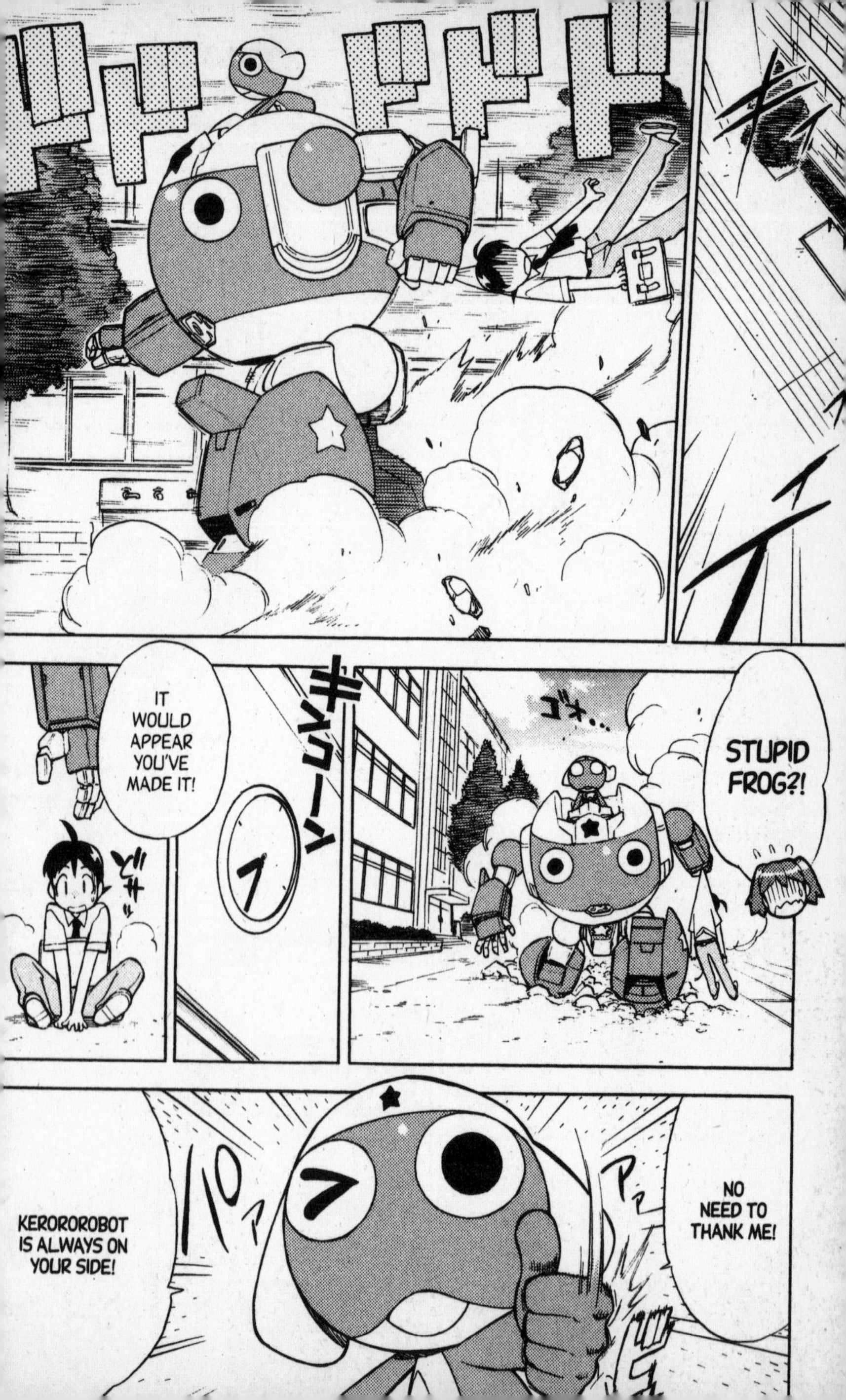
STUPID FROG?!
IT WOULD APPEAR YOU'VE MADE IT!
NO NEED TO THANK ME!
KERORO ROBOT IS ALWAYS ON YOUR SIDE!

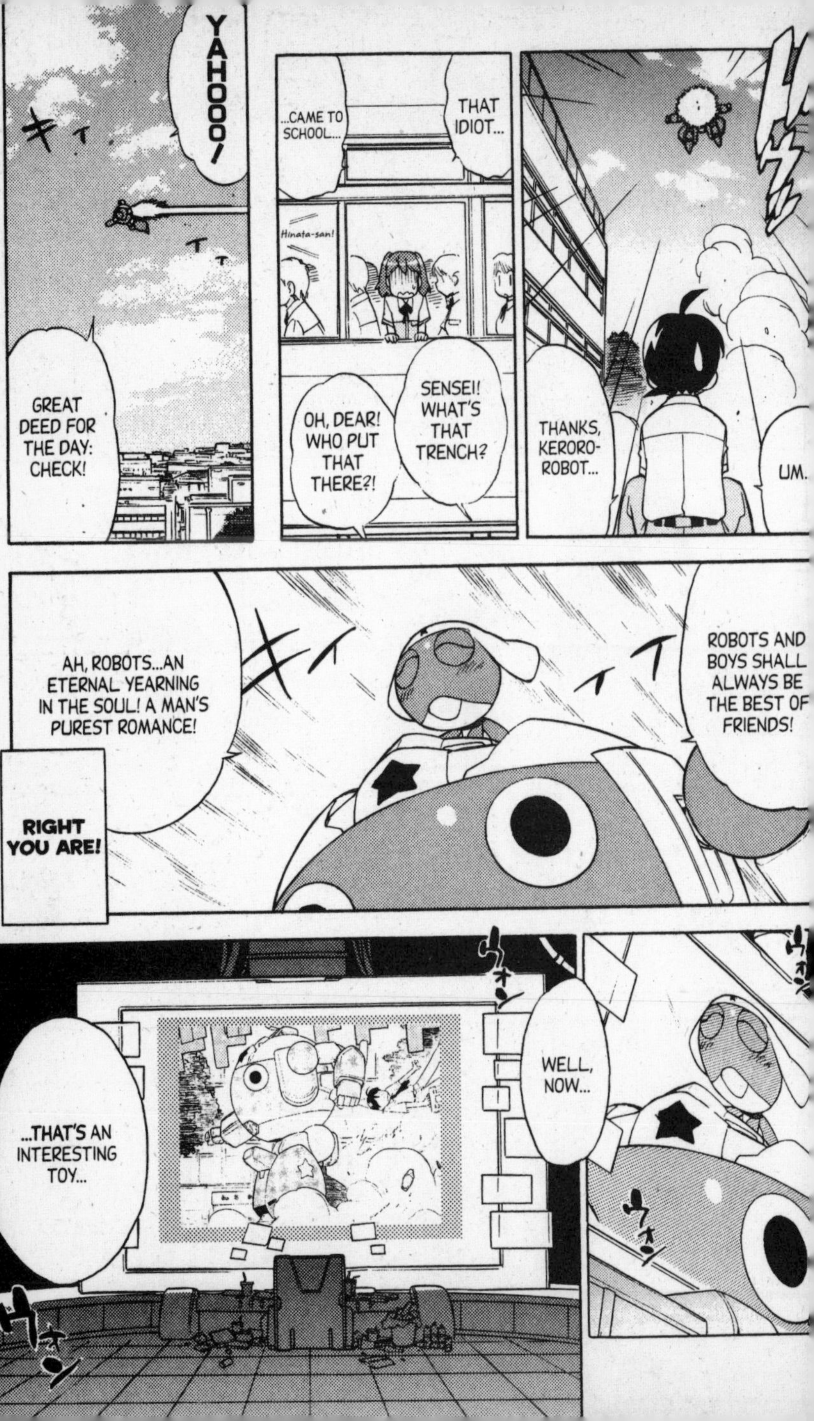
UM.
THANKS, KERORO-ROBOT...
THAT IDIOT...
...CAME TO SCHOOL...
Hinata-san!
SENSEI! WHAT'S THAT TRENCH?
OH, DEAR! WHO PUT THAT THERE?!
YAHOOO!
GREAT DEED FOR THE DAY: CHECK!
ROBOTS AND BOYS SHALL ALWAYS BE THE BEST OF FRIENDS!
AH, ROBOTS...AN ETERNAL YEARNING IN THE SOUL! A MAN'S PUREST ROMANCE!
RIGHT YOU ARE!
WELL, NOW...
...THAT'S AN INTERESTING TOY...

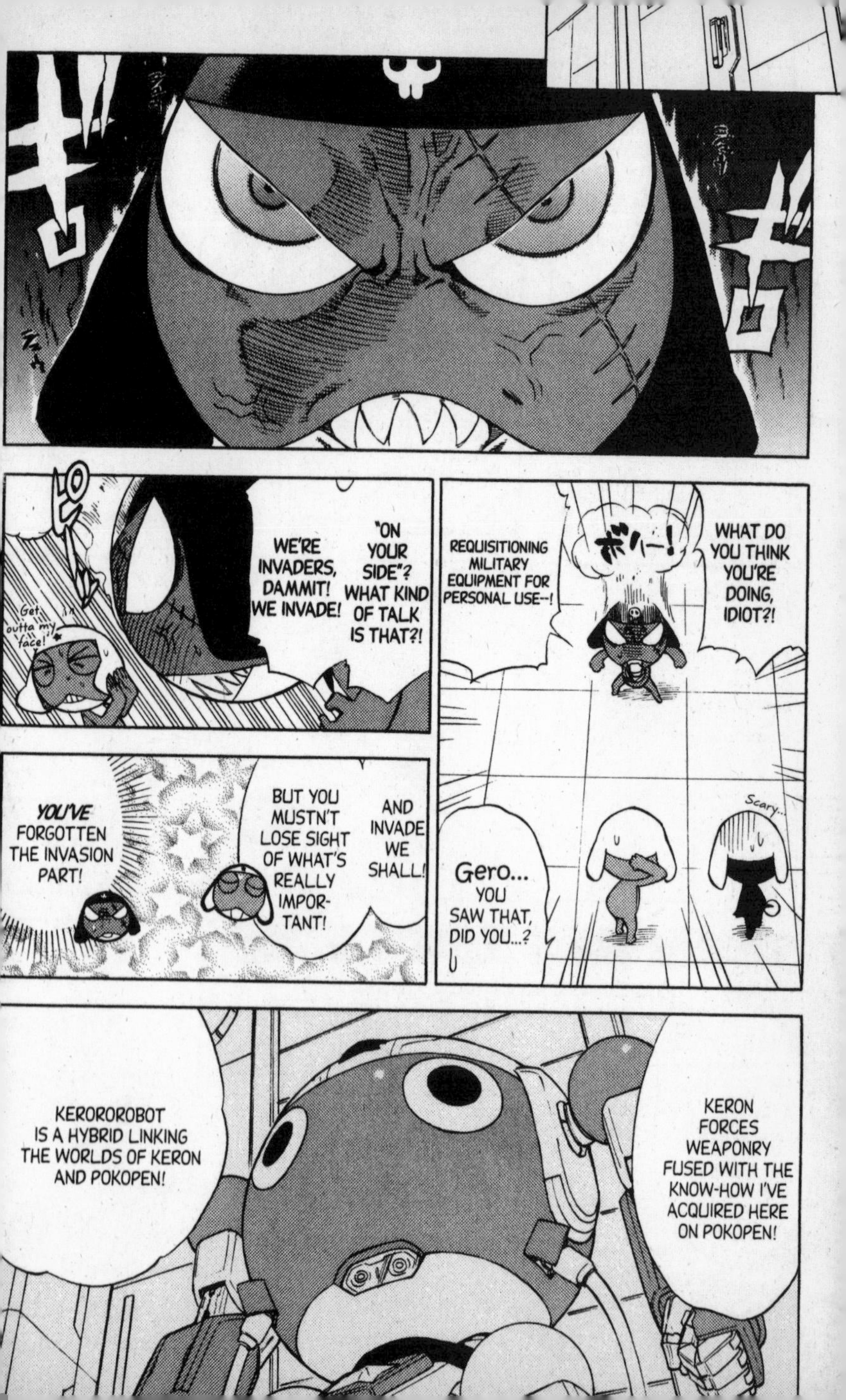
ギロ
ギロ
WHAT DO YOU THINK YOU'RE DOING, IDIOT?!
REQUISITIONING MILITARY EQUIPMENT FOR PERSONAL USE--!
ボハー!
Scary...
Gero... YOU SAW THAT, DID YOU...?
"ON YOUR SIDE"? WHAT KIND OF TALK IS THAT?!
WE'RE INVADERS, DAMMIT! WE INVADE!
Get outta my face!
AND INVADE WE SHALL!
BUT YOU MUSTN'T LOSE SIGHT OF WHAT'S REALLY IMPORTANT!
YOU'VE FORGOTTEN THE INVASION PART!
KERON FORCES WEAPONRY FUSED WITH THE KNOW-HOW I'VE ACQUIRED HERE ON POKOPEN!
KEROROROBOT IS A HYBRID LINKING THE WORLDS OF KERON AND POKOPEN!

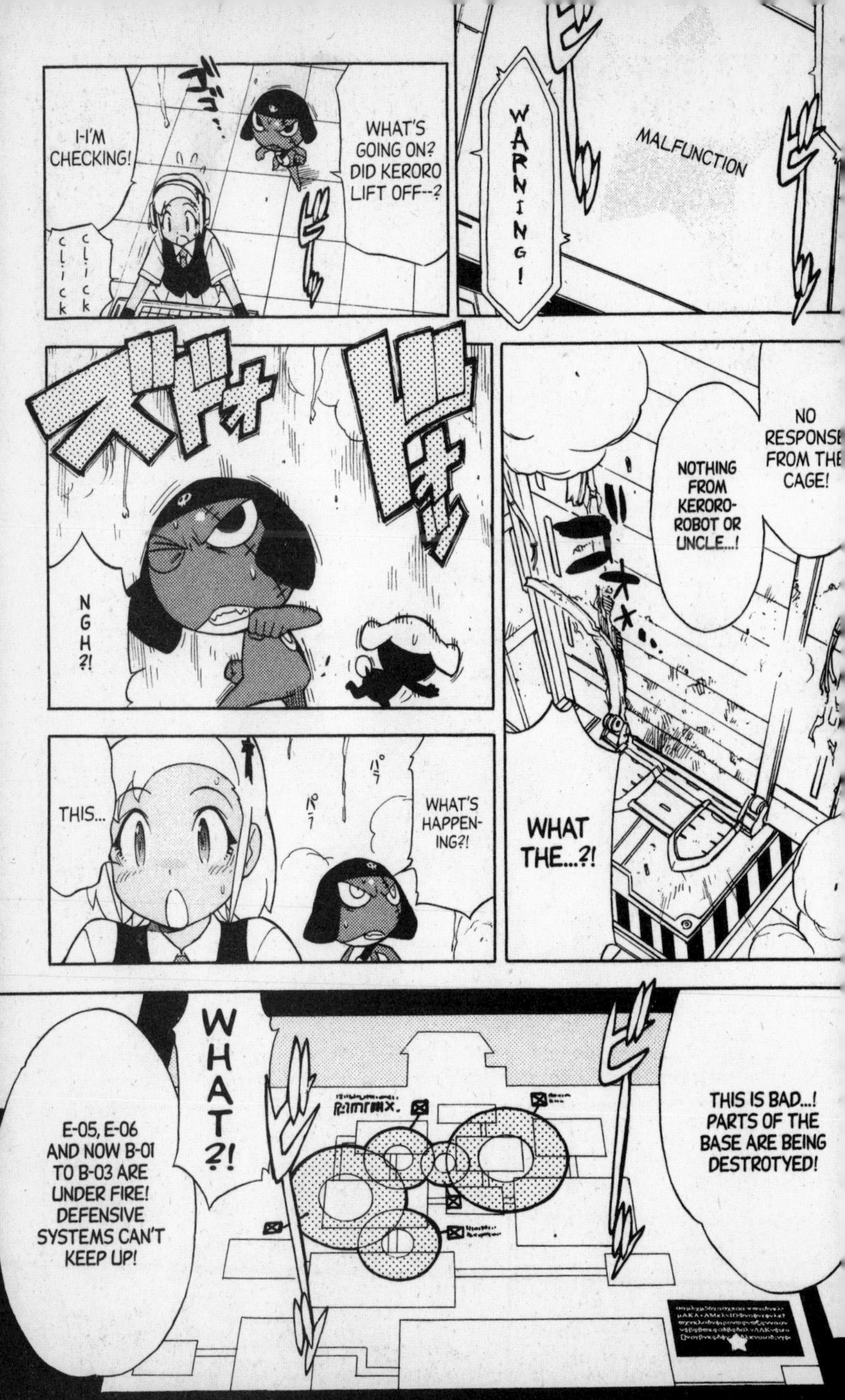
WARNING!
MALFUNCTION
WHAT'S GOING ON? DID KERORO LIFT OFF--?
I-I'M CHECKING!
click click
NO RESPONSE FROM THE CAGE!
NOTHING FROM KERORO-ROBOT OR UNCLE...!
WHAT THE...?!
NGH?!
WHAT'S HAPPEN-ING?!
THIS...
THIS IS BAD...! PARTS OF THE BASE ARE BEING DESTROTYED!
WHAT?!
E-05, E-06 AND NOW B-01 TO B-03 ARE UNDER FIRE! DEFENSIVE SYSTEMS CAN'T KEEP UP!

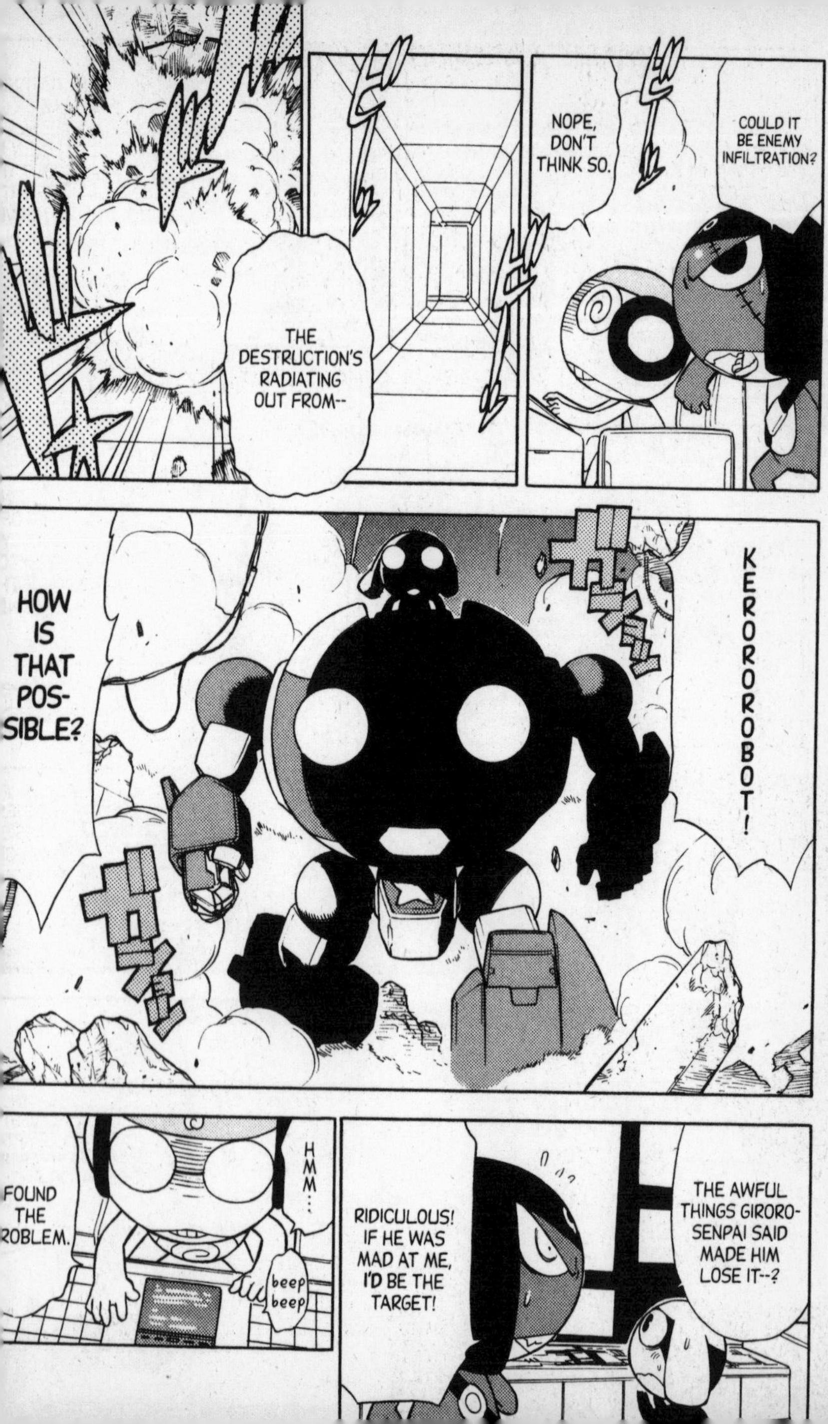
COULD IT BE ENEMY INFILTRATION?
NOPE, DON'T THINK SO.
THE DESTRUCTION'S RADIATING OUT FROM--
KEROROROBOT!
HOW IS THAT POS-SIBLE?
THE AWFUL THINGS GIRORO-SENPAI SAID MADE HIM LOSE IT--?
RIDICULOUS! IF HE WAS MAD AT ME, I'D BE THE TARGET!
HMM...
beep beep
FOUND THE ROBLEM.

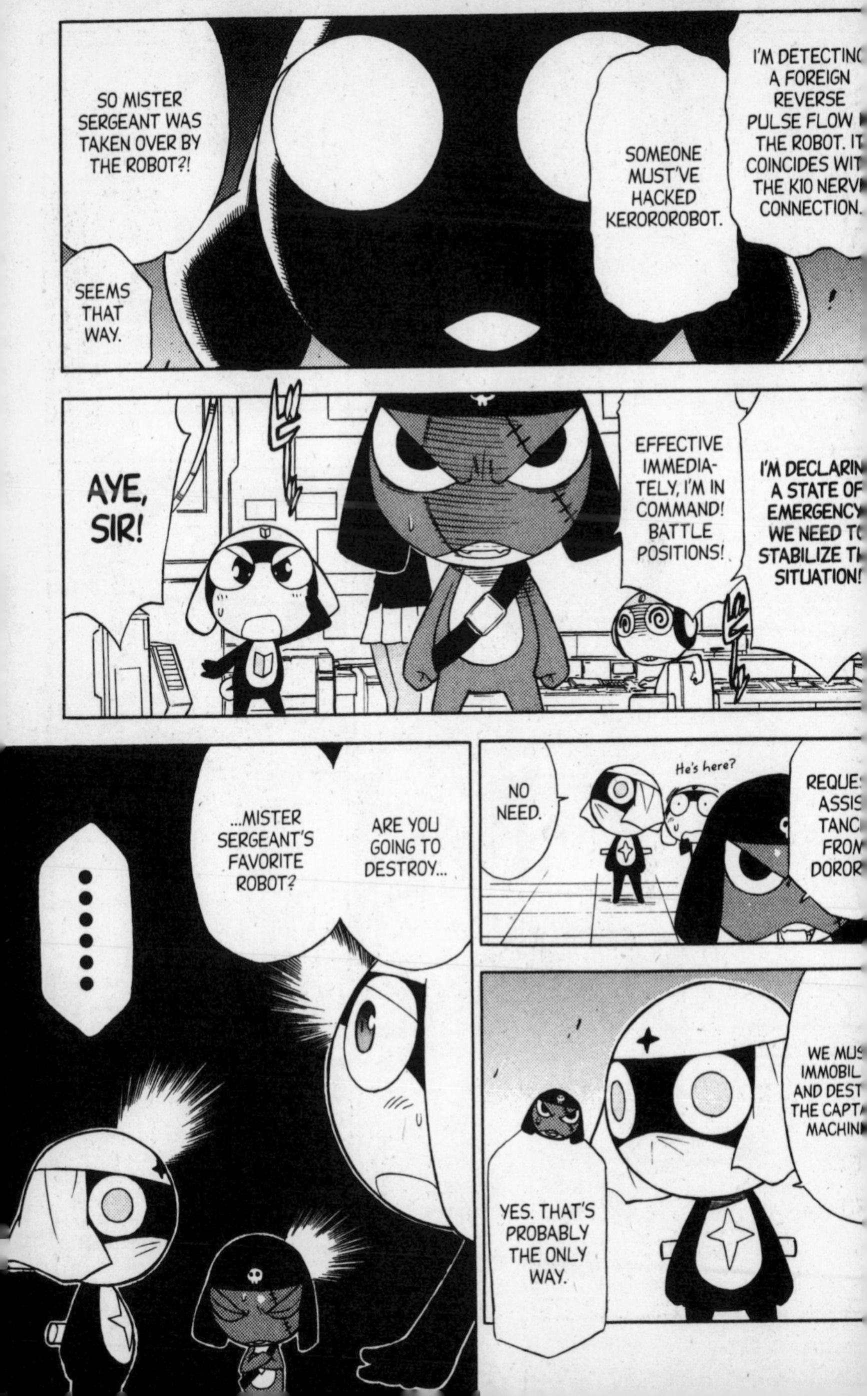

I'M DETECTIN A FOREIGN REVERSE PULSE FLOW THE ROBOT. IT COINCIDES WIT THE K10 NERV CONNECTION.
SOMEONE MUST'VE HACKED KERORO ROBOT.
SO MISTER SERGEANT WAS TAKEN OVER BY THE ROBOT?!
SEEMS THAT WAY.
I'M DECLARIN A STATE OF EMERGENCY WE NEED T STABILIZE T SITUATION!
EFFECTIVE IMMEDIA-TELY, I'M IN COMMAND! BATTLE POSITIONS!
AYE, SIR!
REQUE ASSIS TANC FROM DOROR
He's here?
NO NEED.
WE MUS IMMOBIL AND DEST THE CAPT MACHIN
YES. THAT'S PROBABLY THE ONLY WAY.
ARE YOU GOING TO DESTROY...
...MISTER SERGEANT'S FAVORITE ROBOT?
......

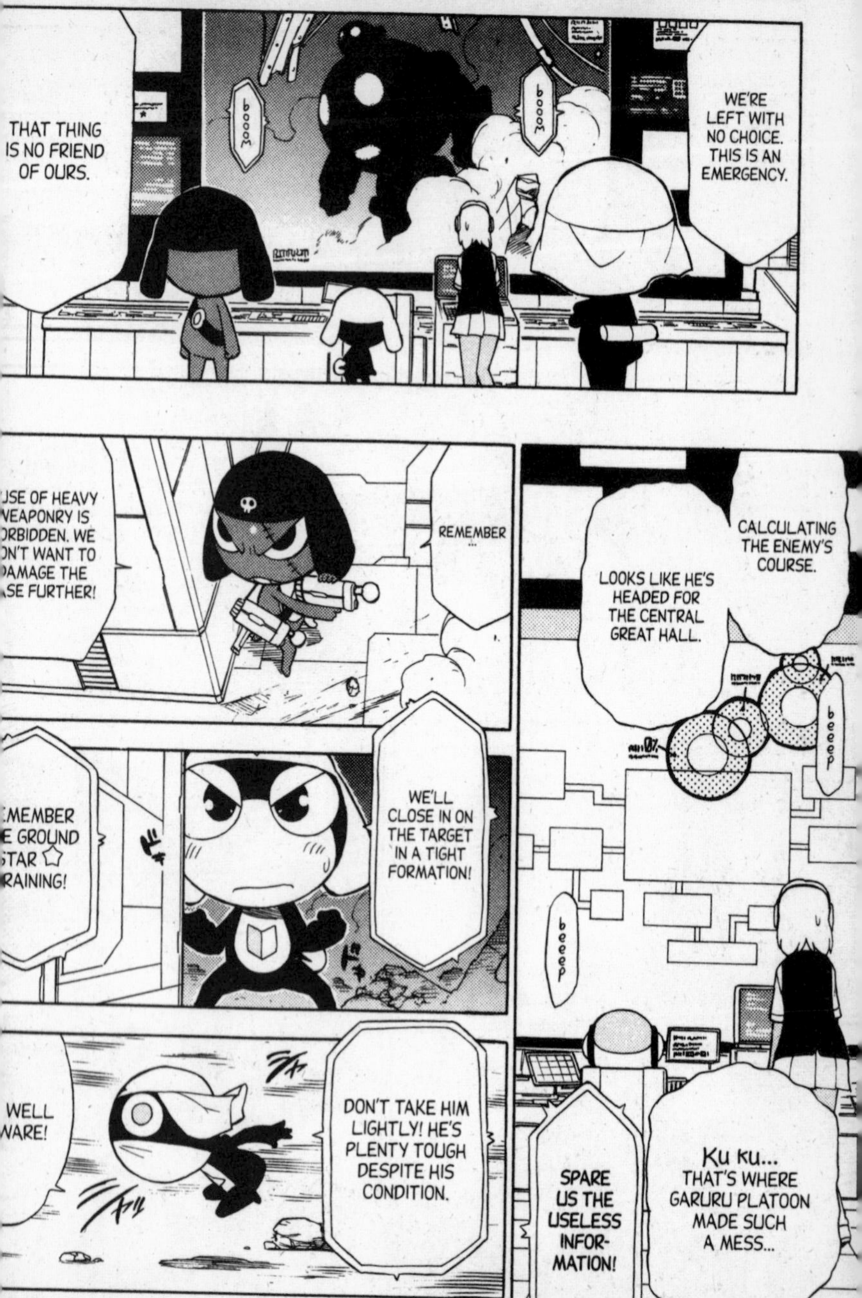
WE'RE LEFT WITH NO CHOICE. THIS IS AN EMERGENCY.
booom
booom
THAT THING IS NO FRIEND OF OURS.
CALCULATING THE ENEMY'S COURSE.
LOOKS LIKE HE'S HEADED FOR THE CENTRAL GREAT HALL.
beeep
beeep
Ku ku... THAT'S WHERE GARURU PLATOON MADE SUCH A MESS...
SPARE US THE USELESS INFOR-MATION!
REMEMBER...
JSE OF HEAVY VEAPONRY IS ORBIDDEN. WE ON'T WANT TO DAMAGE THE ASE FURTHER!
WE'LL CLOSE IN ON THE TARGET IN A TIGHT FORMATION!
EMEMBER E GROUND STAR ☆ RAINING!
DON'T TAKE HIM LIGHTLY! HE'S PLENTY TOUGH DESPITE HIS CONDITION.
WELL VARE!

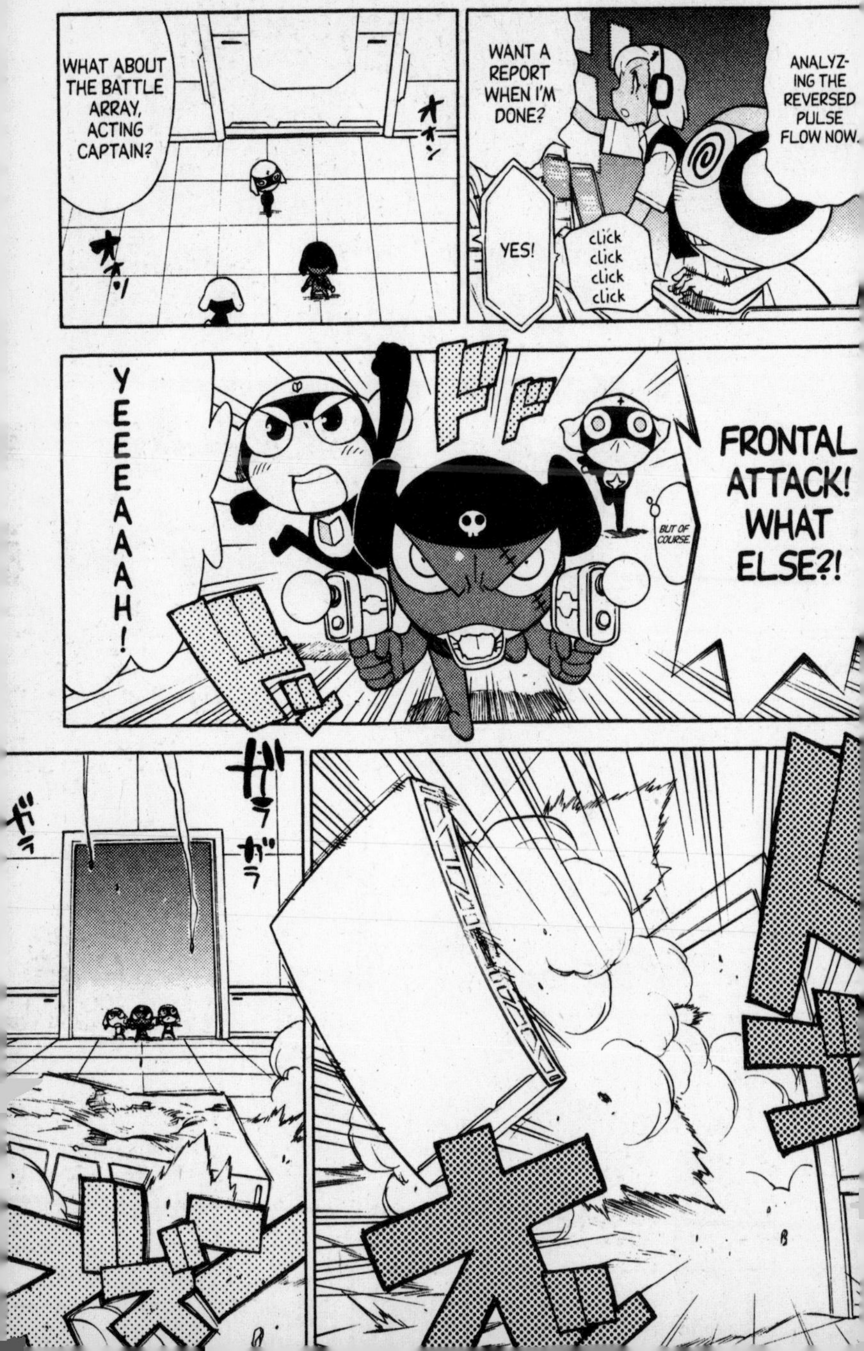
ANALYZ-ING THE REVERSED PULSE FLOW NOW.
WANT A REPORT WHEN I'M DONE?
click click click click
YES!
WHAT ABOUT THE BATTLE ARRAY, ACTING CAPTAIN?
FRONTAL ATTACK! WHAT ELSE?!
BUT OF COURSE.
YEEEAAAAH!

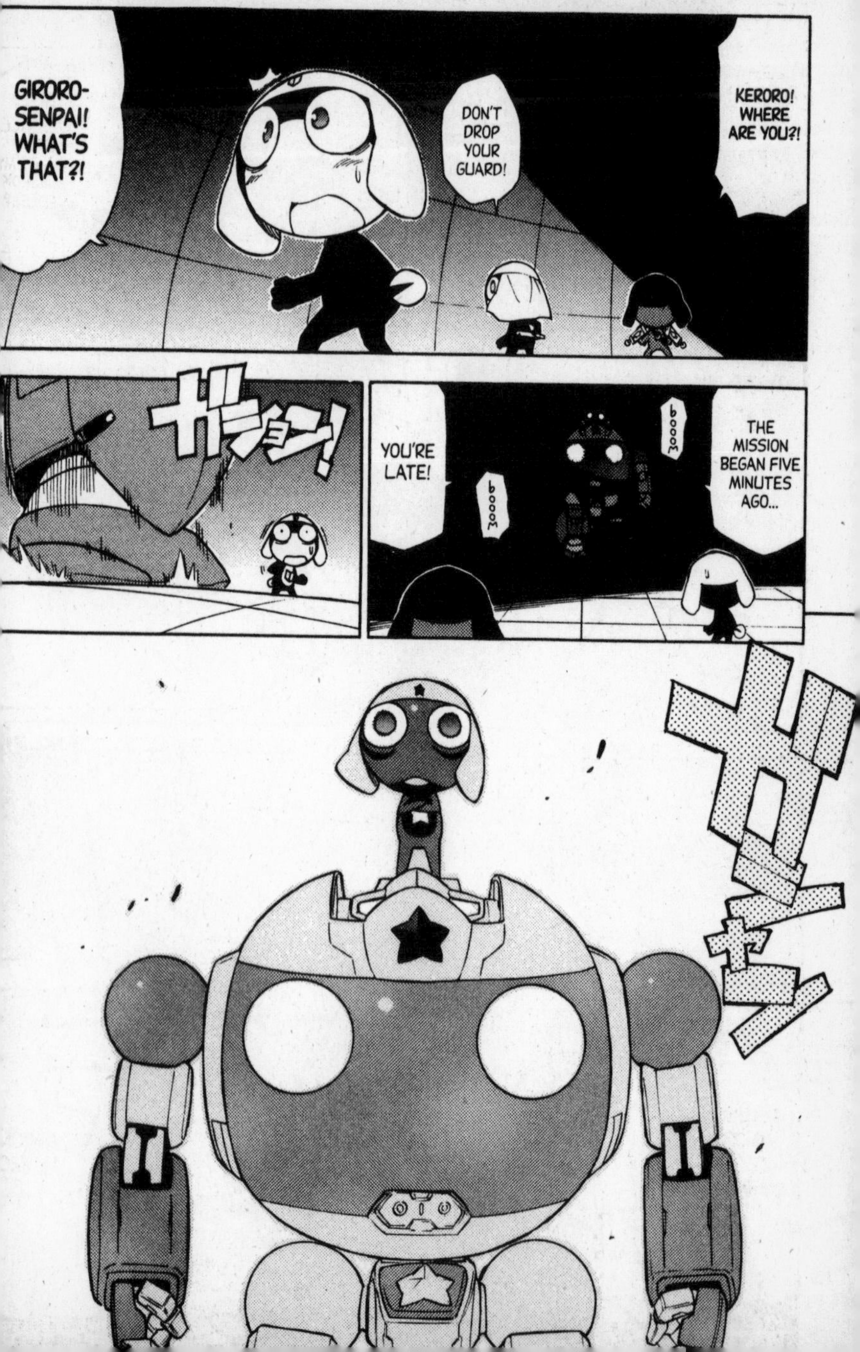
KERORO! WHERE ARE YOU?!
DON'T DROP YOUR GUARD!
GIRORO-SENPAI! WHAT'S THAT?!
THE MISSION BEGAN FIVE MINUTES AGO...
booom
YOU'RE LATE!
booom

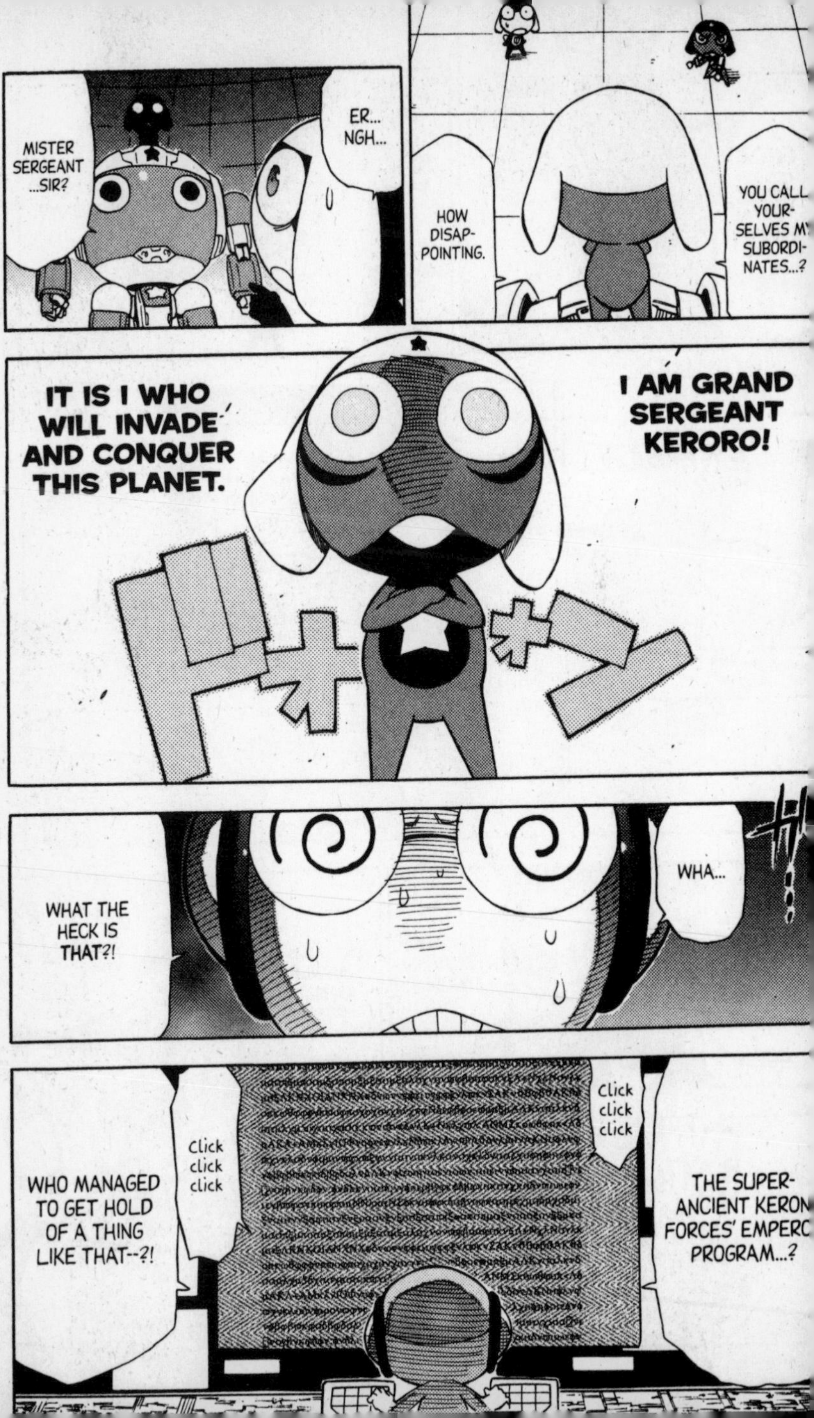
YOU CALL YOURSELVES MY SUBORDINATES...?
HOW DISAPPOINTING.
ER... NGH...
MISTER SERGEANT ...SIR?
I AM GRAND SERGEANT KERORO!
IT IS I WHO WILL INVADE AND CONQUER THIS PLANET.
WHA...
WHAT THE HECK IS THAT?!
THE SUPER-ANCIENT KERON FORCES' EMPERO PROGRAM...?
Click click click
Click click click
WHO MANAGED TO GET HOLD OF A THING LIKE THAT--?!

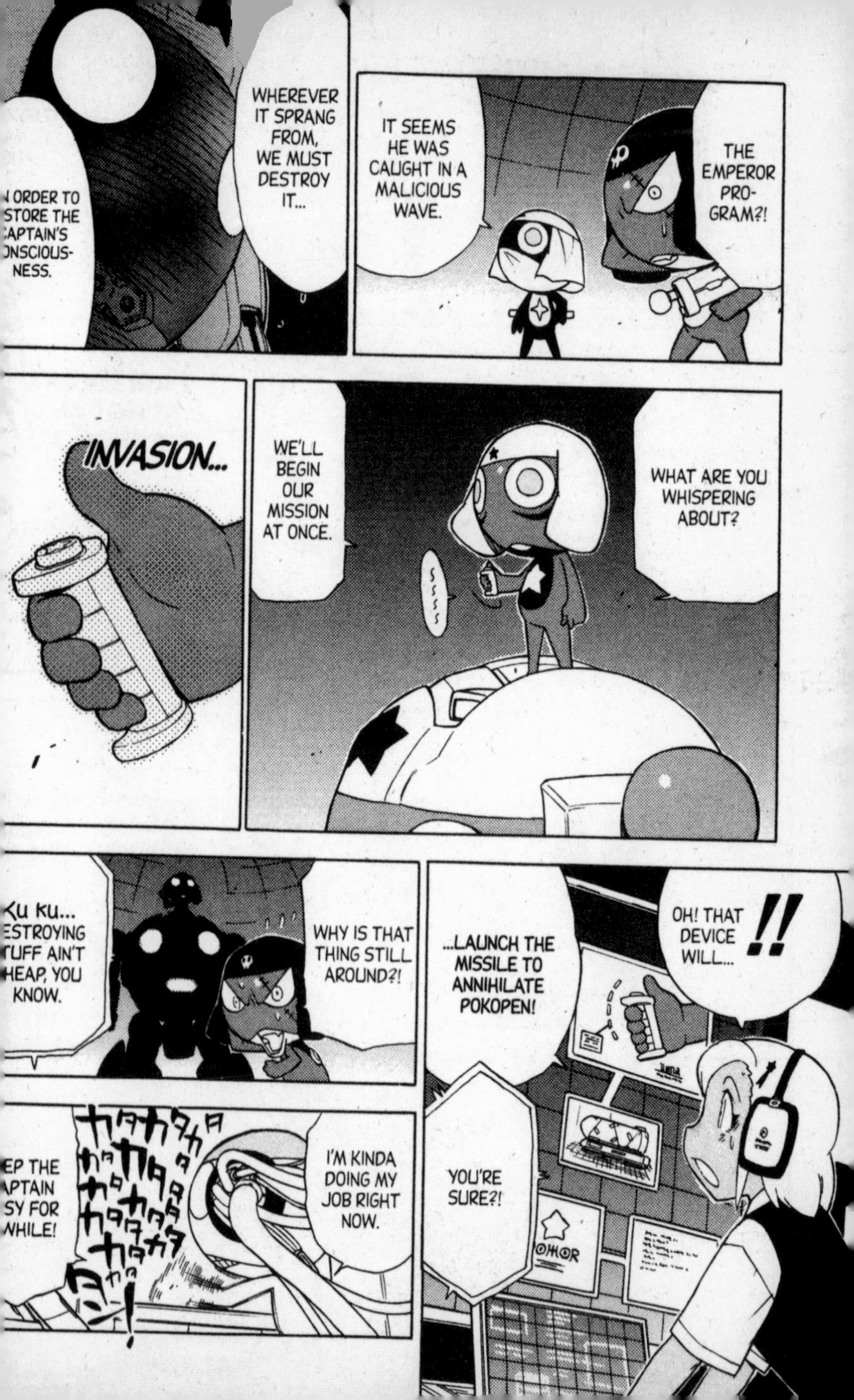
THE EMPEROR PROGRAM?!
IT SEEMS HE WAS CAUGHT IN A MALICIOUS WAVE.
WHEREVER IT SPRANG FROM, WE MUST DESTROY IT...
N ORDER TO STORE THE APTAIN'S ONSCIOUSNESS.
WHAT ARE YOU WHISPERING ABOUT?
WE'LL BEGIN OUR MISSION AT ONCE.
INVASION...
OH! THAT DEVICE WILL... !!
...LAUNCH THE MISSILE TO ANNIHILATE POKOPEN!
YOU'RE SURE?!
WHY IS THAT THING STILL AROUND?!
KU KU... ESTROYING TUFF AIN'T HEAP, YOU KNOW.
I'M KINDA DOING MY JOB RIGHT NOW.
カタカタカタ
EP THE APTAIN SY FOR WHILE!

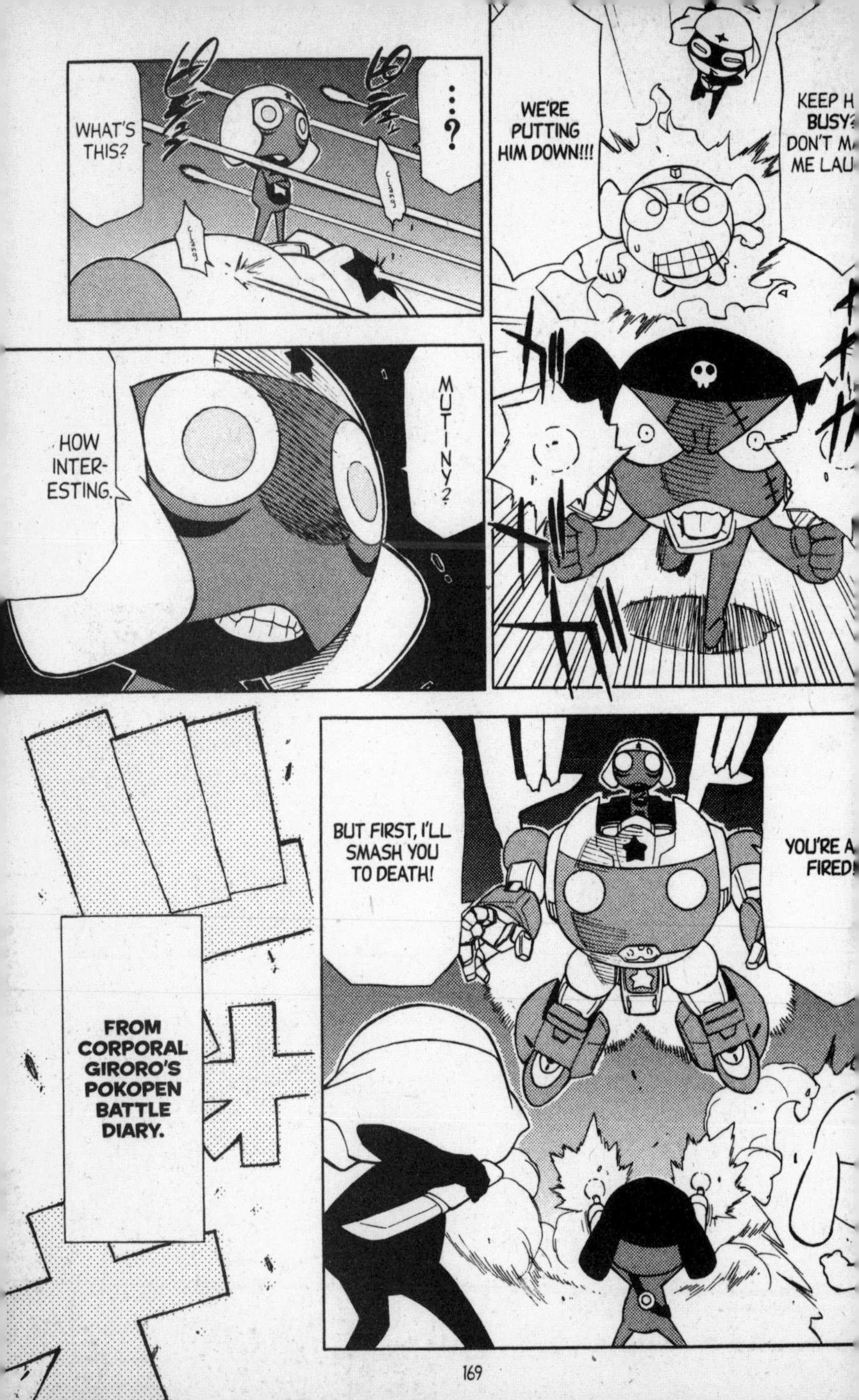
KEEP H
BUSY?
DON'T M
ME LAU
WE'RE PUTTING HIM DOWN!!!
...?
WHAT'S THIS?
clang
clang
MUTINY?
HOW INTERESTING.
YOU'RE A
FIRED!
BUT FIRST, I'LL SMASH YOU TO DEATH!
FROM CORPORAL GIRORO'S POKOPEN BATTLE DIARY.

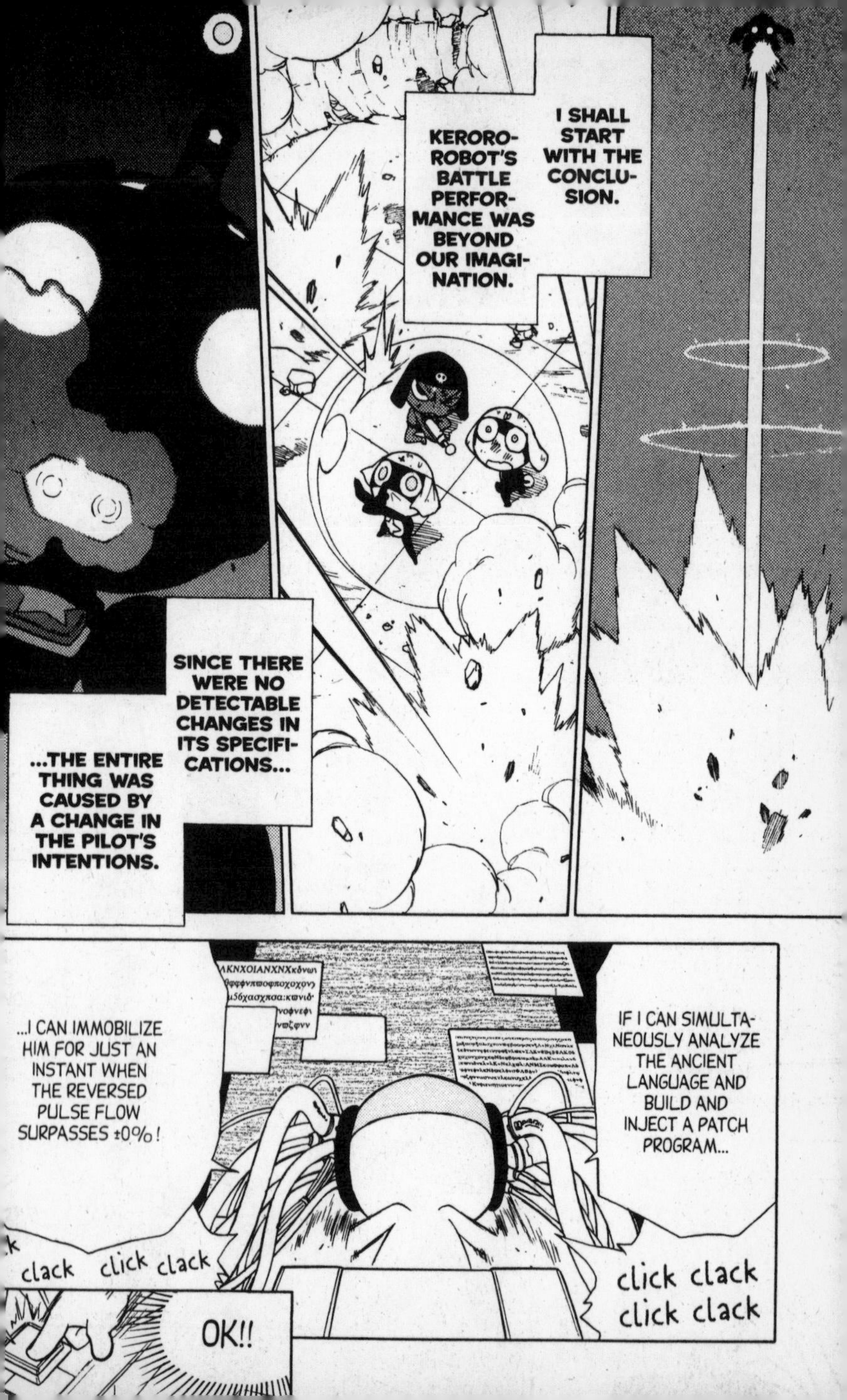
I SHALL START WITH THE CONCLU-SION.
KERORO-ROBOT'S BATTLE PERFOR-MANCE WAS BEYOND OUR IMAGI-NATION.
SINCE THERE WERE NO DETECTABLE CHANGES IN ITS SPECIFI-CATIONS...
...THE ENTIRE THING WAS CAUSED BY A CHANGE IN THE PILOT'S INTENTIONS.
IF I CAN SIMULTA-NEOUSLY ANALYZE THE ANCIENT LANGUAGE AND BUILD AND INJECT A PATCH PROGRAM...
click clack click clack
...I CAN IMMOBILIZE HIM FOR JUST AN INSTANT WHEN THE REVERSED PULSE FLOW SURPASSES ±0%!
clack click clack
OK!!

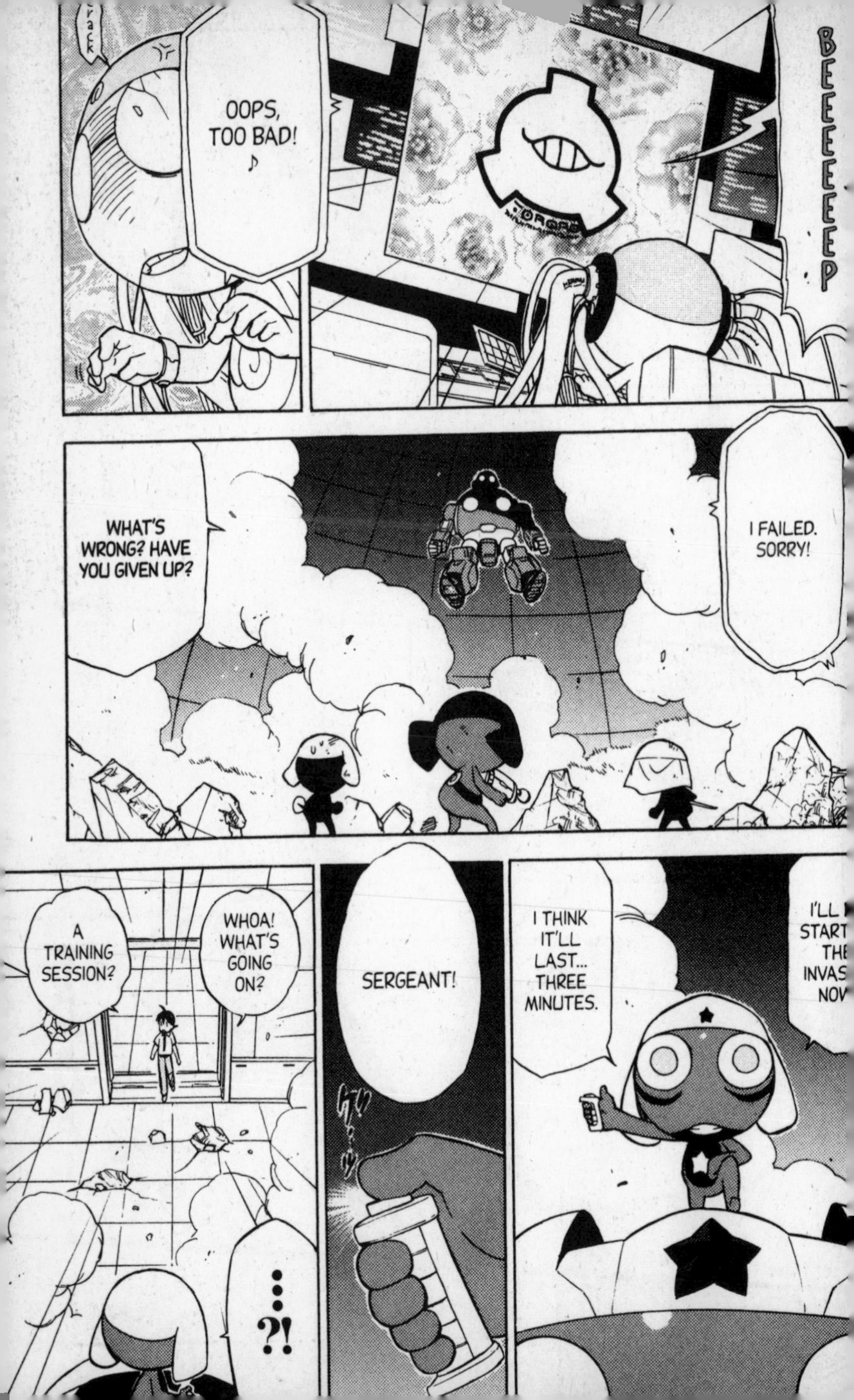
BEEEEEEEP
crack
OOPS, TOO BAD! ♪
I FAILED. SORRY!
WHAT'S WRONG? HAVE YOU GIVEN UP?
I'LL START THE INVAS NOV
I THINK IT'LL LAST... THREE MINUTES.
SERGEANT!
WHOA! WHAT'S GOING ON?
A TRAINING SESSION?
...?!

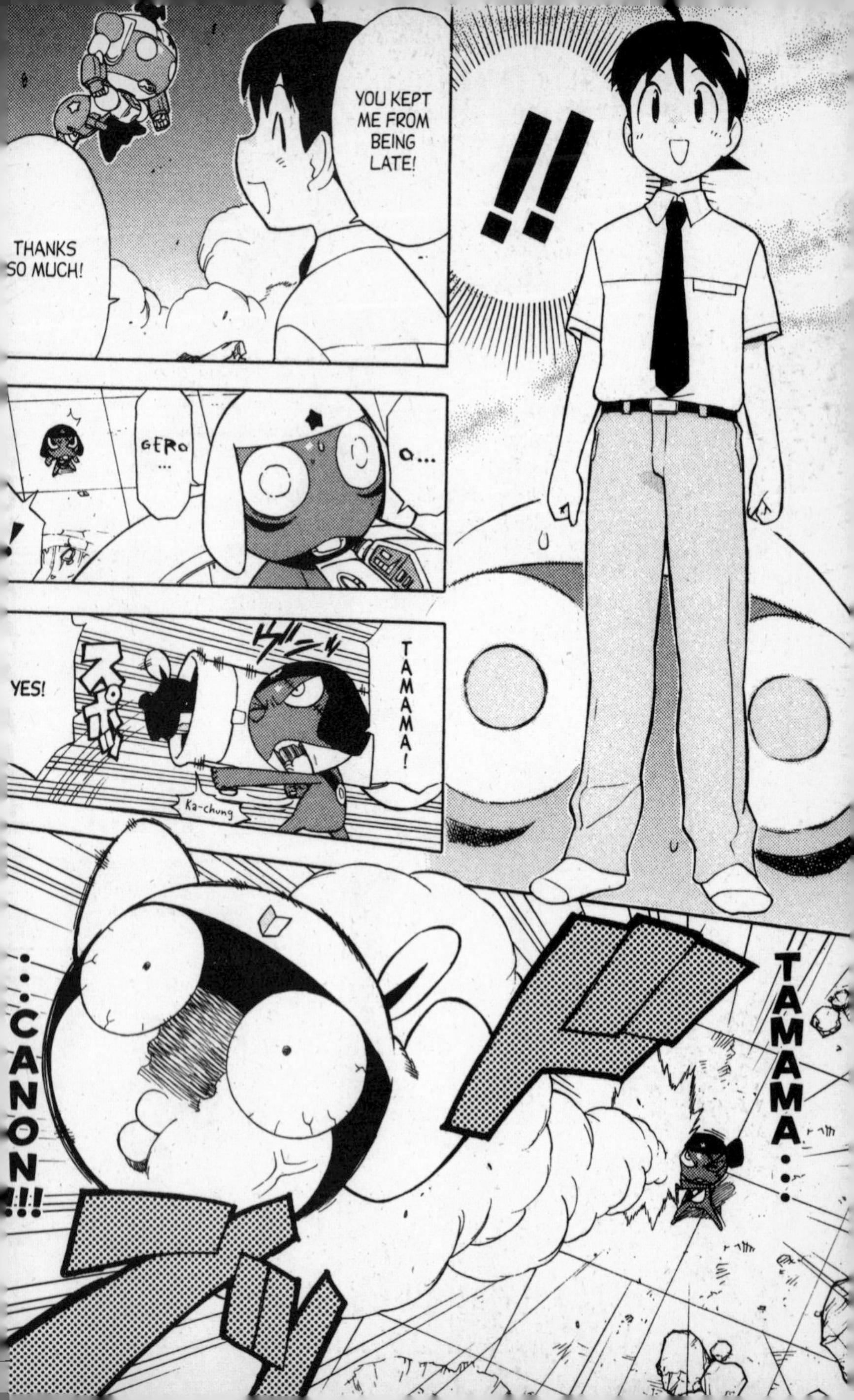
!!
YOU KEPT ME FROM BEING LATE!
THANKS SO MUCH!
O...
GERO...
TAMAMA!
YES!
Ka-chung
TAMAMA...
...CANON!!

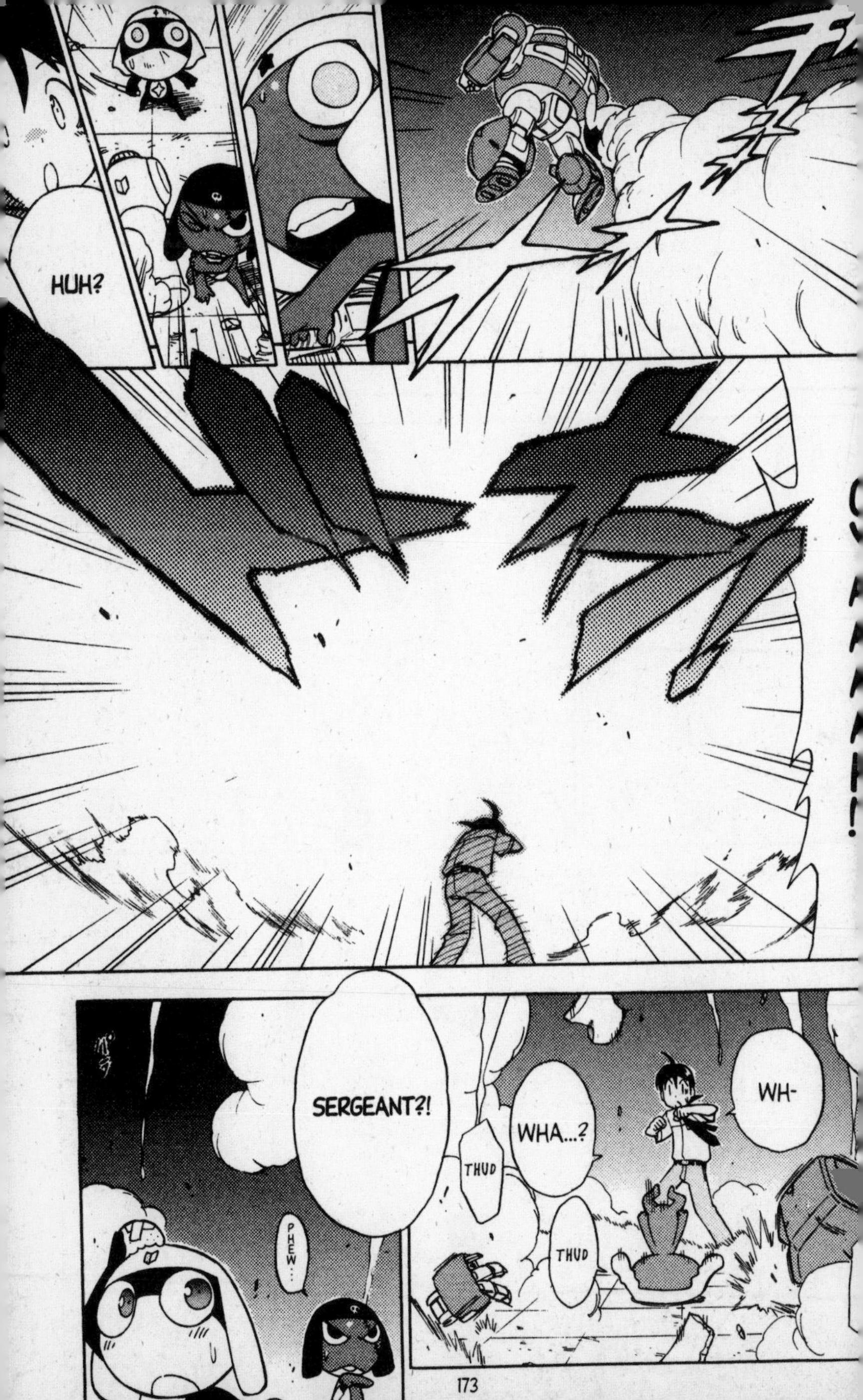
HUH?
WH-
WHA...?
THUD
THUD
SERGEANT?!
PHEW...

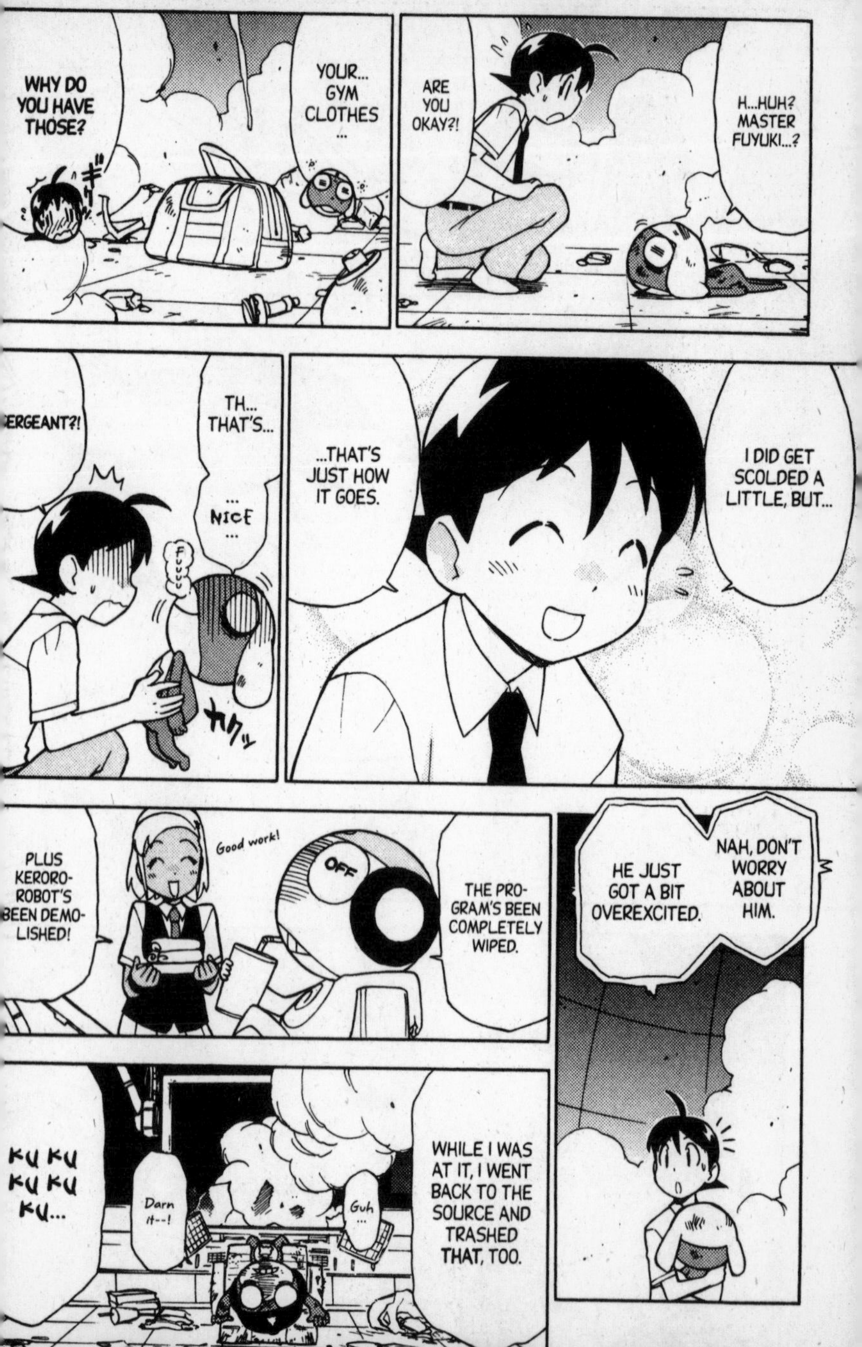
H...HUH? MASTER FUYUKI...?
ARE YOU OKAY?!
YOUR... GYM CLOTHES ...
WHY DO YOU HAVE THOSE?
I DID GET SCOLDED A LITTLE, BUT...
...THAT'S JUST HOW IT GOES.
TH... THAT'S... ...NICE...
ERGEANT?!
NAH, DON'T WORRY ABOUT HIM.
HE JUST GOT A BIT OVEREXCITED.
THE PRO-GRAM'S BEEN COMPLETELY WIPED.
OFF
Good work!
PLUS KERORO-ROBOT'S BEEN DEMO-LISHED!
WHILE I WAS AT IT, I WENT BACK TO THE SOURCE AND TRASHED THAT, TOO.
Guh ...
Darn it--!
KU KU KU KU KU...

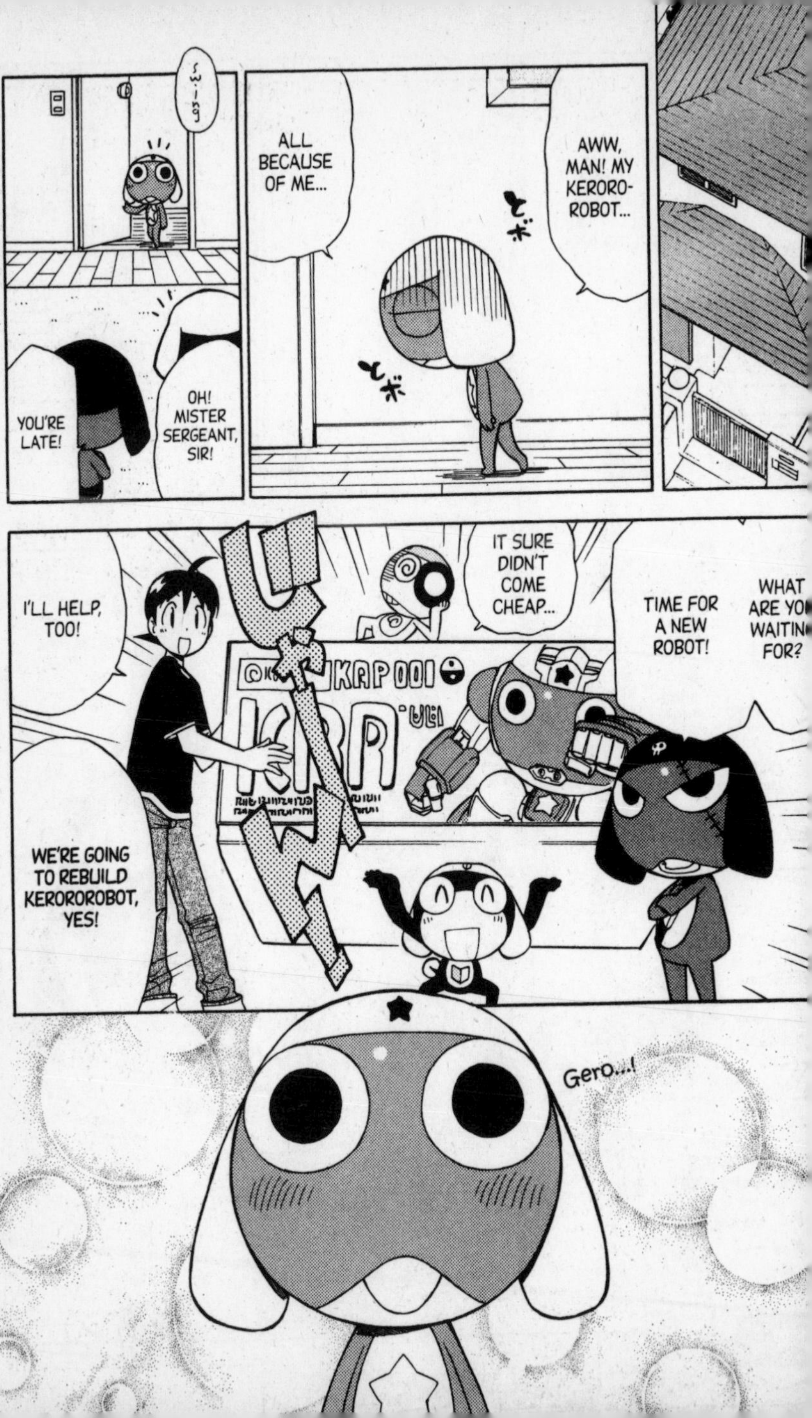
AWW, MAN! MY KERORO-ROBOT...
とボ
とボ
ALL BECAUSE OF ME...
s-w-i-n-g
...
OH! MISTER SERGEANT, SIR!
YOU'RE LATE!
WHAT ARE YO WAITIN FOR?
TIME FOR A NEW ROBOT!
IT SURE DIDN'T COME CHEAP...
I'LL HELP, TOO!
WE'RE GOING TO REBUILD KERORROBOT, YES!
Gero...!

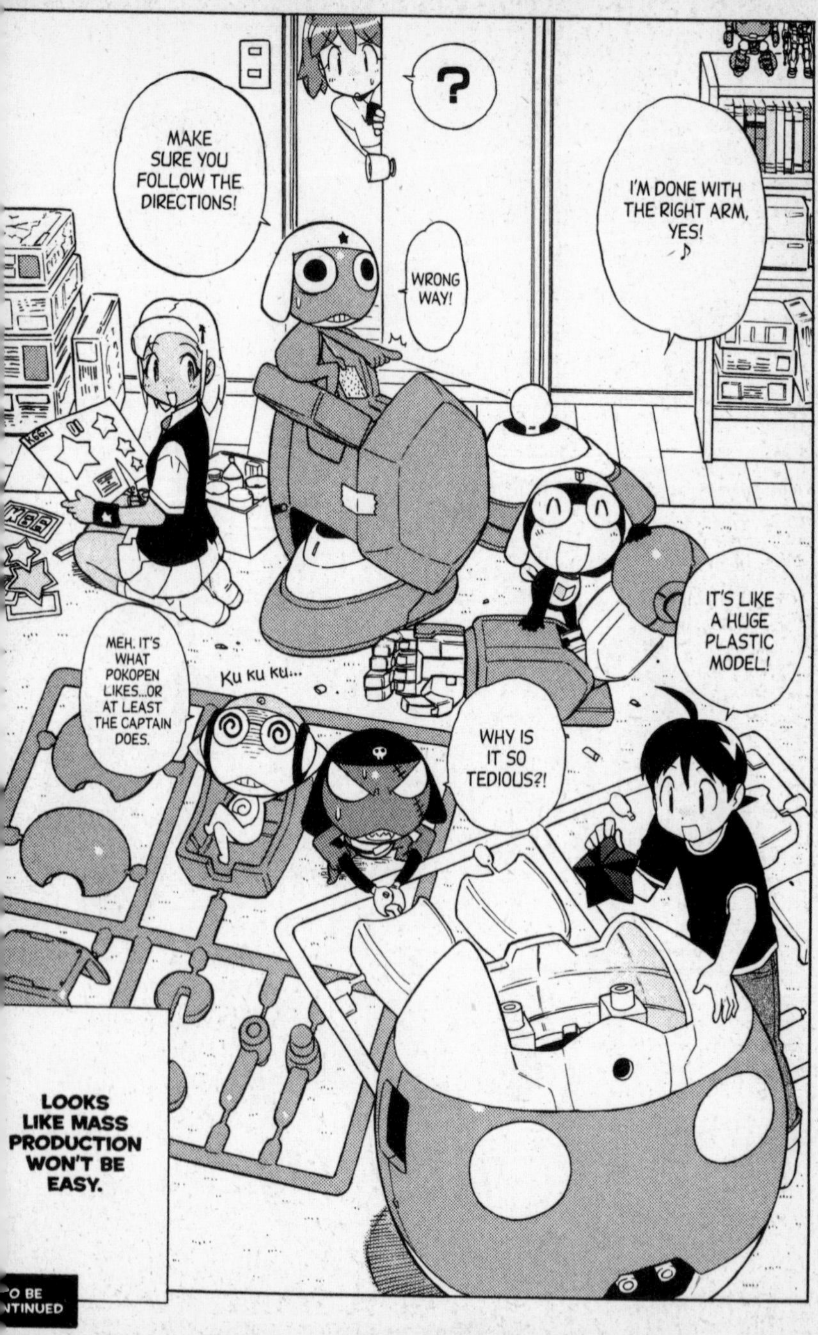

?
I'M DONE WITH THE RIGHT ARM, YES! ♪
WRONG WAY!
MAKE SURE YOU FOLLOW THE DIRECTIONS!
IT'S LIKE A HUGE PLASTIC MODEL!
WHY IS IT SO TEDIOUS?!
Ku ku ku...
MEH. IT'S WHAT POKOPEN LIKES...OR AT LEAST THE CAPTAIN DOES.
LOOKS LIKE MASS PRODUCTION WON'T BE EASY.
O BE
NTINUED

JAPAN STAFF

CREATOR
MINE YOSHIZAKI

BACKGROUNDS
OYSTER

FINISHES
GOMOKU AKATSUKI
TOMMI NARIHARA
634
EIJI SHIMOEDA
RYOICHI KOGA

TO BE CONTINUED
IN VOLUME 20

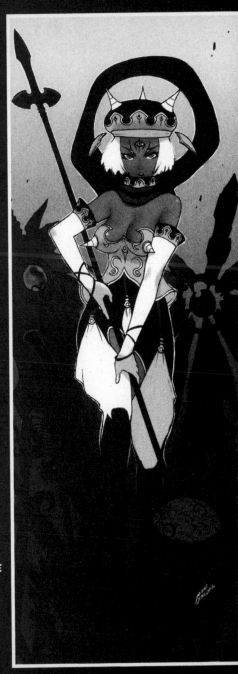

ANGOL FEAR

EARTH IS A RARE PLANET
IN THE GALAXY--IT'S BEEN
VISITED BY ANGOLS THREE
TIMES IN ITS HISTORY,
STARTING WITH ANGOL
TIA IN THE CRETACEOUS
PERIOD, ANGOL FEAR AT
THE END OF THE 16TH
CENTURY, AND NOW ANGOL
MOA, AND YET IT STILL
EXISTS. ANGOL FEAR PAID
EARTH A VISIT TO CHECK
UP ON HER COUSIN, ANGOL
MOA, WHO'D BEEN SENT
TO JUDGE THE PLANET.
SHE HAS THROWN HERSELF
INTO THE BATTLE OF THE
SPIRIT SWORDS OF THE
TIME. ALTHOUGH ALL THREE
USE THE SAME WEAPON,
THE LUCIFER SPEAR, THEY
ARE MADE OF IRIDIUM (IR),
COBALT (CO) AND TITANIUM
(TI), RESPECTIVELY.

IN THE NEXT VOLUME OF

SGT FROG™

KERORO GUNSO

FORGET A LAND INVASION, THE NEW STRATEGY IS TO CONQUER THE SEAS! BUT WAIT—THAT'S NOT SGT. KERORO AND HIS GANG THREATENING FISHING BOATS AND KIDNAPPING NATSUMI WHILE THE KIDS ARE ON A BEACH VACATION!! JUST WHO ARE THESE THESE STRANGE, NEW KERONIANS AND WHY ARE THEY STATIONED AT THE BOTTOM OF THE OCEAN? BETTER YET, WHAT ARE THEY PLANNING ON DOING TO THE EARTH?!

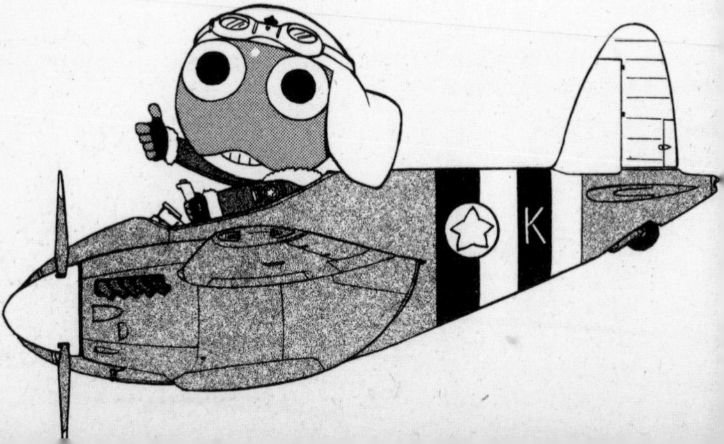
K

TOKYOPOP Insider
Stu Levy, May 2010

Hi everyone! Most of you don't know me but please allow me to introduce myself. While my parents named me Stuart Joel Levy, I really just go by "Stu". Ever since I was a child, people would tease me about being a food, calling me "Beef Stu" and the like. Even in Japanese, I get variations (although I'm 「スチュウ」 "Su-chu" whereas "stew" the food is actually 「シチュー」 "Shi-chu").

Now that we've gotten that sorted out, let me explain why I'm writing this. At TOKYOPOP, we decided to start a new column in our manga called "TOKYOPOP Insider" where some of our staff can write something casually – whatever's on their mind. I guess it's sort of a paper-based blog. I thought I'd be the first one to give it a go and see what you guys thought.

It may be hard to believe but it's been 13 years since I founded TOKYOPOP. Wow, time flies! Along with me, you manga readers have matured as well. We've seen some of our favorite series end, others begin, lots of content go online, and books evolve. Many more people know and love Japanese culture than when I first started – and I'm proud that I was a part of making that happen.

So, let me say ありがとう！("arigatou" - "thank you") to all of you for being interested in manga, Japan, and otaku culture overall. It's been a whirlwind of a ride over the past 13 years, but I've enjoyed every thrilling moment of it – working day and night for a passion that we all share.

This summer we're doing something I've wanted to do for years but never had the guts. I'm going on the road with Dice (from TOKYOPOP) and a very talented group of fans (the "Otaku Six") and we're going to search the nation for "America's Greatest Otaku" as well as give away lots of TOKYOPOP swag. Who knows what will happen – it's a crazy endeavor since we'll all be living on a humongous bus for 3 months – but my goal is to meet as many of you in person as I can (www.Americasgreatestotaku.com).

The details will be online but please come out and say hi if we're in your neighborhood – I'd love to meet you!

今後とも宜しくお願いします！("Kongo tomo Yoroshiku onegai-shimasu!"which roughly translates as "Looking forward to it!")

Cheers!
-Stu

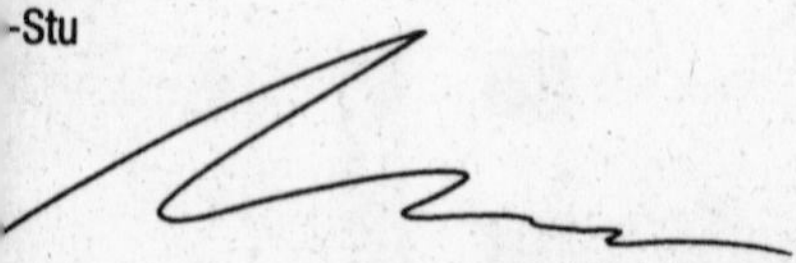

A TOKYOPOP® Manga
E-mail: info@TOKYOPOP.com
Come visit us online at www.TOKYOPOP.com

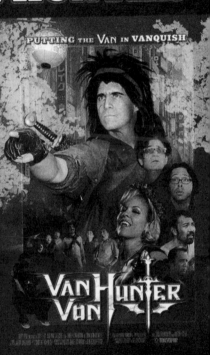

DISCOVER HOW IT ALL BEGAN

AN EVIL, ANCIENT AND HUNGRY, IS ROAMING THE
BADLANDS OF THE OLD WEST. IT SPARES NOT MAN,
WOMAN NOR CHILD, DEVOURING ALL THAT STAND
BEFORE IT. ONLY ONE MAN CAN STOP IT...A MYSTERIOUS
PRIEST WITH A CROSS CARVED INTO HIS HEAD. HIS NAME
IS IVAN ISAACS, AND HE WILL SMOTE ALL EVIL IN
A HAIL OF HOT LEAD. HALLELUJAH.

MIN-WOO HYUNG'S INTERNATIONAL MANWHA SENSATION RETURNS
WITH SPECIAL COLLECTOR'S EDITIONS FOR FANS OLD & NEW!

© MIN-WOO HYUNG, DAIWON C.I. INC.

The World Is Back, and It Will Surprise You!

.hack//link

TOKYOPOP

Two years after the popular video game The World was shut down, Tokio Kuryuu cannot wait for The World R:X to come out. Unfortunately for him, he forgets to reserve a copy and finds himself without access. That is, until a beautiful new transfer student suddenly and mysteriously forces Tokio into the game and makes him her servant!

Preview at www.TOKYOPOP.com/hack_Link

STOP!

This is the back of the book.
You wouldn't want to spoil a great ending!

This book ... left
format. Si...
get to exp...
asking for ...
and far m...

8 7 ... or

10

THE MANGA REVOLUTI...